The Chocolate Lover's Guide™

TO THE PACIFIC NORTHWEST

Food, Lodging, and Fun Things to Do
in Oregon, Washington, and
Southwest British Columbia

BY BOBBIE HASSELBRING
The Chocolate Traveler

Wordsworth Publishing
Beavercreek, Oregon

Printed in the United States.

ISBN 0-9665619-0-2

Cover design: Marty Urman, MU Graphics
Interior design and layout: Marty Urman, MU Graphics
Proofreaders: Elise Campbell and Anne Weaver
Fact checker: Elise Campbell
Award design and layout: Anne Weaver

Wordsworth Publishing
P.O. Box 311
Beavercreek, OR. 97004
(503) 632-4610
(503) 632-6754 (fax)
hasselbring@msn.com

Publisher's Cataloging-in-Publication
(Provided by Quality Books, Inc.)

Hasselbring, Bobbie, 1951-
        The chocolate lover's guide to the Pacific Northwest :
food, lodging, and fun things to do in Oregon,
Washington, and Southwest British Columbia / by Bobbie
Hasselbring. -- 1st ed.
        p. cm.
        Includes index.
        ISBN: 0-9665619-0-2

        1. Restaurants--Northwest, Pacific--Guidebooks.
2. Bakers and bakeries--Northwest, Pacific--Directories.
3. Confectioners--Northwest, Pacific--Directories.
4. Chocolate. 5. Northwest, Pacific--Guidebooks.
I. Title.

TX907.3.P323H37 1998   647'.95795'05
                             QB198-1132

For Anne—Always.

The
Chocolate
Lover's Guide™
TO THE PACIFIC NORTHWEST

Table of Contents

Contents

Contents

Acknowledgements

No book is the work of one person and *The Chocolate Lover's Guide* would never have happenned without the advice, council, help, and belief of many. The author's thanks and gratitude go to: Anne E. Weaver, without whose continued support, confidence, and love, this project would never have been completed. In addition, the author wishes to thank my dear friends and colleagues Carla Perry, Marilyn McFarlane, and Gabrielle Kraft. My gratitude goes to Marty Urman for her wonderful artistic skills and to Elise Campbell for her excellent fact-checking and proofreading. I offer my grateful thanks to my excellent physicians, Louisa Silva, M.D., and Anita Cignolini, M.D., for keeping my body going throughout 9 months of traveling and chocolate tasting.

Thanks also to Heidi Yorkshire, Marilyn Gilbaugh, Gerry Frank, Nancy Olsen, Michael Castleman, Marguerite Clark, Pauline Weaver, Scott Bruess, Vickie Foster, Tammy and Marge Arndt, Cheryl Rolstad, Shirley Alderson, Lou Childers, Barbara Watcher, Tom Dundas, Chuck Nerger, Donna and Vermont McAllister, Jan Simmons, Judy McLane, Myra and Roger Plant, Rhonda Cox, Michael Burtram, Wayne Purcell, Keith McCrea, Bobbye and Doug Boger, Bob and Nita Hempfling, Jeannie Schnyder, Marilyn and Dan Lowewke, David Campiche, Debbie and Steve Demarest, Joyce Woodward, Wendy Floyd, Emma O'Campo, Charlotte Morgan, Carol McGough, Carolee and Dennis Casey, Pebby Kuan, Crissy Barnett, Dan Durant, David Newton, Chris Volk, Joe Figone, Melissa Henniger, Trevor Logan, Steve Bennette, Peter Goldfarb, Cindy Nelson, Eleni Skalbania, David Tikkanen, Vickie Pratt, Peggy Thompson, Judy Ahola, Goody Cable, Shelly Sabin, Niki Price, Christine Danzer, Laurie Asin, Stacie Smith-Blosser, Julia Schroeder, Barbara and Dick Yunker, Scout and Max Weaver, and members of the Northwest Association of Book Publishers.

And the hundreds of restauranteurs, chefs, pastry chefs, bakers, chocolatiers, and ice cream makers who shared their chocolate, their stories, and their goodwill.

Chocolate Dreams

What a long, strange, and wonderful trip this has been. When I started on *The Chocolate Lover's Guide to the Pacific Northwest*, I thought I could "knock out" this project in a few months. I didn't realize that the Pacific Northwest encompasses a huge territory and that hundreds of chefs, pastry chefs, bakers, chocolatiers, and ice cream makers are doing incredible things with chocolate here.

I also didn't know that *The Chocolate Lover's Guide* isn't just about chocolate. *The Chocolate Lover's Guide to the Pacific Northwest* is about people's hopes and fears and dreams, including my own. Chocolate, though wonderful in itself, is just a medium like paint for a painter. The people in this book have used chocolate to change their lives, to mold their aspirations, to vanquish their fears, and to make their dreams into reality.

Great chocolate products, with few exceptions, aren't being made by anonymous corporate America. It's being made by *individuals* with hopes and dreams and passions. People like the European pasty chef who gave up working in glamorous luxury resorts and opened a tiny pastry shop in Bend, Oregon, so his kids could have a great place to grow up. Or the civil engineer in Winthrop, Washington, who traded constructing bridges for building mammoth-sized chocolates. Or the baker in Cashmere, Washington, who bakes outrageously wonderful rustic hearth breads, including chocolate bread, in her home-based shop in the middle of a pear orchard so she can do what she loves and still be with her small children. Or the woman in Redmond, Oregon who wanted to bring a bit of "culture and gentility" to this rugged desert town, so she opened an English tea room. Or the man in Portland, Oregon who took on a broken-down chocolate company with the dream of restoring it to its former glory. All of them and hundreds more let me look into their lives, taste their chocolate, and, for a moment, share in their dreams. For that I am ever grateful and enriched.

I started with the mission of finding and directing people to the best sources of chocolate in the Pacific Northwest. *The Chocolate Lover's Guide* does that. It also, I hope, helps support and promote small business owners, the dreamers who dare to step out of line and listen to their own rhythm. It is my dream that chocolate lovers will read *The Chocolate Lover's Guide to the Pacific Northwest* and buy the products listed. For every bite you take of the wonderful chocolate produced by the people in this book, you'll be sharing in someone's chocolate dream.

Your's Gratefully in Chocolate, Bobbie Hasselbring

YOUR GUIDE TO
Chocolate Bliss & More

Chocolate Desserts, Candy, Baked Goods, Frozen Treats. *The Chocolate Lover's Guide to the Pacific Northwest* is the first and only comprehensive guide to everything chocolate in the Pacific Northwest. If you're fortunate enough to live in the Pacific Northwest, you know that it is one of the most beautiful and bountiful places on earth. You also know it's a place of great food, including terrific chocolate. Pacific Northwest chefs, bakers, and confectioners make some of the most delectable chocolate desserts, candy, baked goods, and frozen treats and beverages in the world. And *The Chocolate Lover's Guide to the Pacific Northwest* is your personal guide to enjoying the best chocolate the Pacific Northwest has to offer.

Chocolate Facts, Tips, Quotes, and Profiles. To make enjoying chocolate even more enjoyable, *The Chocolate Lover's Guide* features fascinating facts about your favorite indulgence. Some of the best restaurateurs, chefs, bakers, and candymakers in the Pacific Northwest share their secrets and tips about chocolate. We also give you some mini-profiles, so you can meet some of the personalities behind some of the best chocolate in the Pacific Northwest.

Chocolate Happenings. *The Chocolate Lover's Guide* also leads you to terrific chocolate happenings. Throughout the book, you'll find notes about chocolate events.

Terrific Places to Stay, Great Things to Do. While exploring the wonderful world of Pacific Northwest chocolate, you need great places to stay and other fun things to do. *The Chocolate Lover's Guide to the Pacific Northwest* lists some of the best lodging in each area and not-to-miss places and fun things to do.

GETTING THE MOST FROM YOUR
Chocolate Lover's Guide

The Chocolate Lover's Guide to the Pacific Northwest is organized so that it's easy to use and easy to find the best chocolate wherever you live or travel in the Pacific Northwest.

Divided by Regions. *The Guide* is divided geographically by region. Our Pacific Northwest includes Oregon, Washington, and southwest British Columbia. This geographic division will enable you to follow a route as if traveling by car from one destination to another. It will allow you to make chocolate treks, getting the most chocolate per mile, whenever the urge strikes.

♥♥♥♥ **Rated by Chocolate Hearts.** Every business listed in *The Guide* produces superior chocolate products or they wouldn't be in the book. Each has been personally tasted and reviewed both by the author and other hand-picked reviewers. Being reviewed did *not* guarantee inclusion in *The Guide*. And **none of the businesses paid to be listed**. In fact, you can't buy your way into *The Chocolate Lover's Guide*. The only way in is to make terrific chocolate.

Each restaurant, bakery, ice cream/yogurt store, and candy shop reviewed received a rating of 0 to 4 chocolate hearts, according to how wonderful their chocolate products are.

> **No hearts** = No recommendation. Stop in a chocolate emergency.
> ♥ = Pretty good, a pleasing experience.
> ♥♥ = Solidly good.
> ♥♥♥ = Excellent.
> ♥♥♥♥ = Chocolate nirvana, the best you can get.

Businesses who made it into *The Chocolate Lover's Guide* and earned a rating all received a door sticker that says "Recommended by The Chocolate Lover's Guide." When you see this sticker, you can be assured you're in for some good chocolate. (Lodging places featured also received stickers, assuring travelers that the accommodations have been reviewed and recommended for chocolate lovers.) In addition, outstanding establishments who earned a ♥♥♥♥ (chocolate nirvana) rating received a special "Award of

Chocolate Excellence." Those who made the Best List earned a "Best List Award."

Why are there only positive reviews? We didn't think our readers wanted *The Chocolate Lover's Guide to the Worst Chocolate*. So we included only the best chocolate in the Pacific Northwest. Our reviews conjure a mental picture of each chocolate item and describe its good points. If there are any negatives, like being a bit too sweet or dry, for instance, we point that out.

Did businesses pay to be in The Chocolate Lover's Guide? Absolutely not. No one can buy their way into the book. Not everyone who was evaluated got into the book. The only way to get in is to offer terrific chocolate. (Or, for hotels, inns, and B&Bs, to be a terrific place for chocolate lovers to stay.)

Are the heart ratings important? You bet! While all the chocolate products listed in *The Chocolate Lovers Guide* are good, there are substantial qualitative differences between a ♥ rating and a ♥♥♥♥ rating. Only the very best in the Pacific Northwest earned the coveted ♥♥♥♥ rating and *The Chocolate Lover's* Award of Chocolate Excellence.

Why do some businesses have no rating? We consider these to be "chocolate emergencies." While they didn't earn our regular rating, other qualities like location make them a good place to stop for a chocolate fix.

Who conducted the reviews? Every dessert, baked item, ice cream/ frozen confection and chocolate candy was tasted, evaluated, rated, and reviewed by the author to ensure consistency in ratings. In addition, many of the products were reviewed by a second chocolate reviewer. A few were reviewed by as many as 3 reviewers. All were evaluated on taste, texture, presentation, and originality.

The ratings were based on the chocolate items sampled by the reviewer(s). In some cases, we sampled 1 or 2 items. In others, we sampled several. In all instances, the rating was based on an *average* of items sampled.

Although the author has been a chocolate lover for more than 40 years and a professional writer for nearly 20, the reviews are the author's *opinions*. You may or may not agree with them. The ratings and reviews are intended only as a guide for chocolate lovers, not as set-in-concrete fact. Also, it is our intention that the information presented here be as accurate and up-to-date as possible. However, we recognize that chefs and bakers move on, businesses change hands, and menus don't stay the same. We apologize if you don't find the same items or level of quality we found when we reviewed certain establishments. We also encourage you to let us know if and when you find discrepancies by writing to us at the address provided in the Back Talk/Talk Back section at the end of this book.

How can I get my favorite place into the next edition of The Chocolate Lover's Guide to the Pacific Northwest? Fill out the Back Talk/Talk Back form at the end of this book and we'll do our best to evaluate it.

Words
YOU NEED TO KNOW

Chefs, bakers, and chocolatiers use terms, many of them foreign, that you may or may not be familiar with. To get the most from the reviews, you should know these terms (approximate pronunciation in italic).

Bombe- (*bomb*)- A cylindrical or bomb-shaped dessert consisting of mousse or ice cream with mousse.

Chocolate buttercream- A very light frosting made from chocolate, egg whites, sugar, and butter.

Coulis (*cou-lee*)- Thin puree or sieved sauce made of fruit or vegetables.

Couverture (*co-va-tur*)- Chocolate for dipping or coating. A highly-refined chocolate with a higher cocoa butter content (about half its weight) than eating or baking chocolate. It forms a thin, hard, shiny shell.

Creme anglaise (*crem anglaze*)- A light vanilla sauce or thick custard made from milk, vanilla bean, egg yolks, and sugar.

Creme brulee (*crem bru-lay*)- Baked custard cream with a burnt sugar topping.

Creme chantilly or **chantilly cream**- Whipped cream flavored with vanilla.

Creme fraiche (*crem frash*)- A mature and tangy cream that's made from heavy cream and buttermilk or sour cream that has soured and thickened to the consistency of yogurt.

Curcocao (*cur-a-cow*)- Bitter orange liqueur.

Fondant- Sweets made from boiling a sugar syrup and kneading it into a creamy, smooth paste. It's often used to make a soft icing. May be flavored with liqueurs.

Frangipanne or **frangipan** (*frang-a-pannie*)- A light almond sponge cream often used in cakes and pastries.

Florentine (*floor-en-teen*)- A large, flat biscuit made from nuts and candied fruits covered on one side or one-half with chocolate.

Ganache (*ga-nash*)- A smooth cream made from mixing high-quality chocolate (couverture) and boiled cream.

Gianduja (*gan-du-ja*)- In France, Italy, and Switzerland, the term used for nougat. Made from equal amounts of almonds or other nuts, sugar, and high-quality chocolate (couverture).

Gateau or **gateaux** (*gat-toe*)- Layers of sponge cake filled and covered with buttercream.

Genoise (*gen-wa*)- The classic sponge cake in which the batter is heated slightly before baking.

Madeleines (*mad-e-lynns*)- Shell-shaped sponge cakes.

Marjolaine (*mar-jo-lane*)- A dessert made of sponge cake, custard cream, buttercream and cake crumbs.

Meringue (*mer-ang*)- A frothy mixture of egg white and sugar that's oven-dried (not baked).

Mousse (*moose*)- A light dessert consisting of whipped cream, egg yolks, boiled sugar, and flavoring.

Mousseline (*moose-a-leen*)- An egg-sugar base to which lightly whipped cream is added.

Nougat or **noughat** (*no-gat*)- A paste made from almonds or other nuts, beaten egg white, sugar or honey and high-quality chocolate (couverture).

Pain (*paan*)- French word for bread.

Pot de creme (*po-da-crem*)- Custard baked and served in a cup.

Praline (*pray-leen*)- Paste made from sugar, almonds, and other nuts.

Profiterolles (*pro-fit-er-olles*)- Small cream puffs filled with cream and covered with a sauce.

Puff pastry- Thin, alternating layers of butter and dough.

Roulade (*ru-lad*)- Rolled cake.

Sabayon (*sa-ba-yon*)- A foaming sauce made from eggs, sugar, and spirits. Italians call it zabaglione or zabaione.

Sacher torte (*soc-r tort*)- A chocolate cake invented by Sacher, a famous pastry chef and owner of a renowned pastry shop in Vienna.

Sorbet (*sor-bay*)- A well-flavored, semi-frozen ice.

Soufflé (*soo-flay*)- A very light, baked or steamed pudding or dessert.

Sponge cake- A light yet rich cake.

Tuile (*tweel*)- Thin, crisp biscuit often made with ground almonds and slightly curved like a roof tile (tuile means roof tile in French). Used in making small serving baskets or decorative garnishes for desserts.

Zabaglione or **zabaione** (za-ba-yon)- An Italian dessert made with egg yolks, sugar and wine (usually Marsala), whisked until frothy. The French call it sabayon.

AMERICAN VERSUS EUROPEAN-STYLE CHOCOLATES
We often refer to **"American-style"** or **"European-style"** chocolate. In general, European chocolates are darker (semi- or bittersweet) and tend to be less sweet. Some believe European-style chocolates have more flavor. American chocolates, in contrast, have more added sugar and often use milk chocolate.

Raw Egg Warning: There is some risk of salmonella contamination in recipes using uncooked eggs (very rare in the Pacific Northwest). If you choose to make a recipe with raw eggs, use only fresh, uncracked eggs and refrigerate dish promptly after making. Don't serve to anyone with compromised immune system (infants, very elderly, chronically ill, or pregnant women).

Portland and Surrounding Communities

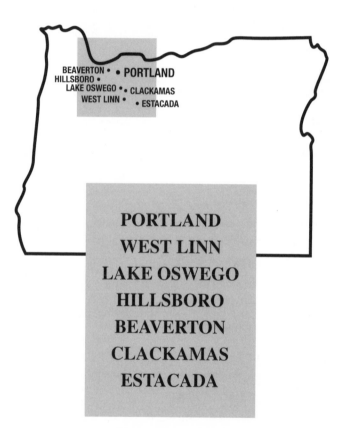

BEAVERTON • • PORTLAND
HILLSBORO •
LAKE OSWEGO • • CLACKAMAS
WEST LINN • • ESTACADA

PORTLAND
WEST LINN
LAKE OSWEGO
HILLSBORO
BEAVERTON
CLACKAMAS
ESTACADA

The Rose City is a most livable city. Some compare it to San Francisco 50 years ago. Less urban than Seattle or Vancouver, B.C., Portland is bisected by the Willamette River and boasts one of the largest urban parks in the country.

Great Things to Do

• **Check Out Packy and Friends**. **Oregon Zoo**, 4001 SW Canyon Road, **Portland**, OR. (503) 226-1561. Portland grows some of the best elephants in the country. The Oregon Zoo (formerly the Washington Park Zoo) has an international reputation for elephants, including Packy, Portland's unofficial mascot. The zoo recently added an African Rain Forest exhibit filled with fascinating animals of East Africa.

• **Become a Mad Scientist for a Day**. **OMSI**, 1945 SE Water Avenue, **Portland, OR**. (503) 797-4000. The Rose City has one of the best science museums in the country. With 6 exhibit halls, dozens of interactive displays, live demonstrations, a planetarium, and the wrap-around, 5-story Omnimax theater, kids and adults will sure to find plenty to keep them fascinated.

• **Do Saturday Market**. **Portland Saturday Market**, 108 W Burnside, **Portland, OR**. (503) 222-6072. Ever wonder where Portlanders get all those tie-dyed shirts? At the strange and wonderful Saturday Market. Rain or shine, the eclectic outdoor market comes to life every Saturday and Sunday from March through Christmas, selling unique gifts, exotic foods, and fresh fruits and vegetables. Entertainers play music, sing, dance, juggle and eat fire.

• **Go Wine Touring**. People don't often associate Oregon with fine wines, but the state produces some of the best, especially pinot noir. Several excellent wineries are located in Washington and Yambill Counties, just a few miles from Portland. Take a picnic and make a day of it. Check out these and other area winemakers: Amity Vineyards (**Amity, OR**. 503-835-2362), Elk Cove Vineyards (**Dundee, OR**. 503- 985-7760), Oak Knoll Winery (**Hillsboro, OR**. 503-648-8198), Ponzi Vineyards (**Beaverton, OR**. 503-628-1227), Rex Hill Vineyards (**Newberg, OR**. 503-538-0666), and Tualatin Vineyards (**Forest Grove, OR**. 503-357-5005.)

• **Enjoy the Gardens**. **Washington Park**, Portland, OR. (503) 223-4070. Portland is renown for its lovely gardens, especially the **International Rose Test Gardens** and the **Japanese Garden** in Washington Park, in the city's West Hills. If you're a rose fan, you'll be fascinated by the dozens of rose varieties, all marked for easy identification.The Japanese Garden, designed by Professor P. Takuma Tono of the University of Tokyo, will feed your senses and your soul.

• **Read a Book**. Portland has the distinction of having the most bookstores per capita of any city in the United States. **Powell's City of Books**, (1005 W Burnside, **Portland, OR** (503) 228-4651), which occupies an entire city block, is the second largest independent bookstore in the country.

Terrific Places to Stay

Heathman Hotel, 1001 SW Broadway, **Portland, OR.** (503) 241-4100/(800) 551-0011. The Heathman is one of Portland's finer city hotels. Situated in the heart of downtown, just a few blocks from lively Pioneer Square, the historic hotel prides itself on exquisite service and features 150 guest rooms and 47 suites, all well-appointed with desks, good reading lamps, arm chairs, color televisions, honor bars, and phones with data ports. Extra amenities include 24-hour room service, terry robes, Lord and Mayfair toiletries, hair dryers, clock radios, valet parking, and a complimentary 400-title movie library. The air-conditioned rooms have windows that open, especially appreciated with Portland's mild climate. The guest rooms tend to be a bit small, which may be why many guests gather in the historic lobby lounge with its 2-story ceilings, couches and overstuffed chairs and tables, paneled walls, cozy fireplace, and vibrant red carpets. Guests are entertained here with piano or jazz performances. Up a grand staircase is the Mezzanine Bar and lending library stocked with books of authors who have stayed at the hotel. A few steps away is the Heathman Restaurant (see review). For guests who need to burn a few calories, the sunny fitness suite on the 3rd floor features 2 treadmills, a stairstepper, an exercise bike, free weights and benches, and a color TV.

Hotel Vintage Plaza, 422 SW Broadway, **Portland, OR**. (503) 228-1212/(800) 243-0555. Located in the heart of Portland's downtown shopping and cultural district, Hotel Vintage Plaza is exactly what a sophisticated urban hotel is supposed to be. The guest rooms and suites are beautifully-appointed in rich colors and prints that reflect the hotel's vintage wine theme. On the topmost floor, the Starlight Rooms feature conservatory windows for stargazing and excellent views of the city. The 2-story townhouse suites have deep, 2-person jetted tubs. All the rooms have honor bars, terry robes, and toiletries. Extras include valet service, complimentary newspapers, morning coffee, wine and cheese in the evening, turn down service, and room service from the hotel's excellent restaurant, Pazzo Ristorante (see review). The lobby features easy chairs, couches and tables, a fireplace and live piano music. An adequate 24-hour workout room in the basement has a handful of aerobic and weight training equipment.

Restaurants

3 Doors Down

1429 SE 37th Avenue, Portland, OR. (503) 236-6886

♥♥♥♥ Owner and chef Dave Marth's and owner/manager Kathy Bergin's **3 Doors Down** is a casual and popular neighborhood bistro. On weekends, the line of waiting diners spills onto the sidewalk. They serve Italian/Northwest cuisine such as Fra Diavolo, a delightful mix of prawns, mussels, clams, scallops, and kalamata olives in a sumptuous broth served over fettuccini. Their imaginative and delicious pasta, salmon, steak, seafood, and rabbit dishes change every 2 weeks. But it's Dave's desserts that have earned them our highest accolade. The **Double Chocolate Mousse Cake with Raspberry Puree** is a light, flourless mousse cake with an intensely chocolate bittersweet chocolate ganache frosting surrounded by a tangy raspberry sauce. The blending of textures and rich chocolate taste is chocolate nirvana.

It was at 3 Doors Down we learned that white chocolate can make an incredible dessert. Their **White Chocolate Bread Pudding with Bourbon Sauce** is 2 thick slabs of white chocolate bread custard covered with a rich bourbon sauce topped with soft raisins and a sprig of mint. Served warm, the pudding is tender with crispy edges. The intense sauce makes you want to lick the plate! It's dessert you won't soon forget.

Getting there: *Located "3 doors down" from the corner of Hawthorne and 37th.*

Caffee Mingo
807 NW 21st, Portland, OR. (503) 226-4646

♥♥♥♥ **Caffee Mingo**, a small trattoria on hip NW 21st, has a casual ambiance that borders on industrial funk with wooden tables and chairs, black and green tile floors, open metal shelves of wine bottles, large, classroom-style light fixtures, a blond wine/food bar, and hot salsa music. They serve dinner, with entrees like ravioli, gnocchi, risotto primavera, penne with beef braised in Chianti and espresso, and polenta with Italian sausage. Their nod to chocolate is the **Torte de Cioccolata**, a generous wedge of alternating layers of hazelnut meringue and chocolate mousse topped with a thick layer of ganache. Simply served on a hand-painted plate, this torta is a wonderfully rich blending of hazelnut and dark chocolate flavors. The mousse is thick and dense with an intense chocolate flavor and meringue adds a soft chewiness. The ganache is melt-in-the-mouth delicious. It's so satisfyingly rich you could share this dessert—or not.

Getting there: *On 21st between Johnson and Kearny.*

Caprial's Bistro and Wine
7015 SE Milwaukie Avenue, Portland, OR. (503) 236-6457

♥♥♥♥ **Caprial's** is a small bistro with tile floors, blue-green walls, blonde wood cloth-covered tables for 2 or 4, open racks of wine, and a scattering of ceramic raku pieces. Specials are printed in colored chalk on a big chalkboard. (Much to the relief of their ever-expanding crowd of loyal fans, Caprial's is scheduled to be remodeled and double in size summer '98.) Their lunch entrees include salads like grilled chicken with pear dressing, roasted hazelnuts, and gorgonzola, and sandwiches like grilled eggplant with roasted red peppers, tomato and provolone, and roasted turkey on grilled basil French bread with bacon, gruyere, and arugula. At dinner, they offer a half-dozen entrees like tandoori-style fish, wild mushroom pasta, and grilled smoked pork chops, plus nightly specials.

Desserts change every month, but chocolate lovers can count on a couple of standards—Chocolate Turtle Torte with Caramel Sauce and Chocolate Silk with Raspberry Sauce. The **Chocolate Turtle Torte** starts with a flaky pastry crust, followed by a $1^1/_2$-inch layer of caramel and pecan, then a $1^1/_2$-inch layer of intensely dark chocolate truffle, topped with a thin layer of chocolate ganache. This entirely successful dessert is chewy and buttery, a wonderful combination of melt-in-the-mouth dark chocolate and soft caramel flavors. If you love caramel and chocolate, you'll be in heaven with this one.

Caprial's Chocolate Silk with Raspberry Sauce is a generous wedge of dark cookie crust filled with 2 inches of dark chocolate silk topped with an inch of ultra-light hazelnut cream, served with raspberry sauce and whipped cream. It's wonderful! The cookie crust has a rich cinnamon-chocolate flavor and a good crunchiness. The silk and hazelnut cream both have a delicate, silky texture.
Getting there: On Milwaukie at Bybee.

Esplanade at Riverplace (Riverplace Hotel)
1510 SW Harbor Way, Portland, OR. (503) 295-6166
♥♥♥♥ Esplanade's ambiance is richly elegant—faux-painted walls in warm rusts and browns, original paintings and prints, dark blue cloths and tiny vases of fresh flowers gracing the tables, large windows overlooking the Willamette River and the marina. They serve breakfast, lunch, and dinner, with dinner specials that change weekly. Dinner entrees include duck with fruit sauce, medallions of beef with dried cherries and pinot noir, tortellini with chicken and sundried tomatoes, and lamb with lemon and herbs. Specials often include fresh fish dishes like halibut with truffle oil and steelhead with fresh fava beans.

Desserts, the forte of veteran pastry chef Colin Cameron, include his **Chocolate Sampler**, 8 small desserts, which change every few weeks, each with appropriate sauces. The **White Chocolate Cheesecake with Passion Fruit Sauce** is a $1^1/_2$-inch button of cheesecake with dark chocolate crust, topped with a pale yellow passion fruit glaze that gives the dessert a bright, fresh tropical taste. **The Dark Chocolate Madeleine with Coffee Creme Fraiche** is a thick, fudgy cookie with a deep chocolate flavor. The coffee sauce adds a subtle java flavor.

Colin's **Ultimate Chocolate Brownie** is a small triangle that's rich, more like fudge than a brownie, that's chock full of nuts and intense chocolate flavor. The **Chocolate Raspberry Bombe** is a 2-inch round of milk chocolate raspberry mousse that's enrobed in dark chocolate and garnished with milk and white chocolate drizzles and raspberry sauce. The mousse is very light with a delicate raspberry flavor and the dark chocolate coating adds a lovely snap to this rich dessert.

The **Chocolate Hazelnut Frangipane Tartlet with White Chocolate Creme Anglaise** is a delicate 3-inch-round chocolate tart cup filled with chopped roasted hazelnuts and chopped dark chocolate. The tart has a fresh-baked, soft-crunchy texture and the hazelnuts add a good chewiness. The creme anglaise adds a light creaminess. Be sure to eat this one first as the creme anglaise can quickly cause the tartlet to become soggy. **Mascarpone Fudge Truffle** comes with a milk chocolate coating and has a cheesy-chocolaty goodness. The Chocolate Sampler is completed by a scoop of **Chocolate Decadence Ice Cream** that is creamy and intensely chocolaty.

> **Chocolate boots energy. It provides quick-release calories. The energy derived from a chocolate bar is two and a half times that of pure carbohydrate.**

The **Triple Chocolate Terrine**, the Esplanade's most requested chocolate dessert, is a 4x5-inch slab of white chocolate, milk chocolate, and dark chocolate mousses swirled so that each bite has a different flavor. It's attractively presented on a bed of red raspberry and blackberry sauce and garnished with a dark chocolate triangle and fresh flowers. The white chocolate mousse is light, not overly sweet, with a subtle creamy flavor. The milk chocolate mousse has a rich, milky flavor and the dark chocolate mousse is intensely chocolate. All are incredibly creamy, melting effortlessly on the tongue. The berry sauces, some of the best this reviewer has tasted, have just the right sweet-tart balance. This is one wonderful terrine, chocolate lovers.

Getting there: Off Front Avenue in the Riverplace complex.

L'Auberge

2601 NW Vaughn Street, Portland, OR. (503) 223-3302

♥♥♥♥ Outside **L'Auberge** looks like a European inn. Inside this French restaurant has an Old World feeling with burgundy carpeting, peach and forest green walls, cloth-covered tables with hurricane lamps and flowers, and paned and stained glass windows. Off the comfortable bar area, there's a lattice-enclosed patio with hanging fuschia baskets where diners enjoy outdoor dining.

The dinner menu, which changes weekly, features entrees like duck, rack of lamb, filet mignon, roasted pheasant, portobello mushroom ravioli, and potato-crusted Alaskan halibut. They also offer pre-fixe dinners and 5-course, regional meals, which feature the dishes and wines of different regions in France.

Desserts change every couple of months and may include chocolate treats like their wonderful **Triple Chocolate Cake**, a warm, bittersweet individual cake baked in a tartlet pan and inverted on a bed of mulled cabernet sauvignon sauce and vanilla bean ice cream. It's simply garnished with white chocolate glaze, cocoa powder, and a fresh pansy. This is a heavenly dessert with a warm, rich, gooey center of milk chocolate ganache. The cabernet sauce lifts this dessert from excellent to extraordinary. The vanilla bean ice cream is rich and clean-tasting. Go for this one, chocolate lovers!

Two Mousse Gateau is a 4-inch round tower of bittersweet and white chocolate minted mousses surrounded by chocolate and almond sponge cake on a chocolate genoise cake base. It's beautifully served with fresh orange slices, honey citrus sauce, sliced almonds, and tiny fresh flowers. This is a fresh, minty, ultra-light dessert. The white mousse is delicate without being airy; the more dense chocolate mousse has a smooth texture with a deep chocolate flavor. The honey citrus sauce adds a bit of tartness. This makes a lovely, light end to a meal.
Getting there: On the corner of NW Vaughn and 26th.

Paley's Place
1204 NW 21st Avenue, Portland, OR. (503) 243-2403
♥♥♥♥ In a converted house on NW 21st, **Paley's** offers diners a quiet respite with white walls, cloth-covered tables with votives, hand-painted plates, and fresh flowers. Weather permitting, guests can dine on the wide, covered front porch. The bar features booth-style seating with small tables for casual knoshing. They serve lunch and dinner with entrees like pork tenderloin with applewood smoked bacon, roast squab, and wild salmon, among others. Pastry chef Jennifer Flanagan offers a delectable **Hot Pecan Brownie with Caramel Ice Cream** that's definitely a cut above. The 3x4-inch brownie is served warm in a hand-painted shallow bowl in a pool of dark chocolate sauce with chopped pecans and a scoop of caramel ice cream. This dessert is wonderfully rich with a deep chocolate flavor. The pecans provide a delightful counterpoint to the soft brownie and the dark chocolate sauce has a perfect chocolate taste. This gooey dessert is chocolate comfort food!

Paley's **Warm Chocolate Soufflé Cake with Honey Vanilla Ice Cream** is a 4-inch individual soufflé served warm with ice cream, chopped peanuts, drizzles of chocolate sauce, cocoa, and powered sugar. The outside is soft with slightly crispy edges and inside is rich with gooey, liquid chocolate. The honey vanilla ice cream, made in-house, is rich yet light with the delicate flavors of vanilla and honey.

Getting there: Corner 21ˢᵗ and Northrup.

Pazzo Ristorante (Hotel Vintage Plaza)
627 SW Washington, Portland, OR. (503) 228-1515
♥♥♥♥ At casually elegant **Pazzo**, patrons dine at wooden booths or cloth-covered tables with wooden chairs surrounded by peach-colored walls, large pillars covered with mirrors, over-sized glass ceiling fixtures, and a big, open kitchen that dominates an entire wall. They serve lunch and dinner with a large selection of pastas like angel hair with clams, rock shrimp, and scallops, pasta tubes with Italian sausage, red chard, marinara, and ricotta, and smoked salmon ravioli. Other selections include rib eye, braised lamb, stuffed pork chop, chicken with prosciutto and sage, and veal with mushrooms and marsala.

For dessert, **Semifreddo alla Gianduja**, is a double layer, semi-frozen mousse that's made with bittersweet chocolate and hazelnuts. It's served on a hand-painted plate in a pool of espresso creme fraiche sauce and it's simply garnished with fresh flowers. This dessert doesn't look fancy, but the flavor and texture are terrific. It has the perfect blending of hazelnut and dense chocolate flavors and the texture is ultra-creamy and cool. The espresso creme fraiche has an excellent, rich coffee flavor that doesn't dominate. You'll really love this one, chocolate lovers.

The **Tiramisu** is a 3x4-inch rectangle, 3¹/₂ inches high that has alternating layers of rum and espresso-soaked lady fingers and lightly-sweetened mascarpone cream that's dusted with dark cocoa powder and served on fresh cream, garnished with sliced strawberries and fresh flowers. This classic Italian dessert isn't easy to make well, but they know the secret. The soaked lady fingers are subtly flavored, not drenched with rum and espresso and the delicate mascarpone has just the right amount of sweetness. The fresh cream sauce adds a nice lightness to this delectable dessert.

Traveler's note: As The Guide went to press, talented pastry chef Diana Vineyard left Pazzo. Vineyard shared her recipes with Pazzo, but we can't guarantee you'll find the same quality.
Getting there: In the Hotel Vintage Plaza, on Broadway at Washington.

Ron Paul Charcuterie
1441 NE Broadway, Portland, OR. (503) 284-5347
Other Portland location:
Ron Paul Express, 507 SW Broadway, Portland, OR.
(503) 221-0052

♥♥♥♥ Located in a historic building, **Ron Paul Charcuterie** offers a casual atmosphere with tile floors, blonde wood tables and chairs, huge windows, and a big display case full of desserts, salads (couscous, chicken, pasta, tomato-cucumber, potato, fruit, szechuan), and hot entrees (lasagne, chicken verde casserole, quiche, pizza, polenta torte), all available to eat in or to-go. They serve lunch and dinner, with dinner entrees (which change every week) like linguine, salmon, pork chops, white bean ragout, and herbed goat cheese ravioli. They offer more than a dozen desserts like their signature **Chocolate Buttermilk Cake**, an impressive 6 inches high with 2 layers of dark chocolate cake filled and frosted with chocolate ganache. The cake is moist and slightly tangy with a rich chocolate flavor and the ganache is delightfully smooth. This is a great basic chocolate cake, chocolate lovers!

Is Chocolate an Aphrodisiac? The Mayan Emperor Montezuma thought so. He always drank the chocolate drink, chocolatl, before visiting his harem.

Cup of Heaven is a chocolate bourbon soufflé with a brownie crust, served warm with whipped cream. The top is an intensely chocolaty cake-like brownie. Dip your spoon in and you'll find a veritable pool of gooey chocolate. This is a rich delight.

Black Angus is the name of their big, 5-inch round cookie that combines 3 kinds of Belgian chocolate and espresso. Packed with walnuts and chocolate chips, this very chocolaty cookie is slightly crunchy on the outside, soft and chewy inside.
Getting there: On Broadway at NE 15th Avenue.

Wildwood
1221 NW 21st Avenue, Portland, OR. (503) 248-9663
♥♥♥♥ **Wildwood** is a large, airy space with contemporary decor—blond wood tables and chairs, skinny blonde and metal stools at the bar, tiny artsy ceiling lights, retro 50's tiger-striped booths, faux- painted walls in subtle mustards and browns, original paintings and prints, and an open kitchen with a food bar and brick oven. They serve lunch, dinner, and Sunday brunch, with entrees like leg of lamb, chicken with cornmeal dumplings, Oregon rabbit with cracked pepper spatzle and marionberry sauce, and grilled eggplant with penne pasta, tomato, baby spinach, and golden raisin vinaigrette. If you're lucky, pastry chef Jennifer Welshhons will be serving her **Chocolate Banana Strudel**, 2 big wedges of flaky, paper-thin phyllo pastry filled with a heavenly chocolate brownie base with walnuts and ganache, and bananas sautéed in bourbon caramel. It's served slightly warm with caramel ice cream and garnished with chocolate and caramel sauces. The combination of the

delicately crunchy phyllo and the soft, rich chocolate mixture is divine, chocolate lovers. The caramel ice cream is creamy and buttery and the chocolate/caramel sauces are rich.

If you want something a bit lighter, Jennifer's **Frozen Chocolate Soufflé** is light and airy, standing an impressive $2^1/_2$ inches above its baking dish. It's decorated with thin wedges of hazelnut espresso biscotti, thin, dark and white chocolate triangles, chocolate swirls, a dusting of cocoa and powered sugar, and a dollop of chocolate sorbet. The flavor is a subtle milk chocolate and the texture is a cross between a very light mousse and pudding. The biscotti is delicate with a good hazelnut flavor.

Wildwood also serves a variety of homemade ice creams and/or sorbets. The **Candied Orange Chocolate Ice Cream**, this reviewer's favorite, is a wonderful pairing of chocolate and orange flavors that's creamy without clinging to the palate.
Getting there: On 21st at Overton.

Zefiro
500 NW 21st, Portland, OR. (503) 226-3394
♥♥♥♥ One of Northwest Portland's favorite restaurants, **Zefiro** is decorated in minimalist style—blonde wood floors, lime sherbet green walls, black booths and chairs, white tablecloths, tiny art gallery lights, a few black and white photos, and large windows overlooking 21st Avenue. They serve lunch and dinner, with a menu that changes every couple of weeks. Dinner selections may include dishes like Asian risotto, grilled striped bass, grilled veal chop, Alaskan Chinook salmon, and grilled baby chicken in an Algerian marinade of ginger anise seed, and saffron. Chocolate lovers won't be disappointed by their ever-changing dessert menu, which can include **Chocolate Marjolaine,** 2 slabs (2x4-inches) of rich hazelnut meringue layered with finely-chopped hazelnuts and frosted with chocolate ganache. It's presented on a large, white plate with a generous amount of espresso creme fraiche and garnished with caramelized sugar and whole caramelized hazelnuts. The meringue is thick and rich, with a lovely creaminess that's punctuated with chewy hazelnuts. The ganache has a heavenly deep, dark chocolate flavor. The espresso creme fraiche, which isn't sweet, has a light creaminess that compliments this truly decadent dessert.
Getting there: NW 21st at Glisan.

Assagio
7742 SE 13th Avenue, Portland, OR. (503) 232-6151
♥♥♥ Brown-rust colored faux-painted and stenciled walls, upbeat Italian music, concrete floors, and cloth-covered tables with votive candles, and big windows all contribute to **Assagio's** casual

trattoria atmosphere. They serve dinners, offering their own rustic hearth breads and a large selection of fresh pastas like farfalle with yellow squash, zucchini, eggplant, mushrooms, and tomato sauce, spaghetti with a spicy sauce of black olives, capers, garlic, olive oil, and tomato, and pasta braids tossed in sun-dried tomato cream sauce with capers and gorgonzola. The entree and dessert menus change monthly, but diners can count on their signature **Salame di Cioccolata**, chocolate salami studded with pine nuts, dried cherries, cranberries, and raisins, served with creme anglaise. The 2 (2$\frac{1}{2}$-inch) round slices are rich and crunchy, with a fruity sweetness. There's not much chocolate flavor here, but each bite offers the flavor of cranberry, cherry, and pine nuts that slowly reveal themselves on the tongue. The light creme anglaise provides a delicate accent to this rich salami.

Their **Gianduja Gelato** is cool and creamy without being clingy. While the chocolate flavor is subtle, the terrific taste of roasted hazelnuts comes on strong. **Torta di Cioccolata con Pannadi Amaretto** is a chocolate mousse cake served with amaretto-flavored whipped cream. It's soft, creamy-dry, melting on the tongue instantly, leaving a lovely, delicate chocolate flavor. The amaretto cream is a good pairing with the chocolate.

Assagio's **Tiramisu** is a 4-inch square of espresso-soaked lady fingers layered with mascarpone cheese and cocoa powder. The lady fingers are well-flavored, though a bit too soaked for this reviewer's taste. The mascarpone is light rather than being sweet. *Getting there: On 13th at Lambert.*

Brasserie Montmatre

626 SW Park, Portland, OR. (503) 224-5552

♥♥♥ Casual, hip, happening, **Brasserie Montmatre** has all the ambiance of a popular Parisian café. The black and white tile floor, black ceilings onto which customers toss signed playing cards, a long bar, cloth and paper-covered tables (with crayons provided), large framed drawings from their popular crayon contest on the walls, and live jazz all contribute to the excitement. They're open for lunch, dinner, and weekend brunch. Starters include pate, clams, and fried brie, among others. Dinner entrees include dishes like grilled venison, roast chicken, Oregon Snapper Nicoise (snapper with Roma tomatoes, garlic, caper berries, and olives), and filet mignon with peppercorn and brandy sauce.

Their chocolate selection includes a delectable **Chocolate Hazelnut Cake with Coffee Cream**. It comes as a 4-inch round individual cake dusted with powered sugar and cocoa, floating in a bed of creamy, latte-colored coffee sauce. The good-textured dark chocolate cake is moist and wonderfully gooey on the bottom. The bits of hazelnuts add chewiness and the coffee cream has a light coffee flavor that compliments the chocolate.

We could not review their **White Chocolate Mousse with Raspberry Sauce** because it was late when we arrived and constant opening the refrigerator had caused the mousse to fall and lose its texture.

Getting there: Downtown near the Park Blocks.

Genoa
2832 SE Belmont, Portland, OR. (503) 238-1464

♥♥♥ One of Portland's best restaurants, **Genoa** has been serving sumptuous 7-course, fixed-price Northern Italian meals for 26 years. More recently, they've begun serving 4-course meals on weekdays. Diners always have a seafood, poultry, or meat selection and a choice of 7 different desserts. While the menu and desserts change regularly, there are always at least 2 intensely chocolate desserts that feature the dense taste of bittersweet chocolate. Their **Torta de Santa Maria**, our favorite, is a delightfully rich, fruity blend of raisins marinated in Grand Marnier, ground toasted hazelnuts and European chocolate flourless cake crumbs, frosted with chocolate buttercream. The chocolate-raisin-nut flavor combination is both unusual and delicious.

Their **La Victoire** is a **Chocolate Soufflé** served with a pistachio sauce that is very light with a densely chocolate flavor. The pistachio custard sauce adds an interesting contrast to the chocolate.

Genoa's traditional **Cassatta** is 7 layers of lemon pound cake speckled with candied orange peel and chocolate with ricotta cheese and Grand Marnier cream. It's all frosted with rich chocolate butter cream. It's a light Italian classic.

The **Michaneglo** is a light chocolate cake with a swirl of almond-flavored frangipanne filling frosted with chocolate espresso buttercream. The almond filling is intense. Plan on sharing this almost too-rich dessert.

Getting there: Located in Southeast Portland on the corner of 28ᵗʰ and Belmont.

Heathman Restaurant and Bar (Heathman Hotel)
1001 SW Broadway, Portland, OR. (503) 241-4100

♥♥♥ Large windows overlook busy Broadway in the contemporary **Heathman Restaurant and Bar**, the restaurant that Executive Chef Philippe Boulot put on the culinary map. The decor is simple and understated—cloth-covered tables with tiny votive lights, black leather and wood arm chairs, and beige walls. The only real colors are Andy Warhol Endangered Species animal prints that dominate one end of the restaurant. The menu, which changes seasonally, features dishes like wild Chinook salmon, baked rockfish and shrimp mousse wrapped in spring cabbage, braised rabbit in cider, and steak a la bordelaise. Pastry chef Susan Boulot does the chocolate honors with offerings like **Chocolate Gourmandise**, a warm chocolate cake draped in chocolate sauce served with homemade vanilla ice cream. The individual cake is tiny—about 2 inches around—but it's rich, with an ultra-dark chocolate flavor, and exquisitely gooey texture. The chocolate sauce is wonderfully rich and the vanilla ice cream adds a cool, clean creaminess to this decadent chocolate dessert. It's a winner for true chocolate lovers.

> *"The secret of working with chocolate is 20 years of practice. You have to work with it enough that you can feel when it's right."*
>
> – Janele Smith,
> chocolatier,
> Fenton and Lee,
> Eugene, Oregon

Susan's **Malted Milk Chocolate Ice Cream Sandwich** features 2 thick, 4-inch chocolate fudge cookies that sandwich malted chocolate ice cream and chopped Whoppers. It's garnished with swirls of creme anglaise and chocolate sauce. The cookies are chocolaty and fudgy with a nice crunch and the malted chocolate ice cream has plenty of malted flavor. However, because the ice cream is quite soft and the cookies thick and crisp, the ice cream tends to squirt out when you take spoonful. Good flavor, but this reviewer would like to see the malted ice cream served firmer to make this delightful dessert easier to eat.

The Fine Chocolate Tart is a 4-inch round thin biscuit that's filled with fudgy ganache. It's cradled in a large pool of pistachio cream that's topped with finely-chopped pistachios. The biscuit is rich and crisp. The ganache is thick, melting instantly in the mouth, and the pistachio cream is rich, yet subtle.

Traveler's note: The boisterous Heathman Bar is right across from the restaurant. If you're looking for a quiet meal, request a table furthest from the bar.
***Getting there:** On Broadway at Salmon.*

Higgins
1239 SW Broadway, Portland, OR. (503) 222-9070
♥♥♥ **Higgins** is a hip, urban place with blonde wood floors, a pressed tin ceiling, purple/olive curtains, large windows, and white cloth-covered tables with tiny table lamps. They serve Northwest cuisine at lunch and dinner with entrees like curried red lentil cakes, lamb shank with carrot charmoula, spinach and 3 cheese cannelloni, and Alaskan spot prawns, Willapa Bay oysters, and rockfish and chorizo.

Desserts, which change twice a month, often include at least 1 chocolate item like **Chocolate Malt Custard with 3 Different Chocolate Chip Cookies**. It comes in a 4x8-inch shallow, oval baking dish, dusted with powered sugar and garnished with a dollop of lightly-sweetened whipped cream, a wedge of chocolate, and 3 tiny chocolate chip cookies. The custard is ultra-creamy, dancing lightly over the tongue, with an interesting blend of malt and light chocolate flavors that invites another bite. The cookies are crisp and full of chocolate chips.

Getting there: Downtown on Broadway at Jefferson.

London Grill (Benson Hotel)
309 SW Broadway, Portland, OR. (503) 295-4110
♥♥♥ Located down a grand stairway from the lobby of the historic Benson Hotel, the **London Grill** has been feeding visitors and locals for more than 30 years. The ambiance is traditional— oak paneling, arched ceilings, candle-style chandeliers, and fresh flowers on each cloth-covered table. They serve breakfast, lunch, and dinner. Entrees are timeless dishes like salmon filet, garlic and herb roasted chicken, pan seared veal chops, and mustard crusted rack of lamb.

The dessert menu, which changes every couple of weeks, is sure to please chocolate lovers with a number of chocolate offerings like warm chocolate bread pudding, chocolate almond soufflé, or dark Godiva cheesecake. The desserts are all artfully presented and garnished with fresh raspberries, kiwis, blood oranges, and strawberries. Their **White Chocolate Grand Marnier Mousse** comes piped into a lovely white chocolate swan floating in a pool of raspberry puree. The mousse is light-as-air with a subtle Grand Marnier flavor. The swan has a creamy, not overly sweet flavor, and the raspberry puree is lip-smacking tart-sweet.

Their **Mousse Trio**, white chocolate, milk chocolate, and Grand Marnier mousses, comes in tiny dark and white chocolate cups. The white chocolate mousse is light and subtly flavored. The Grand Marnier mousse is the same delightful mousse described above and the milk chocolate mousse has a good chocolate flavor, though its texture is slightly grainy.

The **Tri-colored Terrine** is a triangle of silky white, dark, and milk chocolate. It's garnished with strings of dark chocolate, swirls of caramel puree, and fresh fruit. The terrine is rich, with an excellent blending of the 3 chocolate flavors, and the caramel puree is thick and buttery.

Getting there: In the Benson Hotel on Broadway at Oak.

Papa Haydn
5829 SE Milwaukie Avenue, Portland OR. (503) 232-9440

Other Portland location:

Papa Haydn West, 701 NW 23ʳᵈ, Portland, OR. (503) 228-7317

♥♥♥ **Papa Haydn East** is a small, casual neighborhood place with blonde wooden chairs and tables, ceiling fans, windows overlooking Milwaukie Avenue, and one of the biggest dessert display cases you'll see. They serve lunch and dinner, with offerings like salads, reuben and black forest ham sandwiches, and hot entrees like scallops carbonara, pork stew, and lamb shank with couscous. For many, however, desserts are the real draw. Papa Haydn East and Papa Haydn West are dessert central for Portland. They offer more than 15 different desserts, all of them over-sized and beautiful. **Autumn Meringue**, their signature chocolate dessert, is alternating layers of Swiss meringue and dark chocolate mousse, enrobed in dark chocolate with big, fluffy ribbons of dark chocolate on top. This incredibly rich, chocolaty dessert's mousse is thick, more like pudding than mousse. The Swiss meringue provides a sweet lightness and crunch.

Marjolaine is a big 7x2-inch slab that starts with a layer of meringue/praline crust with an inch of dark chocolate mousse, an inch of hazelnut meringue that's topped with creme fraiche and streaks of dark chocolate. This marjolaine has a terrific combination of soft and crunchy textures and chocolate, hazelnut, and praline flavors. Yum!

Their **Chocolate Raspberry Terrine** features 2 layers of thick mousse separated by a layer of raspberry, served with a tart and tangy raspberry sauce. The mousse is velvety with an intense chocolate flavor and the raspberry sauce provides the flavor of fresh raspberries. This is a major chocolate hit, chocolate fans!

Black Velvet comes with 4 inches of brandy and espresso mousse that's wrapped in genoise cake and glazed in dark chocolate. The brandy and espresso give the mousse a lovely, rich depth, while the genoise adds a bit of contrasting texture.

Triple Chocolate Torte is an impressive 6 inches tall with 4 layers of dark chocolate buttermilk cake filled with espresso ganache, glazed with milk chocolate frosting, and garnished with thick ropes of dark chocolate. The cake is moist and fine-textured. The espresso ganache doesn't detract. In fact, one reviewer, who isn't a coffee fan, loved this basic chocolate cake.

Papa Haydn offers plenty of goodies for non-chocolate fans like strawberry tart, NY cheesecake, Key Lime cheesecake, Irish coffee charlotte, berry cobbler, and blackberry streusel tart.

Getting there: *In the Sellwood neighborhood, on Milwaukie at Ramona (next to the Yukon Tavern).*

Red Star Tavern and Roast House (5th Avenue Suites)
503 SW Alder, Portland, OR. (503) 222-0005

♥♥♥ **Red Star** is a hip and happening Tuscan bistro with soaring boxed ceilings, large murals, big pillars, over-sized marble and glass light fixtures, hardwood floors, yellow faux-painted adobe walls, burgundy booths and white-clothed tables, dramatic flower arrangements, an open brick oven and rotisserie, and 40's jazz wafting on the air. Their dinner menu, which changes every 3 months, features dishes like cedar planked salmon, lemon chicken with rosemary, pork loin with mustard cure, and fisherman's stew (scallops, crab, prawns, new potatoes, and roasted vegetables).

All of pastry chef Tim Daly's desserts are elegantly served without being fussy and the portions are quite generous. His **Tazo Earl Grey Tea and Bittersweet Chocolate Custard** is a baked custard (pot de creme) that comes in a large porcelain coffee cup topped with a dab of chantilly cream, candied orange zest, and crushed chocolate. It's served with 2 rolled orange snap cookies. The custard, infused with Early Grey tea and flavored with bitter orange, has a depth not often found in custard. The texture is silky smooth and the orange zest and chocolate on top add a contrasting crunch.

Granny Pearl's Banana and Chocolate Bread Pud'n, is a big triangle of bread and chocolate cake bread pudding that incorporates grandmother Pearl's banana bread recipe. It comes with rum creme anglaise and bittersweet chocolate sauce with slices of caramelized banana and chocolate curls. The pudding is tasty, but is light on chocolate flavor. The texture is satisfyingly chewy. By itself, the anglaise has a strong rum flavor, but with the pudding, it's quite complimentary.

> **Chocolate prevents cavities.** The American Dental Association says chocolate contains a protein that blocks the formation of plaque. Cocoa butter in chocolate helps rinse out plaque-causing sugar and other food particles that cause cavities.

Tim's **Chocolate Frenzy**, this reviewer's favorite, keeps getting put back on the menu by popular demand. It's a layer of sour cream chocolate cake that's topped with a huge scoop of homemade cocoa ice cream. The dessert is garnished with milk and dark chocolate sauces, 3 dollops of whipped cream, crushed chocolate, and chocolate curls. This, chocolate lovers, is intense chocolate! The sour cream cake adds a wonderfully sharp contrast to the dark, sweet ice cream. As you dig into the ice cream, you'll be pleasantly surprised to find a cinnamon-flavored, white chocolate truffle buried in the center. The chocolate sauces combine for a rich, smooth flavor. Go for this one, chocolate lovers, when you want a serious chocolate fix.

Getting there: SW Alder at 5th.

Rimsky-Korsakoffee House
707 SE 12th Street, Portland, OR. (503) 232-2640

♥♥♥ In a big, brick red Old Portland style house, **Rimsky-Korsakoffee House** is a dessert and coffee house that's a little different. In the livingroom-parlor of the old house, guests are entertained by live classical music from a grand piano. There are several small tables for 2 or 4, each dedicated to a different composer. Just for fun, one of the tables slowly rises and falls—so slowly that it usually goes unnoticed by hapless guests until it's too late and everyone else is laughing. The upstairs bathroom is a must-see—painted with fish, plants, and blue water so that it appears you're under water, a pair of feet and a dock dangle from the ceiling while a bearded mannequin in formal clothing and silver boots reclines in the corner with a lap full of colorful fish. From early evening until midnight (an hour later on weekends), they serve tea, coffee, and espresso drinks, and a variety of desserts. Their house special is **Mocha Fudge Cake**, a thin 4x4-inch square of fudgy cake that's drizzled with a light glaze. While it doesn't look impressive, this cake is melt-in-the-mouth delicious. It's slightly crusty and crumbly on top; velvety creamy in the center. The glaze gives it a slightly fruity taste. It's delicious!

They regularly serve other chocolate desserts like Chocolate Pot de Creme and Chocolate Fool, a combination of raspberry mousse, chocolate pot de creme, and chocolate candy. In addition, they offer other chocolate desserts as specials.

Getting there: On SE 12th at Alder.

Southpark
901 SW Salmon Street, Portland OR. (503) 326-1300

♥♥♥ One of Portland's newest additions to the culinary scene, **Southpark** is a seafood grill and wine bar situated in the cavernous space formerly occupied by B. Moloch/Heathman. With its blond wood floors, big faux-painted pillars, tiny artsy lights, dark green booths, blonde wood tables with votives, big mirrors, and a large Parisian-style mural dominating one wall, Southpark is a casually boisterous place that invites diners to enjoy. Their menu features entrees like grilled grape leaf salmon, halibut with Venetian sweet and sour sauce, and terra cotta monk fish with olives, artichokes, roasted shallots, and preserved lemon. For those who don't like fish, they offer a veal and a chicken dish. Chocolate lovers can look forward to chocolate delights like **Chocolate Soufflé**, a 4-inch round individual soufflé that's served warm with a small pot of raspberry sauce. This dessert has an ultra-rich chocolate flavor. The top crust is slightly crispy; the middle, a soft cake-like texture. The delicate raspberry sauce adds a nice contrast without overwhelming the chocolate flavor. Or you may want to try the **Tartufi**, a big, fist-sized ball of homemade milk chocolate ice cream that's been rolled in chocolate shavings. The suprise is a small grappa-soaked truffle in the center. The milk chocolate ice cream is rich and creamy without clinging to the palate. The chocolate shavings add a good chocolate flavor and a bit of chewiness. The center truffle shouts, "Grappa" and can dominate if you take too big a bite, but in tiny portions, the grappa truffle gives an interesting accent to the milk chocolate ice cream.

Getting there: Right off the Park Blocks near the Portland Art Museum.

Café de Amis
1987 NW Kearny, Portland, OR. (503) 295-6487
♥♥ **Café de Amis** is a small, light-filled neighborhood restaurant with big windows with lacy café curtains, white cloth-covered tables with fresh flowers, and a scattering of photos and prints on white walls. Their dinner menu, which changes seasonally, includes entrees like braised lamb shanks, grilled pork loin, Salmon troisgros, and duck with blackberry sauce, among others. Steven Smith, the pastry chef, whips up desserts like **Walnut Banana Cake with Banana Caramel Ice Cream**, 2 layers of banana walnut cake filled and frosted with dark chocolate topped with chocolate curls and a dusting of powered sugar. The cake is moist and dense with a strong banana flavor. The frosting is thick, almost fudgy. The banana caramel ice cream offers a lovely blend of buttery caramel and banana flavors.

Getting there: On the corner of 20th and NW Kearny.

Fiddleheads
6716 SE Milwaukie, Portland, OR. (503) 233-1547
♥♥ **Fiddleheads** is hip and upscale with its tall ceilings, textured green and mustard walls, persimmon wainscoting, bold geometric patterns, and Native American art. Open for brunch, lunch, and dinner, entrees favor regional ingredients and include dishes like Juniper Grilled Venison, Prime Rib with Pinot Noir Sauce, Oregon Chicken with fresh herbs, and Winter Steelhead. Their menu, including the dessert menu, changes seasonally. Chocolate lovers can always count on at least 1 chocolate selection such as **Chocolate Marquise with Huckleberry Sauce**, a 4-inch slab of dense chocolate that's served pate style with drizzles of huckleberry sauce, whipped cream, homemade cookies, chopped hazelnuts, and a tiny rosebud. The texture is dense and slightly crumbly with a medium chocolate flavor that's satisfying. The lightly sweetened cream adds a creamy lightness and the huckleberry sauce is appropriately sweet-tart.

Getting there: In the Sellwood district, on Milwaukie near Bybee.

Jake's Famous Crawfish

401 SW 12th, Portland, OR. (503) 226-1419

♥♥ Venerable **Jake's Famous Crawfish** has been wooing Portlanders with fresh seafood for more than 100 years. Situated in the old Whitney Grey Building on the corner of 12th and Stark, Jake's is a step back in time with dark green carpets, Victorian chandeliers, historic murals, cozy wooden booths, bent wood chairs and tables, and velvet embossed wallpaper. Their lunch and dinner offerings, which rely heavily on fish, include dishes like Jake's cakes (crab, crawfish, and salmon), sturgeon, Alaskan halibut, pecan-crusted catfish, and tuna with cranberries, orange zest, and port. For those who don't care for fish, they offer steaks and chops.

Their signature chocolate dessert is **Jake's Famous Truffle Cake**, a generous 1-inch tall wedge that's dusted with powered sugar and served with a dollop of whipped cream and raspberry melba sauce. It's rich, thick, and fudgy with a chocolate flavor that doesn't overpower. The sweet, thick raspberry sauce nicely compliments the cake. This is a rich one you can share with a friend.

Their other ode to chocolate is **Chocolate Hazelnut Mousse**, a milk chocolate mousse that's laced with hazelnut liqueur and garnished with a tiny dollop of whipped cream and chopped roasted hazelnuts. It's a generous serving that comes in a tall sundae glass. The mousse is ultra-light, almost airy, and melts in the mouth instantly. The hazelnut flavor is light, not overpowering, and the chopped hazelnuts offer a nice crunch. This is a darned good mousse, chocolate lovers.
Getting there: On 12th at Stark.

Jake's Grill (Governor Hotel)

611 SW 10th, Portland, OR. (503) 241-2100

♥♥ When the old Governor Hotel was renovated, they asked McCormick and Schmick, the folks who run Jake's Famous Crawfish and a number of other successful restaurants, to open **Jake's Grill**. It was a good choice. The restaurant's 20-foot boxed ceilings, mahogony columns, original mosaic tile floors, long mahogany bar, and bent wood chairs and tables lend just the right casual, clubby ambiance. They serve breakfast, lunch and dinner. Paper menus, which are printed daily, offer dishes like steaks, chops, poultry, and old favorites like blue cheese steak, chicken marsala, chicken pot pie, macaroni and cheese, and even meatloaf with hot fanny gravy.

They serve **Jake's Famous Truffle Cake**, which is made at Jake's Famous Crawfish (see review), as well as **Chocolate Mousse**. Whole Jake's Truffle Cakes are also available at Made in Oregon stores.
Getting there: In the Governor Hotel on 10th at Alder.

Opus Too

33 NW 2nd Avenue, Portland, OR. (503) 222-6077

♥♥ Situated in Portland's Old Town District, **Opus Too** is 2 long, narrow rooms—1 with an open kitchen, long counter, and wonderful stained glass ceiling; the other features wooden tables and chairs, 2 large stained glass light fixtures, and a beautiful lead and beveled glass window. An open doorway from the kitchen dining room leads to Jazz de Opus, the restaurant's clubby lounge that features live nightly jazz. Opus Too serves lunch and dinner. Their large dinner menu relies heavily on their mesquite grill, offering dishes like filet, rib eye, New York, lamb, chicken, salmon, ahi tuna, snapper, steelhead, and halibut, among others. Their nightly fresh sheet features entrees like macadamia encrusted Ahi with ginger butter and honey razor clams.

For chocolate lovers, their signature chocolate dessert is **Chocolate Decadence**, a thick, nearly flourless torte that's served with commercial chocolate syrup and a dollop of whipped cream. It's very thick and fudgy, melting in the mouth smoothly and quickly.

Their **Espresso-Chocolate Swirl Cheesecake**, this reviewer's favorite, starts with a chocolate cookie crust that's topped with 2 inches of creamy chocolate espresso cheesecake. With flecks of finely-ground espresso and swirls of chocolate, it's a soft blend of coffee and chocolate flavors that java lovers will appreciate.

The big wedge of **Chocolate Peanut Butter Torte** features an inch layer of dense chocolate decadence that's punctuated with chopped walnuts and an inch of thick peanut butter-cream cheese, that's topped with an inch of fudgy ganache. The peanut butter layer is velvety with an intense peanut butter flavor. Paired with the chocolate layers, it's very rich, almost too rich for this reviewer's taste.

Getting there: NW Couch at 2nd.

Marco's Café and Espresso Bar

7910 SW 35th Avenue, Portland, OR. (503) 245-0199

♥♥ **Marco's** is a pleasant neighborhood restaurant with latte- and country blue-colored walls, hanging plants, café curtains on big windows, wooden tables and chairs and an open kitchen and espresso bar. The effect is comfortable, neighborly. They serve breakfast, lunch, and dinner. They're known for their all-day breakfasts, including cheese blintzes and French toast made from broiche dipped in egg and grilled. At lunch, they serve salads and inventive sandwiches like eggplant with feta cheese, cucumber, tomatoes and sprouts with hummus, and BLT with bacon, Swiss, lettuce, tomato, guacamole, and herb mayonnaise. Dinner entrees, which change regularly, always include 2 vegetarian dishes, and selections like salmon and mixed grill. Their dessert case tempts choco-

Portland &
Surrounding
Communities

late lovers with the signature **Chocolate Velvet**, a thick chocolate cookie crust, 2 inches of chocolate mousse and 2 inches of whipped cream. The crust is crumbly and chocolaty, the mousse is rich, though not as creamy as it could be, and the whipped cream is real, not canned.

An entirely successful dessert is pastry chef Annie Peterson's **Milk Chocolate Hazelnut Ice Cream**. It's a big scoop of milk chocolate ice cream studded with plenty of chopped, roasted hazelnuts and served with a chocolate chip hazelnut biscotti. The ice cream, which Annie makes the old fashioned way with ice and rock salt, has a rich chocolate-hazelnut flavor, and is smooth and creamy without clinging to the tongue. The biscotti is big—6x2-inches—and crisp without being too hard. It has a good flavor with plenty of chocolate chips and bits of hazelnut.

> **Chocolate is for Lovers.**
> **Chocolate contains phenyl-ethylamine, an anti-depressant and nervous system stimulant. It creates a state of euphoria similar to feelings of love.**

Chocolate Orange Roulade is 3 thin layers of dark chocolate cake rolled around whipped cream that's been flavored with Triple Sec and pieces of fresh orange. It's served with creme anglaise and orange sections. This ultra-rich cake is moist with a lovely combination of orange and chocolate flavors. The creme anglaise is thick and rich, almost like custard.

Chocolate Crackle Cookie is a big, 4-inch round, dark chocolate cookie that's dusted with powdered sugar. It's soft and chewy like a soft brownie with a slightly crunchy top.

Marco's also serves a large selection of espresso drinks, many of them with chocolate. Their **Bella Mocha** is espresso and steamed milk with Guittard white chocolate and cocoa powder. It's rich and chocolaty and the white chocolate gives it a deep creaminess. Yum! *Getting there: In Multnomah Village, on SW 35th at Multnomah.*

Rose's Restaurant
12329 NE Glisan, Gresham, OR. (503) 254-6545
♥♥ **Roses's Restaurant** is back! That's good news for patrons who, for more than 40 years, enjoyed Rose's deli sandwiches piled high with thin slices of meats and cheeses and their incredibly huge cakes and pastries. Several years ago, the venerable 3-restaurant/bakery establishment was purchased and 2 locations and the bakery quickly closed. Then 3 years ago, Mike Roberts and Carol

Johnston bought the remaining Gresham restaurant and set about to recapture Rose's former glory. They serve breakfast, lunch, and dinner, including a daily $2.95 breakfast special as well as lunch and dinner specials. You can still get many of the old favorites like giant deli sandwiches including their famous Reuben sandwich, cheese blintzes, and chicken matzo ball soup. Dinner selections include pot roast, lasagna, top sirloin, meatloaf and gravy, and prime rib.

Save lots of room for one of Roses's 30 desserts, including their impossibly huge pastries and cakes. Although Rose's Bakery is gone, they farm out their baking to a couple of local bakeries who use Rose's original recipes to create desserts like the **Florentiner**, a 6-inch macaroon crescent shell that's filled with milk chocolate cream and dipped in chocolate. The cookie is delicately crunchy and the chocolate cream is silky and light without being airy.

Their **Black Forest Cake**, at 7 inches high, has 7 layers of medium chocolate cake separated by layers of whipped cream, Kirsch cherries, and Kirschasser Liqueur, all frosted with whipped cream and shaved chocolate. The cake is moist and the filling adds a subtle, fresh cherry flavor that's refreshing.

Rose's Pecan Fudge Cake is 5 layers of fudge chocolate cake speckled with chopped pecans and frosted with chocolate buttercream. This cake has plenty of pecan flavor and the buttercream is thick and fudgy.

Their 7-inch **Almond Roca Cake** features 6 layers of chocolate champagne cake lined and frosted with chocolate buttercream and chunks of Almond Roca. The ultra-light buttercream compliments this light cake and the Almond Roca candy pieces add a sweet almond surprise. Their **German Chocolate Cake**, one of the best we've had, is a satisfying variation on an old theme. Instead of the usual milk chocolate cake, it comes with 6 layers of a moist, super dark chocolate cake separated by alternating layers of pecans and coconut and praline filling. It's topped with coconut and pecan and frosted with chocolate buttercream. This excellent cake is rich, moist, and deeply chocolaty. The coconut-nut filling has a good coconut flavor without being overly sweet and the buttercream frosting is light-as-air.

Rose's **French Silk Cake**, their tallest cake, is 8 layers of ultra-dark chocolate cake filled and frosted with a milk chocolate buttercream, garnished with a darker buttercream and a dark chocolate fan. The cake is moist with an even texture. The frosting is incredibly creamy and compliments the deep chocolate flavor of the cake.

Death by Chocolate, one of the only normal-sized desserts they offer, is a dense, flourless cake with a thin walnut crust, followed by 2 layers of fudgy chocolate that sandwich a layer of chocolate mousse. True chocoholics will love this thick, fudge-like dessert.

Their **Rocky Road Brownie** is a 2x4-inch bar that starts with a thin layer of chewy brownie that's topped with a mound of tiny marshmallows and chopped walnuts that's covered in chocolate. More candy than brownie, this reviewer found this brownie too sweet.
Getting there: On Glisan at 122nd in the Menlo Park Plaza.

The Berlin Inn
3131 SE 12th, Portland, OR. (503) 236-6761
♥♥ Dark wood, white walls, lacy curtains, stained glass, blue-clothed tables, and prints of the Bavarian countryside decorate this German restaurant, **The Berlin Inn**. They serve traditional German dishes for lunch and dinner like schnitzel platter, smoked salmon veggie potato cakes, sauerbrauten (beef marinated in red wine, herbs, and seasonings), chicken cordon bleu, and alder smoked pork chops. Chef/owner Karen Bauer, who trained under Jicava's Jack Elmer, bakes in the European tradition. She uses less sugar, sponge cake that is brushed with liqueurs, and many imported products like European preserves, which don't use sugar. The result are desserts like her **Black Forest Cake**, that starts with a thin vanilla cookie crust, followed by 3 layers of chocolate sponge cake that have been brushed with cherry brandy, a layer of sour cherry filling and light chantilly cream. It's an interesting blending of flavors, but the sour cherry filling tends to dominate the light cake and cream.

Her **Grand Marnier Truffle Cake** is 3 layers of the same chocolate sponge cake brushed with orange brandy, layered with Grand Marnier truffle filling and a milk chocolate mousse, topped with chocolate ganache. This dessert has lovely, soft textures and a nice combination of orange and chocolate flavors. The **Apricot Cappuccino Cake** features alternating layers of chocolate sponge cake and espresso chantilly cream, highlighted with imported apricot preserves and garnished with candied coffee beans. Again, Berlin Inn achieves soft textures with this dessert and the coffee and apricot combination is a unique and successful pairing.

Chocolate Espresso Silk Torte has 2 ($1^1/_2$-inch) layers of light chocolate sponge cake layered with semi-sweet chocolate espresso mousse, finished with whipped cream. The cake, mousse, and cream all provide soft, melt-in-the-mouth textures and the mousse has a good chocolate flavor.
Getting there: On 12th at SE Powell.

American Palate

1937 NW 23rd Place, Portland, OR. (503) 223-6994

♥ In a bright blue converted house, **American Palate** is a casual, neighborhood spot with scuffed wooden floors, sponge-painted beige walls, cloth-covered tables with small candle-stick lamps, bent wood chairs, and paintings by local artists. Their dinner menu changes weekly, with offerings like herb crusted halibut, salmon with spicy pepper puree, roast chicken breast with morel mushroom sauce, and angel hair pasta with goat cheese and walnuts. Chef Kimmy Wartena makes a variety of desserts that all have a downhome look and taste. Her **Chocolate Cookie Sandwich with Malted Ice Cream** features 2 (4-inch) crisp chocolate cookies topped with granulated sugar that sandwich a thin layer of chocolate malted ice cream. The cookies have a spicy rather than chocolate flavor and are difficult to cut with a spoon. The chocolate malt ice cream is tasty with a light malt flavor.

The **Chocolate Swirl Cheesecake** is a generous wedge of very tangy cheesecake with plugs of dense Valhrona chocolate cheesecake throughout. This reviewer would have liked a sweeter chocolate cheesecake. However, if you eat the vanilla and chocolate cheesecake together, it's quite satisfying.

Flourless Cake with Strawberries and Whipped Cream is 2 diamonds of thin (1/2-inch) cake that sandwich fresh, sliced strawberries and whipped cream, garnished with a dollop of whipped cream. The cake is like a moist, fudgy brownie and the fresh strawberries add a fruity lightness to the dessert.

Getting there: On Vaughn Street at NW 23rd Place.

Bread and Ink Café

3610 SE Hawthorne, Portland, OR. (503) 239-4756

♥ A light and airy restaurant serving breakfast, lunch, and dinner, **Bread and Ink Café** is a favorite with Hawthorne area residents. They serve sumptuous breakfasts (don't miss their home-fried red potatoes) and interesting lunch fare such as enchilada verde, grilled salmon sandwiches, and moussaka. For dinner, they offer 5 or 6 entrees, which change regularly. Their desserts, which have an Italian flair, include **Il Diplomatico,** a torte of rich chocolate mousse sandwiched between layers of rum and espresso-soaked pound cake, frosted with chocolate ganache. The mousse is thick and rich and blends well with the smoky, intense rum flavor.

Their **Cassatta Siciliana** features thin layers of pound cake with lightly sweetened ricotta, candied orange peel, and bittersweet chocolate frosted with espresso-flavored chocolate ganache. The pound cake is light and lemony and the frosting is densely chocolate flavored yet surprisingly light. The pieces of candied orange peel are a bit large and can distract from the overall effect.

Their **Chocolate Pot de Creme** is like biting into the inside of a dark truffle. It's a thick, creamy, dense chocolate custard flavored with Meyer's dark rum and garnished with whipped cream. You must love dense, dark chocolate to enjoy this dessert.

Getting there: *Located in Southeast Portland at the corner of 36th and Hawthorne.*

Montage

301 SE Morrison Street, Portland, OR. (503) 234-1324

♥ **Montage** is a quirky blend of Generation-X hip and fine dining. It's a place of sharp contrasts. The restaurant is located in the industrial district under the Morrison Street bridge, yet features beautifully-set linen covered tables. The wine list is intelligent and extensive, but the bright, red uni-sex, graffiti-filled bathroom looks like something you'd find in a rock and roll club. The menu features Southern Cajun dishes like blackened catfish and Jambalaya as well as macaroni and Spam. Their desserts include **Mississippi Mud Pie**, a huge slab of mocha almond fudge ice cream topped with whipped cream and cookie crumbs with an Oreo cookie crust so thick it doesn't cut with a fork. The piece is generous, but the crust lacks chocolate flavor.

Instead, we'd recommend the **Chocolate Pot de Creme**, a creamy, light chocolate egg custard. It's served with forgettable shortbread cookies, but the custard is one of the better ones we've tasted.

Getting there: *Located under the Morrison Bridge at the corner of 3rd and Morrison, just off Martin Luther King Boulevard (Highway 99).*

Chocolate Event!

RiverPlace Chocolate Invitational. Sample an array of chocolate delights from award-winning Portland chefs. Taste wines and coffee blends specially selected to match different types of chocolate. Proceeds benefit the Children's Museum. Held in February at the RiverPlace Hotel, 1510 SW Barbur Way, Portland. Call (503) 228-3233 for more information.

Portland Steak and Chop House (Embassy Suites)

121 SW Third Avenue, Portland, OR. (503) 223-6200

♥ In the renovated old Multnomah Hotel, circa 1912, the **Portland Steak and Chop House** has just the right ambiance for a steak place—red naugahyde booths, dark wood wainscoting, wooden blinds, dark wood arm chairs, white cloth-covered tables, and 30's and 40's piped-in jazz. They serve lunch and dinner, offering interesting pizzas like roma tomato and roasted garlic, smoked salmon and brie, and Italian chicken sausage and mushrooms, as well as entrees like roasted half-chicken, pork tenderloin, and portobello mushroom steaks from their wood-fired oven. They offer plenty of steaks and chops—New York, filet, sirloin, porterhouse, pork chops, veal chops and lamb chops. They also serve a few seafood and pasta dishes.

For chocolate lovers, the **Grand Marnier Triple Chocolate Cake** is 4 half-layers of medium chocolate cake soaked in simple syrup and Grand Mariner, filled with mocha frosting (chocolate sabayon) and raspberry, and frosted with bittersweet ganache. The cake is moist and fudgy with a lilt of orange flavor. The sabayon is light and creamy with a good mocha flavor. The ganache has a creamy texture, but its chocolate flavor is overwhelmed by the Grand Mariner.

The **Hazelnut Chocolate Tart** is a wedge of chocolate crust, followed by a half-inch layer of chocolate truffle caramel with finely ground hazelnuts and a half-inch layer of espresso cream. It's garnished with commercial chocolate sauce and shaved chocolate. It's nutty and chewy, with more hazelnut than chocolate taste. The espresso cream is so subtle it gets lost.

The **White Chocolate Mousse**, the most successful of their chocolate desserts, comes piped in a lacy, praline cup, served on a bed of raspberry coulis and creme anglaise. Nicely presented, the mousse is very light; the praline cup is crispy and buttery; and the raspberry/creme anglaise adds a subtle raspberry flavor to this light-as-air dessert.
Getting there: On 3ʳᵈ between Pine and Ash.

Toulouse
71 SW 2ⁿᵈ Avenue, Portland, OR. (503) 241-4343
♥ Located in an Old Town building, **Toulouse** has exposed brick walls, blonde wood floors, tall windows overlooking 2ⁿᵈ Avenue, and an open kitchen with a wood-fired grill and rotisserie. They serve lunch and dinner, focusing on mesquite and rotisserie cooked meats and comfort foods like mashed potatoes and root vegetables. Dinner entrees include steamed Alaskan halibut with pink grapefruit, rabbit fricassee with thyme, wild mushrooms and feta in phyllo, duck with herb wild rice, risotto primavera, and herb crusted lamb.

For dessert, their **Double Chocolate Terrine** is a 4x4-inch slab of dense chocolate mousse and white chocolate/hazelnut praline mousse (the contrasting colors form a "T") with a thin layer of chocolate soufflé on the bottom and a thin layer of chocolate ganache on the outside. It comes on an over-sized plate in a pool of raspberry coulis and creme fraiche, all dusted with cocoa and powered sugar. The chocolate mousse is thick, almost fudgy; the white chocolate mousse has a light hazelnut flavor that's not overpowering. The ganache, though a bit sticky, has a good chocolate flavor, but the raspberry puree is quite tart.

Their **Opera Cake** is a 3¹/₂-inch square of alternating layers of chocolate soufflé, almond meringue, chocolate mousse, and espresso buttercream that's topped with a thin layer of chocolate ganache, in a pool of mint anglaise, garnished with chocolate fans. This moist opera cake is a complex blending of many flavors that work, but it's overwhelmed by the minty flavor of the anglaise. If you like Opera Cake, we'd suggest ordering it without the mint sauce.

Getting there: *On 2ⁿᵈ at Ash, just south of Burnside.*

Bakeries

Three Lions Bakery
1138 SW Morrison, Portland, OR. (503) 224-3429
Other Portland Locations:
135 NW 5ᵗʰ Ave, Portland, OR. (503) 224-9039
4147 SE Division, Portland, OR. (503) 236-4783
501 N Graham, Portland, OR. (503) 287-8556
♥♥♥♥ Walk into **Three Lions Bakery** and you'll be overwhelmed by the beautiful and delicious European-style pastries, cookies, cakes, and tarts. Their **Mocha Nut Fudge Brownie** is a 2x4-inch bar with a wonderfully crunchy top and a soft, chewy middle. The combination of coffee and chocolate is rich and wonderful. Even a non-coffee drinking reviewer commented, "This is a great brownie!"

Their **Peanut Butter Fudge Bar** has a soft, rich peanut butter center enrobed in dark chocolate and topped with chopped peanuts. This devilishly delicious bar melts in the mouth like a chocolate meltaway. It's terrific!

Three Lions offers several cakes and tortes by the slice or whole like their **Mocha Whipped Cream Torte**, a chocolate genoise (light cake) filled with chocolate mousse, and frosted with mocha buttercream. It's topped with dark chocolate sauce and a mocha bean. The cake is ultra-soft, the mousse light, and the mocha buttercream is delicate. The intense coffee flavor is one java lovers will enjoy.

Their **Chocolate Bombe** is a dome-shaped cake filled with chocolate mousse and chocolate sponge cake that's coated with dark chocolate ganache. It's incredibly rich yet light and delicate. The mousse melts quickly in the mouth. The cake, mousse, and ganache combine for a rich, delicious treat that's not to be missed.

The **French Fudge Cake** is 4 layers of moist chocolate fudge cake filled and frosted with chocolate ganache and topped with truffles. This is a wonderful basic chocolate cake—rich, intensely chocolate flavored. The cake is moist, the ganache fudgy. It's a real dark chocolate lovers delight.

Their **Chocolate Eclair** is huge—8x5 inches and 4 inches high! The delicate pastry has just the right chewiness and it's completely filled with sweet cream. Even the chocolate icing on the top is of wonderful quality. We think is this the best eclair you'll find in the Pacific Northwest!

Three Lions also serves a few breakfast items as well as soups, sandwiches, and weekly hot entrees at lunch.
Getting there: (Morrison location) In downtown Portland, on Morrison at 11ᵗʰ.

Giving Chocolate the Squeeze. In 1828, Dutchman C.J. Van Houten invented the chocolate press, which squeezes out some of the cocoa butter and gives chocolate a smoother consistency (a process known as "dutching").

Joseph's Dessert Company
3436 SE Milwaukie, Portland, OR. (503) 231-0989
(special orders)
♥♥♥ In a little, unmarked storefront on Milwaukie Avenue, self-taught baker and pastry chef, Joseph Vasquez, and his crew turn out some of the best by-the-piece desserts you can buy in Portland, many of them chocolate. They use good quality Callebaut and Guittard chocolate and make everything from scratch, including their own toffee, glazes, and shells. Joseph, a dedicated chocolate lover, makes several chocolate desserts like **Double Chocolate Cake**, a 3¹/₂ inch round individual cake that's 2 layers of sour cream chocolate cake filled and frosted with chocolate ganache. The cake is moist with the tangy flavor of sour cream and the ganache is thick, fudgy, and smooth with a deep chocolate flavor.

His **Chocolate Cappuccino Toffee Cake**, this reviewer's favorite, is a 5x5x2-inch slice of thin layers of dark chocolate chiffon cake sandwiching 2 layers of chocolate-espresso mousse that are topped with whipped cream and chunky almond toffee pieces. It's a wonderful blending of textures—soft cake, smooth mousse, and crunchy toffee. The mousse offers a lovely combination of espresso and chocolate flavors and the toffee adds a buttery accent.

Joseph's Tiramisu is 2 layers of coffee- and rum-soaked sponge cake that's layered with whipped cream and mascarpone and topped with cocoa. The textures are soft and smooth and the cake is delicately soft, not overly wet. Although this tiramisu doesn't have the cheesy mascarpone flavor of some recipes, the rum flavor speaks with authority without overwhelming.

Coconut Cake is a 5x2x4-inch slice of 3 layers of white cake filled and frosted with white chocolate buttercream, topped with shredded coconut, and garnished with a tiny chocolate fan. The cake is ultra-soft while the coconut adds a chewy contrast. The white buttercream is delicate and not overly sweet. Coconut fans will enjoy this one.

White Chocolate Carrot Cake is another 3$^1/_2$-inch round individual cake that has 2 layers of moist carrot cake with walnuts, coconut, and pineapple filled and frosted with white chocolate buttercream and garnished with shredded white chocolate and white chocolate curls. This spicy cake is coarse textured with plenty of nuts, coconut, and pineapple to add a satisfying toothiness. The white chocolate buttercream is creamy and slightly tangy.

You can special order any of Joseph's dozen or so cakes, cheesecakes, tortes, and tarts whole by calling the bakery 3 days in advance. Or you can get his desserts by the slice at restaurants like **Flying Saucer Café, Common Grounds, Palio, Wild Heron, Thai Orchid**, and the **Hawthorne Café**, as well as retail outlets like **Cheshire Cat, Favorites Bakery, Zupan Markets, Pasta Works, Burlingame Market, Palisades Market, Wizer Grocery**, and **Strohecker's Markets**.
Getting there: SE Milwaukie at Rhine (special orders only).

Delphina's Neighborhood Baking Company
3310 NW Yeon, Portland, OR. (503) 221-1829
♥♥ Primarily a wholesale bakery, **Delphina's** runs a small retail operation in an unlikely industrial location where they sell a variety of breads (baguettes, seed semolina, olive, hearth, Swedish limpa, challah, Italian, rye, etc.), muffins, cookies, and brownies. Their **Chocolate Chip Cookie** is a full 6 inches of buttery goodness packed with chips. Their **Chocolate Fix Cookie** is a thick, 4-inch chocolate cookie with white chocolate chips that has a slightly crumbly-springy texture and good chocolate flavor.

Their **Mocha Swirl Pound Cake** is a dense, even-textured cake with a subtle coffee flavor. Their **Chocolate Yogurt Coffee Cake**, is a 4 inch square that's 2 inches high. It's a soft, moist cake that's topped with a thick layer of cinnamon sugar-chocolate chip topping. It's not long on chocolate flavor, but this cinnamon-rich coffee cake is tasty.

Their **Mocha Brownie** is a 3-inch square topped with chopped walnuts. Its cake-like texture and good chocolate flavor combine to make this a satisfying brownie. The **Chocolate Hazelnut Scone**, an 8-inch wedge filled with hazelnuts and chocolate chips, is less successful—a bit dry and crumbly. Their **Chocolate Croissant**, while flaky and buttery, needs more chocolate.

Getting there: On the way to St. Johns. Highway 30 (Yeon) just before 29th.

Piece of Cake Catering and Desserts
7858 SE 13th Street, Portland, OR. (503) 234-9445
♥ In a converted barn-style house decorated with small, gaily-painted wooden tables, **Piece of Cake** is a casual, funky place where people can buy **cakes, cheesecakes, tortes**, and **frozen desserts** by the slice or whole. They also make special order wedding cakes. Using no mixes and no shortening, self-taught baker and owner, Marilyn DeVault, says they make "grandmotherly" desserts. Their desserts are down home and reasonably priced rather than sophisticated. For chocolate lovers, Piece of Cake offers **Double Chocolate Fudge**, 2 layers of extra-dark chocolate cake that's frosted and filled with chocolate fudge frosting. The cake is very moist and fine-textured and the frosting soft. **Chocolate Chantilly Cake** offers 2 layers of the same dark chocolate cake frosted with cream cheese frosting and topped with a lacy pattern of dark chocolate. Though it's a bit sweet, the sour cream frosting provides a nice accent.

Chocolate Espresso Cake features 4 layers of the fudge cake with alternating layers of soft, silky espresso and fudge frosting. Their **Frosted Brownie** is 2x4 inches of dense fudgy brownie with a scattering of chopped hazelnuts that's topped with their fudge frosting.

Piece of Cake offers plenty of non-chocolate items like their **Irish Oatmeal Cake**, a moist oatmeal spice cake that's topped with a mixture of coconut, almonds, and caramel and frosted with cream cheese frosting. It's a soft, spicy, cinnomony treat. **Herman's Apple Rum Cake**, named after Marilyn's late father, is 2 layers of spicy cake packed the big pieces of apples, raisins, and walnuts. It's full of fruity goodness, though we found it a bit sweet.

Getting there: In the Sellwood neighborhood, on 13th at Bidwell.

Chocolate Shops

Bernard C.
4768 NW Bethany Boulevard, Portland, OR. (503) 690-8982
♥♥♥ (See review under Bernard Callebaut, Candy Shops, Victoria.)
Getting there: In Bethany Village.

JiCava's Chocolates and Pastries

4733 SE Hawthorne Boulevard, Portland, OR. (503) 234-8115 ♥♥♥ (chocolates)/ ♥♥♥ (cakes, tortes, pastries) If it's chocolate you want—from fine European filled chocolates, to delicate pastries and towering fudge tortes—you can find it at **JiCava's.** Their chocolate tastes like none other because they've developed their own formulations, blendings of different chocolate, to create unique dark, milk, and white chocolate. In their confectionery line, they feature delicate filled **European chocolates** in marvelous shapes such as leaves, shells, and fanciful swirls. The chocolate has just the right deep, rich flavor and snap as you bite into it and the fillings are incredibly creamy. They also feature **American chocolates**, which tend to be larger and not quite as creamy. In addition, the chocolatiers at JiCava's love to make **chocolate shapes**—cats, pigs, boxes, shells, cars, company logos. They also make chocolate shapes to order.

Their extensive line of pastries incude **Swiss Pastries**, thick boat-shaped cookie crusts dipped in chocolate and filled with raspberry, peanut butter, or other delightful flavors and garnished with a light chocolate cream and chocolate sprinkles. Their **Chocolate-dipped Spritz**, one of our favorites, is a buttery, flaky, melt-in-your-mouth spritz cookie dipped in dark chocolate. Their **Chocolate Monster Cookie** is a big, soft chocolate cookie dipped in chocolate with white chocolate drizzles. Their **Chocolate Brownie** (or the smaller **Chocolate Brownie Stick**) is a light, slightly crumbly brownie dipped entirely in chocolate and covered with chocolate drizzles. Their large **Rum Balls** have a dark, almost smoky flavor that makes you want more.

JiCava's also specializes in towering multi-layered cakes of soft, delicate cake and creamy fillings and frostings. They come in a variety of chocolate flavors, including **Fudge, 7th Heaven** (seven different kinds of chocolate), **Black Cherry Mousse, Chocolate Raspberry, Mint Chocolate Cheesecake, Chocolate Rum, Chocolate Mint, Austrian Gateau**, and **French Silk**. Unfortuntately, the cakes don't come by the slice, only in 6" or 9" cakes. If you call ahead, you can order your cake with any combination of cake flavors, fillings, and frostings.

Getting there: In Southeast Portland on the north side of Hawthorne between 46th and 47th.

Chocolatier Profile –

Iva Elmer
JaCiva Chocolates and Pastries
Portland, Oregon

Iva Elmer is an energetic woman, in love with life, with people, and with chocolate. When I first met her, she was hurrying out the door of her candy/bakery shop in Southeast Portland with a towering stack pastry boxes. There was a "chocolate emergency." One of her customers running a special on JiCava's eclairs had run out. In a moment, we were off, dispensing smiles, hugs, and, of course, chocolate.

Iva learned the chocolate trade from her Swiss husband, Jack, a European-trained pastry chef and chocolatier who started baking cakes at age 6. Iva and Jack worked side-by-side for years, first out of their basement, then later in the shop on Hawthorne, perfecting their chocolate formulations and building a loyal clientele. When Jack had a massive stroke in 1991, Iva took a larger role in running the business. A silver-haired woman with a quick smile and hearty laugh, Iva supervises, manages, bakes, decorates, delivers, and mothers the company's nearly 50 employees.

She routinely works 80-hour weeks, but doesn't seem to mind. "What else would I do?" she says smiling. "When you love what you do, it doesn't seem like work"

She recalls one night after the store was closed when a man pounded on the door, begging to be let in. He said his wife needed chocolate. He bought a pound of JiCava's European Chocolates. His wife got her chocolates and Iva earned the man's unswerving loyalty. He buys a pound of chocolates for his wife every week.

Iva eats chocolate every day. She says, "People ask, don't you get tired of chocolate? Not me. I love it."

She believes the secret to JiCava's success is that they never stop trying to improve their products. "Never think you have the best, the ultimate," she says. "Everything, even our chocolates, can be improved."

Moonstruck Chocolatiers
608 SW Alder, Portland, OR. (503) 241-0955
♥♥♥ (chocolates and cakes/pastries)/ ♥♥♥♥(chocolate drinks)

Although **Moonstruck Chocolatier** is only 5 years old, the company has gained a strong following among fans of artisan chocolates. Known for selecting only the finest quality cocoa beans and adding little sugar, Moonstruck chocolate has close to 70% cocoa content (most commercial chocolate has half the amount). Their signature chocolates are their **truffles**, whose fillings come right out of the Northwest: huckleberries from Mt. Hood, Chardonnay and Pinot Noir from the Willamette Valley, pear and apple brandy from Clear Creek Distillery, fruit preserves from Glenmore Farms. They come in flavors like **Pure Gold**, a dome of dark chocolate filled with Drambue and honey, decorated with a tiny fleck of edible gold. It's rich tasting with a center that's slightly stiff, but smooth. The **Oregon Wild Huckleberry** is milk chocolate molded into a berry shape with a white chocolate and huckleberry center. Creamy and berry good!

> **Chocolate "Blooms."** Ever noticed a white film that can develop on chocolate? This is chocolate bloom. It can form on chocolate that's been exposed to a high temperature. Bloom means the cocoa butter has crystallized and risen to the surface. It doesn't affect the flavor, but it does affect the smoothness. It may also mean your chocolate isn't fresh.

Their **Cinnamon Roll Latte**, shaped like a tiny cinnamon roll, has a milk chocolate center with a strong cinnamon flavor with subtle coffee undertones that's been enrobed in milk chocolate. It's breakfast for chocolate lovers. For even more coffee flavor, the **Italia** is a dark chocolate pyramid with white chocolate on top and a dark chocolate espresso center. The espresso flavor is a bit heavy for this java lover.

Raspberry Chambord comes with a dark chocolate center with an intense raspberry flavor. Their **Clear Creek Pear Brandy Truffle** (Apple Brandy also available) has a soft center with the strong, clear flavors of pear and brandy.

Overall, their truffles are lovely to look at with distinct flavors. However, their centers are often a bit too stiff for this reviewer's taste.

For really soft centers, their **Cream Cones**, miniature ice cream cone shapes with ultra-soft centers, are the ticket. The **Peanut Butter Banana**, a milk chocolate cone with a whipped peanut butter and banana center, is rich and full of peanut butter flavor. Their

Vanilla Bean Cream Cone has dark chocolate covering a white center. It has a good dark chocolate flavor.

Even more whimsical are their **Hot Fudge Sundae** and **Banana Split**. The Banana Split comes with a white basket, a chocolate top, "whipped cream," chopped nuts, and a tiny cherry on top with a white and chocolate center. They're cute, but, perhaps because of the many components, they lack distinct flavors. Kids are sure to love them.

At the **Moonstruck Chocolate Bar** on Alder, they sell **individual cakes** like their **Tiramisu**, 2 layers of soft cake filled and frosted with mascarpone and dusted with cocoa. The cake is moist, if a bit overwhelmed by the flavor of rum. The mascarpone is thick with a good, sweet cheesy flavor.

Their **Chocolate Cheesecake**, this reviewer's favorite, is a 4-inch round cake that starts with a $1/2$ inch of dark cookie crust, then 2 inches of chocolate cheesecake that's topped with a thin layer of ganache and shaved chocolate and garnished with chocolate curls. The result is a light, creamy, cheese-chocolate combination. The chocolate crust adds a punch of dark chocolate flavor and the ganache topping is appropriately rich.

Their **German Chocolate Cake**, also a 4-inch cake, is 3 thin layers of dark chocolate cake separated by light chocolate buttercream and topped with a buttery coconut mixture. It's garnished with buttercream rosettes and dark chocolate cookie crumbs. The cake offers a deep chocolate flavor, the buttercream is light and creamy, and the coconut topping isn't overly sweet.

Also at the Moonstruck Chocolate Bar, chocolate lovers can get a large assortment of **chocolate drinks** like their **Cinnamon Roll Latte**, a rich chocolatey concoction that has a real cinnamon kick. Their **Mondo Berry Ice Teaser**, which is made with Tazo Tea's Berry Iced Tea Concentrate, dark chocolate, and milk, is refreshing with a wonderful berry flavor.

Moonstruck chocolates and cakes (including full-sized ones) are sold at a variety of retail locations around Portland, including **Wizer's Lake Grove, Wizer's Oswego Foods**,and **Strohecker's** grocery stores, and a number of candy shops like **Toutes Sweet**. *Getting there*: *On SW Alder at 6th*.

Van Duyn's   ✗
P.O. Box 10384, Portland, OR. (503) 227-1927
Portland retail stores:
Beaverton Mall, 3205 SW Cedar Hills Boulevard, Beaverton, OR.
(503) 646-0809

Clackamas Town Center, 12000 SE 82nd Avenue, #1020, Portland, OR. (503) 659-1031

Lloyd Center, 1212 Lloyd Center, Portland, OR. (503) 281-2421

Menlo Park, 12307 NE Glisan, Portland, OR. (503) 252-5033

Pioneer Square, 617 SW Morrison, Portland, OR. (503) 221-4940

Factory "seconds" store:

2360 NW Quimby, Portland, OR (503) 227-9327

Also in Vancouver Mall, Vancouver, WA.

♥♥♥ Van Duyn's is back and getting better all the time! That's great news for Northwesterners who grew up with the venerable candy company. Established in 1927 by talented candymaker, Neuman Van Duyn, Van Duyn's was Portland's premiere candy company for 60-plus years. The company was sold in the 1980's to investors who knew nothing about making candy and, for a dozen years, the company and the quality of its candy went downhill. Fortunately for chocolate lovers, Van Duyn's was rescued in 1991 by Sean Gilronan and his family. Their mission is to return the company to its former glory—and they're doing a good job of it. By resurrecting Neuman Van Duyn's family recipes and making their candy in small batches with traditional equipment and good quality ingredients, the company is again making excellent chocolates.

Van Duyn's **European truffles** are 1$\frac{1}{2}$-inch domes of milk or dark chocolate covering lovely soft centers. The hand-dipped coating is the right thickness with a good snap to it and the flavors are distinguishable, but subtle. The **Dark Chocolate** comes with a dark chocolate ganache center with a deep chocolatey flavor. **Amaretto**, with its medium-dark center and chopped almonds on top, has just a lilt of amaretto. **Raspberry** comes with a milk chocolate center with pink "strings" on the coating for identification and a good fruity flavor. Other truffle flavors include **Black Forest, Grand Marnier, Irish Cream, Kahlua**, and **Milk Chocolate**.

A signature chocolate for Van Duyn's is their **Truffle Mint**, 1$\frac{1}{2}$ inch flat disks in milk or dark chocolate with whipped milk chocolate centers flavored with a fresh mint flavor that doesn't overpower. One reviewer, who isn't a mint fan exclaimed, "These are really good!"

Another signature chocolate is their **Cherribons**™, their version of cherry cordials. They use Hood River cherries, which are dipped in sweet fondant and then twice dipped in dark or milk chocolate and wrapped in pretty foil. The thick coating holds in the soft, not overly sweet, liquid center and its cherry. Fans of cherry cordials will cheer!

Cream Caramels are 1$\frac{1}{2}$ inch squares of firm, chewy caramel enrobed in dark or milk chocolate. We found them a bit too chewy and lacking in buttery flavor. In contrast, the Savannah, which isn't chocolate at all, but a concoction of butter, brown sugar, and nuts, is wonderfully buttery and melt-in-the-mouth delicious. It's an old time flavor your grandmother would remember.

Neuman, named after the firm's founder, is a tiny teddy bear filled with peanut butter cream and tiny bits of peanut. It has a soft peanut butter flavor. **Cranberries and Cream** comes as 2 thin pieces of white chocolate studded with pieces of dried cranberry. The white chocolate is subtle, not overly sweet, and the tangy cranberry bits shout, "Cranberry!"

One of this reviewer's favorites is the **Oregon Blackcap**, a chocolate molded to resemble the Oregon berry. It's filled with an ultrasoft lavender center punctuated with tiny bits of blackcap berry. It has a wonderfully intense blackcap flavor.

Van Duyn's **Rocky Road** is a bit different. It has big pillows of homemade marshmallow, walnuts, and whipped milk chocolate. While the it melts in the mouth with a soft chocolate flavor, this reviewer would like to see a bit more chocolate with all that marshmallow.

Vandango's™, their version of turtles, are big 3-inch puddles of chocolate, caramel, and big pieces of roasted pecans, almonds, cashews, or macadamia nuts. They don't skimp on the nuts and the caramel and nuts make this candy wonderfully chewy. The caramel they use in Vandango's™ is appropriately soft and buttery. It's a terrific combination.

Van Duyn's also makes a line of **sugar-free chocolates** that are the best these reviewers have tasted. While no sugar-free can compare to chocolate made with sugar, these tasty chocolates are naturally sweetened and have no after taste.

Van Duyn's packaging is beautiful and imaginative. Their standard gold and blue boxes with gold ribbon are attractive, but their gift boxes and tins, some in purples, pinks, and gold foils, are exquisite.
Getting there: The factory seconds store is at NW 23rd and Quimby. The other stores are located in area malls.

Candy Basket
1924 NE 181st Avenue, Portland, OR. (503) 666-2000 (factory and retail store)
Other area location:
248 E Main, Hillsboro, OR. (503) 648-2611
♥♥ Started as a small, family operation back in 1938, **Candy Basket** is a wholesale/retail candy manufacturer that specializes in

American style, machine-enrobed candies made with Guittard chocolate, fresh cream, butter, and no preservatives. They're also known for their 21 foot chocolate cascade or chocolate waterfall, 2,800 pounds of melted chocolate that cascades over marble and bronze into a big pool in the factory store's entryway. They make a large selection of **old fashioned truffles** with whipped centers. They're small, 1-inch squares in dark or milk chocolate with flavors like **Filbert, Mocha Velvet, Mint, Double Chocolate, Mocha,** and **Rum**. The centers melt instantly on the tongue, but this reviewer found most of the flavors, with the exception of mint, a bit indistinct.

Their line of **creams**, which are the size of a quarter and have slightly stiff centers, come in a rainbow of flavors, including **Coconut, Raspberry, Marionberry, Lemon, Orange, Maple, Vanilla, Strawberry, Coffee, Rum Butter**, and **Chocolate**. The **Chocolate Cream**, which comes with a milk chocolate center and milk chocolate coating with chocolate sprinkles, has a good creamy milk chocolate flavor. **Marionberry**, with its dark chocolate coating and pink center, offers the fresh taste of berries.

They also make golf ball-sized **ganache-filled truffles** in **Grand Marnier, Kahlua, Amaretto**, and **Double Chocolate**. Enrobed in milk chocolate, they have a good chocolate flavor, though the centers are a bit stiffer than some we've enjoyed.

Their **Jell Sticks** are a big 4 inches and come in milk or dark chocolate. **Orange Jell** sticks have a good, firm jelly texture and a fresh orange flavor. **Seafoam** is a 2x1-inch log of honeycomb enrobed in chocolate that is a bit sweet for this reviewer's taste.

Candy Basket's **Peanut Butter Cups** are a bit different. Peanut butter cream is poured directly into 3-inch paper candy cups and just a tiny dollop of chocolate is piped onto the top. Not a lot of chocolate flavor, but our peanut butter reviewer says it has a good peanut flavor. The **Peanut Butter Squares** are 1-inch squares of the peanut butter cream punctuated with bits of wafer and topped with milk chocolate. They're creamy and chewy.

Their **Caramels** are something special. Enrobed in milk or dark chocolate or plain, the caramel is extra soft with a good, buttery flavor. **Beaver Paws**, their version of turtles, are 3-inch dollops of caramel, chopped walnuts, and milk, dark, or white chocolate. They're a nice blending of chewy and soft textures and chocolate, caramel, and walnut flavors. Their **Butter Almond Toffee** is a 1-inch square of firm, buttery toffee enrobed in milk chocolate, topped with chopped almonds. This buttery, crunchy candy will make you give up commercial toffee.

They also make a line of **sugar-free candy** for those who can't consume sugar.

In addition to their retail locations, Candy Basket candies are available at **Made in Oregon** stores, **Harry and David**, and at licensee Candy Basket stores in Bend, Manzanita, and Springfield.
Getting there: Although they have a Portland address, the factory store is actually in Gresham on 181st at San Rafael (near Halsey).

Ice Creamery

Tillamook Ice Cream Restaurant
12890 NW Cornell Road, Portland, OR. (503) 641-8013
Other Portland location:
10805 NE Halsey Street, Portland, OR. (503) 257-5129
♥♥♥ Portlanders can rejoice because Tillamook Ice Cream has come to town. Although you won't find the huge selection of flavors available at the Tillamook Creamery on the coast, chocolate lovers will find flavors like **Chocolate, Chocolate Chip Mint, Chocolate Chunk Yogurt, Chocolate Moose Light, Chocolate Peanut Butter, Coffee Almond Fudge, Cookies and Cream**, and **White Chocolate Sundae**. (For complete review, see Tillamook Ice Cream, Tillamook, OR.)
Getting there: The Cornell store is in Cedar Mill; the Halsey store is in the Gateway district.

Hello Milk Chocolate. In 1876 when Daniel Peter of Switzerland added milk to chocolate, milk chocolate was born.

SDK's
388 SW 2nd Avenue, Portland, OR. (503) 227-8983
♥♥♥ If you've never tasted frozen custard, you're in for a sensual treat at **SDK's**. It has the rich flavor of ice cream, the lightness of gelato, and the texture of pure satin. Frozen custard melts on the tongue like soft ice cream, but has more structure like hard ice cream or gelato. SKD's offers only 2 flavors each day. If you're lucky, owner Steve Keeler will be serving up his Cocoa Cream, a satiny custard with a light chocolate flavor.

Traveler's note: At press time, SDK wasn't planning on renewing their lease after summer '98 at their downtown location. If you can't find them at their 2nd Avenue location, call information. They're worth finding!
Getting there: On SW 2nd Avenue in downtown Portland a few blocks south of the Morrison Bridge.

WEST LINN

Bugatti's Ristorante Italiano

18740 Willammette Drive, West Linn, OR. (503) 636-9555

♥♥♥ **Bugatti's** is a simple yet hip retreat off busy Highway 43 that's decorated in gold, rust, and mustard-colored faux-painted walls and tables draped with green cloths and brown butcher paper with crimson napkins. Dinner, which changes seasonally, includes a large selection of pastas like angel hair with toasted pine nuts, tomatoes, arugula, and feta, rigatoni with braised lamb, garlic, rosemary, and proscuitto, and fettuccine with cream sauce with cremini mushrooms and chicken. Second course offerings include grilled salmon, chicken with fontina and capers in marsala sauce, tiger prawns in garlic, oregano and brandy, and veal scaloppini.

Their signature chocolate dessert is **Fallen Chocolate Soufflé**, a 4-inch round of soft, dark chocolate cake that comes slightly warm and covered with a big mound of freshly whipped cream. It's served simply on a black plate with homemade chocolate sauce, a sprig of mint and a dusting of powered sugar. This rich, moist soufflé melts on the tongue almost instantly. The cream, which is barely sweetened, adds a lovely lightness to the rich chocolate flavor. The lip-smacking chocolate sauce adds a satisfying gooeyness.

Bugatti's also offers **Chocolate Sorbet**, which comes with 2 generous scoops and a crispy, lacy triangle cookie. The sorbet has an intense chocolate flavor and the cookie is buttery with a crispy bite.

Getting there: On Willamette Drive (Highway 43) at Fairview.

Hidden Springs Café

19389 Willamette Drive, West Linn, OR. (503) 635-3580

♥♥ Tucked into a strip mall just off busy Highway 43, **Hidden Springs Café** is a lovely little neighborhood restaurant featuring good-quality food in a comfortable atmosphere. Serving lunch, dinner, and Sunday brunch, Hidden Springs offers burgers, focaccia bread sandwiches, pasta, fish, chicken, and unusual gourmet pizzas like pesto pine nut and Northwest Smoked salmon. Save room for their **Chocolate Brownie**, a 4-inch square of chocolate delight. It's moist with just the right texture—not too dense or too cakelike—with large pieces of walnuts, and it's topped with a creamy layer of fudge frosting.

Getting there: On Willamette Drive at Hidden Springs Road.

LAKE OSWEGO

La Provence Bakery and Bistro
15964 SW Boones Ferry Road, Lake Oswego, OR.
(503) 635-4533
♥♥♥♥ A bright, sunny respite off busy Lower Boones Ferry Road, **La Provence Bakery and Bistro** is the kind of place you want to linger over a hearty soup, a sumptuous salad, or a sandwich on their homemade bread at lunch or, for dinner, filet mignon, chicken breast, lamp chops, or pasta dishes, all cooked with a French flair. Do save room for dessert because pastry chef and owner, Didier Blanc-Gonnet, creates desserts and pastries that are both beautiful to look at and wonderful to eat. He uses a blend of French and Belgian chocolate that isn't overly sweet. His mousses, which he makes with an Italian meringue, are incredibly light and smooth without being frothy.

His **Square Chocolate Mousse Cake** is a 4-inch square of alternating layers of chocolate mousse with chocolate cake infused with rum extract. The whole thing is encased in dark couverture chocolate and garnished with white chocolate and large chocolate curls. While rich, this dessert is amazingly light. It comes off the tongue cleanly and invites another (and another) bite.

Chocolate Basket is dark chocolate molded to look like a basket and filled with a thin layer of white cake with kirsch syrup on the bottom and raspberry mousse. It's garnished with chocolate curls. This refreshing dessert is one to order on a hot summer day.

The **Chocolate Orange Mousse Cup** is a molded dark chocolate cup filled with chocolate cake infused with rum extract, then filled with chocolate mousse and orange mousse. It's garnished with large chocolate leaves. Again, light, smooth mousse and rich, perfect chocolate.

Chocolate Pear Tart is a thick shortbread crust filled with a layer of chocolate and topped with sliced pears in glaze. As the flavors blend in the mouth, the first impression is "Oh pears;" the next, "Ah chocolate;" then it's, "This is delicious!" The tarts are kept refrigerated. Let your's warm up a bit before enjoying.

La Provence is also known for excellent French style breads, which are made with a sponge of apple and vinegar instead of yeast, giving them a sweet-tart taste and long shelf life.
Getting there: On Boones Ferry near Bryant.

Amadeus

148 B Avenue, Lake Oswego, OR. (503) 636-7500

♥ A shiny grand piano graces the entrance of second-floor **Amadeus,** a charmingly intimate restaurant decorated with showy bouquets of fresh flowers, crystal chandeliers, cloth-covered tables, Indian throw rugs, antique furniture and pieces of old evening clothing. They serve lunch and dinner with a focus on classic dishes like seafood Caesar, escargot, rack of lamb, bouillabaisse, Viennese schnitzel, chateaubriand, and duck a l'orange. Their nod to chocolate is their **Chocolate Silk Pie**, a small, 2-inch high wedge that comes with a graham crust and garnished with sliced almonds and Hershey's chocolate sauce. The pie is silky and creamy, but the crust is a bit soft and the commercial chocolate sauce adds little. *Getting there: In downtown Lake Oswego, on B Avenue at 2nd Street.*

Ice Creamery

Tillamook Ice Cream

37 SW A Avenue, Lake Oswego, OR. (503) 636-4933

♥♥♥ Lake Oswego's **Tillamook Ice Cream** store resembles an old fashioned burger café and is a favorite with local families. Although you won't find the huge selection of flavors available at the Tillamook Creamery on the coast, chocolate lovers will find flavors like **Chocolate, Chocolate Chip Mint, Chocolate Chunk Yogurt, Chocolate Moose Light, Chocolate Peanut Butter, Coffee Almond Fudge, Cookies and Cream**, and **White Chocolate Sundae**. (For complete review, see Tillamook Ice Cream, Tillamook, OR.)

Getting there: On A Avenue at State.

BEAVERTON

Pavillion Bar and Grill (Greenwood Inn)

10700 SW Allen Boulevard, Beaverton, OR. (503) 626-4550

♥♥♥ This reviewer was suspicious of a motel restaurant located in the hinterlands of Beaverton's surburbia, but was pleasantly surprised with what Executive Chef Kevin Kennedy has done with the Pavillion Room. The dining room itself is pleasant, if a bit dated (a remodel is scheduled)—a beautiful Columbia River basalt sculpture-waterfall surrounded by live plants dominates the center of the sunroom whose walls and ceiling are covered in cedar lattice. They serve breakfast, lunch, and dinner, focusing on regional cuisine that changes seasonally. Insisting on the freshest ingredients, Chef Kevin even has an herb garden outback overlooking Highway 217! His dinner menu includes dishes like coriander crusted ahi tuna, crab cakes, pecan crusted catfish, apple smoked prime rib, venison chops, roasted eggplant and fresh mozzarella strudel, and rosemary smoked duck.

At dessert, the focus shifts to pastry chef Liz Smith whose beautifully presented desserts reflect well on the apprenticeship she served at the Sonoma Mission Inn. The dessert menu also changes seasonally and always has at least 1 chocolate item to choose from such as the **Bittersweet Chocolate Grand Marnier Mousse**. It comes as 3 small, piped dollops of chocolate mousse that have large, dark chocolate disk "hats." It's garnished with bright yellow Grand Marnier sauce, candied orange peel, blood oranges, and a chocolate shortbread cookie—an artful presentation. The mousse is rich and ultra-creamy and the sauce adds a lovely citrus contrast to the rich chocolate. The chocolate disks have an appropriate snap and the shortbread cookie is rich and buttery-crumbly.

Chocolate Hazelnut Torte is a generous wedge of dark Guittard chocolate torte flavored with bits of toasted hazelnuts and Frangelico. It comes on a bed of lavender/Meyer lemon-infused syrup with lemon zest, and fresh raspberries. The cake has a wonderful, creamy texture that contrasts with the chewy crunch of hazelnut pieces. The syrup adds a flowery-lemony lightness to this rich dessert.
Getting there: On Allen Boulevard at Highway 217.

Ice Creamery

Tillamook Ice Cream
11485 SW Scholls Ferry Road, Beaverton, OR. (503) 579-4292
♥♥♥ Although you won't find the huge selection of flavors available at the Tillamook Creamery on the coast, chocolate lovers will find flavors like **Chocolate, Chocolate Chip Mint, Chocolate Chunk Yogurt, Chocolate Moose Light, Chocolate Peanut Butter, Coffee Almond Fudge, Cookies and Cream**, and **White Chocolate Sundae**. (For complete review, see Tillamook Ice Cream, Tillamook, OR.)
Getting there: On Scholls Ferry Road, across Highway 217 from Washington Square.

HILLSBORO

Candy Basket
248 E Main, Hillsboro, OR. (503) 648-2611
♥♥ (See review under Candy Shops, Portland, OR.)
Getting there: On the main thoroughfare in Hillsboro.

CLACKAMAS

Michele's Chocolate Truffles

14698 SE 82nd Drive, Clackamas, OR. (503) 656-0220

♥♥♥ Ten years ago, chocolatier Michele Chergwin was a stay-at-home mom with 4 kids and a hobby making chocolate truffles. Today, she's head of **Michele's Chocolate Truffles**, a wholesale/retail chocolate company offering 32 different types of **truffles** and other **chocolate candies**. Naturally, truffles are her signature candy. About the size of a large jaw breaker, these machine-enrobed truffles (a few are still hand-dipped) are made with Guittard chocolate. The coatings have a nice snap to them and the centers are ultra-creamy, with a buttery melt-in-the-mouth softness and subtle flavorings that don't hit you over the head. Her **Irish Cream Truffle** has a milk chocolate shell with a buttery, semisweet chocolate center with just a lilt of Irish Cream flavoring.

The **Berries and Cream Truffle** features a dark chocolate shell with a creamy white center that's flavored with blackberry brandy and cream. It's light, subtle, and very creamy. **Kahlua** has a dark chocolate covering with a dark chocolate center that's melt-in-the-mouth smooth. However, the kahlua flavor is so subtle, one reviewer mistook this for dark chocolate.

Michele's **Caramel Truffle** is an interesting variation. A milk chocolate coating is filled with a milk chocolate center that's been smoothly blended with caramel, which gives a caramel flavor without the chew. If you like caramel, you'll enjoy this one.

Michele makes 3 types of **Chocolate-covered Caramels—Orange, Chocolate**, and **Vanilla**. The caramel is medium-soft and chewy. The Orange Caramel has a subtle orange flavor. The Chocolate Caramel is more chocolate flavor than caramel flavor. The Vanilla Caramel, this reviewer's favorite of the bunch, has a more traditional buttery caramel flavor.

Suzy's Chews, Michele's version of Turtles, are interesting 4-inch patties of caramel, macadamias, pecans, almonds, and cashews covered in chocolate. They're good and chewy!

Their **Toffee Bar**, a 3-inch bar enrobed in milk chocolate and topped with chopped nuts (almond or macadamia) has a wonderful crispy bite and an excellent buttery flavor. Heath Bar eat your heart out! The **Rocky Road Bar** is 2 inches high, 4 inches long and has a whipped chocolate center that's packed with peanuts, a thin layer of homemade marshmallow, and covered in dark chocolate. It's good, but this reviewer wishes they'd be a bit more generous with that soft, pillowy marshmallow.

Michele's chocolates are also available at retail locations around Portland, including the **Candy Jar** in John's Landing, **Captain Beans** in Clackamas Town Center, and **Coffee's On** in Gresham. *Getting there: Off 205 take exit 12; right on Highway 224, ¹/₂ mile to the second industrial complex on the left. Watch for the "Chocolate" sign.*

ESTACADA

Harmony Baking Company, Inc.
221 SW Wade Street, Estacada, OR. (503) 630-6857
♥♥ Southeast of Portland in the little timber town of Estacada, **Harmony Baking Company** has been bringing people of every stripe together over hearty breakfasts and fresh baked goods. At Harmony, loggers, environmentalists, conservatives, liberals, church-goers and non-believers all agree—owner Linda Lawrence's omelets, home-fried potatoes, and fresh-baked bagels, doughnuts, and breads are terrific. The atmosphere is country-casual with maple tables and club chairs. In the summer, you can eat outside under umbrellas on the tiny patio.

For lovers of chocolate, Linda's **doughnuts** aren't to be missed. Made fresh every morning, they're impeccably fresh with that wonderfully crisp bite outside, soft chewiness inside. Her **Buttermilk Bar**, at 4x2-inches, is dense and chewy with a generous topping of chocolate glaze. Her **Chocolate Cake Doughnut,** with chocolate glaze and chopped walnuts on top, is soft and springy.

At a big 10 inches, the **Raised Chocolate Twist** is one of the biggest we've encountered. It's soft, raised dough, twisted into a braid and slathered with plenty of chocolate glaze. Her **Bavarian Cream** is 5-inches round and puffy, and filled a generous amount of creamy custard. Yum!

Linda's **Chocolate Layer Cake**, a new addition to her baking line, is 3 layers of extra dark chocolate cake filled and frosted with dark chocolate buttercream. We found the coarse-textured cake didn't measure up to her excellent doughnuts.
Getting there: Wade Street at 3ʳᵈ Avenue.

OREGON

North Oregon Coast

GEARHART
CANNON BEACH
• SEASIDE
•
• NEHALEM
BAY CITY
OCEANSIDE
• TILLAMOOK
• PACIFIC CITY

GEARHART
SEASIDE
CANNON BEACH
NEHALEM
BAY CITY
TILLAMOOK
OCEANSIDE
PACIFIC CITY

From Astoria to Lincoln City, Oregon's north coast is known for its rugged beauty—steep cliffs that plunge into the Pacific, fog-shrouded rocks filled with nesting seabirds, uncrowded beaches littered with gray driftwood twisted and worn into fantastic shapes by the water.

Great Things To Do

• **Step Back in Maritime History. Columbia River Maritime Museum**, 1792 Marine Drive, **Astoria, OR**. (503) 325-2323. If you've ever wondered what it was like 100 years ago on the Columbia River, stop by this fascinating maritime museum with its galleries full of old seaman's relics and restored boats. Be sure to take the self-guided tour on the lightship Columbia, moored just outside the museum.

• **Spot Eagles. Twilight Eagle Sanctuary**, 8 miles east of **Astoria, OR**. Bird lovers will want to take a little side trip 8 miles inland to see about 50 bald eagles roosting. The Sanctuary is off Highway 30 on Old Highway 30.

• **Check Out The Giant Sitka Spruce.** Highway 26, **Klootchy Creek near Seaside, OR**. If you live in the area, you've probably driven past the "Giant Sitka Spruce" sign. Next time, turn in, get out of your car, and get up close and personal with this 750 year old forest giant. At 216 feet high, with a diameter of 17 feet, a circumference of 56 feet and a crown spread of 93 feet, it's the largest Sitka Spruce in the United States. They've built a walkway around this incredible tree, so you can walk around it and get a real feel for one of nature's miracles.

• **Ride A Warbird. Tillamook Air Museum,** 6030 Hanger Road, **Tillamook, OR**. (503) 842-1130. Located in old WWII blimp hangers, the Tillamook Air Museum offers a glimpse at the history of air flight. There are more than 20 restored warbirds like the P-51 Mustang, a theater, an exhibit room with photos and historic air relics, and a flight simulator where you can get the feel of what it was like to fly these old planes.

• **Get with the Cheese. Tillamook Cheese Factory,** 4175 Highway 101 N, **Tillamook, OR**. (503) 842-4481. Ever wonder how they make cheese? You can find out at Tillamook's premiere tourist draw, the Tillamook Cheese Factory. Visitors can take an interesting self-guided tour, sample cheese, buy gift items, and then belly up to the 2 ice cream stations to sample some of the freshest ice cream in Oregon (see review).

• **Shuck Some Oysters. Pacific Oyster Company**, Highway 101, **Pacific City, OR**. (503) 377-2323. In tiny Pacific City, on a pier with a terrific view of the water, stop at the Pacific Oyster Company and get a bag of some of the freshest oysters you'll ever shuck.

Terrific Places To Stay

Inn at Spanish Head, 4009 Southwest Highway 101, **Lincoln City, OR**. (800) 452-8127. Built right into the side of a steep cliff overlooking the raging Pacific, the Inn at Spanish Head is as close as you can get to the ocean without getting wet. The Inn has 10 stories, the top floor occupied by a lounge and restaurant, the first floor by meeting rooms, spa, sauna, and exercise room. Each of the 110 rooms, many with kitchenettes, feature a glass wall with a sliding glass door and balcony that afford some of the most spectacular ocean views on the coast. On the patio, protected from the ocean winds by a see-through screen, is a heated swimming pool.

Sand Dollar Bed and Breakfast, 606 N Holladay, **Seaside, OR**. (800) 738-3491. If it's homey you crave, you'll like the Sand Dollar Bed and Breakfast. Located a walkable few blocks from the popular downtown area, the Sand Dollar is a 1920's bungalow with 2 large guest rooms and private baths, both decorated in a simple country motif. The south room has a queen bed and 2 twin beds in an alcove area for the kids. Both rooms share a tiny sitting room with television, VCR, phone, and small refrigerator. Innkeepers Bob and Nita Hempflinger bring early coffee or tea to the sitting room and serve a full, delicious breakfast which may include Nita's chocolate-stuffed French toast.

GEARHART

Pacific Way Bakery and Café
601 Pacific Way, Gearhart, OR. (503) 738-0245
♥♥♥♥ **Pacific Way Bakery and Café** is a pleasant, sunny café with hardwood floors, mustard-colored walls, and plum-colored tables, that invites patrons to sit a while, enjoy a cup of coffee, and a treat from baker/owner Lisa Allen's heavenly oven. You can get a sandwich like a Pacific club, roast beef, or BLT, all served on homemade bread. Or you can order one of their unusual pizzas like cilantro chicken or apple chicken sausage. But save room for Lisa's chocolate desserts. The desserts change regularly, but chocolate lovers are likely to run into a **Chocolate Velvet Torte**, a rich graham/nut crust that's covered with 2½ inches of velvety, dark chocolate torte, topped by a thin layer of rich ganache, and garnished with slivered almonds on the sides. This is a creamy chocolate delight, chocolate fans.

Lisa's **Chocolate Caramel Pecan Tart** has a nut crust with a layer of thick, buttery caramel that's topped with ganache and garnished with white chocolate squiggles. The nut crust adds a nice crunch to the creamy caramel and the ganache lends just the right dense chocolate flavor.
Getting there: Corner of Pacific Way and Cottage in Gearhart.

SEASIDE

With all of its candy and ice cream shops, Seaside's main street downtown may have the distinction of having more calories per block than any other Oregon coastal town.

Restaurants

Nostalgic
521 Broadway, Seaside, OR. (503) 738-0693
♥♥ **Nostalgic** is a breakfast, lunch and dinner café, which serves the usual breakfast offerings, seafood, pasta, chicken, steaks, burgers, and an interesting array of German specialties, including wiener schnitzel and bockwurst and sauerkraut. Save room for their **homemade ice cream**, including several chocolate varieties. Made with no fillers, no preservatives, and no eggs, Nostalgic's ice cream is rich (20+% butterfat) with little air. They make 40 different flavors, about 15 chocolate flavors. They usually have 4 chocolate flavors on hand, including their **Chocolate Fantasy**, semi-sweet chocolate ice cream with hunks of chocolate brownie. This flavor won an award at Seaside's Chocolate Lover's Festival in 1997. Their **Double Chocolate Macadamia Nut** is semi-sweet and dark chocolate ice cream with chopped macadamia nuts—chocolaty, creamy, nutty. Plain **Chocolate** is creamy with a light chocolate flavor. Their **White Chocolate Peanut Butter** won't satisfy a chocolate craving, but it's full of peanut butter flavor.

> **Chocolate Happening!**
> **Seaside Chocolate Lover's Festival, January 31.** Don't miss this annual chocolate lover's delight. Samples from restaurants, bakeries, and chocolatiers. For more information, call the Seaside Chamber of Commerce (800) 444-6740.

Getting there: *In downtown Seaside, on Broadway just after you cross the river bridge.*

Bakery/Pastry Shop   closed 8/11

Harrison's Bakery
601 Broadway, Seaside, OR. (503) 738-5331
♥♥♥ Chris and Tom Hurner run **Harrison's**, Seaside's only from-scratch bakery and it's a good one. In the back, Tom cranks out giant Danish, cinnamon rolls, muffins, doughnuts, cookies, and

North
Oregon
Coast

other goodies. (He learned from Portland's JaCiva baker, Jack Elmer.) Chris works the front—waiting on customers, swapping gossip with locals, calling everyone "darlin'" or "hon," making people feel like family. One of their specialties is **Pecan Royale**, a cookie crust with a thick layer of chopped pecans and caramel enrobed in dark chocolate. It's rich and delicious. Their **Chocolate Raspberry Cake** is 4 layers of dark chocolate cake filled with raspberry and chocolate, frosted with a mousse-like chocolate icing, and covered with chocolate ganache, decorated with chocolate sprinkles.

Their **Chocolate Doughnuts**, both old fashioned and raised, get special kudos. They're incredibly fresh, soft on the inside, slightly crunchy on the outside. The raised doughnuts are so tall, you can barely get your mouth around them. The icing is rich and chocolaty without being too sweet. They're some of the best doughnuts this reviewer has ever tasted.

If you're lucky, they'll have some of their **Chocolate Truffles,** big scoops of velvet smooth dark chocolate truffle filling dipped in milk chocolate—very sensuous.
Getting there: In downtown Seaside, on Broadway between Holladay Street and the bridge that crosses the river.

Chocolate Shops

Phillips Candies of Seaside
217 Broadway, Seaside, OR. (503) 738-5402
♥♥♥♥ At 100 years old, **Phillips Candies** has the distinction of being the oldest—and one of the best—candy shops on the Oregon coast. They sell a huge selection of **fresh chocolate candy** as well as salt water taffy and caramel corn. It's made on-site, by hand, ensuring it's fresh and delicious. Phillips' **Rocky Road**, a big seller, is a very light, whipped chocolate with big hunks of marshmallows and finely-chopped walnuts. It's creamy, yet the chocolate has a satisfying snap when you bite into it. Their **Butter Rum Creams** are dark chocolate surrounding a creamy center made with 150-proof rum and finely-chopped walnuts. Phillips's **Chocolate-covered Caramels** are buttery and chewy. **Orange Straws**, chocolate with an orange jellied center, have an intense orange flavor.

Truffles average
Taffy good

Seafoam, a coastal favorite, is a rich chocolate covering a honeycomb-like center. Their **Pecan Patties** are caramel and pecans covered with chocolate. **Peanut Crunch** is a crunchy, rich peanut butter center covered with chocolate. Their **Fudge** is creamy and rich, the kind your grandmother used to make—or you *wished* she made.

Their **truffles** are what 87-year-old owner Marguerite Phillips calls "old fashioned" truffles. Instead of creamy ganache, they have a stiffer, whipped chocolate center. Their **Truffle Mints** combine the flavor of creamy chocolate with cool mint. Phillips' chocolate truffles have an intense chocolate flavor that makes you want to reach for another.

Getting there: On the main thoroughfare in downtown Seaside, just past the river bridge.

Chocolatier Profile –

Marguerite Phillips, owner
Phillips Candies of Seaside
Seaside, Oregon

*"I taught myself to dip chocolates," says 87-year-old **Marguerite Phillips**, the owner and matriarch of Phillips Candies of Seaside, smiling mischievously. "I dipped a bunch of cherries and the pin setter from the bowling alley next door came by and asked if he could taste them. He didn't like them. I'd dipped them in unsweetened baking chocolate."*

Marguerite Phillips has learned a thing or two about making good chocolates since then. In 1927 when she was in high school, Marguerite went to work for the candy company, then Pool's Candies. A dozen years later, she and her husband bought and expanded the business and renamed it Phillips Candies of Seaside.

One of the things she's learned over the years is the value of using good ingredients.

"Use only the best," she says knowingly. "We use the best Nestles chocolate they make. People will tell you they use this kind or that kind of chocolate. But every company makes a lot of different grades of chocolate. A brand name means nothing. We use only the top grade of Nestles."

Today, Marguerite Phillips is silver-haired, but her hand-shake is firm, her eyes bright and full of merriment. Other family members may be involved in the business, but there's no doubt she's still running the show. She chuckles, "You know, I've eaten a ton of chocolate. As long as you eat chocolate, you'll live a long time."

Tom N Larry Candy
133 Broadway, Seaside, OR. (503) 436-0526
Other North Oregon Coast Location:
Sandpiper Square, Cannon Beach, OR. (503) 436-0526
♥♥♥♥ **Tom N Larry Candy** makes only 4 types of candy—

Chocolate Fudge, Penoche (brown sugar) Fudge, Almond Toffee, and Peanut Brittle. They've been making it for 67 years. When you've been specializing in a making a few candies for so many years, you're bound to get good at it, very good. Their Chocolate Fudge, which is made with big chunks of walnuts, is extra creamy with a light chocolate flavor. While it's not chocolate, their Penoche Fudge, is addictively good. Their Almond Toffee is melt-in-the-mouth buttery and it's loaded with almonds. The Peanut Brittle crispy and buttery, full of peanuts.

Getting there: On the main thoroughfare in downtown Seaside, a few blocks up from the beach.

Portland Fudge Company
102 Broadway, Seaside, OR. (503) 738-0602
♥♥ A funny name for a company based in Seaside, the Portland Fudge Company specializes in a variety of fudge—Chocolate, Chocolate Walnut, Chocolate Amaretto, Chocolate Peanut Butter, Chocolate Pecan, Peanut Butter, and Maple Walnut, as well as Rocky Road and Divinity. You can watch them cook their fudge on-site in large copper kettles and work it by hand on marble slab tables. Made without artificial ingredients, colorings, or preservatives, the fudge is creamy without being too sweet. The nut varieties have plenty of big chunks of nuts.

Getting there: On the main thoroughfare in downtown Seaside, 2 blocks up from the beach.

Chocolate Marches to War. During World War II, the U.S. government commissioned Milton S. Hershey to make a chocolate bar Allied soldiers could carry into war.

CANNON BEACH

Wayfarer Restaurant (Surf Sand Resort)
1190 Pacific Drive, Cannon Beach, OR. (503) 436-1108
♥♥♥ The Wayfarer Restaurant and Lounge is a casual place with great views of the beach and famous Haystack Rock. They serve pasta, steak, chicken, and a wide range of seafood, including Northwest salmon and steamer clams. Save room for their Chocolate Ganache, a thick slice of bittersweet chocolate filling with pecan praline crust, garnished with drizzles of homemade caramel sauce. The crust is flavorful and nutty, providing a nice contrast to the velvet smooth chocolate. The caramel sauce is buttery and not overly sweet. Wayfarer won second place in 1997 in Seaside's Chocolate Festival with this dessert.

Their **Bailey's Chocolate Mousse** is a large serving of melt-in-the-mouth creamy mousse garnished with a generous serving of whipped cream and chopped chocolate. It has a medium chocolate flavor that's enhanced by a delicate overlay of Bailey's Irish Cream. *Getting there: On the south side of Cannon Beach, off S Hemlock at West Gower.*

Chocolate Shops

Tom N Larry Candy
Sandpiper Square, Cannon Beach, OR. (503) 436-0526
♥♥♥♥ (See review under Seaside.)
Getting there: Off the main street in Cannon Beach in Sandpiper Square.

Bruce's Candy Kitchen
256 N Hemlock, Cannon Beach, OR. (503) 436-2641
Bruce's Candy Kitchen, with its pink and white facade and large candy making area, is a popular landmark in Cannon Beach. They're known for their huge variety of chewy salt water taffy, but they also make **chocolate candy**. Their **Crabs** have a thin covering of dark or milk chocolate, caramel, and big pieces of pecans. Lots of nutty flavor, but not much chocolate. Their **Double Chocolate Truffle** is small as truffles go with an intense chocolate flavor and a thick chocolate covering. Their **Raspberry Jell Stix** has good raspberry flavor. Their **Peanut Butter Meltaway** is light on peanut butter taste, but melts in the mouth. We'd skip the **Tingaling**, a strange combination of crushed peanut brittle, mint, and chocolate.
Getting there: Bruce's is located on the north end of downtown Cannon Beach on Hemlock.

Picnic Basket
163 2nd Avenue, Cannon Beach, OR. (503) 436-1470
Picnic Basket owner Wayne Schwietert has been cranking out 11 different kinds of fudge to tourists and locals for more than a dozen years. The fudge is chewy and sweet. We found the best flavors were **Chocolate** and **Chocolate Walnut** as the added flavorings seemed to overwhelm the chocolate taste. Their pretty rainbow of fudge flavors include **Chocolate, Chocolate Walnut, Milk Chocolate, Vanilla Walnut, Penoche, Chocolate Peanut Butter, Vanilla Chocolate Swirl, Chocolate Praline, Maple Walnut, Amaretto Chocolate Swirl**, and **Mint Chocolate Swirl**.

They also sell 24 flavors of **Tillamook Ice Cream**, including **Chocolate, Chocolate Chip Mint, Chocolate Peanut Butter, Rocky Road, French Silk, Cookies and Cream**, and **Cookie Dough**.
Getting there: In downtown Cannon Beach, on 2nd between Hemlock and Spruce.

NEHALEM

Beverage Bin and River Gallery

35840 Highway 101, Nehalem, OR. (503) 368-5295

♥♥ You wouldn't expect **fudge** in this wine/espresso/gallery, but **The Beverage Bin and River Gallery** offers a small and tasty selection. Their **Chocolate Walnut** is melt-in-the-mouth creamy with large pieces of walnuts. Their **Chocolate Peanut Butter** is a bit grainy and a bit sweet for this reviewer. For java lovers, **Espresso Fudge** tastes like a cup of hearty sweetened espresso.

Getting there: Can't miss it. Highway 101 (7ᵗʰ street) passes right through Nehalem.

BAY CITY

ArtSpace Gallery and Café

Highway 101 and 5ᵀᴴ Street, Bay City, OR. (503) 377-2782

♥♥♥ Located halfway between Garibaldi and Tillamook, **ArtSpace Gallery and Café** is an unexpected gem of sophistication and good eating on the Oregon coast. Unlike the kitschy tourist gift stores in nearby towns, ArtSpace is a fine art gallery showcasing Northwest artists, especially Northwest artists of the 1930's and 40's. The café serves interesting lunch offerings like homemade soups and oyster burgers. For dinner, they offer fresh fish, chicken dishes, oysters, and fettuccine. Chocolate lovers will enjoy their **Sour Cream German Chocolate Cake**, 3 layers of medium chocolate cake filled with coconut filling and frosted with a semi-sweet chocolate buttercream frosting. The cake is just the right texture and the coconut filling is buttery with large chunks of walnuts. The buttercream frosting is melt-in-the-mouth creamy.

Their **Chocolate Decadence with Raspberry Sauce** is a dense wedge of dark, fudge-like cake served with sweetened raspberry sauce and a dollop of whipped cream. The bittersweet chocolate makes the cake chocolaty without being sweet and the sweet raspberries offer a nice contrast.

Getting there: Right off Highway 101.

TILLAMOOK

Tillamook Ice Creamery

4175 Highway 101 N, Tillamook, OR. (503) 842-4481

♥♥♥ It used to be a quaint little place where you could buy fresh Oregon ice cream and cheese right from the creamery. But the

Tillamook Ice Creamery has gone big time tourist with a huge facility, acres of parking, multiple gift shops, and long lines. It's still a great place to buy some of the freshest and best **ice cream** in Oregon. Fresh from the creamery does taste better! Their ice cream contains 13.5% butterfat, yet is as flavorful as some of the premium ice creams with higher fat levels. It's creamy and comes cleanly off the tongue.

They carry about 40 regular flavors as well as several "lite" and sugar-free varieties. This reviewer's favorite chocolate flavor (and Tillamook's #1 chocolate seller) is **Chocolate Peanut Butter**, a medium chocolate taste with big chunks of peanut butter. Their **German Chocolate Cake** is the same creamy chocolate ice cream filled with pieces of fudge brownie and coconut. It's chocolate lover's delight! Other chocolate flavors include **Chocolate, Chocolate Chip Mint, Cookie Dough, French Silk, Rocky Road,** and **White Chocolate Sundae**.

> *"Chocolate and the king are my only passions."*
> **– Queen Maria Theresa of France in the 1600's**

Traveler's tip: Crowds can be big and lines long during peak summer months. Try a visit in spring, fall, or even the winter.
Getting there: *On Highway 101 on the north side of Tillamook.*

OCEANSIDE

If you stay on Highway 101, you'll miss beautiful Cape Meares and the tiny town of Oceanside.

Roseanna's Oceanside Café
1490 Pacific Avenue, Oceanside, OR. (503) 842-7351
♥♥ **Roseanna's** is a popular restaurant perched right above the beach with great views of the ocean and the towering coastal rocks. Their lunch offerings include hot and cold sandwiches served with soup, chowder or a salad, and egg scramble with shrimp/cheese or veggies. Dinners include chicken, filet, penne pastas, and several Northwest fish selections cooked in a variety of interesting ways, such as dijon citrus, lemon herb butter, and Cajun spiced with chutney butter. For the chocolate lover, they offer **Chocolate Caramel Crunch Cake**, a 4-inch square that's a single layer of dark chocolate cake topped with a layer of caramel, whipped cream, and cara-

melized almonds. The cake is very moist and the caramelized almonds and whipped cream add a nice compliment.

Their **Tollhouse Pie** is tollhouse filling with large chunks of walnuts and chocolate chips served in a flaky pie crust. It's chewy and cookie-like. Ask for it served warm with a scoop of vanilla ice cream.

Getting there: Off Highway 101, follow the signs to the Three Capes Scenic Drive. Then follow the signs to Oceanside. Roseanna's is on Pacific Avenue right next to the post office and the beach wayside.

PACIFIC CITY

The Riverhouse
3440 Brooten Road, Pacific City, OR. (503) 965-6722

♥♥♥ **The Riverhouse** is an intimate restaurant snuggled right along side the Nestucca River. The food is tasty and portions generous. Lunch fare includes hot and cold sandwiches, soup, chowder, and salads. Dinner includes such favorites as broiled coast salmon, oysters with bacon and Swiss cheese, and spinach-mushroom crepes. Some evenings they feature live music from Northwest musicians like blusey-voiced Kate Sullivan. They make their own desserts on-site, including their **Chocolate Cake**, 5 layers of dark chocolate cake filled and frosted with a light chocolate buttercream frosting. Yum! This moist cake is what chocolate cake should taste like.

Their **Chocolate Amaretto Mousse** is light-as-air. Its flavor is more amaretto than chocolate. If you need a real chocolate hit, opt for the chocolate cake.

Getting there: Follow the signs off Highway 101 to Pacific City. The Riverhouse is on the main road from the highway.

Bakery

The Grateful Bread Bakery
34805 Brooten Road, Pacific City, OR. (503) 965-7337

♥♥♥ Laura and Gary Seide have been baking up bread and other oven delights in Pacific City for a half-dozen years. **The Grateful Bread Bakery** is a from-scratch bakery that uses good ingredients like Callebaut Chocolate and Dutch process cocoa. The results show in their **Cream Cheese Chocolate Brownie**, a thin layer of moist, cake-like brownie, topped with an inch-thick layer of cheesy topping. Unlike most cream cheese brownies, this one isn't overly sweet. The topping is rich and cheesy and gives a good contrast to the dark chocolate brownie—one of the best this reviewer has tasted. Their **Chocolate Chunk Cookie** is huge—a half-inch thick and 5 inches across. It's a tollhouse type cookie that's soft and chewy inside with a crunchy outside, crammed with chunks of dark chocolate the size of a quarter.

The bakery also serves omelets and other breakfast items, a large selection of soups like garlic potato and corn and cheese chowder, sandwiches, burgers, pizza, and vegetarian specials.

Getting there: On the main street in Pacific City just a few doors down from the Riverhouse Restaurant.

Fleuri (Sutton Place Hotel)
Vancouver, British Columbia

TRIPLE CHOCOLATE CROISSANT PUDDING

Makes 6 servings

6 cups milk
³/₄ cup granulated sugar
5 eggs
4 cups cubed croissants
¹/₃ cup (2 ounces) milk chocolate chips
¹/₃ cup (2 ounces) white chocolate chips
¹/₃ cup (2 ounces) dark semi-sweet chocolate chips

Preheat oven to 350 degrees. Butter a deep (at least 2") 8-inch pan.

In a large bowl, combine the milk and sugar. Add the eggs and beat until well combined. Place the cubed croissants in the prepared cake pan and pour the milk mixture over the croissants. Fold in chocolate chips.

This warm custard-like bread pudding isn't long on chocolate flavor, but it's loaded with comfort.

Place the cake pan in a large baking pan. Pour boiling water around the cake pan to reach half way up the sides of the cake pan. Bake for 45 minutes or until set in center. Serve warm.

From *The Chocolate Lover's Guide Cookbook,* Pacific Northwest Edition.

South Oregon Coast

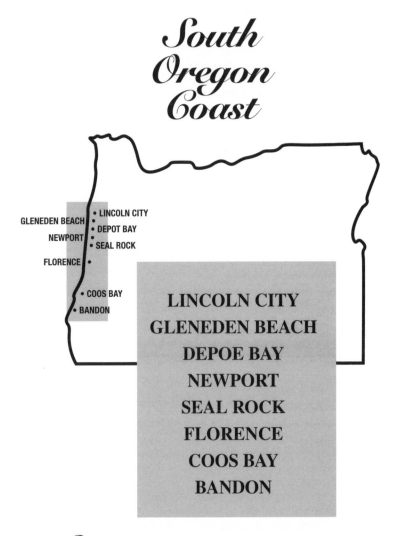

GLENEDEN BEACH
NEWPORT
FLORENCE

- LINCOLN CITY
- DEPOT BAY
- SEAL ROCK
-
- COOS BAY
- BANDON

LINCOLN CITY
GLENEDEN BEACH
DEPOE BAY
NEWPORT
SEAL ROCK
FLORENCE
COOS BAY
BANDON

Some say the South Oregon coast is a bit tamer than the North Oregon Coast. Don't believe it! With soaring cliffs and spectacular scenery like Cape Perpetua Scenic Area, near Yachats, as well as interesting coastal towns like Newport, the southern half of the Oregon coast has plenty to offer visitors.

Great Things to Do

• **Catch a Kite**. **Catch the Wind Kite Shop**, 266 SE Highway 101, **Lincoln City, OR**. (541) 994-9500. Kite flying is almost a religion with some along the Oregon Coast and the grand cathedral for kite enthusiasts is Catch the Wind. They offer kites in all sizes and prices, from simple to incredibly elaborate. They'll also throw in a bit of flying advice.

• **Watch Whales**. December through April Whale is spoken along the Oregon coast as the great grays make their way back to summer waters in Alaska. Often the whales come close enough to shore that they can be easily seen from headlands (their spouts can often be spotted from local restaurant windows!). If you want an even closer look, several whale watching outfitters like **Deep Sea Trollers** (541) 765-2248) and **Tradewind Charters** (541) 765-2345) in **Depoe Bay** and **Sea Gull Charters** (541) 265-7441) and **Newport Sport Fishing** (541) 265-7558) in **Newport Bay** offer whale-watching tours.

• **Visit the Aquarium**. **Oregon Coast Aquarium**, 2828 SE Ferry Slip Road, **Newport, OR**. (541) 867-3474. "Free Willy" star Keiko, the famous orca whale, put the Oregon Coast Aquarium on the map. Even without their star attraction, the Aquarium has plenty to offer, especially the beautiful and surreal Jelly Fish exhibit.

• **Learn about the Sea. Hatfield Marine Science Center**, 2030 S Marine Science Drive, **Newport, OR**. (541) 867-0100. While you're in an ocean-going mood, check out the Hatfield Marine Science Center, which features free displays, nature walks, and even a working tide pool.

• **View a Historic Lighthouse. Yaquina Head Natural Area**, **Newport, OR**. Just north of Newport above Agate Beach is the 1873 restored Yaquina Head Lighthouse, which is open to the public. The surrounding area offers an intertidal area full of interesting wildlife, hiking trails, and million dollar panoramic views.

• **Get Sandy. Oregon Dunes National Recreation Area Headquarters**, 855 Highway Avenue (intersection of Highway 101) **Reedsport, OR**. (541) 271-3611. More than 50 miles of sandy dunes, many of them more than 600 feet high, stretch along the Oregon coast from Florence southward to North Bend. You can hike the dunes, swim in the many fresh water lakes, or enjoy riding your off-road vehicle (check the headquarters map to see where it's allowed).

• **Go on Safari. West Coast Game Park Safari**, 6 miles south of **Bandon, OR**. (541) 347-3106. This park lets visitors view wild things like lions, tigers, and elk.

Terrific Places to Stay

Salishan Lodge, 7760 Highway 101 N, **Gleneden Beach, OR**. (541) 764-3600/ (888) 725-4742. If you want the feeling of staying in your own private lodge, Salishan Lodge is for you. Guest rooms and suites are situated in individual buildings tucked into rolling hills facing Siletz Bay. They feature open-beamed ceilings, gas fireplaces with rock faces, balconies, mini-bars, in-room coffee, televisions with remote, honor bars, plush robes, and covered carports. With comfortable couches, overstuffed chairs, and occasional tables, the suites have a genuine homey feel. The main lodge building features stone floors covered with colorful throw rugs in native patterns, a fireplace room with couches and overstuffed chairs, wrought iron chandeliers, lamps, and tables, and a paneled, well-stocked library with large windows, good reading lamps, and comfy chairs and couches. Guests can dine in the Dining Room (see review) or the more casual Sun Room. Salishan is famous for its golf, including a par 72 course, driving range, and putting green. There are also wooded nature trails, complete fitness center with exercise room, large indoor pool, sun deck, whirlpool, and men's and women's saunas.

Sylvia Beach Hotel, 267 NW Cliff, **Newport, OR**. (541) 265-5428. No phones, no TVs, no data ports, no exercise room. Sylvia Beach Hotel, housed in a 1910 building perched above the pounding surf, is meant for quiet relaxation. A historic landmark, the Sylvia Beach Hotel harkens back to a simpler time when fun meant writing, reading, doing puzzles, or playing board games by a roaring fire. Named after the late bookstore owner and patron of literature, Sylvia Beach, the hotel's 20 rooms, all with private baths, are named and decorated after famous writers like Colette, Mark Twain, Gertrude Stein, Oscar Wilde, and Edgar Allen Poe. The Agatha Christie room, for instance, a corner room with magnificent views of the ocean, is decorated in deep greens—forest green walls and carpeting, green and rose floral drapes, quilts, and couch, even the tile on the working fireplace has green tiles. "Clues" are left around the room for guests to discover. The Poe Room has dark wallpaper, crimson bedding, a big black raven, and a small pendulum suspended over the bed. The 3rd floor livingroom has good views, a fireplace, happily mismatched and comfortable overstuffed chairs, ottomans, and couches, all with good reading lamps and a coffee and tea room close-by. There's a well-stocked lending library in the alcove where guests can select a book to enjoy. A full breakfast with fresh fruit, baked goods, cereals, eggs, pancakes, and meats is included at the hotel's Tables of Contents Restaurant (see review). *Traveler's note: Allergy alert— there's a resident cat.*

Inn at Face Rock, 3225 Beach Loop Road, **Bandon, OR**. (541) 347-9441. The Inn at Face Rock is a terrific place to watch the storms roll in at Bandon, storm capitol of the Oregon coast. Located on Bandon's scenic Beach Loop, many of the rooms offer good views of the Pacific. The spacious ocean-view suites are particularly suited for families with king or 2 queen beds, fireplaces (logs provided), kitchenettes, coffeemakers, and refrigerators. Guests can enjoy the 9-hole golf course, outdoor spa, private beach access, and guest laundry. Dining is available at Christophe, the Inn's fine dining restaurant (see review).

LINCOLN CITY

Closed 8/14 *Restaurant*

Chamelon Café
2145 NW Highway 101, Lincoln City, OR. (541) 994-8422
♥♥ With its white walls with pastel green and rose trim, original artwork, cloth and glass-covered tables, blond chairs, and jazz filling the air, **Chamelon Café** is a casual and pleasant retreat from the bustle of Highway 101. For lunch and dinner, they offer Mediterranean dishes like spanakopita, tabouli, and falafal, vegetarian offerings like portobello mushrooms and spinach cakes, and pasta dishes like linguine with spinach, walnuts and gorgonzola. Their chocolate desserts include **Chocolate Ganache**, a thin wedge of crunchy, toasted walnut crust topped with a half inch of thick, creamy ganache. It's served with a buttery, homemade caramel sauce. It's a rich variation on a chocolate standard that chocolate lovers will surely enjoy.

They also serve a **Chocolate Espresso Mousse** that comes piped into a large wine glass, served with real whipped cream and dark chocolate shavings. The mousse is an excellent blend of espresso and chocolate flavors with a creamy texture. The whipped cream, which has little sweetening, adds a fresh taste.
Getting there: *On Highway 101 between 21ˢᵗ and 22ⁿᵈ streets in Lincoln City.*

GLENEDEN BEACH

Chez Jeannette
7150 Gleneden Beach Loop, Gleneden Beach, OR. (541) 764-3434
♥♥♥ **Chez Jeannette** is situated in a cozy 1920's cottage complete with fireplace, wall sconces, blue and gold patterned wallpaper, and cloth-covered tables with fresh flowers and flickering candles. They serve dinner entrees like veal medallions, rack of lamb, roast pork with garlic, red wine, peppercorn, and juniper berry sauce, and chicken in olive oil with a sauce of golden raisins, white wine vinegar, fresh thyme, rosemary, pine nuts, and veal stock, as well as nightly seafood, game, and pasta specials. Their **Mocha Fudge Torte** comes on a delicate, buttery cookie crust.

The filling has a deep chocolate flavor and is so thick and fudgy that it's chewy.

Their **Hazelnut Milk Chocolate Mousse** comes in a tall coffee glass topped with a whole hazelnut. It's light-as-air with a delicate milk chocolate flavor. The creamy texture of the mousse is punctuated by chewy bits of hazelnut.

Getting there: One-quarter mile south of Salishan Lodge on Old Highway 101.

Dining Room at Salishan Lodge
7760 Highway 101 N, Gleneden Beach, OR. (541) 764-3600

♥ Subdued lighting, wooden wall carvings, upholstered booths and arm chairs, cloth-covered tables with pink oil lamps, and large windows that overlook lighted evergreens all contribute to the pleasant ambiance at Salishan Lodge's Dining Room. They serve fish selections like alder planked salmon, peppered sturgeon, halibut, and pancetta-wrapped scallops as well as meat and poultry dishes like beef tenderloin, NY steak, lamb chops, duck breast, and pork chops. Their desserts, which change seasonally, may include **Warm Chocolate Pudding**, a baked pudding with a cake-like texture accented with tiny bits of hazelnuts that's slightly crispy on the outside, soft and moist on the inside.

The **Liquid Center Chocolate Cake** is a 3-inch round cake that's served warm and garnished with a ribbon of dark chocolate and raspberry and chocolate sauces. It has a dark chocolate flavor that's especially intense in the soft, liquid center.

The **Chocolate Creme Brulee Napoleon**, one of the most successful of the selections, comes as 3 (8-inch) disks of phyllo that have been brushed with warm chocolate sandwiched with chocolate creme brulee and whipped cream. The creme brulee is smooth with a light milk chocolate flavor while the crispy phyllo adds a great crunch.

They serve **Chocolate Mousse** in a variety of styles—in a chocolate cup, in a triangle wedge, or in a chocolate tower. In the cup, it's flavored with chocolate liqueur and garnished with a chocolate swirl, chocolate sauce, and a dollop of whipped cream. The triangle mousse has a light milk chocolate flavor. When it's served in a tall box of dark chocolate, it's flavored with almond paste. Although the flavors are all good, the texture of the mousse is a bit grainy.

Getting there: On Highway 101 in Gleneden Beach. Watch for the signs.

DEPOE BAY

Tidal Raves
279 NW Highway 101, Depoe Bay, OR. (541) 765-2995
♥♥♥ **Tidal Raves** has simple decor—light yellow walls with green trim and a simple seashell mural. With huge windows providing an unobstructed view of the pounding surf and wind-sculpted rocks, it doesn't need more. They serve lunch and dinner with emphasis on fresh seafood with some creative innovations like stir-fried prawns and scallops, cornmeal grilled snapper with Southwest spices, crab with penne, white sauce, and Bandon cheddar, Thai BBQ prawns, and scallops with penne, feta, garlic, fried tomatoes and kalamata olives. The few non-fish dishes include lemon rosemary chicken, pork tenderloin, and NY steak. Their signature chocolate dessert is the **Chocolate Truffle Cake**, a thin slice of dark, rich truffle served with vanilla and raspberry-citrus sauces and garnished with roasted hazelnuts. This is an ultra-silky dessert with an excellent chocolate flavor. The vanilla sauce, speckled with flecks of vanilla bean, is light and the raspberry-citrus sauce is refreshing.

You can also order the **Chocolate Chunk Cookie with Tillamook Vanilla Bean Ice Cream**. At 7 inches, this giant cookie is thin and crisp on the outside, slightly soft on the inside and loaded with nuts and chunks of Guittard chocolate. It's the closest this reviewer has come to a homemade chocolate chip cookie. Served with Tillamook ice cream, it's a real treat.
Getting there: *On Highway 101 in Depot Bay.*

NEWPORT

Tables of Contents (Sylvia Beach Hotel)
267 NW Cliff Street, Newport, OR. (541) 265-5428
♥♥♥♥ **Tables of Contents,** the author-themed Sylvia Beach Hotel's (see review) restaurant, has 2 seatings on weekends and 1 during the week for their pre-fixe dinners. They include an appetizer, salad, homemade bread, an entree like scallops with saffron sauce, vegetable, starch dish, dessert, and beverage—a real bargain. Desserts change regularly, but one of their standards is **Chocolate Oblivion**, a flourless torte that comes topped with ganache and white chocolate with whipped cream. It's creamy and rich with an incredibly dense chocolate flavor. The whipped cream is only slightly sweetened and adds a freshness to this devilishly chocolaty dessert.

Another regular on their menu is their **Chocolate Poppers A'Cage**, bite-sized almond brownies topped with a milk chocolate buttercream. Pop these babies in your mouth and you may forget all about those greasy jalapeño poppers. These little brownies are rich and chewy with buttercream that is so light it almost floats away.

Travelers note: There isn't always a chocolate dessert on their pre-fixe menu, but if you call up and whine a bit, they'll accommodate you.
Getting there: *On the corner of Cliff and NW 3rd.*

Whale's Tale
452 SW Bay Boulevard, Newport, OR. (541) 265-8660
♥♥♥♥ Whale's Tale is a cozy, casual place along Newport's waterfront that looks like a boathouse with crab boxes, huge whale bones, harpoons, and a dingy hanging from the ceiling. For more than 20 years, they've been delighting locals and tourists alike with breakfast, lunch, and dinner. They're known for hearty breakfasts like the Logger, 2 eggs, potatoes, biscuits and gravy, ham, or sausage and the Deckhand, ham, sausage, 3 eggs, potatoes, biscuit, and gravy. Dinner entrees include seafood selections like fresh scallops, prawns, and cioppino, as well as lasagne and German sausage, ham, sauerkraut, and black bread. For dessert, chocolate lovers should try their signature **Mousse in a Bag**, a 3x4 inch "sack" of dark chocolate filled with white chocolate mousse and covered with fresh, sliced strawberries, and whipped cream. The chocolate sack is thin and crisp with a wonderfully deep chocolate flavor. The white chocolate mousse is light, almost lemony. The strawberries add a delightful freshness to this decadent dessert.

Chef Patricia Dickey also makes dessert specials like her **Chocolate Butterfly Truffle Torte**, which won first place in Newport's 1998 Chocolate Classic Competition. It's a thick, dark chocolate torte frosted with white chocolate buttercream and decorated with delicate, dark chocolate butterflies and tiny purple flowers. The truffle is soft and silky with an excellent dark chocolate flavor. The white chocolate is creamy without being overly sweet.
Getting there: *In Newport's historic bay front district on Bay Boulevard at SW Fall Street.*

ARR Place
143 SW Cliff Street, Newport, OR. (541) 265-4240
♥♥♥ ARR Place is a comfortable breakfast-lunch place where locals and tourists alike come to enjoy the ocean views and let their kids scamper around the play area set aside for them. The menu offers largely breakfast items—corned beef hash, huevos rancheros, eggs Benedict, French toast, waffles, pancakes, and scrambled with spinach, onions, mushrooms and seasoned ground beef. For lunch, they offer burgers, chili, Asian chicken salad, and soups. The desserts, which change at the chef's whim, usually include at least one chocolate item like their **Mocha Fudge Torte**, a

large wedge that's dusted with powered sugar. It's very moist with a deep, rich chocolately flavor with a texture that's a cross between cake and a truffle center. Yum!

Getting there*: On 2ⁿᵈ and Coast behind the Green Gables Bed and Breakfast.*

Canyon Way Restaurant and Bookstore
1216 SW Canyon Way, Newport, OR. (541) 265-8319
♥♥♥ **Canyon Way Restaurant and Bookstore** is a place for book lovers and dessert lovers. The bookstore stocks more than 20,000 titles; the restaurant a dozen or so desserts, many of them chocolate. The restaurant serves lunch and dinner. At lunch, the atmosphere is casual with wooden tables and chairs and a menu that offers dishes like cod fingers, crab cakes, a large selection of salads as well as hot sandwiches like fish, Cajun turkey, teriyaki, and shrimp melt. At dinner, candles, linen, folded cloth napkins, and subdued lighting transform the ambiance. Dinner entrees include seafood dishes like salmon, Yaquina Bay oysters, saffron steamed mussels, and sautéed prawns; meats like filet mignon, New York, prime rib and chicken; and pasta dishes like prawns and fettuccine, shrimp Alfredo, and spicy seafood pasta.

Most diners can't resist the dessert case stocked with delights like **Chocolate Peanut Butter Cake**, 4 layers of dark chocolate cake alternately filled with a thick ganache and a fluffy peanut butter cream. The cake is moist and medium-textured; the peanut butter cream is light and silky with a subtle peanut flavor.

Their **Hazelnut Chocolate Torte** comes as a big wedge of brownie-like torte that's packed with hazelnut pieces, topped with ganache, and garnished with hazelnuts. It's thick, chewy, and fudgy with lots of chocolate flavor.

The **Chocolate Hazelnut Brownie Fudge Square** is 2 (4x6-inch) cake-like brownies sandwiched with a thick layer of whipped cream and chocolate hazelnut cream. It's all topped with a thick chocolate fudge and roasted hazelnuts. The brownies are moist and cakey and the hazelnut cream has a mousse-like texture. The fudge topping has an intense, dark chocolate flavor.

Their **Chocolate Cheesecake** is a large slice of graham-nut crust that's topped with 3 inches of milk chocolate cheesecake and whipped cream. It has a cheesy tang that's just right. **French Silk** starts with a crumbly, cinnamon-flavored crust that's topped with an ultra-creamy chocolate cream.

The **German Chocolate Cake** is 4 layers of the same dark chocolate cake that's in the Chocolate Peanut Butter Cake, but this one is filled with creamy coconut and frosted with milk chocolate buttercream. The coconut filling isn't overly sweet and the buttercream has a soft, subtle chocolate flavor.

Getting there: Between Hurbert and Bay Boulevard.

Champagne Patio

1630 N Coast Highway, Newport, OR. (541) 265-3044

♥♥ Attached to a wine shop, **Champagne Patio** is a small restaurant with 15 wooden tables and chairs, royal blue carpeting, and wine box engravings and wine bottles decorating the walls. They serve lunch and occasional wine dinners. They offer cold deli sandwiches like ham, roast beef, turkey, braunschweiger, and Tillamook cheese; hot sandwiches like cheddar, ham and pineapple, Monte Cristo, and Reuben; as well as salads and razor clam chowder served with homemade Swedish bread. Desserts change daily and often include a chocolate dessert like **Chocolate Shortbread Tart**, a wedge of shortbread crust that's topped with 2 inches of brownie-like cake and real whipped cream. The cake is soft, the shortbread crust crisp and buttery, and the whipped cream, which is barely sweetened, adds a wonderful accent. It's a most satisfying combination.

Getting there: Highway 101 between 17th and San-bay-o Streets.

> **Melts in Your Mouth.**
>
> Cocoa butter is the fat of the roasted cocoa beans. It melts at lower temperature than other vegetable oils. The faster a chocolate melts in your mouth, the more cocoa butter it has.

SEAL ROCK

Fudge, Etc.

10449 NW Pacific Coast Highway, Seal Rock, OR. (541) 563-2766

♥♥ If you've got a yen for **fudge** while making your way down the coast, stop at **Fudge, Etc**. You can't miss the Homemade Fudge sign fronting the tiny shop along the coast highway. Proprietor Karen Hohnstein handmakes several varieties of fudge using Guittard Chocolate, cream, butter, and no preservatives and sells them in big, 2x2 inch chunks. She sells 2 basic varieties: **All American**, traditional fudge with or without walnuts, and **Fudge Supreme**, a darker chocolate that comes with or without nuts. All American is soft and creamy without being overly sweet. The Fudge Supreme, this chocolate lover's favorite, has a deep rich chocolate flavor. It definitely has more chocolate punch than most fudge. Using All

American Fudge, their **Chocolate Peanut Butter** comes with big chunks of peanut butter (unsweetened) that give a lovely sweet/ salty combination. Other variations include **Amaretto, Vanilla, Irish Cream**, **Butterscotch**, and **Penoche**.

Traveler's note: The fudge is especially fresh and moist in the summer when business is hopping.
Getting there: *On the east side of the highway in Seal Rock. Watch for the "Fudge" sign.*

FLORENCE

BJ's Homemade Ice Cream
2930 Highway 101 N, Florence, OR. (541) 997-7286
Other Florence location:
1441 Bay Street, Florence, OR. (541) 902-7828
♥♥♥♥ If you're looking for excellent **ice cream** on the Oregon coast, head for **BJ's Homemade Ice Cream**. Owner and ice cream maker, Brian Cole uses the old fashioned batch method of making 1 flavor or batch at a time rather than making hundreds of gallons of vanilla base and then adding flavors. His recipes have been in his family for more than 90 years (his father owned Cole's Ice Cream in 1917). He uses only the best ingredients—high-quality Guittard chocolate, fresh cream and whole milk from a local, family-owned dairy in Eugene, egg yolks, and cane sugar (not less expensive corn syrup). He also puts in plenty of condiments like roasted nuts, fresh bing cherries, and caramel in the more than 50 flavors he makes. The result is rich, creamy ice cream with 14.2% butterfat that doesn't cling to the tongue. His 6 ounce scoops are big enough to please.

Oregon Trail is a double chocolate ice cream with blackberry marbling and roasted hazelnuts. The chocolate ice cream has deep chocolatey flavor, the blackberry actually tastes fresh, and the roasted hazelnuts add a nice crunch.

If you like caramel, try **Tortal** (an off-shoot of Turtles), double chocolate ice cream with loads of buttery caramel and Oregon English walnuts. It's like having a chocolate caramel sundae on a cone. His **Peanut Butter Cup**, some of the best this reviewer has tasted, is loaded with huge chunks of peanut butter.

Chocolate Almond is made with Mission almonds, which are smaller and tend to hold their crispness in the ice cream after roasting. The milk chocolate ice cream has a soft, subtle chocolate flavor.

Chocolate Chip is packed with big Guittard chocolate chips. His **Chocolate Cheesecake** uses real NY cheesecake base with chocolate marbled in. The result is ice cream that's tangy and cheesy like cheesecake.

His **Mint Chip** features Creme de Menthe ice cream with pieces of Andies Mints. Mint fans will love this one. **Grasshopper** uses the same Creme de Menthe ice cream with Keebler Grasshopper cookies crumbled into it.

Rocky Road fans won't have to look far for the marshmallows and walnuts. They're loaded in this version. **Bittersweet Nugget**, one of this reviewer's favorites, is double chocolate ice cream loaded with Guittard chocolate chips. It's a major chocolate hit!

They also sell most of their flavors in lower-fat yogurt versions which are surprisingly good.
Getting there: The Highway 101 store is on the east side of the highway in Florence. The Bay Street store is on the Florence Old Town Loop.

COOS BAY

Blue Heron Bistro
100 W Commercial, Coos Bay, OR. (541) 267-3933
♥♥♥ **Blue Heron Bistro** is casual place with blonde wood tables and chairs, a tile floor, skylights, and an L-shaped bar. Open for lunch and dinner, they serve entrees that reflect their proximity to the ocean such as blackened red fish, snapper and salmon Vera Cruz, New Orleans oysters, and non-fish items like pasta, and German bratwurst. For dessert, they usually offer a **Chocolate Pie**, with a pressed-in pastry crust, 3 inches of dark chocolate cream, 2 inches of real whipped cream, and dark chocolate shavings. The crust, which has some whole wheat added, has a nutty flavor; the cream is thick with a good chocolate flavor.

Their **Chocolate Almond Torte**, another standard, starts with a graham crust, then a $1/2$ inch layer of ganache, 3 inches of chocolate mousse, and a layer of almond-flavored whipped cream, garnished with chocolate shavings. The mousse is light and creamy; the ganache is very thick and rich. The almond whipped cream adds a subtle, nutty flavor.

Their **Truffle Cake**, this reviewer's favorite, is 6 layers of dark chocolate cake with alternating layers of ganache and whipped cream. The whole cake is covered with a layer of whipped cream. This multi-layered cake is dramatic to look at and wonderful to

eat. The medium-textured cake has just the right moistness; the ganache is rich and fudgy; and the whipped cream adds a nice lightness. The slice is huge. Plan to share it—or not.
Getting there: Highway 101 and Commercial.

Cranberry Sweets
1005 Newmarket Street, Coos Bay, OR. (541) 888-9824
♥♥ (See review under Chocolate Shop, Bandon.)
Getting there: On Newmarket near Schomenan.

BANDON

Christophe (Inn at Face Rock)
3225 Beach Loop Drive, Bandon, OR. (541) 347-3261
♥♥ The glass atrium with good ocean views, cloth-covered tables with small frosted oil lamps, colorful plates, stainless and wicker chairs, plants, and ceiling fans all contribute to a casual, yet elegant dining area at **Christophe**. They serve breakfast, lunch, and dinner, with dinner selections like filet mignon in creamy cognac, green peppercorn, and black pepper sauce, chicken with gorgonzola, lobster in beurre blanc, poached salmon, pasta dishes, and grilled steaks, chops, and chicken. Their signature chocolate dessert is **Chocolate Decadence**, a slim wedge of flourless torte served with blackberry coulis swirled with thinned whipped cream. Made with semi-sweet Belgian chocolate, this decadence has an intense chocolate flavor and a silky texture. The tart blackberry sauce cuts the sweetness of the chocolate.
Getting there: South of downtown on the Beach Loop.

Lord Bennett's Restaurant and Lounge
1695 Beach Loop Drive, Bandon, OR. (541) 347-3663
♥♥ **Lord Bennett's** is a contemporary, second-story restaurant on the dramatic Bandon Beach Loop. Its white walls, tall, narrow windows, wood tables and chairs, cloth placemats and napkins, and track lights contribute to a casual ambiance that fits the beach. They serve lunch and dinner with evening entrees including seafood dishes like shrimp sautéed in butter with garlic, sherry and lemon, and sole stuffed with shrimp, ricotta cheese, herbs and vegetables. Non-fish dishes include steaks, lamb, pork loin, and fettuccine Alfredo. They always offer several chocolate desserts, including their **Chocolate Hazelnut Cake**, a yellow cake with tiny hazelnuts pieces that's filled and frosted with a milk chocolate buttercream. The cake is moist and well-flavored and the buttercream is light and silky.

Their **Chocolate Espresso Mousse** is piped into a large wine glass and garnished with bits of roasted espresso beans. The mousse is the right light texture. However, the ground espresso beans in the mousse, which contribute an interesting flavor, interfere with the dessert's creamy texture.

The **Kahlua Coffee Cheesecake** is more successful in using espresso beans. It comes with a graham cracker crust, $2^1/_2$ inches of kahlua coffee cheesecake, and a thin layer of dark chocolate ganache, garnished with toasted espresso beans. The cheesecake is tangy with plenty of cheese flavor. The coffee-kahlua flavor is subtle and the ganache rich.

German Chocolate Cake is 3 layers of dark chocolate cake filled and topped with a coconut/walnut mixture, then frosted on the sides with dark chocolate buttercream and garnished with chopped walnuts. The medium texture cake has a solid, chocolaty flavor and the coconut mixture is chewy.
Getting there: On Bandon's Beach Loop.

Bandon Boatworks Restaurant
275 Lincoln Avenue SW, Bandon, OR. (541) 347-2111
♥ Situated out on South Jetty, the **Boatworks** is a terrific place to watch storms roll in. Large windows, a dozen 4-person tables covered with bright blue cloths, straw mats, and fresh flowers give the place an inviting feel. They're open for dinner with plenty of seafood like catch of the day, snapper, oysters, and prawns. There is also filet, teriyaki or marinated chicken and prime rib. Their nod to chocolate is **Chocolate Mousse**, a half-cup portion served with a dollop of whipped cream. It's a hearty mousse, creamy, yet still light. A bit of brandy and almond extract give it a nice depth.
Getting there: On Bandon's South Jetty.

Grateful Bread Bakery
Pacific City, Oregon
CREAM CHEESE BROWNIES

Makes 24 brownies

Brownie Layer:
1 ½ cup melted butter
3 cups granulated sugar
6 eggs
1 teaspoon vanilla
1 ½ cups all-purpose flour
1 ½ cups cocoa powder

Cream Cheese Layer:
2 8-ounce packages cream cheese
2 eggs
³/₄ cup granulated sugar
2 tablespoons all-purpose flour
1 teaspoon vanilla

For Brownie Layer:
Preheat oven to 350 degrees. Butter a 9x13-inch baking pan.

Combine the butter and sugar in the bowl of an electric mixer and beat well. Add the eggs 1 at a time, beating well after each addition. Beat in vanilla. Add flour and cocoa and stir to combine. Do not over mix.

Grateful Bread's Cream Cheese Brownies have the rich flavor of chocolate with the wonderfully tangy flavor of cream cheese.

For the Cream Cheese Layer:
Place the cream cheese, eggs, sugar, flour and vanilla in the bowl of a food processor and blend until smooth.

Pour most of the brownie layer into the prepared pan, reserving a small amount for topping.

Spread the cream cheese batter over the chocolate and smooth with a spatula. With a spoon, dollop six portions of the reserved chocolate batter on top of the cream cheese. Using the tip of a knife, swirl the chocolate topping into the cream cheese layer.

Bake 55-60 minutes. Cool completely in pan before cutting.

From *The Chocolate Lover's Guide Cookbook*,
Pacific Northwest Edition.

OREGON

Willamette Valley

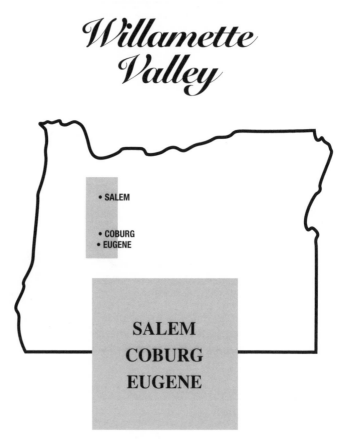

SALEM
COBURG
EUGENE

*S*andwiched between the Coast Range and the Cascades, Oregon's Willamette Valley stretches from just outside of Portland to the north to Eugene in the south. Its verdant soil grows a number of agricultural products, from flowers to some of the best pinot noir grapes in the world.

Great Things to Do

• **Hunt for Antique Treasures**. **Aurora Historic District, Aurora, OR**. In a village many think time has forgotten, antique hunters will find a bonanza of antique shops and period buildings. On the National Register of Historic Places, Aurora, Oregon is a pleasant place to spend an afternoon looking for that special treasure.

• **Sip a Bit of the Vine**. There are enough excellent wineries in the Willamette Valley to keep a dedicated wine lover happy for many weekends of tasting. So many, in fact, that it's wise to get a winery map from the **Oregon Wine Advisory Board** (1220 NW Naito Parkway, Suite 400, **Portland, OR**. Call (800) 242-2362) before planning your wine excursions.

• **Take a Trail Ride**. **Flying M Ranch**, 23029 NW Flying M Road, **Yamhill, OR**. (503) 662-3222. Just 10 miles west of the little town of Yamhill, the Flying M Ranch, with its log cabin style lodge, offers visitors a chance to take a horse ride with local cowboys. Afterward, you can grab some grub at the ranch's restaurant.

• **Visit an Abbey**. **Mount Angel Abbey, Mt. Angel, OR**. (503) 845-3030. This 100-year-old seminary, perched on a hilltop just a few miles—and a world away—from the state's capitol, Mt. Angel Abbey is a pastoral place to visit. The library, built by an acclaimed architect from Finland, is well worth a tour. Call for visiting hours.

• **Stroll through the Deepwood Gardens**. **Deepwood Estate**, 1116 Mission Street SE, **Salem, OR**. (503) 363-1825. This Victorian beauty, built in 1894, has become a urban oasis with its conservatory, gardens, and hiking trails. There's a small fee to tour the home, but the gardens and trails are free.

• **Get Under Cover**. **Covered Bridge Society of Oregon**, PO Box 1804, **Newport, OR**. The Willamette Valley boasts nearly 50 covered bridges, wonderful remnants of a by-gone era. The best way to tour them is to get a map from the Covered Bridge Society of Oregon (send a SASE with 2 first-class stamps), pack a picnic, and head out.

• **Go for the Crafts**. **Saturday Market**, High at Broadway, **Eugene, OR**. April through December, Eugene hosts an eclectic open air market of crafts, food, music, and merriment. It's a great place to pick up a gift or just enjoy some interesting people watching.

Terrific Places to Stay

The Campbell House, 252 Pearl Street, **Eugene, OR**. (541) 343-1119. Conveniently located in the National Historic District within walking distance of Eugene's downtown shops and restaurants, The Campbell House is much like a small European hotel. A lovely home built in 1892 and completely restored into an inn, the Campbell House features 14 beautifully decorated rooms, each with their own bath, television, and telephone. Although all of the rooms are lovely, some are quite small. You might want to splurge on one of the larger rooms. For really special occasions, there's a spacious suite with large windows, high ceilings, and a jetted tub for 2. Coffee or tea is delivered to your room in the morning and a full breakfast is served in the dining room overlooking the garden. Breakfast includes delicacies freshly baked at the inn.

The Oval Door, 988 Lawrence, **Eugene, OR**. (541) 683-3160. Shaded by large maples on the corner of West 10th and Lawrence Streets, The Oval Door Bed and Breakfast is within easy walking distance of Eugene's downtown. Built in 1990 as an inn, The Oval Door features 4 spacious rooms, each with its own private bath, beautifully decorated in a country style that is elegant rather than fussy. Innkeeper Judy McLane pays close attention to detail and provides niceties such as Perrier, magazines in each room, fluffy robes, hair dryers, and an assortment of toiletries. A shared Jacuzzi bathroom features candles, music, books, and bubbles to relax away your cares. An excellent cook, Judy makes a full, delicious breakfast, often featuring her homemade breads.

SALEM

Restaurants

Gerry Frank's Konditorei
310 Kearney Street SE, Salem, OR. (503) 585-7070

♥♥♥♥ Sixteen years ago, Barney Rogers and Gerry Frank decided to capitalize on Gerry's fame as a chocolate cake judge and open **Gerry Frank's Konditorei**. They specialized in gourmet cakes and dessert lovers have been lining up ever since. Though they serve breakfast, lunch, and dinner, it's their fabulous desserts, especially dramatic, multi-layered cakes, they're known for. If you like chocolate cake, you're destined to find one you like such as the **Grand Marnier Mousse Torte**, that comes with a thick walnut crust that's topped with $1/2$ inch of dark ganache, 2 inches of mousse, and frosted with a light chocolate mousse. It's a good creamy/chewy combination. Or you might try the **Kahlua Mousse Torte**, the same as above except with a subtle kahlua flavor. The **Fudge Truffle Cake** is 5 layers of chocolate cake frosted and thickly filled with a fluffy milk chocolate cream. It's light and creamy.

If you're more of a traditionalist, you'll enjoy **Gerry's Chocolate Cake**, 6 half-layers of dark chocolate cake filled and frosted with chocolate buttercream. The cake is moist and the buttercream is light, almost fluffy.

Their **Fantasy Raspberry Rum Espresso Cake** has 6 half-layers of dark cake filled with thin layers of raspberry cream and frosted with dark chocolate ganache. This ultra-moist cake has a deep chocolate flavor complimented by raspberry. If you want even more chocolate flavor, try the **Black Out Cake**, this reviewer's favorite. It's 3 layers of medium chocolate cake that's filled with dark chocolate buttercream and frosted with a lighter chocolate buttercream. It's moist with a dense chocolate flavor that invites another bite.

The **Fudge Brownie Cake** comes with 6 half-layers that are loaded with chocolate chips and frosted and filled with chocolate buttercream. It's thick and fudgy. The **Coconut Mounds Cake** is 4 layers of dark chocolate cake that's filled with chocolate buttercream and coconut cream and topped with whole almonds and a thin layer of ganache. Moist, chewy, full of coconut flavor, this excellent cake will make coconut lovers weep for joy.

They also carry a large selection of dessert bars like **Rocky Road Brownie, Blondies**, and **German Chocolate Brownies**, but the real treats are the cakes.
Getting there*: At Commercial and Kearney.*

Chocolatier Profile –

Gerry Frank, co-owner
Gerry Frank's Konditorei
Salem, Oregon

"I'm a chocoholic by inheritance," **Gerry Frank** *says, smiling broadly. "My father was a chocoholic. I grew up in a chocoholic home. I hardly remember any desserts at home that weren't chocolate."*

In political circles, Gerry Frank is best known as former U.S. Senator Mark Hatfield's chief-of-staff and right hand man. In chocolate circles, he's known as the Oregon State Fair's one and only chocolate cake judge and co-owner of Konditorei, a pastry shop and restaurant in Salem that's renown for towering chocolate cakes.

"As I grew up, I did everything I could do to increase my chocolate intake," says Gerry. "In the Army during World War II, we were on chocolate bar rations. We had to eat 3 of them a day because they couldn't get fresh food to us. Everyone in my unit complained about the chocolate bars, but I loved them. We lived on them for a week or so."

Gerry's love of chocolate was well-known to friends and colleagues. In 1959, when Mark Hatfield won the Oregon governor's race, the new governor asked the Oregon State Fair Commission to appoint Gerry judge of the chocolate cakes at the Oregon State Fair. "We started with 3 cakes in the back room," Gerry recalls. "Over the years, we've had as many as 120 cakes. Now 500 people come to watch this fool judging and I entertain them with chocolate stories and chocolate jokes."

When Hatfield moved onto the Senate, Gerry put his love of chocolate to work judging a number of chocolate contests for U.S. Senate employees. He's judged national chocolate cake contests for major magazines and innumerable chocolate contests around the Northwest.

Gerry and long-time friend, Barney Rogers, wanted to go into business together. Since Gerry was by then known for chocolate cakes, they decided to go into the chocolate cake business. "We didn't know anything about the chocolate cake business," he admits. "But it took hold. Last year, we served 100,000 people in this little place. Ours is probably the largest gourmet cake business in the Northwest."

There's a good reason Gerry Frank is called Mr. Chocolate Cake.

Candy Shop

Euphoria Chocolate
401 Center Street, #130, Salem, OR. (503) 362-5451
♥♥♥♥ (See review under Chocolate Shops, Eugene.)
Getting there: *In the Salem Center Mall, near High and Chemeketa Streets.*

Ice Cream/Candy Shop

Curly's Homestyle Ice Cream
2280 Mission, Salem, OR. (503) 399-1394

Closed 8/1(

♥♥♥ (ice cream)/♥♥ (candy) Family-owned **Curly's** has been making **ice cream** from milk and cream from their own dairy right next door for more than 25 years. Travelers can sample their very fresh, 12% butterfat ice cream in the distinctive pink and white ice cream parlor. Chocolate lovers will find chocolate flavors like **Chocolate Peanut Butter**, which is a creamy chocolate flavor with large hunks of peanut butter, as well as **Chocolate Lovers Chocolate, Chocolate Chip Mint, Pastachio Nut Fudge**, and **Chocolate Almond**. Or they can try Curly's **Nutty Ice Cream Bars**, 4-inch squares of premium vanilla ice cream dipped in nuts or nuts and toffee and thickly covered in dark chocolate. It's the best dipped ice cream bar we've tasted.

Curly's also uses their own cream, butter, and milk to make hand-dipped, American-style **creams**, **chews**, and **nuts**. They offer soft, subtle flavors that fill the mouth as they melt. Their **Chocolate-covered Caramel** is a buttery, medium-soft version that's chewy. **Dark Chocolate Mint** is a dark chocolate center covered in chocolate that's fresh-tasting without being overpowering. Their **Rum Truffle**, the size of a quarter, has a soft rum flavor.

Getting there: On Highway 22 (Mission) a few blocks past the airport.

COBURG

A little, historic town a few miles north of Eugene, Coburg is a great place to hunt for antiques or pick up a bit of chocolate.

Candy Shop

Larsen's Fine Candies
91012 S Willamette, Coburg, OR. (541) 686-5783
♥♥♥ Ruth Larsen started making candies 12 years ago as a hobby. Today, she owns and operates **Larsen's Fine Candies** and ships her **chocolates** nationwide. She uses Merckens Chocolate and her recipes are time-tested. Many come from a candymaker who made confections for the Czar of Russia. This is a candymaker who takes the time to do things right like hand double-dipping the chocolates.

Ruth carries a selection of large, satiny **truffles** in some unusual flavors, including **Very Berry, Vanilla Nut, Vanilla Buttercream, Pineapple, Orange, Mint, Maplenut, Lime, Lemon, Coconut, Cherry Pecan, Chocolate Mint, Chocolate Buttercream**, and **White Satin**. Most satisfying!

Larsen's is known for their **jelly sticks** and they should be. The raspberry and orange flavors are vibrant and alive and not overly sweet. They're also famous for their **Hazelnut Clusters**, a full 2 ounces of chocolate and roasted nuts with a creamy hazelnut butter in the center. They also come in **Almond** and **Peanut**. Her **Chocolate-covered Caramel** is firm and chewy with a rich, buttery flavor.

They also carry a large selection of **creams**, many in the same flavors as the truffle line. Her **Raspberry Buttercream,** with little bits of raspberry in the buttercream, is especially intense and delicious.

Getting there: Take the Coburg exit off I-5. Larsen's is on the main thoroughfare in downtown Coburg.

EUGENE

A vibrant college town, Eugene has plenty of great restaurants, bakeries, and confectioners to please the most discriminating chocolate lover.

Restaurants

Adam's Place

30 East Broadway, Eugene, OR. (541) 344-6948

♥♥♥♥ **Adam's Place** may just be the best restaurant in Eugene. With linen tablecloths, fresh flowers on each table, rich navy and rose carpeting and upholstery, tall ceilings, dark wood trim, and a fireplace in the dining room, it's sophisticated and classy without being stuffy. Owner Adam Berstein has created a place you'd go for a special occasion, but one that's casual enough for lunch. The lunch menu includes a variety of hot sandwiches, including a portabello mushroom steak sandwich, salads, and several entrees like Louisiana bourbon chicken and herb encrusted Oregon oysters. For dinner, they offer Hawaiian ahi, filet mignon with a merlot infused demi glaze, wild salmon, and rack of lamb, among others.

Chocolate feels like love. Phenylethylamine, a chemical found in chocolate, is produced by the brain when you're in love.

Do save room for their **Black Bear Pie**, an incredibly creamy triple mocha Grand Marnier cake. Beautifully presented, it comes on a large, hand-painted Italian plate with *Adam's Place* stenciled in cocoa and garnished with whipped cream, drizzles of caramel, and a fresh strawberry. It features an ultra-creamy mousse-like cake sandwiched with thin sponge cake that's topped with a thin layer of chocolate ganache. Rich, yet surprisingly light, this a dessert that's utterly satisfying.

Getting there: On the Broadway pedestrian mall between Oak and Willamette.

Café Zenon

898 Pearl Street, Eugene, OR. (541) 343-3005

♥♥♥♥ Put together great cooks, pastry chefs, and bakers and challenge them to be creative and what you get is **Café Zenon**, an ever-popular Eugene restaurant with an international flair. Open 363 days a year, serving breakfast, lunch, and dinner with menus that change 4 times a day, Café Zenon is sure to have something to please every palate. For breakfast you can order such dishes as Greek eggs, eggs Florentine, pesto eggs, or chilaquiles con huevos. For lunch or dinner, they offer a variety of "small plates," which can include chili relleno, pate, or antipasto. They also offer international soups, interesting salads, seafood, vegetarian dishes, veal, beef, lamb, and pork, duck, venison, and chicken dishes.

If you think their entree menu is large, wait until you see their huge, 4-tier dessert case, brimming with dozens of beautiful and imaginative desserts. When this reviewer visited, there were at least a dozen chocolate desserts available. Truly a chocolate lover's paradise! Their **Zenon Chocolate Cake** is an impressive 3 layers of moist, dark chocolate cake with a sour cream frosting that contrasts beautifully. It's a house favorite—and a favorite of this reviewer.

Their **Cappuccino Torte** is 3 layers of light chocolate cake flavored with cinnamon and filled and frosted with a whipped cream frosting. It's most refreshing!

Their **Coffee Toffee Torte** is a very dense, fudge-like torte with a thin Heath Bar crust and topping, garnished with deep, dark, thick fudge dollops. This one is almost too rich.

Zenon's **Chocolate Bourbon Pecan Torte** is a very dark, creamy chocolate torte infused with tiny bits of chopped pecan and topped with finely chopped pecans. Their **Chocolate Hazelnut Torte** is a light chocolate cake with a thin layer of sweetened whipped cream frosted with thick dark fudge and topped with coarsely chopped hazelnuts.

In addition to a number of other tortes and cakes, they offer other chocolate delights such as **Double Chocolate Pecan Cream Cheese Brownies, Chocolate Rum Pecan Pie**, and **Chocolate Bread Pudding**. They also make their own **ice cream**, including chocolate and black forest chocolate.

Zenon changes their desserts regularly. Or as their extensive dessert menu says, "Our dessert selection varies by the season and by the baker's whim…" Not to worry. At Zenon, you're sure to find chocolate desserts that delight.
Getting there*: Downtown at the corner of 9th and Pearl Streets.*

Willie's on 7th
388 West 7th Street, Eugene, OR. (541) 485-0601
♥♥♥♥ We review **Willie's on 7th** because it is one of the better restaurants where you can enjoy individual slices of **Sweet Life Patisserie's decadent chocolate cakes** (see review under Bakeries in this section). Willie's, owned and operated by long-time restaurateur Johnny Saleeby, is located in a grand old bungalow. Guests dine in the former parlor and living room where the original woodwork, fireplace, rich burgundy carpeting, and floral upholstered

arm chairs add to the ambiance. Open for lunch and dinner, their lunch menu includes London broil steak sandwich, a variety of large, international salads, burgers, pasta, and fresh fish. This reviewer enjoyed Willie's flavorful grilled salmon with brandy butter sauce served with a compote of thinly sliced apples and onions, rice pilaf, and seasonal vegetables crisp cooked to perfection. Their dinner menu includes a large variety of gourmet entrees, including broiled quail, prawns, veal marsala, scallops, apricot-rosemary pork, and Beef Diane, among others.

For dessert, they carry a large sampling of **Sweet Life's chocolate cakes**, including the light mousse-whipped cream **September 7th Cake, Bailey's Irish Cream Mousse Cake, Raspberry Rhapsody**, and **Chocolate Truffle Cake**, among others. *Travelers note: The selection can vary, so if you have a favorite, call ahead.* ***Getting there****: On the corner of West 7th and Lawrence Streets.*

Chanterelle
207 East 5th Avenue, Suite 109, Eugene, OR. (541) 484-4065
♥♥♥ When Conde Nast surveyed 8,000 food lovers nationwide for their favorite restaurants, Eugene's **Chanterelle** came in 37th. No other restaurant in Oregon or Washington made the top 50. A classically-trained European chef, Ralf Schmidt has been delighting diners for 14 years with timeless dishes like tournedo of beef, rack of lamb provencale, coquille St. Jacques, and veal scallopini marsala. For dessert, he offers a **Chocolate French Silk Pie** made with Belgian chocolate, butter, and eggs. It has a light chocolate flavor and an incredibly smooth texture that slips across the tongue. He also serves **Heren Creme**, a German chocolate dessert flavored with rum that's a cross between a mousse and a light chocolate pudding.
Getting there*: Chanterelle can be a little hard to find. It's tucked in the very back of the Fifth Avenue Pearl Building, on the corner of Fifth and Pearl Streets.*

Bakeries/Pastry Shops
Palace Bakery
844 Pearl Street, Eugene, OR. (541) 484-2435
♥♥♥♥ **Palace Bakery** is the baking arm of Café Zenon (see review). While they don't have the incredible selection of cakes, tortes, and pies carried at Café Zenon, they have a few like **Peanut Butter Pave, Chocolate Fudge Cake, Chcolate Coconut Pecan Pie**, and **Turtle Tarts**. (Like Café Zenon, the selection changes regularly.) You can also get Café Zenon's wonderful baguettes at the bakery, as well as a variety of other breads, rolls, and scones.
Getting there*: On Pearl at High Street.*

Sweet Life Patisserie
1200 W 4th Street, Eugene, OR. (541) 683-5676

♥♥♥♥ Tucked in a old garage behind a modest house on West 4th Street, Cheryl Reinhard and her sister, Catherine, turn out what are arguably the best chocolate cakes in Eugene. Made with organic flours, Guittard chocolate, fresh butter, pure extract flavorings, and fresh seasonal fruits, **Sweet Life Patisserie's cakes** are distinctively rich and beautiful and some of the best this reviewer has tasted. Unfortunately, even if you live in the area, you may have never heard about this wonderful bakery. They bake only whole cakes and sell them primarily to local restaurants, for weddings, or as special orders. They make a dozen different chocolate cakes and a half dozen chocolate tortes using imaginative ingredients such as kirsch soaked cherries, caramelized bananas, white chocolate chunk mousse, hazelnut toffee, cinnamon chocolate mousse, and ginger orange marmalade.

The finest quality cocoa beans are said to come from South America – Brazil, Ecuador, and Venezuela.

Their **September 7th Chocolate Cake** is a chocolate sponge cake filled with whipped cream and frosted with a light chocolate mousse. The combination of fluffy mousse and whipped cream make this dessert surprisingly light and wonderfully delicious.

Their **Bailey's Irish Cream Cake** is a dark chocolate cake with a Bailey's chocolate mousse filling and frosted with a Bailey's white chocolate buttercream. The cake is perfectly-grained and rich. The mousse filling is creamy with a dense chocolate taste. The white buttercream frosting is surprisingly delicate and not overly sweet.

Sweet Life's **Raspberry Rhapsody**, this reviewer's favorite, is a dense, dark chocolate cake with dark Chambord mousse filling, frosted with dark chocolate fudge buttercream and topped with sweetened, thickened raspberries. The blending of the moist, dark chocolate cake and raspberry is wonderfully fresh.

The **Chocolate Truffle Cake** is a dense dark chocolate dome cake with chocolate chunks, chocolate mousse, and frosted with a thick chocolate ganache. It's a major chocolate hit!

On a whim, Cheryl made this reviewer a **Chocolate Raspberry Almond Crunch Cake**, something that doesn't appear on their menu. This kind of spontaneous creativity is how they come up with new creations. It's a moist, dark chocolate cake filled with a thin layer of chopped almond toffee and a generous layer of dark chocolate Chambord mousse, frosted with dark chocolate ganache and chopped almond toffee and topped with sweetened, thickened raspberries. The combination of the almond toffee, chocolate, and raspberries is rich and satisfying.

> **"What's the best chocolate? It's not milk chocolate or bittersweet chocolate. It's the chocolate you like. I know a woman who loves the chocolate in Almond Joy. For her, that's the best chocolate. It's what you like. That's the best."**
>
> **– Iva Elmer, owner JiCava's Chocolates and Pastries**

They also make other delightful chocolate desserts such as **Chocolate Raspberry Fudge Cheesecake, Chocolate Mousse in a Hazelnut Crust** (Chocolate Silk), **Fudge Brownies, Double Fudge Tea Cookies, Chocolate Dipped Strawberries, Chocolate Rum Balls with Glaze** (called hedgehogs because they have spikes), and **White Chocolate Clam Shells With Raspberry Mousse** (Mousse on the Half Shell).

The good news is that Cheryl and Catherine can make you a Chocolate Raspberry Almond Crunch Cake or another of their imaginative creations if you call a day ahead and place an order. Or you can sample their wares at various restaurants around town, including **Jamoca's on 18th**, **Joe Fredericos, Hilda's, Studio One, North Bank**, and **Willie's on 7th**. Or you can get married, just so you can taste their wedding cakes.

Getting there: To pick up call-ahead orders, Sweet Life Patisserie is located just off Blair Street on West 4th. For single servings of their desserts, check in the phone book for the restaurants listed above.

Metropol Bakery
296 E 5th, Eugene, OR. (541) 687-9370
Other Eugene location:
2580 Willakenzie Road, Eugene, OR. (541) 344-1457
♥♥♥ A busy, bustling European style bakery inside the popular 5th Street Market, **Metropol Bakery** bakes up a number of wonderful **chocolate cakes**. Their **Chocolate Raspberry Mousse Cake** is a densely dark, moist chocolate cake layered with dark fudge and raspberry puree frosted with sweetened whipped cream. Yum!

Their **Hazelnut Marjolaine** features alternating layers of dark chocolate, hazelnut Frangelico and buttercream topped with a light chocolate buttercream frosting and chopped hazelnuts. This dessert is rich with a good nutty flavor.

Metropol's **German Chocolate Cake** is 3 layers of light chocolate cake sandwiched with thick layers of creamy coconut and frosted with a light chocolate buttercream frosting. It's a delight for German chocolate cake lovers.

Their **Metropol Chocolate Cake** is 3 layers of dark chocolate cake. The tangy white cream cheese frosting is a lovely contrast to the rich chocolate cake. It's satisfying indeed!

For the non-chocolate lover, Metropol also makes a large number of pies, including marionberry, lemon chiffon, apple crumb, as well as carrot cake, and lemon bars.
Getting there: *Metropol's main location is in the downtown Market District in the 5th Street Public Market at 5th and Pearl Streets.*

Chocolate Shops

Euphoria Chocolate Company
6 West 17th Avenue, Eugene, OR. (541) 343-9223
Other Eugene locations include:
199 E 5th Street, Eugene, OR. (541) 345-1990
Valley River Center, Eugene, OR. (541)343-3995
Also in Salem
♥♥♥♥ **Euphoria Chocolate Company** has made a name for itself in the Willamette Valley with its large, melt-in-your mouth **truffles**, some of the best these reviewers have tasted. Made with fresh cream, liqueurs, and high-quality chocolate without added sugar, Euphoria truffles must be refrigerated and have a very short shelf life. This makes mailing the truffles troublesome, but ensures they are always fresh, creamy, and delicious. Their flavors include **Toasted Almond, Grand Marnier, Milk Chocolate, Double Chocolate, Hazelnut, Oregon Mint Dark And Milk Chocolate, Amaretto, Kahlua Cream,** and **Kona Coffee.**

In addition to their signature truffles, Euphoria covers just about everything in dark and milk chocolate, including **Marshmallows, Graham Crackers, Oreos, Milano Cookies**, and **Apricots**. They also **mold** their chocolate into a variety of fun shapes such as giant lips, aspirin, and cars. We tried their **Chocolate Cheesecake**, individual cakes made with a dark cookie crust with a layer of dark chocolate cheesecake topped with a sweetened sour cream frosting. While the cheesecake is very creamy, it lacks the cheesy tang of truly great cheesecake. We'd stick with their terrific truffles.
Getting there: *Euphoria's original retail outlet is located downtown on the corner of 17th and Willamette. Their 5th Street store is downtown at 5th and Pearl Streets. Their Valley River location is in the Valley River Mall.*

Chocolatier Profile –

Bob Bury, owner
Euphoria Chocolate Company
Eugene, Oregon

Bob Bury, *the founder and owner of Euphoria Chocolate Company, says he was weaned on great chocolate. As a child, his grandmother dipped premium chocolates for a now-defunct candy company in San Francisco. Bob says there were always large blocks of good chocolate around the house.*

"Instead of giving me cookies, mom would chisel off hunks of this great chocolate for me to take to school," Bob recalls. "I learned to appreciate high-quality chocolate early on."

Even as a youngster, Bob experimented with baking with great chocolate. "My mother was a good cook, so I learned to cook and to bake at an early age," he says.

By the time he was in college, he was an accomplished baker. "At potlucks, people would always say to me, 'You bring dessert.'"

After college, Bob traveled in Europe, sampling some of the best chocolate in the world. "For months, we lived on chocolate," Bob says, laughing. When he returned, he took what he'd learned and his long-held appreciation for great chocolate a step further and formed Euphoria Chocolate Company.

"I felt there was niche in this area that was beyond See's and more approachable than Godiva," he said. His vision became refrigerated truffles made with only fresh cream, liqueurs, and high-quality chocolate without added sugar. Back then, he made the truffles in a friend's café.

Today, Euphoria Chocolate Company employs as many as 60 people, depending on the season. They're just moving into a new 10,000-square foot production facility and are looking to expand their retail operation.

Fenton and Lee Chocolatiers
35 E 8th Avenue, Eugene, OR. (541) 343-7629/(800) FENTON-1

♥♥♥♥ Janele Smith's **Fenton and Lee Chocolatiers** specializes in using Northwest products like hazelnuts, cranberries, and strawberries in high-quality Guittard chocolate. Because she uses fresh or freeze-dried fruits and nuts rather than flavored syrups, the flavors are wonderfully intense. Her **Buttercrunch**, hazelnuts or pistachios with chopped nuts sprinkled on top and dipped in chocolate, is crisp and buttery. Her **Cherry with Dark Chocolate** jumps up and hollers, "Fresh cherries!" The **Caramel**, which they coat with dark or milk chocolate or cover with nuts and chocolate is creamy without being overly sweet.

Fenton and Lee's **Espresso Tea Wafers**, finely-ground espresso beans in dark chocolate, are a must for espresso lovers. For a more unusual treat, try their **Ginger Tea Wafers** with finely ground ginger and dark chocolate. It'll wake up your tastebuds!

Fenton and Lee also makes a variety of **molded chocolate shapes** in dark or milk chocolate, including horseshoes and cars. For the northwest gardener in your life, consider one of their **Chocolate Cream-filled Slugs.**

They will wrap your box of chocolates in beautiful handmade paper with jute ribbon for a special Northwest touch. Fenton and Lee chocolates are also available by mail order.
Getting there: *Downtown on 8th Street between Willamette and Pearl Streets.*

Chocolatier Profile–

Janele Smith, owner
Fenton and Lee
Eugene, Oregon

Janele Smith, *a tall woman with a contagious smile and quick laugh, used to teach pre-school. Today, her "babies" are delightful chocolates made with fresh and dried Northwest fruits, nuts, and berries.*

Before 1969, Janele didn't even like chocolate. Then she tasted some high-quality chocolate while living in Los Angeles and she was hooked. When she and her husband moved back home to Oregon in 1980, she became intrigued with the idea of dipping hazelnuts, cherries, almonds, strawberries, raspberries, and other Northwest products in great chocolate. The result was Fenton and Lee Chocolatiers.

Without any experience or background in working with chocolate, Janele quit her teaching job and worked for a year on chocolate recipes. She leased a space and opened her business with 2 accounts.

Looking back, she smiles and says, "You hit a point where you either step out there and take a risk or you become a grumpy old lady."

In 1992, Fenton and Lee claimed the Confection of the Year Award from the National Association of Specialty Foods in Manhattan. Their entry was a line of tea wafers, thin dark or milk chocolate disks made with finely ground espresso beans, ginger, or hazelnuts. It's a product that remains popular with customers today.

Fenton and Lee is mainly a wholesaler with 60% of their business done on the east coast. Fortunately, Eugene, Oregon, has its own retail outlet where Janele and her crew experiment with new products. Using Guittard Chocolate's molding line, which has more cocoa butter in it, they hand-dip and hand-mold everything. They make chocolate sculptures like gold-leafed and carved yule logs. They make French creams, with dense, heavy cream centers, cream-filled chocolates, and various fruits and nuts dipped in chocolate.

Named after Janele's grandfathers, Fenton and Lee has a serious-sounding name, but Janele keeps the business fun. She carries a French cream she calls Nipples of Venus, a chocolate cherry cream with tiny, pink tufts that resemble, well, nipples. During the city's annual celebration, she also carries milk and dark chocolate cream-filled slugs. In fact, customers are greeted with a giant, 9 pound chocolate slug they make to be auctioned for charity—and for fun.

Ice Creamery

Geppetto's Ice Cream
861 Willamette, Eugene, OR. (541) 343-2621
Gepetto's serves Prince Puckler's **ice cream**, a Eugene company that's drawing a loyal following. Not as rich as the super-premium ice creams, Prince Puckler's is a tasty, not-overly-creamy dairy treat. Gepetto's gets points for their generous servings and their many chocolate flavors. They carry **Chocolate Chip**, **Rocky Road**, **Bittersweet Nugget**, **Chocolate Lover's Chocolate**, **Galaxy**, a malted chocolate with white chocolate and dark chocolate chips, and **Muddy River**, malted chocolate ice cream with caramel swirl.
Getting there: Downtown at 8th and Willamette.

BELGIUM BITTERSWEET CHOCOLATE ICE CREAM

Makes 1 gallon

1 ¹/₃ cups half and half
²/₃ cup whipping cream
¹/₄ cup coffee
7 tablespoons granulated sugar, divided
2 tablespoons plus 2 teaspoons butter
8 ounces Belgium bittersweet chocolate, broken into small pieces
4 egg yolks

Combine the half and half and cream in a small sauce pan. Heat over medium heat until tiny bubbles form around the edge of the pan. Do not boil!

Make a simple syrup by combining the coffee and 3¹/₂ tablespoons sugar in a small pan and simmering over medium heat for a few minutes. When syrup is ready, stir in the butter and chocolate and melt over low heat.

While whisking constantly, pour the scalded cream into the melted chocolate mixture until well combined.

An ultra-rich, custard-like ice cream with a coffee undertone, Rhododendron Café's Belgium Chocolate Ice Cream will make you swear off those cheap imitations in the supermarket. Now this is ice cream, chocolate lovers!

In a large bowl, whisk together the remaining 3¹/₂ tablespoons sugar and the egg yooks. Slowly whisk the hot chocolate mixture into the yolk-sugar mixture. Refrigerate until chilled. Pour into ice cream freezer and freeze according to manufacturer's directions.

See *Raw Egg Warning*, page 17.

From *The Chocolate Lover's Guide Cookbook*, Pacific Northwest Edition.

Southern Oregon

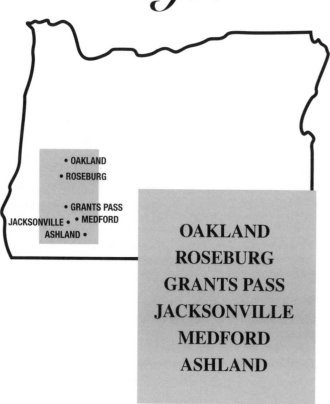

- OAKLAND
- ROSEBURG
- GRANTS PASS
- JACKSONVILLE • • MEDFORD
- ASHLAND •

OAKLAND
ROSEBURG
GRANTS PASS
JACKSONVILLE
MEDFORD
ASHLAND

For those who live in Portland, Southern Oregon might seem like a vast, empty place between Eugene and California. Instead, it's a vibrant area full of fascinating small towns and some of the most dramatic scenery in Oregon.

Great Things to Do

• **Sip the Vine.** The area around **Roseburg** is beginning to rival the Willamette Valley for wineries. There are now 6 wineries where you can tour and taste to your heart's content: **Callahan Ridge** (541) 673-7901; **Henry** (541) 459-5120; **Umpqua River** (Denino) (541) 673-1975; **La Garza** (541) 679-9654; **Hillcrest** (541) 673-3709; and **Girardet** (541) 679-7252. Call for hours and directions.

• **Go on Safari. Wildlife Safari**, Route 99, 4 miles west of I-5, **Roseburg, OR.** (541) 679-6761. If you can't afford an African safari, Roseburg's Wildlife Safari isn't a bad alternative. You drive through rolling hillsides dotted with African and North American wildlife. While the drive-thru can get frustratingly crowded during travel months (imagine a bumper-to-bumper traffic jam on twisting dirt roads), the Wildlife Village is a good place for kids to stretch and run about.

• **Hunt for Antiques. Jacksonville, OR.** Just 15 miles from Medford and Ashland, the historic town of Jacksonville is a haven for antique buffs. Not only does the town have excellent antique shops, the entire town is living 19th century history. Stroll through hundred-year-old buildings, explore the Jacksonville pioneer cemetery, or enjoy some of Jacksonville's great restaurants like Bella Union and the Jacksonville Inn.

• **Enjoy a Concert Under the Stars. Britt Festival, Jacksonville, OR.** (541) 773-6077/(800) 882-7488. Every year between June and September, people flock to the Britt Festival in Jacksonville for jazz, bluegrass, folk, country, and classical music as well as dance and musical theater. The open-air venue under the stars make the performances all the more special.

• **Explore a Volcano.** Only 2½ hours from Ashland, **Crater Lake National Park**, via Highway 138 or 62, **Crater Lake, OR.** (541) 594-2511, is Oregon's only national park and has some of the bluest and deepest water you'll ever see. Boat tours are available in the summer months They've recently completed a spectacular $15 million restoration of the park's historic lodge.

• **Go Shakespeare. Oregon Shakespeare Festival**, P.O. Box 477, **Ashland, OR.** (541) 482-4331. Ashland, Oregon, is known the world over for the annual Shakespeare Festival that runs February through October. Productions of the Bard play out on 3 theaters, including the wonderful outdoor Elizabethan Theater.

• **Ride the Rogue River. Ashland, OR.** Enjoy a half, full or multi-day trip down the beautiful Rogue River. You can customize your trip—everything from champagne moonlight cruises, overnight trips, scenic mild snooze cruises, to wild whitewater adventures. **Rogue River Hellgate Excursions** (800) 648-4874; **Adventure Center** (541) 482-5139; **Rogue Wilderness Adventures** (800) 336-1647.

Terrific Places to Stay

Touvelle House Bed and Breakfast, 455 N Oregon Street, **Jacksonville, OR**. (800) 846-8422/(541) 899-8938. In a historic town filled with bed and breakfast inns, you have to be pretty special. And special is just what Touvelle House Bed and Breakfast is. Located a few blocks from downtown, the huge 1916 Craftsman strikes an impressive pose. Broad porches with thickly padded chairs invite guests to rest a while under the oak trees. Inside, rich wood paneling, built-in cabinetry, and broad, square-beamed ceilings lend a stately air. Each room is distinctly decorated—some with European antiques, others with quilts that hark back to pioneer times, still others with art deco pieces. All 6 guest rooms feature private baths, thick robes, air conditioners, and turn down service with truffles by Jody, a local chocolatier. Guests can enjoy the pool or spa or watch television or read in the library. The full breakfast may include dishes such as baked grapefruit, herbed polenta and egg burritos with salsa.

Chanticleer Inn, 120 Gresham Street, **Ashland, OR**. (541) 482-1919. Words like "homey," "comfortable," and "restful" come to mind when visiting Chanticleer Inn. Long one of Ashland's most popular bed and breakfasts, Chanticleer is an Arts and Crafts bungalow that's surrounded by beautiful gardens. The common room has a rock fire place, period built-ins, and comfortable couches and chairs that invite a read by the fire. The 6 guest rooms, all with private baths and phones, are simply decorated with oak antiques and down comforters. Breakfast is hearty and may feature such delights as artichoke heart quiche, fresh fruit, and juice.

The Peerless Hotel, 243 Fourth Street, **Ashland, OR**. (800) 460-8758. The railroad workers who used to board here wouldn't recognize the old Peerless Hotel. The 1900-era brick building has been lovingly restored and is now a small, elegant hotel. The small lobby is richly decorated in deep reds and forest greens and features an inviting fireplace. Hardwood floors gleam under brightly-colored Oriental carpets. A garden room off a small courtyard has comfortable chairs and tables for reading and relaxing. It's also where breakfast is served to guests. The 4 guest rooms and 2 suites all have jacuzzi or clawfoot tubs and showers, handmade Italian linens, cable music with 30 channels, and air conditioners. Each room is uniquely decorated with period antiques and artist-rendered murals. One room, for instance, has lovely painted flowers that cascade down from the ceiling. Another features a faux archway with a stone path and garden.

Country Willows, 1313 Clay Street, **Ashland, OR**. (800) 945-5697/(541) 488-1590. A 7-minute drive from downtown Ashland, Country Willows is a stylishly rebuilt 1896 home set on 5 picturesque acres surrounded by flower beds, maples, and, of course, willows. The blue frame inn features a wisteria-covered verandah and a swinging bent willow chair under a big willow tree where guests can relax and enjoy the pastoral view. The den, with its stone fireplace, has TV, movies, games, and puzzles. The inn's 4 guest rooms in the main house all have air conditioning and private baths and are decorated with country flair. Three suites are nestled in the blue and white barn out back behind the swimming pool, hot tub, sun deck, and garden. The Sunrise Suite, is a large, open space with a white-washed pine interior. It features a private deck with mountain views, gas fireplace, microwave, mini-refrigerator, king bed, a 2-person shower, and an old-fashioned tub for 2 with a bay window and skylight. The guest cottage right off the duck pond offers a white iron queen-sized bed, woodstove, and kitchenette. In the morning, Country Willow guests enjoy a full breakfast on the sun porch, which may include dishes like eggs and feta cheese in phyllo wrappers, French toast with strawberry butter, or a Mexican casserole. Convivial hosts Dan and David are pros at making guests feel welcome, offering good suggestions for restaurants and area highlights, as well as extra touches like fluffy robes, an always-full cookie jar, and bicycles.

OAKLAND

Who'd think the Rice Hill exit between Cottage Grove and Roseburg would be a chocolate oasis? If you're 1 of the 3 travelers who don't know about the drive-ins (1 on the south side of the freeway; 1 on the north) that serve huge scoops of local Umpqua ice cream, sundaes, and milkshakes, read on.

Ice Creameries

K & R Drive-In
201 John Long Road, Oakland, OR. (541) 849-2570

♥♥♥ For 25 years, Ruth and Ben Emry have been serving some of the biggest and best **ice cream** cones in the Northwest at their **K & R's Drive-In** at the Rice Hill exit interchange off I-5. A small serving is 6-7 ounces or 2 scoops of 1 flavor; a medium is 11-12 ounces of up to 2 flavors; and a large is a full 16 ounces of up to 3 flavor choices. For dogs only, they offer a 1-scoop dish of vanilla ice cream with a doggie bone. They serve 35 flavors of Umpqua ice cream, a locally-made product that's rich without being cloyingly creamy. For chocolate lovers, they offer **Chocolate Cheesecake, Mocha Almond Fudge, Cookie Dough, Chocolate Chip, Chocolate Mousse Pie, Double Chocolate Almond, Cookies and Cream, Fudge Pie**, and **Chocolate Chip Mint**. The Fudge Pie is a real chocolate lover's delight with rich chocolate mocha ice cream with chunks of Oreo cookies and Chocolate.

While you're waiting for your cone, enjoy K & R's entertaining and often philosophical signs. "It's never too cold for ice cream" is one chocolate lovers can embrace. If you've got a bad attitude, another sign says, expect to be charged $10 extra. They won't let you use their bathroom and if you want ice water, it'll cost you 25 cents, but the ice cream is definitely worth a stop.

Getting there: *About 20 miles north of Roseburg at the Rice Hill exit off I-5 (south side).*

Quickies Drive-In

621 John Long Road, Oakland, OR. (541) 849-2500

♥♥♥ You may have seen the "I Love Quickies" bumper stickers. They come from Quickies Drive In, where they sell 34 flavors of Umpqua ice cream, hard ice cream shakes, and giant sundaes. Like their competition across the freeway, "small" servings of ice cream are really huge—2 big scoops. For the chocolate lover, they offer **Chocolate, Brownie ala Mode, Chocolate Peanut Butter, Chocolate Chip, Triple Chocolate, Rocky Road, Chocolate Chip Mint, Chocolate Cheesecake, Chocolate Almond,** and **Old South Fudge Pie.**

Getting there: *Take the Rice Hill I-5 exit #148.*

ROSEBURG

Teske's Germania Restaurant

649 SE Jackson, Roseburg, OR. (541) 672-5401

♥♥ Walk into **Teske's Germania Restaurant** and you'll feel like you've stepped into a Bavarian inn. The exposed brick walls, tall ceilings, flowered wallpaper, toll-painted cross timbers and plants in the window create a lovely ambiance that's not overdone. Run by long-time restauranteurs Marian and Ernst Teske, the restaurant offers a large selection of pork, beef, veal, and fish dishes such as polish sausage served with hot German potato salad and sauerkraut. One of their specialties is wild boar sausages and steaks from the Teske's own ranch.

Save room for Ernst's signature **Black Forest Cake**, 3 layers of fine-grained, dark chocolate cake layered with cherries, whipped cream, and sherry, topped with whipped cream and shaved chocolate. Unlike many Black Forest Cakes, this is wonderfully light with cherries that taste fresh and not too sweet.

Ernst also serves a **Chocolate Cake** made with 3 layers of the same dark chocolate cake filled with dark chocolate ganache and white chocolate ganache, frosted with milk chocolate and garnished with chocolate shavings and whipped cream. The cake is light without being airy and rich tasting and the frosting is creamy.

Getting there: In historic downtown Roseburg on Jackson between Oak and Cass.

Brandy's Restaurant
2566 NE Stephens, Roseburg, OR. (541) 673-3721
♥ If you're feeling international and can't decide what to eat, **Brandy's** is the place to go. Their motto is "a taste of Europe" and they're not kidding. In a neat restaurant decorated in forest green and white, chef/owner Brandy Stumpee serves up dishes like chateubrian from France, weiner schnitzel from Germany, pork tenderloin from Switzerland, and moussaka from Greece, among others. Her lunch menu includes homemade soups, salads, and interesting sandwiches like eggplant and chicken or veal parmesan.

Dessert includes her signature **Chocolate Crunch Ice Cream Cake**, a wedge of thick layers of chocolate ice cream and coffee ice cream sandwiched between crunchy layers of walnuts, butter, and chocolate. The result is a surprisingly light and refreshing dessert. The ice cream is high quality and the chocolate crumble-nut layer adds a delightful crunch. It's an ice cream lover's delight!

Brandy's **Pistachio Chocolate Cake** has a half-inch layer of dark chocolate cake, followed by a layer of whipped cream, a layer of pistachio cake, more whipped cream, and another layer of dark chocolate cake, all frosted with a rich, dark chocolate buttercream and garnished with chopped pistachios. The cake is moist and the pistachio flavor is a nice change of pace.

If you're watching your waist-line or need to eat lower fat, check out **Brandy's Chocolate Cheesecake**, which she says is low-fat (though it doesn't taste like it). It starts with a dark chocolate cookie crust, followed by a white chocolate cheesecake sandwiched with a thin layer of strawberry filling and topped with a milk chocolate ganache. It's creamy and light with subtle flavors.
Getting there: On Stephens between Stewart Parkway and Newton Creek.

GRANTS PASS

Legrand's
323 NE E Street, Grants Pass, OR. (541) 471-1554
♥♥♥♥ **Legrand's** is an intimate dinner house decorated with simple wooden tables and chairs, dark green carpets, and rose-colored walls that show off original photos and art prints. They offer a classical French menu with innovative touches with dishes such as rack of lamb in cumin sauce, squid, shrimp, and eggplant sauté, duck with orange or pepper sauce, veal piccatta or marsala,

chicken dijon, and beef with béarnaise, among others. Chocolate lovers should definitely make room for pastry chef/owner Daniel Legrand's **Chocolate Mousse Cake**. Five inches high, it starts with a thin layer of chocolate sponge cake, topped with chocolate mousse, a layer of meringue, another sponge cake, and more chocolate mousse topped with chocolate shavings. The result is wonderful. The mousse is velvety. The sponge cake melts in the mouth. The chocolate flavor is rich and deep and the meringue adds a lovely rich moistness.
Getting there: *On E at 9th.*

The Brewery
509 SW G Street, Grants Pass, OR. (541) 479-9850
♥♥ Situated in the original 1886 brick brewery building on the edge of downtown, **The Brewery** oozes old time ambiance with exposed bricks, wood tables and chairs, booths, and plenty of old bottles, wooden beer cases, and kegs. Their menu includes prime rib, pepper steak, filet mignon, enchiladas, beef stroganoff, chicken and seafood dishes. Their desserts come from **The Chocolate Affair**, a storefront bakery and chocolate shop a few blocks away, which is owned by the same folks. Chocolate Affair's chocolate candies are unremarkable, but their desserts, which are available whole or by the slice, are quite good. The Brewery offers several, including their **Peanut Butter Chocolate Cheesecake,** that has an Oreo cookie crust, an incredibly creamy peanut butter cheesecake topped with a rich, chocolate ganache. They also have a **Fudge Pie** that's a dense brownie-like wedge served with Kona coffee ice cream. It's moist and rich with an intense chocolate flavor and the cool coffee ice cream is a good contrast.

Traveler's note: Parking and the entrance is in the back.
Getting there*: At the corner of SW G and 5th.*

JACKSONVILLE

Bella Union
170 W California, Jacksonville, OR. (541) 899-1770
♥♥♥♥ **Bella Union** has a friendly, bistro atmosphere that both locals and tourists alike find irresistible. Tall ceilings, exposed brick walls, scuffed wooden floors, an open kitchen and a central bar all contribute to the casual feeling. Their large menu features soups, interesting sandwiches like Cajun calamari steak and buffalo burgers, pizza, and pastas (spaghetti, fettuccine, ravioli, canneloni, linguine, and tortellini) with a variety of sauces. Chocolate lovers should save room for Bella Union's desserts, which are the best in town. Their signature **Mudpie** is 5 inches of mocha ice cream on a chocolate cookie crust, topped with whipped cream and chocolate shavings in a pool of their homemade chocolate sauce. The ice

cream is rich and refreshing. The chocolate sauce is heavenly. This is a wonderful interpretation of an often poorly-done dessert.

Bella Union's **White Chocolate Cheesecake** comes with a hazelnut crust, 2¹/₂ inches of white chocolate cheesecake topped with hot fudge drizzles. The cheesecake is thick, creamy and cheesy. The fudge sauce looks nice, but gets lost in this tangy dessert.

Their **Double Chocolate Decadence** is a flourless cake that's topped with fudge sauce and surrounded by a homemade custard raspberry sauce. Although it's only a half inch tall, this cake is exquisitely rich and chocolaty—like biting into the inside of a thick truffle. The custard sauce adds a creamy lightness.

The **Dark Chocolate/White Chocolate Mousse** comes layered in a stemmed glass garnished with white chocolate shavings. The light, ultra-creamy texture invites another bite. And another, and another.

Bella's **Cappuccino Mousse Torte** is one of their rotating desserts, so you may or may not find it on the menu when you visit. It comes with a hazelnut crust, a fudge layer, a mocha mousse layer, topped with mocha whipped cream. The fudge is thick, creamy, and fudgy. The mocha mousse adds a delightful coffee flavor. And the mocha whipped cream is light and fluffy. The combination makes for a rich dessert that lingers on the tongue.
Getting there: On the main street downtown.

Jacksonville Inn
175 E California, Jacksonville, OR. (541) 899-1900
♥♥ With its exposed brick walls (reputedly with specks of gold in the mortar), red carpeting, white linen tablecloths, and fresh flowers on each table, the **Jacksonville Inn** has plenty of ambiance. The main upstairs dining room is lighter and brighter; the downstairs dining area more cellar-like. Both serve from the large, award-winning dinner menu that includes dishes such as rabbit loin marinated in olive oil, garlic and fresh tuna, prawns with feta, and filet mignon with portabello mushrooms. The bistro menu, which is served in a small, casual downstairs area, offers lighter (and less expensive) fare such as pasta, chicken, sole, NY and prime rib sandwiches.

For dessert, chocolate lovers will find an **Imported Belgian Chocolate Mousse** that comes with an Oreo cookie crust, 2¹/₂ inches of light, yet very rich chocolate mousse that's topped with an inch of whipped cream and chocolate shavings. The mousse is light and ultra-creamy and the crust adds a nice chocolate crunch.

The **White Chocolate Mousse with Raspberry and Strawberry Swirl** is a beautiful dessert that comes in a stemmed glass. The mousse is rich and thick, but the texture could be a bit smoother. The fruit adds a light sweetness.

The **Chocolate Truffle Cake** is a flourless torte that's topped with ganache. It has a rich flavor and the ganache melts in the mouth. *Getting there: On the main thoroughfare downtown.*

Candy Shop

Mama Georgie's

115 California, Jacksonville, OR. (541) 899-2010

Mama Georgie's carries a variety of sweets—gummi bears, hard candies, handmade caramels, peanut brittle, caramel corn, gourmet syrups and jams, as well as a small selection of Dreyer's Ice Cream flavors. The draw for the chocolate lover is **Jody's Truffles.** This Rogue River wholesale candymaker uses Callebaut chocolate, fresh whipping cream, sweet cream butter, pure flavors, and liqueurs. She makes 13 different types of truffles, including **Brandy, Grand Marnier, Kahlua**, and **Chocolate**. She also makes **Nut Clusters** and firm and chewy **Chocolate-covered Caramels.** *Getting there: On the main thoroughfare downtown.*

MEDFORD

Genessee Place Restaurant

203 Genessee Street, Medford, OR. (541) 772-5581

♥♥♥ Situated in a converted house in a residential area a few blocks from downtown Medford, **Genessee Place** is a popular spot for lunch or dinner. It's pleasantly decorated in rose, green, and white with lace curtains, linen-covered tables, tall ceilings with white fans, and original paintings. Lunch selections include hot sandwiches, deli sandwhiches, salads, and hot entrees like lasagne and quiche. Dinner includes pasta dishes (lasagne, linguine, fettuccine, tortellini, ravioli), rack of lamb, prime rib, chicken (with orange demi-glaze, parmesan, marsala, or lemon), and scallops, among others. For dessert, they offer a **Chocolate Eclair**, a large, 5-inch eclair crust filled with custard cream and topped with dark chocolate and toasted almonds. The eclair has just the right chewiness and the cream is light and not overly sweet. The chocolate icing has a deep chocolate flavor. Eclair fans will enjoy this.

Their **Chocolate Peanut Butter Mousse** is a layer of milk chocolate mousse and a layer of peanut butter mousse topped with dark chocolate sauce. The chocolate mousse is ultra-light, almost airy; the peanut butter mousse is more dense and creamy with an intense peanut butter flavor. The chocolate sauce adds a deep chocolate flavor. All together it creates just the right chocolate-peanut butter balance.

Genessee almost always has some type of chocolate cake. Their **Chocolate Peanut Butter Cake** is 2 layers of dark chocolate cake filled and topped with peanut butter cream, then frosted with a dark chocolate. The cake is fine-textured and wonderfully moist. The peanut butter is velvety with a rich peanut butter taste. The chocolate frosting is thick and fudge-like. This is a rich one that might prove too much for some.

Getting there: On Genessee off Jackson, across from Tinseltown.

ASHLAND

Ashland is famous as home to the Shakespeare Festival. It should also be known for its great chocolate.

Primavera
241 Hargadine Street, Ashland, OR. (541) 488-1994
♥♥♥♥ Step into **Primavera** and you step into a garden of visual delights. The restaurant was designed by theater set designer Craig Hudson, who designed the Oregon Cabaret Theater, and is adorned with huge murals of the Ballet Russes in brilliant blues, oranges, and purples. The semi-circular dining area features faux marble in blues and rust with carved gold pillars, black chairs, and a shiny black grand piano center stage. The bar area in the adjoining room is equally stunning. Primavera's dinner menu, which changes seasonally and features fresh and organic ingredients, includes such choices as loin of pork, duck breast with red wine juniper sauce, kale-filled chicken breast, filet of beef with gorgonzola and leek and mushroom stuffed eggplant.

Chocolate in the Desert. During the Persian Gulf War, Hershey's Food Corporation developed "Desert Bars," chocolate bars that could withstand 140 degrees of desert heat.

Their signature chocolate dessert is a **Chocolate Truffle Torte**, a flourless chocolate torte that's served with blackberry sauce and garnished with whipped cream, mint sprigs, and almonds. It's incredibly rich and smooth like liquid velvet. One of the best truffle tortes this reviewer has tasted, it's a dessert to die for!
Getting there: Downtown below the Oregon Cabaret Theater.

Chateaulin Restaurant Francais
50 E Main, Ashland, OR. (541) 482-2264
♥♥♥♥ Rich red carpeting and red tablecloths, small tables and

booths, lace curtains, and soft lighting all contribute to the intimate, clubby feel at **Chateaulin**. They offer a shrimp prix-fixe meal with wine or you can order from their dinner menu, which includes dishes like spinach linguine with porcini mushrooms, penne with shrimp, spinach crepes, free-range basil pesto chicken, duck with port wine sauce, filet mignon with peppercorn crust, or free-range veal. You can also order these dishes ala carte. Chocolate standards on their menu include the **Grand Marnier Chocolate Bombe**, a large slice of frozen mousse with a thin layer of sponge cake covered with ganache. It comes in a pool of creme anglaise and is garnished with a tiny chocolate fan. The cold mousse is rich and smooth with a deep chocolate flavor. The sponge cake adds an interesting texture. It's a terrific combination.

The **Chocolate Raspberry Roulade** is dark chocolate sponge cake rolled around a whipped cream filling that's topped with ganache and garnished with raspberry puree flavored with Chambord and a chocolate fan. The cake is extremely light, yet has a rich chocolate flavor. The ganache is silky smooth and the raspberry puree adds a tart contrast.

For a lighter dessert, diners can order a couple of Chambord-flavored **Chocolate Truffles**, large domes chocolate-covered of dark chocolate ganache.

An interesting newcomer that isn't always available is their **Frozen Chocolate Soufflé**, a light chocolate concoction which towers several inches over its small soufflé cup, that is topped with powered sugar. The dessert is ultra smooth with a refreshingly light chocolate flavor. The powered sugar distracts rather than adds to this lovely dessert.
Getting there: On E Main between Oak and Pioneer.

Plaza Café
47 N Main, Ashland, OR. (541) 488-2233
♥♥♥ With exposed brick walls, blonde wooden chairs and tables, and large windows overlooking Main Street, **Plaza Café** is a pleasant, casual place for lunch or dinner. The dinner menu features pasta dishes like red bell pepper linguine and gorgonzola rotini, chicken enchiladas, burgers, and salmon club sandwiches as well as a large selection of daily specials like lemon garlic tuna and nut breaded pork loin. For dessert, their signature chocolate dessert is **Chocolate Silk Pie**, which has a walnut praline crust that's topped with a rich chocolate mousse, whipped cream, and chocolate shavings. The crust is crunchy, nutty, and praline-sweet. The chocolate mousse has a firm texture and a deep, satisfying chocolate flavor. It's delightful!
Getting there: On N Main at Water Street.

The Firefly Restaurant

15 N 1ˢᵗ Street, Ashland, OR. (541) 488-3212

♥♥ **Firefly** is a small, continental restaurant with green carpets, white linen tablecloths, small tables and booths, and faux arches that give the place a Mediterranean feel. Their motto is "fine world cuisine" and the menu, which changes 4 times a year, offers dishes from many cultures. Each entree comes complete with side dishes that compliment. For instance, the seared sturgeon comes with coconut lentils, mint red curry, and tamarind and carrot salad. The chicken yakitori is accompanied by teka maki sushi, spinach-seaweed salad, vegetable tempura, and cinnamon broccoli.

The desserts are equally complex and beautifully presented. Pastry chef Dana Keller's **Marjolaine Chocolate Hazelnut Torte** has thin layers of chocolate cake, chocolate ganache, hazelnut meringue, hazelnut cream, chocolate mousse, and dark chocolate. It's garnished with chocolate, caramel, and raspberry sauce, mint, and a tiny cookie. The hazelnut flavor is rich and strong and the combination with the chocolate is delightful. The hard chocolate layer on top makes this dessert impossible to eat daintily. Turn the dessert on its side and dig in.

The **Raspberry, Pistachio and White Chocolate Trifle** is a beautiful layered dessert that's presented in a stemmed glass. Layers of pistachio cake, raspberry and white chocolate mousse are topped with a sprinkling of pistachios and garnished with a star cookie, cookie straws, and mint. The plate comes decorated with swirls of caramel, raspberry, and chocolate sauce and an apple fan. This rich dessert gets points for both presentation and originality. The blending of flavors is interesting, but the raspberry flavor has a tendency to overwhelm the others.

Getting there: On 1ˢᵗ between Lithia and Main.

Beasy's on the Creek

51 Water Street, Ashland, OR. (541) 488-5009

♥♥ **Beasy's on the Creek** is a round restaurant with large windows and a deck that sits 3 stories above Lithia Creek. Its neutral-colored walls with sconces that throw off interesting shadows, upholstered booths and tables, and fireplace all add to its contemporary sopistication. The dinner menu offers plenty of fish choices, including a daily fresh sheet, as well as dishes like black and red (black tiger shrimp and red snapper), Cajun BBQ shrimp in ale, and Blackened snapper. Their steak selection is equally large. Their 1 chocolate dessert is a **Chocolate Pot de Creme**, which is served in a stemmed glass with whipped cream and shaved chocolate. It's very creamy with a smooth, pudding-like texture and a rich chocolate flavor.

Getting there: On Water Street at N Main.

Monet

36 S 2nd, Ashland, OR. (541) 482-1339

♥ **Monet's** lace curtains, upholstered white chairs, floral linen table-cloths, and "Monet colors"—powder blue, white, pinks—all contribute to the peaceful French country charm of this restaurant. Their lunch menu features French onion and a soup du jour, salads, and entrees like linguine with artichokes and sundried tomatoes and chicken breast with leeks and champagne. Dinner includes dishes such as scallops with leeks, mushrooms, and fennel, pork tenderloin with kiwi sauce, and salmon with shallots and wine sauce. For dessert, chef Pierre Verger makes **Chocolate Mousse**, a generous portion served in a delicate almond cookie cup shaped like a tulip. It comes garnished with rosettes of whipped cream, a sprig of mint, and it sits on a bed of swirled cream and strawberry and mango purees. It's a beautiful presentation for an intensely chocolaty mousse.

> **Chocolate is Green.** Every part of the cocoa bean is used. Vegetable fat and theobromine, a stimulant used in medicines, are extracted from the shell. They're ground and fed to cattle. Shells also make great fertilizer and garden mulch, giving the garden a rich, chocolatey flavor.

In the winter, chef Pierre makes a **Buche de Noel** (yule log) of genoise chocolate cake (a light, sponge-like cake) flavored with rum and rolled around raspberry puree and frosted with a milk chocolate/rum buttercream. The cake is moist with more rum than chocolate flavor. The delicate buttercream melts in the mouth.

Pierre's **Ganache** comes on a sweet pastry crust with a layer of almond meal, a thin layer of raspberry preserves, followed by milk and dark chocolate that has been whipped together. It has a light chocolate flavor and rich almond flavor.

Getting there: On 2nd just off E Main.

Cucina Biazzi

568 E Main, Ashland, OR. (541) 488-3739

♥ An intimate Italian restaurant in a converted house, **Cucina Biazzi** is decorated with heavily-textured, sand-colored walls, Italian prints, wooden chairs, cloth-covered tables, throw rugs over hardwood floors, and a wine bottle overflowing with melted wax on each table. Out back, there's a lovely arbor-covered Italian patio with an outdoor fireplace for al fresco dining. Their menu includes 4 courses—antipasti, pasta, an entree, and salad. Entrees include pork, chicken, steak, shrimp, or a seafood stew. Their popular chocolate dessert is **Warm Chocolate Cake with Vanilla Bean Ice Cream**. It comes topped with chocolate sauce. It's a good basic chocolate cake, nothing fancy. The ice cream, which they make on-site, is light and not heavily creamy.

Getting there: Just a few blocks off the main shopping area on E Main Street near 5ᵗʰ.

Bakery

Apple Cellar Bakery and Café

2255 Highway 66, Ashland, OR. (541) 488-8131

♥♥♥♥ You wouldn't know it from the down-home name, but the **Apple Cellar Bakery and Café** is a large, bright bakery specializing in European pastries, cakes, rolls and breads. Everything is made on-site, every day from scratch. Their chocolate items are made with good quality Guittard chocolate. They feature a large selection of **cakes** by the slice or whole such as **White Mousse Cake, German Chocolate, Chocolate Mousse Cake,** and **Carrot**; pies such as apple, marionberry, pecan and pumpkin. They have a large number of **pastries**, including their **Chocolate Decadence Heart**, a heart-shaped flourless cake decorated with a rich dark chocolate buttercream and a white chocolate squiggle. It's thick, fudgy, and full of rich chocolate flavor.

Their **Grand Marnier Mousse** is a tower of white chocolate mousse flavored with Grand Marnier and covered with shaved dark chocolate and topped with a chocolate star. At the bottom is a thick fudge layer and a lightly crunchy chocolate graham crust. The mousse is just the right texture and the Grand Marnier adds a hint of orange flavoring. The chocolate curls and the crust give a bit of crunch. It's the best white chocolate mousse this reviewer has found—a delight!

They make plenty of **cookies**, including **Chocolate Chip, Chocolate Chip Walnut, Peanut Butter, Ginger**, and **Cherry Pecan Chocolate Chip**, among others. Their **Chocolate Florentines** have a thin layer of dark chocolate topped with carmelized almonds and tiny pieces of orange. They're crispy and buttery, but the orange flavor overwhelms the almond flavor. For those who like coconut, try their **Chocolate Dipped Macaroon**, a large mound of sweetened coconut that's soft on the inside, slightly crispy on the outside and dipped in sweet, dark chocolate. With plenty of coconut flavor, it's a macaroon lover's dream.

Apple Cellar also makes a variety of breads and rolls—7-grain, sour, rye, honey wheat, parmesan cheese, olive and roasted pepper. Order one of their huge sandwiches made with your choice of fresh-baked bread and served with their own tasty homemade mayonnaise. Or you can opt for a pasta salad or a hot entree like baked polenta, lasagne, or chicken enchiladas.

Getting there: *Near the junction of Highway 99 and Siskiyou at YMCA Way.*

Candy Shop

Ashland Fudge Company

57 N Main, Ashland, OR. (541) 482-4591

♥♥♥♥ If you're looking for **fudge** or **chocolate candy** in Ashland, look no further than the **Ashland Fudge Company**. They make their products by hand using excellent dark and milk Swiss chocolate (the brand name is highly guarded). The fudge is made from an 1887 recipe from Mackinac Island in Michigan. It comes in **Chocolate, Chocolate Walnut, Chocolate Peanut Butter, Chocolate Cream Cheese**, and **Chocolate Pecan**, as well as brown sugar fudge. It's ultra-smooth and melts in the mouth with a deep rich chocolate flavor that's not overly sweet. It's some of the best fudge this reviewer has eaten!

They also carry a large selection of **Truffles**, which are large, and exquisitely creamy and flavorful. Their **Nut Bark** is a thin sheet of chocolate that's full of fresh roasted nuts. The **Espresso Bark** is delicately thin and lightly crunchy with finely-ground espresso beans. Their **Haystacks**, an old time favorite, taste like fresh coconut with just the right coconut-chocolate ratio. Their **Honeycomb** is huge, buttery, rich, and light-as-a-feather. It's terrific!

Ashland Fudge Company isn't afraid to use a little creativity and have some fun. They make candies like **Doodles**, butterscotch-flavored chocolate covering crispy Chinese noodles, and **Porkers**, caramel, almonds and semi-sweet chocolate all dipped in milk chocolate. Oink!

For those who can't eat sugar, they make a line of **sugar-free chocolate**. They also feature a small selection of excellent **Umpqua Ice Cream**, including **Double Chocolate Almond, Old South Fudge Pie, Cookie Dough, Chocolate**, and **Chocolate Peanut Butter**. **Getting there**: *Downtown on the Plaza.*

Bread and Roses Bakery
Port Townsend, Washington
DEATH BY
CHOCOLATE COOKIES

Makes 2 1/2 dozen 3-inch cookies

1 pound butter
2 1/2 cups granulated sugar
2 eggs
1 tablespoon vanilla
3 3/4 cups all-purpose flour
3/4 cup cocoa powder
2 1/2 teaspoons baking powder
2 teaspoons salt
2 cups semi-sweet chocolate chips, divided
8 oz. high-quality semi-sweeet chocolate, chopped (optional)

These are what we call "industrial-strength chocolate cookies"—hearty cookies with big chocolate flavor.

Preheat oven to 350 degrees.

In a large bowl, cream the butter. Add the sugar and beat until light and fluffy. Add eggs and vanilla and beat well.

In another bowl, stir together the flour, cocoa, baking powder and salt. Add to creamed mixture and stir to blend well. Stir in 2 cups chocolate chips.

Drop by tablespoonful onto greased baking sheet. Bake about 15 minutes or until set. Cool on wire rack.

If desired, melt the 8 oz. semi-sweet chocolate over hot water. Dip 1/2 of each cookie into melted semi-sweet chocolate.

From *The Chocolate Lover's Guide Cookbook*,
Pacific Northwest Edition.

Oregon Cascades

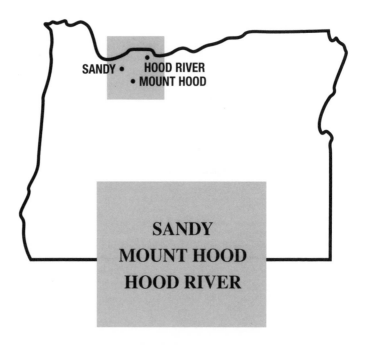

SANDY •   HOOD RIVER
           • MOUNT HOOD

**SANDY
MOUNT HOOD
HOOD RIVER**

*O*regon Cascades Country includes the mighty Columbia River and its fjord-like Gorge, snow-capped Mount Hood at more than 11,000 feet, playground to skiers and snowboarders, as well as seemingly endless miles of forested mountains filled with cascading waterfalls, burbling creeks, and crystalline lakes. Traveling though the Cascades makes one glad to live in the beautiful Pacific Northwest.

Great Things to Do

• **View the Vista. Columbia Gorge Scenic Highway** (Route 30), OR. If you've got the time, getting off Highway 84 and onto the old highway is worthwhile. It's 22 miles of tree-shaded switchbacks and waterfalls. Stop at Crown Point, the art deco vista house, with can't-beat views of the Columbia River and the spectacular gorge.

• **Check Out the Falls. Multnomah Falls,** Highway 84, OR. The Columbia River Gorge is full of beautiful waterfalls, but none rival Multnomah Falls. Cascading 620 feet, Multnomah Falls is the second highest waterfall in the country. During tourist season, the Falls can get busy, but it's worth a stop. There's a stone and timber lodge where you can grab a bite.

• **Grab Some Wind. Hood River, OR.** The conditions are just right on the Columbia near the town of Hood River for world-class windsurfing. Hood River sports a number of board shops where you can rent or buy equipment. Be forewarned, however, conditions can quickly become extremely windy and rough. Beginners should stay near the beaches.

• **Hop a Scenic Train. Mount Hood Scenic Railroad, Hood River, OR.** (541) 386-3556. If a leisurely ride through orchard country is more your style, you can hop aboard the Mt. Hood Scenic Railroad mid-April through December.

• **Climb a Mountain. Mount Hood, OR.** If you've ever dreamed of climbing a challenging mountain, at 11, 245 feet, Mt. Hood presents a challenge. From May-July, it's possible to climb the mountain. However, be aware this mountain can be extremely dangerous. If you're a beginner, go with a guided group like those lead by **Timberline Mountain Guides,** 88220 E Government Camp Loop, **Government Camp, OR.** (800) 464-7704.

Terrific Places to Stay

Timberline Lodge, Timberline Ski Area, **Timberline Lodge, OR.** (503) 231-5400. You can't beat the rustic elegance of historic Timberline Lodge. The National Historic Monument was built as a WPA project during the 1930's and features soaring open-beamed ceilings, massive timbers, intricate wood carvings, over-sized stone fireplaces and hand-crafted Arts and Crafts furnishings. The 3-story structure offers a historic exhibit and gift shop on the first floor. On the second story, chairs and couches grouped around the huge fireplace invite guests to warm themselves. This floor also houses the Cascade Dining Room (see review). The third story offers a small bar area where you can enjoy a toddy or a light meal. The 70 knotty pine paneled guest rooms, all with private baths, are simply furnished with period wooden furniture. The suites with fireplaces are especially cozy on a snowy day. Guests can use the outdoor pool and spa (wonderful when it's snowing).

Columbia Gorge Hotel, 4000 Westcliff Drive, **Hood River, OR**. (541) 386-5566. Overlooking the mighty Columbia River, the Columbia Gorge Hotel brings guests back to long ago elegance. Built in 1921, the hotel has hosted movie stars, presidents, and business moguls. In the 1980's, the old Spanish-style hotel was restored to its original glory and visitors are greeted by an elegant lobby with a green circular couch and a large vase of flowers. Lace curtains hang on the glass doors leading to the Valentino Lounge with its fireplace and tall windows overlooking the Columbia. The 42 guest rooms, all with TVs, phones, and private baths, are individually decorated in a 1920's style and include nicesities like turn down service, flowers, and toiletries. One of the best rooms is the Falls Room, which overlooks Wah-Gwin-Gwin Falls, 206 feet of feathery water that cascades into the Columbia below. Rooms include a bountiful 4-course breakfast in the dining room, which may include fruit, oatmeal, baked goods, eggs, bacon, sausage, hash browns, and buttermilk pancakes.

SANDY

Calamity Jane's
42015 Highway 26, Sandy, OR. (503) 668-7817

♥♥ If you want delicious burgers, head to **Clamity Jane's** on the outskirts of the little town of Sandy. This western theme restaurant offers dozens of big, juicy burgers— from the standard tomato, lettuce, pickle variety to burgers with pineapple and teriyaki. You can even get a peanut butter and marshmallow burger! To go along with all those burgers, they offer big, creamy **milkshakes** in a rainbow of flavors. They come served in a frosty stainless steel mixing container with a dollop of whipped cream. You can mix and match any flavor you'd like. One of our favorites is **Chocolate Coconut**, a soft chocolate flavor with a refreshing lilt of coconut. Yum!
Getting there: On the outskirts of Sandy heading toward Mt. Hood.

Chocolate Shop
The Oregon Candy Farm
48620 SE Highway 26, Sandy, OR. (503) 668-5066

♥♥♥ If you want **chocolates** that are a bit different, try the **Oregon Candy Farm**. Started in 1933, the Oregon Candy Farm is one of the oldest confectioners in Oregon. Twenty years ago, Pat Ruter and her late husband, Don, took over the factory-retail operation on Highway 26 on the way to Mt. Hood and they've used or improved upon the original recipes. Pat uses a high grade of Blommer Chocolate and, as she says, they "put a lot of love and care into every piece of candy."

They carry a large selection of **chocolate-covered creams** in interesting flavors like **Blackberry, Blueberry, Polynesian (Coconut), Strawberry, Orange, Lemon, Maple, Cherry, Chocolate, Raspberry, Peanut Butter, Mint, Mocha**, and **Vanilla**. The cream centers are smooth with bright, fresh-tasting flavors. For instance, the **Rum Cream** is rich without being overpowering. The **Orange Cream** has a fresh citrus flavor. The chocolate coating has a rich chocolate flavor with an excellent snap.

A Candy Farm original is the **Mt. Hood**, a mound of craggy coconut covered in vanilla coating, half-dipped in chocolate. These little "mountains" are slightly crunchy with a good coconut flavor. They make a great gift for out-of-town friends.

A signature candy is their **Rocky Road**, nearly 3 inches tall and packed with walnuts and over-sized, soft, fluffy marshmallow pieces, which they make themselves. It's enrobed in thick layers of milk or ultra-dark chocolate that rocky road fans will love. It's some of the best rocky road we've tasted.

Another candy they're famous for is their **Screen Mint Truffle**, a flat disk of whipped chocolate mint center covered in chocolate. It resembles a melt-away and is slightly crunchy with a cool minty flavor that doesn't come on too strong.

The Finer The Chocolate, The Smoother It Is. The smaller the particles of chocolate, the smoother it is. Smooth chocolate has particles no larger than 30-50 thousandths of a millimeter.

Don't expect the silky ganache associated with today's truffles. The Candy Farm's **Bavarian Truffels** (no misspelling) were developed by candymaker Don Ruter and the pastry chef at the old Rose's Bakery in Portland. The truffle centers, which they call a "paste," are stiffer and thicker than most.

They also carry a good selection of **nuts and chews**. Their **caramel** is buttery and soft. They make a **Chocolate-covered Cinnamon Caramel** that tastes like a buttery, chewy Red Hot. Their **Nougat** comes packed with nuts, plain, or in a surprising mint flavor.

You can buy Oregon Candy Farm chocolates at a variety of retail outlets in Oregon, but you'll get the freshest and best selection at their factory location.

Getting there: About 5 miles east of Sandy at milepost 30.

MOUNT HOOD

Cascade Dining Room (Timberline Lodge)
Timberline Ski Area, Timberline Lodge, OR. (503) 272-3700
♥♥♥♥ Under the expert guidance of award-winning Executive
Chef Leif Benson, **Timberline Lodge's Cascade Dining Room**
has long received accolades from food lovers. The dining room
features simple wooden Arts and Crafts tables and chairs and hardwood floors. During the day, it feels casual enough to wear your
jeans or ski togs while enjoying sandwiches like portabello with
roasted red peppers, Tillamook cheese and pesto mayonnaise or
entrees like penne pasta with pork Dijon. At dinner, the dining
room takes on a more elegant feel with linen tablecloths and candles.
The menu also goes upscale with offerings like apple-braised steelhead, prime rib or pork, cedar wood roasted salmon, and chicken
adobo.

Chocolate lovers won't be disappointed with the chocolate selection. Although desserts change regularly, they have several standards like the **Hazelnut Silk**, a hazelnut-graham cracker crust
topped with creamy dark chocolate silk that's garnished with strings
of white chocolate, whipped cream and chocolate squiggles. It's
creamy and fudgy with an intense chocolate-hazelnut flavor. The
crust adds a lovely chewy contrast.

A Timberline classic is **Chocolate Decadence**, a slice of dense
dark chocolate topped with a light, sweet chantilly cream, and
chocolate curls and served on a bed of raspberry sauce that's not
too tart or overly sweet.

Chocolate Peanut Butter Pie is a thick wedge of graham-walnut
crust with 1$^1/_2$ inches of peanut butter cream crowned with a thin
layer of chocolate and topped with chopped walnuts. This ultra-
creamy dessert has plenty of peanut butter flavor without being
heavy. The nut crust adds a crunchy texture that compliments the
creamy peanut butter.

Chocolate Espresso Cheesecake features a thin graham cracker
crust topped with a generous wedge of chocolate cheese filling,
garnished with chocolate swirls and a rosette of whipped cream.
It's silky and creamy with a wonderful tangy cheesiness that invites another bite.

The **Chocolate Pecan Tart** is only an inch tall, but full of choco-
late-pecan richness. The wedge of chopped nuts and chocolate is
topped with pecan halves and garnished with chocolate curls and a
whipped cream rosette. It's rich and complex tasting with plenty of
chocolate flavor.

Getting there: Sixty miles east of Portland off Highway 26. Watch for Timberline Lodge signs just past Government Camp.

COLUMBIA GORGE

Few areas match the stunning natural beauty of the Columbia River Gorge. Luckily for chocolate lovers, you can also find excellent chocolate there.

HOOD RIVER

Columbia Gorge Hotel
4000 Westcliff Drive, Hood River, OR. (541) 386-5566
♥♥♥ The **Columbia Gorge Hotel's** dining room is stately and elegant with its rose-colored walls, chandeliers, and cloth-covered tables. During the day, ask for a window table for the best river views. They serve breakfast, lunch, and dinner. The dinner menu features entrees like salmon, rainbow trout, rack of lamb, filet mignon, and pork tenderloin. Desserts change daily and they usually have at least 1 chocolate dessert. Their **Chocolate Peanut Butter Terrine** has an ultra-silky filling with a firmer layer of dark chocolate on the outside. It's sliced pate style and served with creme anglaise, and garnished with red and green candied orange peel, a strawberry fan, and a scattering of peanuts. It's a good combination of chocolate and peanut butter flavors.

The **White Chocolate and Dark Chocolate Mousse** comes layered in a slender flute. The dark chocolate mousse is rich and chocolaty; the white chocolate mousse is light with a tangy, almost lemony flavor.

Traveler's note: We were hesitant to review the Columbia Gorge Hotel when we heard the Executive Chef had left and 2 chefs-in-training were at the helm. But the hotel has an excellent reputation and the young chefs proved up to the challenge.
***Getting there**: One hour east of Portland on I-84, exit 62.*

OREGON

Central Oregon

• BLACK BUTTE
SISTERS • • REDMOND
• BEND
SUNRIVER •

BLACK BUTTE

SISTERS

BEND

SUNRIVER

REDMOND

Central Oregon has spectacular scenery with snow-capped Three Sisters, Three-Fingered Jack, Mt. Jefferson, and Mt. Bachelor jutting up from the desert floor. The area is known for sunny weather, brilliant blue skies, and sage- and juniper-scented clean air. It's also a sportsman's paradise with great skiing, white water rafting, hiking and biking trails, fishing and hunting, and many excellent golf courses.

Great Things to Do

• **Powder Ski. Mt. Bachelor, OR**. (800) 829-2442. Skiers on the west side of the Cascade mountains are accustomed to skiing much of the time in "cement," wet, soggy, heavy snow. Just over the mountains in central Oregon's high desert, skiers can enjoy some of the driest powder in Oregon on Mount Bachelor. Ten lifts, 3,100 vertical feet, and miles of groomed Nordic trails make this a primo spot for downhill or cross-county skiers.

• **Walk on Ancient Lava Flows**, **Newberry National Volcanic Monument,** Highway 97 between **Bend and La Pine, OR**. (541) 593-2421. Anyone who knows anything about geography knows that much of the territory was shaped by volcanoes. At Newberry National Monument, you can see a volcanic crater and acres of lava beds. A few miles down the road, you can explore a lava river cave. Be forewarned: the cave is a chilly 40 degrees year round and extremely dark. Wear a jacket, rent one of the lanterns (flashlights *aren't* enough) and wear sturdy shoes for the strenuous, sometimes rocky 1-hour walk. Newberry is generally open Spring through Fall, but call if there is early or late snow.

• **Go Climb a Rock. Smith Rock State Park, Terrebone, OR**. (541) 548-7501. If you're just itching to show off your rock climbing skills, you can do it at Smith Rock State Park. It's a little more than 20 miles north of Bend and features some beautiful and challenging red rock cliffs.

• **Hop a Steam Train**. **Redmond, OR**. You can take a trip back to yesteryear on the **Crooked River Dinner Train**. (541) 548-8630.The steam train makes a 3-hour scenic run through the Crooked River Valley. Complete sit-down dinners are served. Special events and theme rides are offered.

• **Get High On The Desert. High Desert Museum,** 59800 Highway 97, **Bend, OR**. (541) 382-4754. One of the best museums of natural and cultural history in the West, the High Desert Museum showcases fascinating artifacts from local Native Peoples, pioneers, miners, and others who settled the high desert in realistic walk-through diaramas complete with sound effects. The Desertarium features small desert animals such as burrowing and barn owls, pallid bats, and kangaroo rats. Kids can go hands-on in a pioneer cabin, indoor cave, and do-it-yourself puppet show. Outdoor exhibits include walk-through replicas of a pioneer cabin complete with garden and outhouse, a steam-powered sawmill, and animal exhibits, including birds of prey, river otters, porcupines, and rainbow trout. It's a great place for kids and adults and it's completely wheel-chair accessible.

Terrific Places to Stay

Lara House Bed and Breakfast, 640 NW Congress, **Bend, OR**. (541) 388-4064. The honking you hear is geese taking off from

Mirror Pond across the street. That's just one of the reasons Lara House is Bend's oldest bed and breakfast. The 1910 Craftsman bungalow features original wainscoting and mahogany trim, a huge stone fireplace, a wide front porch perfect for relaxing, a sun porch overlooking Baker Park. All 6 guest rooms, which feature separate baths, are spacious and simply, yet elegantly decorated. Guests can use the outdoor spa, ride the bicycles, or watch the TV or VCR in the sun room. The innkeepers don't fuss over guests or provide niceties like toiletries or fluffy robes, but they do serve a large, delicious breakfast.

The Riverhouse, 3075 N Highway 97, **Bend, OR**. (541) 389-3111. You can't stay at a better motor inn than the Riverhouse. Although it's located right on busy Highway 97, the rushing Deschutes River that passes through the property drowns out the traffic and makes you feel like you're in the country. The rooms are spacious, some with kitchens, fireplaces, and/or spas, and rates are more reasonable than many of the nearby resorts. The rooms facing the river are the best. Guests may use the indoor and outdoor swimming pools, 3 whirlpools, saunas, exercise room, indoor Jacuzzi, tennis courts, and the 18-hole golf course. The Crossings (see review) is the Riverhouse's upscale steakhouse. Or you can choose Mai's Chinese Cuisine or the Poolside Café for lighter fare. The lounge offers a light menu and live music 6 nights a week.

BLACK BUTTE

Black Butte isn't really a town. It's a planned residential and vacation community called Black Butte Ranch. It comes complete with golf course, stables, lodge, and a fine restaurant.

Black Butte Ranch Restaurant
Black Butte Ranch, OR. (541) 595-1260
♥♥♥ The **Black Butte Restaurant** has a stunning setting. Shaded by towering Ponderosa Pines and aspens, the tiered restaurant overlooks a lake full of Canada geese and has soaring views of the Three Sisters mountains. The Ranch also serves breakfast, lunch, and dinner. Their specialty is Northwest cuisine, including such specialties as salmon, roasted duck with huckleberry sauce and hazelnuts, and fresh grilled oysters.

Dessert equals the wonderful views. **Alta's Sourdough Chocolate Cake** is a tall, single layer of dark sourdough chocolate cake with a light cinnamon flavor. It's served warm with thick mocha icing and finely-chopped walnuts on top. Named for Alta Brockett, the Ranch's former pastry chef, the cake is warm and rich without being too heavy. The large 4-inch square is plenty to share and we recommend ordering it with vanilla ice cream for that delicious cold-warm contrast.

The Ranch's **Chocolate Walnut Fudge** is served along with the dinner check. It has a light chocolate flavor, isn't overly sweet, and has just the right toothsome feel.

Getting there: Black Butte is located on Highway 20, 8 miles west of Sisters.

SISTERS

Sisters is a quaint town with a western theme. The many interesting shops and proximity to recreational activities like skiing and fishing draw tourists all year.

Hotel Sisters Restaurant
190 Cascade Street, Sisters, OR. (541) 549-RIBS
You won't find a hotel here. You will find Bronco Billy's Saloon and a replica of a 1900's hotel restaurant complete with tall wooden booths and tiny floral print wall paper. Serving breakfast, lunch, and dinner, the **Hotel Sisters Restaurant** specializes in serving good beef—ribs, steak, hot links. They feature Corriente Beef, 50% leaner than other beef and grown with no hormones.

For dessert, they offer **Chocolate Suicide Cake**, which comes from a food distributor. It's 3 layers of very moist, dark chocolate cake, filled and frosted with a thick ganache, topped with melted and molded chocolate chips, and garnished with chopped walnuts. It comes surrounded by swirls of whipped cream and a scoop of vanilla ice cream, all drizzled with chocolate sauce. If this sounds like too much chocolate, they also serve marionberry short cake and apple crisp.

Getting there: On the main street in Sisters, on the corner of Cascade and Fir Streets.

Sisters Bakery
251 E Cascade Street, Sisters, OR. (541) 549-0361
If you want a fresh baked **doughnut**, head for the **Sister's Bakery**. Owner Melissa Ward bakes up a beautiful selection of doughnuts, including **Devil's Food Chocolate** with or without sprinkles or peanuts, huge (10-inch) **Chocolate** and **Maple Bars**, and giant **Bear Claws** with a drizzle of maple or chocolate icing. They're always fresh—soft on the inside with just the right amount of crispness outside.

The bakery also has **brownies—Cream Cheese, Double Fudge**, and **German Chocolate**. We found the cream cheese brownie moist with a light chocolate flavor and tangy frosting. The others were too sweet and sticky.

The bakery also bakes up loaves of fresh breads daily, including French, 8-grain, oatmeal, dill rye, honey sunflower, and cinnamon, among others.

Getting there: The bakery is half a block up from the Hotel Sisters Restaurant on Cascade.

BEND

Restaurants

Café Paradiso

945 NW Bond Street, Bend, OR. (541) 385-5931

♥♥♥♥ We review **Café Paradiso** because it carries a large selection of wonderful **cakes** from the wholesale pastry company, **Sweet Baby Jane's**. Café Paradiso has true coffeehouse atmosphere with its exposed brick walls, modern art, and mis-matched tables and chairs, couches, and overstuffed chairs. They feature espresso drinks and a selection of exquisitely brewed-by-the-cup coffees as well as light lunch and dinner fare. Be sure to order one of their **chocolate cakes** with your brew. **Top Hat** is a dark chocolate cake with the thick wedge of white chocolate mousse filling covered with dark chocolate ganache. The mousse is cheesy rather than sweet and compliments the intense dark chocolate cake.

Brown Velvet is a chocolate mousse with a white chocolate layer with a chocolate cookie crust and ganache topping. It's creamy with a good cookie flavor.

Epitome, this reviewer's favorite, is 4 layers of dense chocolate cake with white chocolate cream and ganache filling frosted with Italian cream. It's a moist, medium-texture cake with just the right chocolate flavor. The Italian cream frosting adds a delightful lightness.

Oops You Got Peanut Butter in My Chocolate is a chocolate mousse cake with peanut butter cream, topped with ganache. It's rich—almost too rich—with an intense peanut butter flavor. This one is definitely for the peanut butter lover.

Getting there: Downtown, on NW Bond Street between Oregon and Minnesota.

Hans

915 NW Wall Street, Bend, OR. (541) 389-9700

♥♥♥♥ **Hans** in downtown Bend is an unassuming little restaurant with the tag line, "Great food. Great place." And it is. Hans serves lunch and dinner, offering such delights as saffron orzo paella, grilled salmon, blackened halibut, and chicken breast in a garlic herb demi glaze.

The draw for chocolate lovers is their towering **chocolate cakes**. Owner and pastry chef Hans Weiss was classically-trained in Austria and has worked in some of the finest restaurants the world over. All of his chocolate desserts are beautiful and have the more subtle, European approach to fine chocolate. His **Sacher Torte** starts with a cookie crust bottom with 6 layers of dark chocolate sponge cake filled with thin layers of raspberry. Then it's covered with chocolate cream and dark chocolate ganache. The sponge cake is soft with just the right amount of chocolate flavor. The raspberry joins the chocolate in a delightful marriage of flavors.

His **Truffle Cake** is chocolate sponge cake, ganache and whipped cream with the slightest touch of rum, covered with chocolate cream and dark chocolate ganache. The mousse filling is light without being too airy.

Hans' **Chocolate Cheesecake** is deliciously unusual. He starts with a cookie crust, adds a layer of chocolate sponge cake, then a thicker layer of chocolate cheesecake, and tops it with dark chocolate ganache. The result is a velvety joining of cheesecake and chocolate.

They also make a variety of chocolate baked goods, including **Chocolate Brownies**, **Chocolate Chocolate Macaroons**, **Chocolate-dipped Florentines**, and **Chocolate-covered Pretzel Cookies**.
Getting there: Downtown on Wall Street between Oregon and Minnesota Streets.

Rosette
150 NW Oregon Ave, Bend, OR. (541) 383-2780
♥♥♥♥ At **Rosette**, you'll find an intimate restaurant with white table cloths and fresh roses at each table. They serve lunch and dinner, offering such dishes as salmon with soy-dijon sauce, duck with marionberry sauce, and shrimp pasta con vodka. Their signature chocolate dessert is their **Chocolate Terrine**. Chocolate hazelnut mousse is whipped and frozen, then cut into triangles, drizzled with homemade caramel sauce, shaved chocolate, and toasted hazelnuts. It looks as beautiful as it tastes. It has the coolness of ice cream, the smoothness of mousse, and the crunch and flavor of toasted hazelnuts. It's delightfully light and refreshing.

Their **Chocolate Gateau** is a flourless chocolate cake with a layer of melted chocolate on top. It's beautifully presented with white and chocolate drizzles, a dab of whipped cream with a mint sprig, and a fresh strawberry cut into a fan. It has a creamy, milk chocolate flavor and the milk chocolate topping adds an interesting toothiness to the dish.

Getting there: Downtown on Oregon between Wall and Bond Streets.

Awbrey Glen
2500 NW Awbrey Glen Drive, Bend, OR. (541) 317-2885
♥♥♥ The **Awbrey Glen Restaurant** at the Awbrey Glen Golf Course overlooks the fairways and has a fine view of Mt. Washington and the Sisters Mountains. The restaurant serves such dishes as grilled salmon, pork porterhouse with papaya mango salsa, and rack of lamb. Their most popular dessert is **Chocolate Decadence Torte**, a creamy, fudge-like, chocolate meringue mousse with a chocolate cookie crust that's garnished with chopped hazelnuts and white chocolate drizzles. The torte is beautifully surrounded with raspberry, creme anglaise, and kiwi puree and has an intense, satisfying dark chocolate flavor.

Getting there: Off Highway 97, go west on Greenwood/Newport, right on Mount Washington Drive.

Broken Top Restaurant
6200 Broken Top Drive, Bend, OR. (541) 383-8210
♥♥♥ **Broken Top Restaurant** at the private Broken Top Golf Course is in the incredibly beautiful clubhouse with lots of natural rock, Northwest native art, sculpture, pottery, and a huge rock fireplace. The restaurant, which is open to the public, has an open kitchen and large windows overlooking a lake and waterfall, fairways, and the mountains. Dinner includes such dishes as venison crusted with pine nuts, cornbread stuffed trout, and sautéed razor clams. Their signature chocolate dessert is a **Chocolate Mousse Cake** that's beautifully presented with white and dark chocolate squiggles and a fan of fresh strawberries. It's 5 inches tall with a spongy layer of chocolate cake that has a light chocolate flavor, followed by a thick layer of intensely chocolate mousse, topped with a creamy smooth ganache.

> **Steel is tempered—cooled, reheated, and cooled—to make it strong. Chocolate is tempered too to make it less likely to melt on store shelves.**

They also serve **Chocolate Mudpie**, a diamond-shaped wedge with a chocolate cookie crust, and layers of chocolate decadence ice cream, bittersweet shavings and roasted hazelnuts, vanilla bean ice cream, Bailey's Cream ice cream, and a fudge topping. The hazelnuts give a good nutty contrast to the ice cream and the fudge topping is chocolaty without being sticky. This is an ice cream lover's treat more than a chocolate lover's treat.

Getting there: Off Highway 97, go west on Greenwood/Newport, right on Mount Washington Drive.

Coho Grill and Catering Service (Orion Greens Golf Course)
61535 Fargo Lane, Bend, OR. (541) 388-3909
♥♥ **Coho Grill and Catering Service** is a pleasant restaurant with large windows overlooking the fairways and a pond full of geese. The lunch menu includes a variety of salads with an ethnic flair such as Greek salmon and Oriental chicken, as well as soups and sandwiches. Their dinner entrees include jerk chicken, pesto crusted salmon, and pork tenderloin, among others. Their chocolate entry is **Chocolate Bourbon Pecan Pie**. It's a crisp tart shell filled with a buttery layer of chocolate filling stuffed with pecans. Served warm, it has a satisfyingly rich, nutty flavor.

Getting there: In the south end of Bend, off Highway 97, turn west on Reed Market Road, then left on Fargo Lane.

Crossings at The Riverhouse
3075 N Highway 97, Bend, OR. (541) 389-8810
♥♥ You wouldn't expect a high-end restaurant in a motor inn, but that's exactly what you get at **Crossings**. The 2-tiered dining room features upholstered, high-back arm chairs grouped around linen-covered tables for 2 or 4. The towering windows overlook the rushing Deschutes River. The dinner menu features plenty of prime beef—filet mignon, porterhouse, New York, tenderloin brochette, and prime rib. For the non-beef eater, they offer salmon, pork chops, chicken, scallops, and scampi. Their spinning bowl salad, which features greens, mandarin oranges, toasted fresh coconut, bay shrimp, and croutons tossed over ice with avocado ranch dressing is a treat.

Crossings' pastry chef gets high marks for presentation of the **Chocolate Sack**. It's 4 ounces of bittersweet Belgian chocolate molded to look like a paper sack, filled with dark chocolate mousse and white chocolate mousse and topped with a white chocolate fan. It's served on a plate of raspberry puree and creme anglaise with seasonal berries. It looks spectacular! The chocolate sack has the perfect dark chocolate flavor with just the right snap when you bite it. The mousse is creamy, but could be a bit smoother.

Getting there: On Highway 97 across from the Bend River Mall.

Bakery/Pastry Shop

DiLusso Baking
1234 NE 1st Street, Bend, OR. (541) 383-8155
♥♥♥♥ **DiLusso's** is the newest entry on the city's baking scene. Located in an unlikely industrial location, people are finding their way to DiLusso's wonderful breads and pastries. Owners Kim and John McGregor, who baked for 10 years in Salt Lake City, bake

everything from scratch, using only the finest ingredients, including Guittard chocolate. Their **Chocolate Raspberry Cake** is 2 layers of moist, dark chocolate cake filled with a layer of raspberry and topped with ganache. The cake has a deep, rich chocolate flavor and the ganache is some of the creamiest this reviewer has tasted.

Their **Chocolate Silk Brownie** topped with chopped pecans is deliciously smooth with a milk chocolate flavor. Ask for this warmed for a real treat. Their **Double Chocolate Biscotti** is a chocolate Italian cookie loaded with chocolate chunks. It's chocolaty and crisp, without the tooth-breaking quality of many of these Italian cookies.

DiLusso's **Chocolate-dipped Peanut Butter Cookie** has a deep peanut butter taste without the usual greasiness. The dark chocolate coating gives a rich, dark chocolate flavor.

Even DiLusso's **chocolate espresso** is terrific. Their **Chocolate Mocha**, served with chocolate whipped cream and a chocolate espresso bean is rich, smooth, and chocolaty.

Don't miss the bakery's line of fine breads, all made from scratch with biga, an Italian starter, that gives their breads a crisp crust and terrific texture. They make breads such as rosemary, olive, ciabatta, golden raisin, sundried tomato, garlic herb, and country. During the holidays, they make a **Chocolate Bread with Chocolate Chunks**.

Getting there: Just west of downtown on 1ˢᵗ Street, north of Greenwood Avenue.

Chocolate Shops

Goody's Soda Fountain and Candy Store
957 NW Wall Street, Bend, OR. (541) 389-5185
Other Oregon Location:
Sun River Village Mall, Building #22, Sun River, OR.
(541) 593-2155
♥♥♥ (ice cream)/ ♥♥ (candy) **Goody's** is THE ice cream and candy shop in Bend. Goody's makes their own everything—ice cream, toppings, chocolate candies, whipped cream, caramel and caramel corn, waffle cones. You name it, they make it. Their ice cream is especially good—rich and creamy. They make **Chocolate** and **Chocolate Almond**. Both have a surprisingly intense chocolate flavor not usually found in ice cream.

Their old fashioned soda fountain, complete with oak back mirror and counter, serves a wide variety of **fountain treats**. You can get a **Turtle Sundae**, ice cream, hot fudge, caramel, whipped cream, nuts, and a cherry. Or **Epress-O-Ly Yours**, coffee ice cream smothered in bittersweet chocolate sauce with all the toppings. They also make **shakes, malts, ice cream sodas, phosphates, floats**, and even **egg creams**.

They make a large line of **chocolate candies** including **Fudge, Truffles, Turtles, Peanut Clusters, Velvets, Fresh Chocolate-covered Cherries, Chocolate-** and **Mint-covered Oreos**, and **Chocolate Potato Chips**. Their **Fudge** is an intense chocolate flavor, though a bit sticky. Their **Turtles** are filled with soft caramel and pecans. The **Dark Chocolate Marionberry Cream** has a tart cream center that contrasts nicely with the chocolate. Their **Double Dark Velvet**, this reviewer's favorite, has a dark chocolatey flavor with a melt-in-your-mouth chocolate center. The **Mint Cindy** is a mint milk chocolate cream center covered with dark chocolate. It's a mint lover's delight.

Fake Chocolate. Carob is not chocolate (you knew that). It's made from the ground-up fruit of a Mediterranean evergreen tree.

Getting there: Downtown on the corner of Wall and Oregon Streets.

SUNRIVER

Sunriver is a planned resort and residential community with all the amenities—golf course, gift shops, movie theaters, grocery stores, and some excellent restaurants.

Meadows at Sunriver Resort
#1 Center Drive, Sunriver, OR. (541) 593-3740
♥♥♥♥ **Meadows,** the restaurant at Sunriver Resort's Lodge, serves breakfast, lunch, and dinner, including dishes like hazelnut crusted salmon and fresh Oregon trout. **Chocolate Pudding Raspberry Cake** is their regular chocolate offering. It's 3 layers of moist, dark chocolate cake filled with ganache, and a "pudding" that's a thick raspberry/ganache combination. Frosted with ganache and garnished with shaved chocolate and a tiny chocolate fan, it's served on a plate of sweetened raspberry puree and vanilla bean sauce sprinkled with chocolate shavings. The presentation is beautiful! The raspberry/ganache filling adds a subtle raspberry flavor and the raspberry puree/vanilla bean sauce (creme anglaise) has just the right sweet/tart taste.
Getting there: Fifteen miles south of Bend on Highway 97, follow the signs to Sunriver Resort Lodge.

Chocolate Shop/Ice Creamery

Goody's Soda Fountain and Candy Store
Sun River Village Mall, Sun River, OR. (541) 593-2155
♥♥♥ (ice cream)/♥♥ (candy) (See review under Chocolate Shop,
Bend, OR.)
*Getting there: Fifteen miles south of Bend on Highway 97, follow
the signs to Sunriver Resort Lodge. The Sunriver Mall is right before you get to the Resort's Lodge.*

REDMOND

Local Grounds
457 SW 6th Street, Redmond, OR. (541) 923-3977
♥ You *can* get a decent cup of java in Redmond and it's at **Local
Grounds**, a pleasant little coffee shop in downtown with big, sun-
filled windows and greenery. They sell soups and sandwiches and
some decent **chocolate pastries**
made with Guittard chocolate.
Their **Hello Dolly Bar** is a substantial cookie bar consisting of
layers of graham crackers, coconut, pecans, and chocolate chips.
It's not overly sweet and has a
good coconut-chocolate flavor.

> **Americans, some of the world's greatest chocolate lovers, consume more than 22 pounds of chocolate per person each year.**

They also carry **Yo Yo's**, sugar
cookies filled with chocolate,
which this reviewer found rather
bland. Instead, opt for their large **Chocolate Chip Cookie**, soft,
chewy, and packed with chocolate chips.

They also sell **chocolate candies** from the **Candy Basket**, including English toffee, Pecan Beaver Paws, peanut truffles, and sugar-
free varieties. (See review under Portland)
Getting there: On the corner of SW Evergreen and 6th Streets.

Wild Rose Tea Room
422 SW 6th, Redmond, OR. (541) 923-3385
Through a narrow hallway and tucked behind several antique shops
is a most unlikely find—the **Wild Rose Tea Room**, an oasis of
British sophistication. Proprietor Bessie Nordahl has filled her little
corner with small tables covered with floral tablecloths, dozens of
beautiful teapots, and the relaxing sounds of song birds. She serves
tea with tiny sandwiches, scones, cookies, or fruit. She also serves
a couple of desserts each day, including her **Double Chocolate
Cream Cheese Brownie**, a dark, chewy layer of brownie followed

by a tangy layer of cream cheese, and another brownie layer. It's frosted with old-fashioned cooked fudge frosting. The cream cheese layer is a nice contrast to the chocolate. The frosting is creamy, if a tad sweet.

Getting there: Downtown on SW 6ᵗʰ.

Ice Creamery/Candy Shop

Cookies and Cream
445 SW 6ᵗʰ Street, Redmond, OR. (541) 548-6561

♥♥ (candy)/♥ (ice cream) It's a 50's style soda fountain, complete with a counter with vinyl-covered stools, red and white tile, and 45 records suspended from the ceiling. At **Cookies and Cream**, which is owned and operated by Toni Jarms and her daughters, they make their own ice cream. They regularly carry **Chocolate** and **Chocolate Almond**. Other times you may find **Chocolate Peanut Butter**, **Cookies and Cream**, **Rocky Road**, and **Raspberry Fudge Ripple**. Their ice cream is a medium-rich product, light on the chocolate flavor, with a good, clean taste.

Their double chocolate biscotti and chocolate shortbread are forgettable, but their **Chocolate Truffle Cake** is rich and creamy.

They also make their own **chocolate candies**, including a large assortment of truffles. Their **truffles** are golf-ball-sized and come with a thin coating that has a good snap to it. Their **Maple Truffle** is creamy with a intense, buttery maple flavor. Their **Almond Cluster**, almonds covered in chocolate, is made with salted, roasted almonds, which give the candy an interesting, salty bite. Their **Coconut Haystacks**, coconut covered with white chocolate and drizzled with dark chocolate, are an interesting twist on an old favorite.

Although this reviewer isn't usually a big fan of **Chocolate-covered Cherries**, the ones at Cookies and Cream are excellent. Dipped with their stems on, these cherries feature a thin, dark shell with a soft, subtle chocolate flavor and liquid centers that are gooey with an intense cherry flavor.

Traveler's note: Due to the heat, they only make fresh chocolates from October through May.
Getting there: Downtown on 6ᵗʰ Street near Evergreen.

OREGON

Eastern Oregon

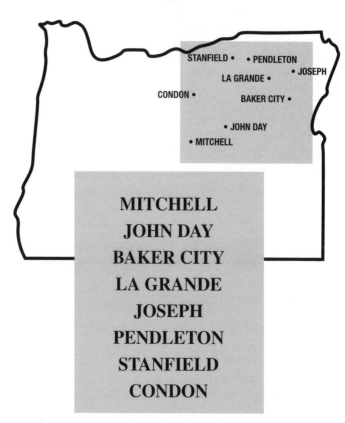

STANFIELD • • PENDLETON
LA GRANDE • • JOSEPH
CONDON •
BAKER CITY •
• JOHN DAY
• MITCHELL

**MITCHELL
JOHN DAY
BAKER CITY
LA GRANDE
JOSEPH
PENDLETON
STANFIELD
CONDON**

astern Oregon is vast and full of surprises. It's a landscape that's ever-changing. One moment you're driving through rolling hills of wheat, golden against brilliant blue sky. A few miles later, the land changes to sagebrush, rugged canyons and dramatic rock formations.

Then, you're in snow-capped mountains thick with pine and deep rivers. Don't nap while passing through this part of Oregon or you'll miss some of the most spectacular scenery in the country.

Who'd expect great chocolate in this big, empty country? We asked a volunteer at the Cant Ranch Sheep Rock Unit Visitor's Center near John Day about good sources for chocolate in the area. She shook her head sadly and said, "Well, there are always Snicker's bars."

She was wrong. Just a few miles down the road, we experienced one of the best chocolate desserts we've eaten. Great chocolate is only one of the wonderful surprises Eastern Oregon has in store for you.

Great Things to Do

• **Dig Fossils. Fossil, OR.** If finding 33 million-year-old fossils interests you, try your luck in the town of Fossil. From I-84 or I-26 take 19 to the town of Fossil. Don't follow the road signs to the fossil beds. Instead, drive into the little town and up the hill to the high school. There behind the baseball field is a hill pockmarked with holes from previous fossil hunters. You'll find impressions in the ash layers of now-extinct species of alder, maple, beech, dawn redwood, and pine. You're allowed to dig about 25 pounds per day. Take a trowel or miner's pick for digging, a box and some paper to wrap up your fragile finds.

• **Go Underground. Pendleton, OR. Pendleton Underground Tours,** (541) 276-0730. You can get a glimpse of Pendleton's wild west history through a fascinating 90-minute tour through the town's underground passageways. Used for safe passage by many of the area's minorities, especially Chinese residents, the underground was home to bordellos, opium dens, and Chinese jails. Make reservations 24 hours in advance. Tours leave from 37 SW Emigrant Avenue.

• **Ride a Narrow Gauge Rail. Sumpter, OR.** The old gold mining town of Sumpter is proud of its boom and bust history. The Narrow Gauge Sumpter Valley Railway, which operates steam locomotives, is a great way to see the 6 miles of tailings dumped by the gold dredges that chewed up Sumpter Valley's grasslands. The trains run from the **Sumpter Dredge Heritage Site** at the edge of town on weekends and holidays throughout the summer months.

• **Go Flea Marketing**. **Sumpter, OR**. Three times a year (Memorial Day, July 4, and Labor Day), the *entire* historic town of **Sumpter** becomes one huge flea market. You'll find a little of everything, including antiques, used tools, baby clothes, toys, and more.

• **Soar In a Gondola**. **Wallowa Lake Tramway, Joseph, OR**. You can get a unique view of the spectacular "Oregon Alps" by taking the Wallowa Lake Tramway 8,200 feet up Mt. Howard. The 4-person gondola is the steepest vertical lift in North America. The 15-minute ride will take you to the top where you can hike trails or eat at the Summit Deli and Alpine Patio.

• **Visit a Bronze Foundry and Galleries**. **Joseph, OR.** The town of Joseph has become known not only for its scenic beauty, but also for its western and contemporary bronze art. You can see how artisans use the "lost wax" cast process to create huge bronze sculptures.

Terrific Places to Stay

DoubleTree Inn, 304 SE Nye Avenue, **Pendleton, OR**. (541) 276-6111. Sandwiched between Highway 84 and rolling wheat fields, the Pendleton DoubleTree is one of this area's best places to stay. Rooms feature the usual nicesities as well as a heated outdoor pool and spa. Guests are invited to exercise at a nearby full-service gym. Like all DoubleTree Inns, guests are greeted with their big, delicious chocolate chip cookies.

Geiser Grand Hotel, 1996 Main Street, **Baker City, OR**. (888) GEISERG. You can live like a timber baron or mining magnate at the Geiser Grand Hotel where a $6 million restoration has brought this 1890's architectural wonder back to full glory. Thirty deluxe guest rooms and suites all feature private baths, crystal chandeliers, and 10-foot windows that open to the cool high desert breezes. Luxurious terry bath robes, full complimentary breakfast, lending video and book library are provided. Even "dog guests" are warmly welcomed with dog biscuits served on doilies. The hotel offers dining in 2 beautiful dining rooms or the casual saloon.

Wallowa Lake Lodge, 60060 Wallowa Lake Highway, **Joseph, OR**. (541) 432-9821. Cradled by the soaring Wallowa Mountains, Wallowa Lake Lodge, sits on 8 acres fronted by a beautiful alpine lake. A former hunting lodge built in the 1920's, it features a comfortable lobby with a large, river rock fireplace and pine log furniture. Twelve beautifully decorated 1-bedroom rooms, 8 2-bedroom rooms, 2 suites, and 8 cozy 1- or 2-bedroom cabins are available. The cabins have a full kitchen and fireplace. The Lodge's restaurant serves breakfast and dinner.

MITCHELL

Blueberry Muffin Café

Highway 26, Mitchell, OR. (541) 462-3434

You've been driving for miles along Highway 26 and you're hot, tired, in need of a stop. You come down a hill and spot the little blue and white house nestled under the shade of a tree. It's the **Blueberry Muffin Café**, a family-owned diner serving homestyle breakfasts, chili, burgers, and, of course, giant blueberry muffins. But for chocolate lovers, the real draw are the old-fashioned **chocolate milkshakes**. Handmade with hard ice cream, the shakes are thick, 20-ouncers you can share with a friend. They also make **Chocolate Cream Pie,** a creamy concoction with a light chocolate taste. Beware, it's topped with whipped topping instead of real whipped cream.

Getting there: Located on Highway 26 between Prineville and Picture Gorge, just on the west edge of the little town of Mitchell (population 250).

JOHN DAY

Grubsteak Mining Company

149 E Main, John Day, OR. (541) 575-1970

♥♥♥ Carol and Bob Phillips' **Grubsteak Mining Company** is truly a culinary oasis in the desert. They offer some of the most flavorful, tender steaks you'll ever eat served with big, foil-wrapped potatoes with all the trimmings, including real bacon bits. But save room for dessert. Their **Chocolate Mousse Pie** is a generous slice of creamy, chocolatey, light mousse nestled in a crisp, buttery chocolate graham cracker crust. They alternate chocolate mousse pie with **chocolate cream pie**. They also serve homemade fruit pies (cherry, peach, berry, etc.). Grubsteak breakfasts are large and delicious too.

Traveler's tip: This place is popular (and one of the only places in town to eat). Make dinner reservations.

Getting there: Highway 26 travels right through John Day. The Grubsteak Mining Company is on this main street in the middle of town.

BAKER CITY

Geiser Grand Hotel

1996 Main Street, Baker City, OR. (541) 523-1889

♥♥♥ Even non-chocolate lovers will appreciate the beautifully-restored **Geiser Grand Hotel** that owner Barbara Sidway and her husband have brought back to its original 1890's Italian Renaissance Revival grandeur. You'll be surrounded by richly-carved mahogany, crystal chandeliers, and gleaming brass in the Grand Dining Room. In the Palm Court, where the stained glass ceiling is the largest in the west, guests enjoy prime rib, steaks, fresh fish, chicken, ribs, and chops. Or order from the lighter saloon menu.

Got a Chocolate Stain?

Use ammonia and water to break down the oil base in cocoa butter and remove the stain.

Their signature chocolate dessert is the **Mudpie Martini**, which comes served in a huge, double martini glass. It's a generous serving of mocha or vanilla ice cream bathed in a pool of dark, hot fudge sauce, covered with Oreo cookie crumbles, and a gob of whipped cream. The rich blending of flavors will have you in chocolate heaven. Or enjoy **Chocolate Mountain**, a dessert inspired by the hotel's mountain views. A soft, rich, Belgian chocolate brownie is covered with vanilla ice cream, hot fudge, and a mountain of whipped cream, topped with a sprig of mint. Both deserts are so generous, they can easily be shared (or not!). After you've sampled these chocolate delights, you'll know why they are the hotel's most popular room service items.

Getting there: Get off I-84 or Highway 26 at the Baker City exit and follow the signs to the Baker City historic district. The Geiser Grand can't be missed since it takes up an entire corner on Main Street.

Tamarack Steakhouse and Saloon
1910 Main Street, Baker City, OR. (541) 523-5576
♥♥ Just up the street from the Geiser Grand Hotel, the **Tamarack Steakhouse and Saloon** offers casual dining in a down home atmosphere. Owner and baker Adrianne Pringle makes a **Chocolate Mocha Cheesecake** that will please chocolate lovers who like a dense chocolate dessert. A thick mocha layer tops a light, creamy chocolate cheesecake with a chocolate cookie crust. It's finished with a dollop of whipped cream.

If you're in the mood for lighter chocolate fare, try the **Amaretto and Chocolate Marble Cheesecake**. More amaretto flavor than chocolate, this cheesecake is exquisitely cheesy and creamy. It's a cheesecake lover's delight.

Getting there: Get off I-84 or Highway 26 at the Baker City exit and follow the signs to Main Street in the historic district. One block from the Geiser Grand Hotel.

LA GRANDE

Lifeline Café
111 Depot Street, La Grande, OR. (541) 962-9568
♥ **Lifeline** is an unusual find in a steak-and-potatoes town like La Grande. Their motto is "healthy, hearty, low-fat cooking." You'll find open-faced, broiled sandwiches like Artichoke Madness, made with artichoke hearts, red peppers, olives, and mozzarella on herbed focaccia. Or Pesto Passion, a baguette topped with pesto, roma tomatoes, feta cheese, and herbed bread crumbs. The original artwork, classical music, and casual atmosphere all add to an enjoyable experience.

Owner and chocolate lover Marty Hart says you can always find a chocolate desert here. Her **Mocha Fudge Pie** is a thick brownie layer topped by a creamy, light chocolate mousse, and whipped cream. She rotates her desserts, so you may find mocha fudge pie one day, triple fudge brownie the next. She serves 6 kinds of **hot chocolate**, including double dark chocolate.
Getting there: *In downtown La Grande on Depot Street.*

*Traveler's Tip: Heading northeast on Highway 82 toward Elgin and Wallowa, you'll see the **Imbler Country Market**. Their sign proclaims "**famous pepperoni**." If you're in need of a little protein to balance out all the chocolate, pick up a few sticks. It's flavorful and spicy without being greasy.*

JOSEPH

The town of Joseph, on Highway 82, is the gateway to the pristine beauty of the Wallowa Mountains and Eagle Cap Wilderness. The soaring, snow-capped mountains that surround the town give the area its designation as the "Switzerland of America." Joseph is not only unusual for its stunning scenery, but also because it's full of art galleries, a bronze foundry, and gift shops that sell high-quality items. It's also the first place we found a 4-heart (chocolate nirvana) dessert.

Old Town Café
8 S Main Street, Joseph, OR. (541) 432-9898
♥♥♥♥ Owner Gail Walter has only been in business here a short while, but judging from the hoards of smiling customers, she and her **Old Town Café** are doing a lot of things right. This breakfast-lunch café serves huge breakfast burritos, mammoth, home-baked cinnamon rolls, a variety of interesting salads, soups, and sandwiches. Smart customers save room for Gail's **Old Town Pie**, a warm chocolate brownie torte with a pecan meringue crust with a

"secret ingredient," topped with vanilla bean ice cream, whipped cream, chocolate sauce, and nuts. The flavors blend beautifully and the contrast between the warm brownie torte and the cold ice cream is heavenly. They also serve a variety of fruit pies, including marionberry, and **Monster Cookies**, large chocolate chippers.
Getting there: Follow Highway 82 into Joseph. Old Town Café is right in the middle of town on the main street.

PENDLETON

DoubleTree Inn
304 SE Nye Avenue, Pendleton, OR. (541) 276-6111
♥♥ You wouldn't expect a chain hotel to come up with a great chocolate cake, but the **DoubleTree Inn's Chocolate Thunder Cake** is a chocolate lover's delight. This cake, which is a staple on their menu, is moist, rich dark chocolate with a surprisingly light fudge frosting loaded with chocolate chips. It'll satisfy your yearning for a good piece of chocolate cake.
Getting there: Across the freeway from the town of Pendleton.

The Cookie Tree Bakery and Cafe
30 SW Emigrant, Pendleton, OR. (541) 278-0343
♥♥ Smell the delicious aromas wafting from the **Cookie Tree Bakery and Café's** ovens and you know why owners Lenny and Kelly Leen have been in business for 14 years. They make all their own baked goods, including huge cinnamon rolls and 32 different flavors of fruit and cream pies (crusts and fillings all homemade), available by the slice or whole. Their **chocolate pies** include **Chocolate Cream**, **Black Forest Cream**, **Chocolate Peanut Butter**, **Toll House Chocolate Chip**, and **German Chocolate**. The **Chocolate Cream Pie** is a thick, rich chocolate cream in a light, flaky crust topped with plenty of real whipped cream and chocolate shavings. The **Black Forest Pie** is creamy, but with more cherry flavor than chocolate. Slices are big and bargain-priced.

They also make a **Chocolate Fudge Brownie**, which is a frosted cake-like brownie with rich chocolate flavor. Their **Peanut Butter Fudge Brownie** is topped with peanut butter whipped with butter into a creamy consistency.

The Cookie Tree also serves delicious-looking breakfasts and lunches at reasonable prices.
Getting there: On Emigrant in downtown Pendleton.

Cakecreations Etcetera

16 SE Court Street, Pendleton, OR. (541) 276-7978
(800) 239-7978

♥ This is cake central for Pendleton. Owner Marilyn French and **Cakecreations** specializes in making beautiful cakes for weddings and other special occasions. You can purchase by the slice or cake. Their **Chocolate Ganache Cake** is a towering triple layer chocolate cake with chocolate fudge filling and chocolate fudge frosting and chocolate ganache. The cake is fine-grained with a very light, creamy fudge frosting/filling with a delicate chocolate flavor. The slice is generous and can easily serve 2.

They also make a cheesy, creamy **Chocolate Ganache Cheesecake** with a chocolate cookie crumb crust. It's a cheesecake lover's delight.

In addition, they make large **chocolate chocolate chip muffins**, **german chocolate brownies**, and **chocolate eclairs**. They also carry (but don't make) an interesting Heath toffee cheese pie and chocolate almond treasure, a rolled filo dough filled with chopped almonds, cashews, and pecans, topped with chocolate and almonds and honey syrup.

Getting there: Just around the corner from The Cookie Tree Bakery.

Chocolate Shop

Toys N' More

339 S Main Street, Pendleton, OR. (541) 276-6095

♥♥ The sign says "flowers, clocks, father's day gifts, fudge, cards, lava lamps" and they're not kidding. **Toys N' More**, an eclectic gift shop in downtown Pendleton, sells everything from lava lamps to Virgin Mary icons, John Wayne picture clocks, and sunglasses. They also sell some of the best **fudge** around and at a reasonable price, which may be why they sell more than 3½ tons of fudge each year. Enjoy the shop and sample their buttery **Milk Chocolate**, **Mint Chocolate Swirl**, **Peanut Butter Chocolate**, **Vanilla Chocolate Swirl**, **Chocolate Nut**, **Double Chocolate Fudge**, and **Amaretto Chocolate Swirl**. Skip the fat-free variety. They also sell **sugar-free fudge** for those who can't eat sucrose.

Chocolate is nutritious. It contains calcium, protein, and riboflavin, one of the B vitamins.

Getting there: Can't miss it on Main Street.

STANFIELD

Wheatland Dairy Cafe
2100 Highway 395 S, Stanfield, OR. (541) 449-3755
You're driving down I-84 and it's hot. An ice cream would hit the spot. The **Wheatland Dairy Café** is a funky little place that serves burgers, hot dogs, and fries. But the real draw is the 39 flavors of **ice cream.** A scoop of ice cream here is the size of a large softball. Their chocolate flavors include **Chocolate, Chocolate Chocolate Chip, Chocolate Peanut Butter, Chocolate Cheesecake, Mocha Almond Fudge, Rocky Road, Espresso Chocolate Pie, Cookies and Cream, Tin Roof,** and **Chocolate Chip.** They also serve **banana splits, sundaes, shakes,** and **malts.**
Getting there: Take the Hermiston exit off I-84. The Wheatland Dairy Café is located on the north side of the freeway junction.

CONDON

If you're like the author, you prefer backroads to interstate highways. A jog off I-84 onto 19, a pleasantly twisted road that meanders through wheatfields and sagebrush, brought us to the tiny pioneer town of Condon.

Country Flowers Deli
201 S Main Street, Condon, OR. (541) 384-4120
♥♥ Condon is 2 blocks long with a scattering of western buildings. In the middle of town, you'll find **Country Flowers Deli** selling high-quality garden and gift items, Powell's Books (yes, *that* famous Portland bookstore), and soda fountain items. It's a place that would be at home in an upscale Portland or Seattle neighborhood. Try their **Double Chocolate Milkshake,** made with hard chocolate ice cream, chocolate syrup, and whole milk, and topped with whipped cream. It's refreshing and more chocolaty than most chocolate milkshakes. They also make old time fountain favorites like a **Black and White,** chocolate ice cream with marshmallow topping and vanilla ice cream with chocolate topping; **brownie sundaes; banana splits; malts; ice cream sodas;** and **floats.** You can even buy a **chocolate Coke** or a fruit phosphate for a trip down memory lane.

Country Flowers Deli also stocks **chocolates** from the Candy Basket (see review under Chocolate Shop, Portland, OR.) and **truffles** by Michele (see review under Clackamas, OR.). If you need lunch, the Deli sells espresso drinks, sandwiches, soups, and salads.
Getting there: Condon is located about halfway between I-84 and I-26 on Highway 19.

Luna Restaurant
Spokane, Washington
MACADAMIA NUT CHIP TART

Makes 1 9-inch tart

Crust:
2 cups all purpose flour
7 tablespoons granulated sugar
3/4 cup cold unsalted butter, cut into bits
1/2 teaspoon vanilla

Filling:
3/4 cup unsalted butter, softened
2 eggs
1/2 cup granulated sugar
1/2 cup all-purpose flour
1/4 teaspoon salt
1 tablespoon vanilla
6 ounces semi-sweet chocolate chips
1 cup macadamia nuts, chopped coarsely

Preheat oven to 350 degrees.

For Crust: Combine the flour, sugar, butter and vanilla in the bowl of a food processor and process until mixed. (Or mix by hand, using a pastry cutter to cut in the butter.) The dough will be crumbly like cornmeal. Press into a 9-inch tart pan or springform pan.

For Filling: In a large bowl with an electric mixer, beat the butter until light. Add the eggs and beat well. Mix in the sugar, flour, salt and vanilla. Stir in the chocolate chips and macadamia nuts by hand.

Spoon into the prepared shell and bake for 45 minutes or until set. Serve warm.

From *The Chocolate Lover's Guide Cookbook*,
Pacific Northwest Edition.

The Chocolate Lover's Guide Best List

Author's Favorite Places To Stay

Oval Door B&B, Eugene, OR.
Peerless Hotel, Ashland, OR.
La Conner Channel House, La Conner, WA.
Schnauzer Crossing, Bellingham, WA.
Big Trees B&B, Bellingham, WA.
Inn at the Market, Seattle, WA.
Edgewater, Seattle, WA.
Four Seasons, Seattle, WA.
Sorrento Hotel, Seattle, WA.
Waverly Place B&B, Spokane, WA.
Larurel Point Inn, Victoria, B.C.
Sutton Place Hotel, Vancouver, B.C.
Wedgewood Hotel, Vancouver, B.C.

Best Chocolate Desserts

MOST BEAUTIFUL CHOCOLATE DESSERTS

La Provence Bakery and Bistro, Lake Oswego, OR.
Georgian Room/Garden Court, Four Seasons Hotel,
    Seattle, WA.
Camille's, Victoria, B.C.
Virazon, Seattle, WA.

BEST CAKES/TORTES

Best Basic Chocolate Cake
Zenon Chocolate Cake, Café Zenon, Eugene, OR.

Epitome, Sweet Baby Jane's (wholesale bakery
only), available at Café Paradiso, Bend, OR.
Black Out Cake, Gerry Frank's Konditorei, Salem, OR.
French Fudge Cake, Three Lions Bakery, Portland, OR.
Chocolate Buttermilk Cake, Ron Paul Charcuterie,
Portland, OR.

Best Specialty Cakes

Raspberry Rhapsody, Sweet Life Patisserie, Eugene, OR.
Double Chocolate Mousse Cake With Raspberry Puree,
3 Doors Down, Portland, OR.
Chocolate Mousse Cake, Legrand's, Grants Pass, OR.
Black Bear Pie (Grand Marnier Cake), Adam's Place,
Eugene, OR.
Truffle Cake, Hans, Bend, OR.
Chocolate Raspberry Cake, DiLusso Baking, Bend, OR.
Chocolate Pudding Cake, Sauci's, Vancouver, B.C.

Best German Chocolate Cake

Rose's Restaurant, Portland, OR.

Best Black Forest Cake

Teske's Germania Restaurant, Roseburg, OR.
Rose's Restaurant, Portland, OR.

Best Chocolate Soufflé/Warm Chocolate Cake

Warm Chocolate Torte, Campagne, Seattle, WA.
Warm Chocolate Soufflé, Bacchus Ristorante
(Wedgewood Hotel), Vancouver, B.C.
Triple Chocolate Cake, L'Auberge, Portland, OR.
Warm Chocolate Grappa Cake with Bittersweet and Milk
Chocolate Sauces, Flying Fish, Seattle, WA.
Cup of Heaven, Ron Paul Charcuterie, Portland, OR.
Gooey Flourless Chocolate Cake with Pecan Filling,
Kaspar's, Seattle, WA.

Best Chocolate Tortes

Chocolate Turtle Torte with Caramel Sauce,
Caprial's Bistro, Portland, OR.
Chocolate Truffle Torte, Primavera, Ashland, OR.
Chocolate Mousse Torte, Il Fiasco (made by Suzanne Leech
Specialty Baking), Bellingham, WA.
Espresso Torte, Fran's Chocolates, Seattle and
Bellevue, WA.
Chocolate Mousse Torte, Tosoni's, Bellevue, WA.
Chocolate Hazelnut Torte, Ship Bay Oyster House,
Eastsound, WA.

BEST TIRAMISU

Marco's Supperclub, Seattle, WA. (for Lush Life
Restaurant)
Deli de Pasta, Yakima, WA.
Pazzo Ristorante, Portland, OR.

BEST CHEESECAKES

Belgian White Chocolate Cheesecake, Gasperetti's,
Yakima, WA.
Caramel Crunch Chocolate Cheesecake, Sweet Cravings,
Spokane, WA.
Mocha Cheesecake, Pastazza, Bellingham, WA.
Wedgie (Frozen Cheesecake), Jim and Kerry's Original
Cheesecake Company, Anacortes, WA.
Chocolate Espresso Cheesecake, Cascade Dining Room,
Timberline Lodge, Timberline, OR.
Truffle Cheesecake with Shortbread Crust, Kaspar's,
Seattle, WA.

BEST SPECIALTY CHOCOLATE DESSERTS

Best Semifreddo
Pazzo Ristorante, Portland, OR.

Best Truffle Cup
Home Fires Bakery, Leavenworth, WA.

Best Chocolate Banana Strudel
Wildwood, Portland, OR.

Best Marjolaine
Zefiro, Portland, OR.
Papa Haydn, Portland, OR.

Best Chocolate Pate
Allegro Café, Vancouver, B.C.

Best Chocolate Ravioli
Ravioli de Banana, Bacchus Ristorante (Wedgewood
Hotel), Vancouver, B.C.

Best Chocolate Bombe
Chocolate Frenzy, Red Star Tavern and Roast House,
Portland, OR.
Chocolate Bombe, Three Lions Bakery, Portland, OR.

Best Chocolate Salami
Assagio, Portland, OR.

Best Chocolate Terrine
Triple Chocolate Terrine, Esplanade at Riverplace,
    Portland, OR.
Chocolate Raspberry Terrine, Papa Haydn, Portland, OR.
Chocolate Terrine (frozen), Rosette, Bend, OR.

BEST PUDDING/CUSTARD/MOUSSE
Best Pot de Creme
Green Gage Plum, West Richland, WA.
Marco's Supperclub, Seattle, WA.

Best Creme Brulee
Valhrona Creme Brulee, Diva at the Met, Vancouver, B.C.
White Chocolate Creme Brulee, Allegro Café,
    Vancouver, B.C.

Best Chocolate Mousse
Triple Mousse, Take the Cake, Spokane, WA.
Chocolate Mousse, La Provence, Lake Oswego, OR.
Chocolate Mousse, Le Crocodile, Vancouver, B.C.

Best White Chocolate Mousse
Grand Marnier Mousse Cups, Apple Cellar Bakery
    and Café, Ashland, OR.

BEST CHOCOLATE BREAD PUDDING
White Chocolate Bread Pudding with Bourbon Sauce,
    3 Doors Down, Portland, OR.
Triple Chocolate Croissant Pudding, Fleuri Restaurant
    (Sutton Place Hotel), Vancouver, B.C.

BEST PIES
Best Chocolate Cream Pie
Cottage Inn, Wenatchee, WA.

Best Tollhouse Pie
Europa, Spokane, WA.
Prospector Pies, Wenatchee, WA.

Best Chocolate Silk Pie
French Silk Pie, Olga Café, Olga, WA.
French Silk Pie, Plaza Café, Ashland, OR.
Chocolate Silk with Raspberry Sauce, Caprial's Bistro,
    Portland, OR.

Best Peanut Butter Pie
Peanut Butter Pie Brandon, Cascade Dining Room,
  Timberline Lodge, Timberline, OR.
Reese's Peanut Butter Pie, Allegro Café, Vancouver, B.C.

Best Chocolate Pecan Pie
The Sanctuary, Chinook, WA.

Best Mud Pie
Bella Union, Jacksonville, OR.

BEST CHOCOLATE/NUT TARTS
Aurora Tart, John Horan Steaks and Seafood, Wenatchee, WA.
Chocolate Nut Tart, Take the Cake, Spokane, WA.

BEST BROWNIES
Chocolate Hazelnut Brownie, Home Fires Bakery,
  Leavenworth, WA.
Cream Cheese Brownie, Grateful Bread Bakery,
  Pacific City, OR.
Peppermint Brownie with Vanilla Mint Ice Cream,
  Duck Soup Inn, Eastsound, WA.
Brownie with Ephemere Frosting, Dilettante Chocolates,
  Seattle, WA.
Flourless Brownie and Chocolate Pecan Turtle Brownie,
  Macrina Bakery, Seattle, WA.
Shortbread Chocolate Brownie, Anjou Bakery and Catering,
  Cashmere, WA.
Hot Pecan Brownie with Caramel Ice Cream, Paley's Place,
  Portland, OR.

BEST COOKIES
Fudgenutter Cookie, Home Fires Bakery,
  Leavenworth, WA.
Chocolate Smudge, Anjou Bakery and Catering,
  Cashmere, WA.
Florentines, Patisserie Daniel, Victoria, B.C.
Almond Squares, Patisserie Bordeaux, Vancouver, B.C.
Chocolate Glob Tea Cookie, Three Lions Bakery,
  Portland, OR.
Peanut Butter Fudge Bar, Three Lions Bakery,
  Portland, OR.
Mountain Bars, Louisa's Bakery and Café, Seattle, WA.
Black Angus Cookie, Ron Paul Charcuterie, Portland, OR.

BEST CHOCOLATE BREAD
Pain Chocolate, Anjou Bakery and Catering, Cashmere, WA.

BEST CHOCOLATE ECLAIR

Three Lions Bakery, Portland, OR.
Le Panier Bakery, Seattle, WA.

BEST CROISSANT

Pain au Chocolat (chocolate croissant), Le Panier Bakery,
Seattle, WA.
Chocolatine (chocolate-hazelnut cream croissant),
Le Panier Bakery, Seattle, WA.

BEST CHOCOLATE COFFEE CAKE

Chocolate Yogurt Coffee Cake, Delphina's Neighborhood
Baking Company, Portland, OR.

BEST ICE CREAM

Chocolate, Chocolate Peanut Butter, and Chocolate
Almond, Ferdinand's, WSU Creamery, Pullman, WA.
Chocolate and Chocolate Almond, Goody's Soda Fountain
and Candy Store, Bend, OR.
Bittersweet Nugget, Peanut Butter Cup, and Tortal
(chocolate and caramel), B.J.'s Homemade Ice Cream,
Florence, OR.

Best Handmade Premium Chocolate Ice Cream
Belgian Bittersweet Chocolate, Rhododendron Café,
Bow, WA.
Chocolate Ice Cream, Il Giardino di Umberto,
Vancouver, B.C.
Chocolate Raspberry, Mallard Ice Cream, Bellingham, WA.
Chocolate Cinnamon Ice Cream, William Tell Restaurant,
Vancouver, B.C.

Best Ice Cream Bars
Nutty Bars, Curly's Ice Cream, Salem, OR.

Best Italian Ice Cream (Gelato)
Choconut and Chocolate Peanut Butter, Mum's Gelati,
Vancouver, B.C.
Gianduja Gelato, Assagio, Portland, OR.

Best Sorbet
Chocolate Cinnamon Sorbet, Chartwell Restaurant
(Four Seasons Hotel), Vancouver, B.C.
Chocolate Sorbet, Mum's Gelati, Vancouver, B.C.

Best Frozen Custard
Cocoa Cream, SDK's, Portland, OR.

BEST CHOCOLATE MILKSHAKES

Ice-Burg Drive-In, Walla Walla, WA.
"Adult" (alcohol fortified) milkshakes, Dilettante
    Chocolates, Seattle, WA.
Sophie's Café, Vancouver, B.C.

BEST CHOCOLATE DRINKS

Cinnamon Roll Latte and Mondo Berry Ice Teaser,
    Moonstruck Chocolates, Portland, OR.
Any of the "fortified" chocolate drinks, Dilettante
    Chocolates, Seattle, WA.
Marco's Café and Espresso Bar, Portland, OR.

Chocolate Candy

BEST CHOCOLATIER (OVERALL)

Fran Bieglow, Fran's Chocolates, Seattle, WA.

BEST (MOST CREATIVE) USE OF LOCAL INGREDIENTS

Chocolate Art, Vancouver, B.C.
Fenton and Lee, Eugene, OR.

BEST TRUFFLES

Most Unusual Truffles
Raspberry Rhapsody Truffle, Chocolate Art,
    Vancouver, B.C.
Basil and Lemon Truffle, Chocolate Art, Vancouver, B.C.

Best Truffles (chocolate enrobed)
Euphoria Chocolate Company, Eugene, OR.
Ashland Fudge Company, Ashland, OR.
Fran's Chocolates, Seattle, WA.

Best Classic Truffles (cocoa dusted)
Chez Daniel, Victoria, B.C.

BEST EUROPEAN CHOCOLATES

(molded and filled)
Bernard Callebaut, Victoria and Vancouver.
Over the Moon Chocolate Company, Vancouver, B.C.
JiCava's Chocolates and Pastries, Portland, OR.

Most Beautiful Molded Chocolates
Over the Moon Chocolate Company (hand-painted),
    Vancouver, B.C.
Bernard Callebaut, Victoria, B.C. and elsewhere.
Native American Chocolate Masks, Chocolate Art,
    Vancouver, B.C.

BEST FUDGE

Cascade Candy Company, La Conner, WA.
Ashland Fudge Company, Ashland, OR.

BEST ROCKY ROAD

Phillips Candies of Seaside, Seaside, OR.
Oregon Candy Farm, Sandy, OR.

BEST PEANUT BUTTER CUP

Baum's, Richland, WA.

BEST SEA FOAM (honeycomb)

Sheri's Sweet Shop, Winthrop, WA.
Ashland Fudge Company, Ashland, OR.

BEST CHOCOLATE-COVERED CARAMELS

Fran's Chocolates, Seattle, WA.
Over the Moon Chocolate Company, Vancouver, B.C.
Candy Basket, Portland, OR.

BEST CHOCOLATE-COVERED CHERRIES

Cookies and Cream, Redmond, OR.
Cherribon™, Van Duyn Chocolates, Portland, OR.

BEST CHOCOLATE-COVERED TOFFEE

Baum's, Richland, WA.

BEST CHOCOLATE-FILLED FIGS

Fran's Chocolates, Seattle, WA.

BEST PEANUT BUTTER-CHOCOLATE COMBO

Frans's Fixations Peanut Butter, Fran's Chocolates, Seattle, WA.

Peanut Butter No Jell, Milton York, Long Beach, WA.

BEST GINGER/CHOCOLATE COMBO

Ginger Tea Wafers, Fenton and Lee Chocolatiers, Eugene, OR.

Fran's Chocolates, Seattle, WA.

BEST HEDGEHOGS

(hedgehog-shaped chocolates filled with hazelnut cream)

Purdy's Chocolates, Vancouver, B.C.

BEST TURTLE-TYPE CHOCOLATE

(chocolate, caramel, nuts)

Vandango's™, Van Duyn Chocolates, Portland, OR.

BEST SUGAR-FREE CHOCOLATES

Van Duyn Chocolates, Portland, OR.

TOLLHOUSE COOKIE PIE

Prospector Pies
Wenatchee, Washington

2 eggs
1 cup butter or margarine, melted
$^1/_2$ cup granulated sugar
$^1/_2$ cup firmly packed brown sugar
$^1/_2$ cup all-purpose flour
1 cup semi-sweet chocolate chips
1 cup chopped walnuts
1 unbaked 9-inch pie shell

Preheat over to 350 degrees.

In a large bowl, beat eggs with an electric mixer until they are light and frothy. Add the margarine and mix well. Beat in the white and brown sugar. Stir in the flour.

This is a delicious, easy-as-pie recipe. It's best served slightly warm with a scoop of vanilla ice cream. For a short-cut, use a ready-made pie shell.

Add the chocolate chips and walnuts and stir by hand to combine. Pour into the unbaked pie shell and bake uncovered for 25 minutes. Cover with an inverted pie tin and continue baking for another 25-30 minutes. The pie should be set in the center. Serve warm with vanilla ice cream, if desired.

From *The Chocolate Lover's Guide Cookbook,*
Pacific Northwest Edition.

Seattle and Surrounding Communities

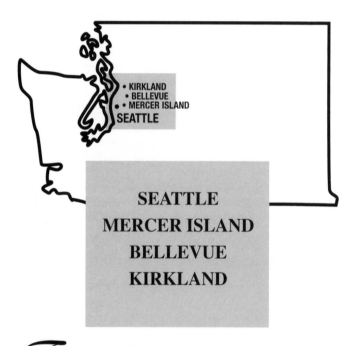

• KIRKLAND
• BELLEVUE
• • MERCER ISLAND
SEATTLE

SEATTLE

MERCER ISLAND

BELLEVUE

KIRKLAND

The City by the Bay, the Emerald City, Home of the Seahawks. None of these names does justice to Seattle's well-deserved culinary reputation. It's a city filled with young, innovative chefs doing incredible things with food and with chocolate.

Great Things to Do

• **Hoop It Up. Seattle Supersonics, Seattle, WA.** (206) 283-3865. For sports fans, a perfect day in the City includes an NBA basketball game with the Seattle Supersonics.

• **Take Me Out to the Ballgame. Seattle Mariners. Seattle, WA.** (206) 622-HITS. Seattle also boasts a national baseball tam. For exciting baseball and mediocre hot dogs, this is the way to go. You can even go on a back stage **Kingdome Tour.** The 1-hour tour takes you into the locker room, press box, playing field, executive suites, and sports museum. For more information, call (206) 296-3128.

• **Go Underground. Underground Tour**, Doc Maynard's, 610 1st Avenue, **Seattle, WA.** (206) 682-4646. Some parts of old Seattle were built an entire story lower than present day shops. You can take a lighthearted look at Seattle's underground history with an Underground Tour.

• **Meet at the Market. Pike Place Market,** Pike Street between Virginia and Union Streets, **Seattle, WA.** Eclectic Pike Place Market with its colorful fish vendors, fresh produce, live music and restaurants may be the #1 tourist attraction in Seattle. It's also where locals in the know go for exceptionally fresh fish, produce, flowers, and other staples. The market is open Monday-Saturday 9-6; Sunday 11-5.

• **Take Wing.** One of the more unique and exciting ways to see Seattle is by seaplane. Fly off the water on Lake Union and take a tour of the city. Or fly over to Victoria or the San Juan Islands. **Kenmore Air Seaplanes,** 950 Westlake Avenue, (206) 486-1257/ (800) 543-9595. **Seattle Seaplanes**, 1325 Fairview Avenue E, (206) 329-9638. If helicopters are more your style, try a heli-tour. **Classic Helicopters** (206) 767-0515.

• **Expand Your Artistic Appreciation. Seattle Art Museum,** 100 University Street, **Seattle, WA.** (206) 654-3100. Internationally recognized for its collections of Asian, African, Native American and modern art, Seattle Art Museum is a must-see for art fans. Recently renovated, the Frye is another stop art lovers shouldn't miss. **Frye Art Museum**, 704 Terry Avenue, **Seattle, WA.** (206) 622-9250.

• **Check Out the Space Needle, Seattle, WA.** (206) 684-8582. Home of the 1962 World's Air, the Seattle Center is famous for the now-classic Space Needle and the mono-rail. The Center also houses the Children's Museum, Pacific Science Center, Opera House, and various theaters.

• **Fly Back in Time. Museum of Flight**, 9404 E Marginal Way S, **Seattle, WA.** (206) 764-5720. If airplanes are your thing, you'll love the more than 50 historic planes on display at the Museum of Flight, including America's first presidential jet.

Terrific Places to Stay

Inn at the Market, 86 Pine Street, **Seattle, WA.** (206)443-3600/
(800)446-4484. If you want to be right in the middle of the excitement of Pike Street and its wonderful market, restaurants, and shops,
Inn at the Market is where to stay. Perched on a hill overlooking
Elliot Bay and Pike Place Market's gaily-colored fish, flower, and
fruit stands, the Inn at the Market is one of Seattle's most sophisticated urban hotels. Leave your car out front for the valet to park.
Walk through a bricked courtyard into the hotel's lobby with its
fireplace and conversation area and you'll be greeted by the friendly,
attentive staff. The personalized service and warm decor have the
feel of a country inn. The rooms are spacious and airy, with large
windows that open to the bay's breezes. Rooms come with televisions, phones, and coffeemakers. Some rooms have kitchenettes.
On the fifth floor, there's a roof-top deck with comfortable chairs
and a spectacular view of the bay and the Olympic Mountains.

Four Seasons Olympic Hotel, 411 University St., **Seattle, WA**.
(206) 621-1700. If you want elegance in Seattle, the Four Seasons
Olympic is an excellent choice. Step into the grand 1924 Italian
Renaissance lobby and you're transported back to a time of opulent, unhurried relaxation, and excellence in service. The hotel's
motto is "defining service" and they do. As a guest, you can have
your bags carried, car parked, washed and detailed, clothes dry
cleaned and/or mended, shoes shined, children watched, and body
massaged. The 450 rooms are decorated in soft pink and rose with
nicesities like hair dryers, fluffy robes, two-line phones, and lovely
toiletries. The health club features an indoor swimming pool, spa,
aerobic, and weight lifting equipment. The hotel features 2 restaurants, the Georgian Room for fine dining, and the plant-filled Garden Court for tea and lighter fare (see review).

The Edgewater Inn, Pier 67, 2411 Alaskan Way, **Seattle, WA**.
(206) 728-7000/(800) 624-0670. A waterside room at the
Edgewater, Seattle's only waterfront hotel, feels like you're sleep-
ing on a boat—without the rocking. You can watch waterbirds,
seals, ferryboats and pleasure and commercial boats right from
your room. With such a location, you'd expect a nautical theme.
But owners of the inn have chosen a rustic lodge decor. The lobby
area features open-beamed ceilings, floor-to-ceiling windows, antler
chandeliers and occasional tables, and a large, river rock fireplace
around which are overstuffed chairs and couches in Native American prints. Guests use this inviting area for enjoying conversation,
drinks, and light snacks. The guest rooms are spacious with peeled
log furniture, crimson carpeting in Native American designs, fluffy
quilts, in-room coffee makers, and hair dryers. There's a casual

restaurant and meeting rooms on-site. The exercise room is minimal, but guests can use a full-service gym nearby for a small fee.

Gaslight Inn, 1727 15th Avenue, **Seattle, WA**. (206) 325-3654. If you're tired of the fussiness of many bed and breakfast inns, you'll enjoy the Gaslight Inn. Veteran innkeepers, Trevor, John, and Steve, provide guests with the information they need and then leave them to enjoy the museum-quality 1906 Arts and Crafts home with its excellent Stickley furniture and collections of decorative glass and Native American artifacts. With plenty of original wood and walls painted in deep, rich colors, Gaslight has a masculine feel that is comfortable. The 9 rooms, half with private baths and some with city views and private decks, all have big quilts and color televisions. One of the best rooms features a gas fireplace. In the morning, guests help themselves to a continental breakfast. *Traveler's note: Allergy sufferers—dogs and cats live on the premises.*

The Sorrento Hotel, 900 Madison Street, **Seattle, WA**. (206) 622-6400. Designed in 1908 in the tradition of an Italian villa, The Sorrento Hotel, with its circular palm-lined driveway, mission style towers, and Italian fountain, greets visitors with Old World charm and hospitality. The Honduras mahogany-paneled Fireside Room's flickering fire and comfortable chairs, couches, and small tables invite guests to enjoy a light meal or afternoon tea. All 76 guest rooms and suites have the charm of elegant private residences and come richly-appointed with European-style furnishings. They feature mini-bars, robes, hair dryers, voice mail, fax, and dataports. The competent and willing staff offer extras like a complimentary town car, daily newspaper, and turn down service that includes a warm hot water bottle on chilly evenings. The 24-hour fitness room is adequate with a treadmill, stepper, and a recumbent bike and free weights. Guests may use a nearby full-service gym for a minimal fee. Breakfast, lunch, and dinner are served at the hotel's elegant Hunt Club restaurant (see review).

Hotel Vintage Park, 1100 5th Avenue, **Seattle, WA**. (800) 624-4433/(206) 624-8000. Situated right in the heart of Seattle's busy downtown district, Hotel Vintage Park is the consummate urban hotel. The small lobby, where guests are served complimentary wine each night, invites with comfortable chairs, couches, and a crackling fireplace. All 126 guest rooms and suites are decorated in rich fabrics and cherry wood furniture and feature hair dryers, bathrobes, private honor bars, 24-hour room service, voice mail and dataports, and complimentary morning newspaper and coffee service. Staff accommodate with valet parking, same-day valet service, and evening turn down. Guests can dine at the hotel's bustling Tulio Restaurant (see review).

Bellevue Club Hotel, 11200 SE 6th Street, **Bellevue, WA**. (425) 454-4424. If you're a sports or fitness fan, the Bellevue Club Hotel is the place to stay in the Puget Sound area. It offers an Olympic-size indoor pool, racquetball and tennis courts, a full gymnasium with an indoor running track, 2 workout studios with the latest aerobic and weight training equipment, daily aerobics programs, sauna, steamroom, and suntanning, as well as professional trainers and massage therapists on staff. If you want a bit more pampering, they offer full-body spa treatments. The Bellevue Club is also a first-class luxury hotel. The hotel's exterior resembles a contemporary Italian villa with a lovely portico and circular driveway, but the interior decor has contemporary Asian influences. Throughout are interesting art pieces like art-glass sconces and ceramicware. Many of the guest rooms, some with decks or patios, have large, floor-to-ceiling doors to let in the breezes and all feature individually-controlled heating and cooling systems, in-room honor bars, large marble-tiled bathrooms with soaking tubs and glass showers, 3 telephones with voice mail and modem hook-up, in-room fax machines, turn down service, and 24-hour room service. Hair dryers, luxury toiletries, fluffy robes, and over-sized bath towels are included. For those who can't stay away from the fitness routine, there's a set of dumbells and an exercise chart in each room. Fine dining is offered in the hotel's Polaris Restaurant or in the Sport Café.

Restaurants

Campagne

86 Pine Street, Seattle, WA. (206) 728-2800

♥♥♥♥ Enter **Campagne** through the inner courtyard and you'll feel like you've discovered a culinary secret. The wall sconces and candles on the cloth-covered tables contribute to the soft lighting and intimate feel of this French restaurant. Dinner entrees include bass grilled and simmered in a lobster, fennel and tarragon broth, rabbit braised with apple cider, bacon and pearl onions, grilled beef tenderloin, and rack of lamb with mustard and fennel crust, among others. For chocolate lovers, they offer their **Warm Chocolate Torte**, a 4-inch, round chocolate soufflé that's dusted with powered sugar and served warm with cinnamon ice cream and 2 triangles of chocolate. It's beautifully garnished with pear and dried fruit compote, creme anglaise, caramel, and chocolate sauce. This wonderful chocolate dessert is like biting into warm, liquid chocolate. The outside of the torte is soft with a slight crispness; the inside rich and gooey. The cinnamon ice cream—refreshing and slightly spicy—is the perfect compliment. Order this one, chocolate fans.

Getting there: Between Stewart and Pine on Post Alley.

Etta's Seafood

2020 Western Avenue, Seattle, WA. (206) 443-6000

♥♥♥♥ **Etta's Seafood's** eclectic decor is retro 50's—fanciful metal railings, skinny tables and chairs, booths in green naugahyde, dark blue ceilings, crimson walls, an oyster bar with a stainless steel bar back, a long wine bar, and large windows overlooking the bay and busy Western Avenue. They serve brunch, lunch, and dinner. Their lunch and dinner selections are heavy on fresh fish such as their signature crab cakes and spice-rubbed pit roasted salmon, broiled sea scallops, sturgeon, and ling cod as well as non-fish selections like pumpkin ravioli. For dessert, try their elegant **Bittersweet Chocolate Fondue with Seasonal Fruits**. The dark chocolate fondue comes in an individual stainless steel fondue cup with warmer, surrounded by a generous selection of fruits like bananas, pears, kiwis, and pineapple. The fondue spreads cleanly over the tongue leaving a deep, rich chocolatey flavor that lingers.

If you're more of a traditionalist, you can dig into their **Old Fashioned Chocolate Cake**, 4 layers of dark chocolate cake filled and frosted with dark chocolate buttercream. It's a solidly good cake with a moist, creamy buttercream.

Or try their **Warm Chocolate Chip Cookies with Cold Milk**. The 2-inch cookies are intensely rich and packed with chips. They're the kind you *wished* your grandmother made.

Getting there: *Just north of Pike Place Market.*

Flying Fish

2234 First Ave, Seattle, WA. (206) 728-8595

♥♥♥♥ **Flying Fish** is one of those totally hip, urban restaurants with big windows offering views of the Sound, tall ceilings, a cement floor, black naugahyde and fabric booths, persimmon, green, and yellow walls, 50's retro ceiling lamps, black and white photos, and a long, blond bar with nice wide seats. Dinner offerings include small plates like Thai crab cake and crispy calamari; large plates like wok-blackened albacore, grilled sturgeon, Thai curry scallops, and buttermilk fried chicken; and platters (meant to be shared) like whole snapper, mussels, and oysters. Their signature chocolate dessert is **Warm Chocolate Grappa Cake**, a 4-inch round cake that's 3 inches high, served warm on a large plate with a scoop of vanilla bean ice cream and a thin tuile cookie on a pool of swirled milk and bittersweet chocolate sauces. It's rich and thick, almost fudgy. With its crusty top and incredibly rich, gooey center, this is what a warm chocolate cake should be. The vanilla ice cream adds a nice lightness and the chocolate sauces are lusciously rich. The tuile cookie is crisp and cinnamony.

Getting there: *First Avenue at Bell.*

Georgian Room/Garden Court (Four Seasons Olympic Hotel)
411 University Street, Seattle, WA. (206) 621-1700
♥♥♥♥ You can't beat the elegant ambiance of the **Georgian Room** at the Four Seasons Olympic Hotel. Antique crystal chandeliers hang from 20 foot ceilings, casting a warm glow over linen-covered tables. White-coated waiters stand at the ready. The dinner menu includes entrees such as smoked salmon with apples and brandy sauce, veal tenderloin with morel mushrooms, duck with figs, rack of lamb, and spiced pheasant. The **Garden Room** with its lush tropical plants, burbling fountain, and large windows, is a pleasant retreat for lunch, light dinner, or afternoon tea. Offerings include linguine, fried chicken, and ginger grilled salmon, and sandwiches such as tomato, mozzarella, avocado and basil.

Whether you eat in the Georgian Room or the Garden Court, you can enjoy Pastry Chef Michel Lassaison's exquisite **chocolate desserts**. Chef Micheal is truly an artist—his highly architectural desserts are almost too beautiful to eat. Go ahead because they're delicious. His **Grand Marinier Parfait** is a frozen white chocolate mousse with nougat that's wrapped in a white chocolate cylinder, topped with candied red and yellow ginger, and served on a bed of poached plums and plum sauce. It's garnished with elegant threads of spun sugar and chocolate leaves. The mousse is light and refreshing. The ginger adds an interesting bite and the plum sauce has just the right tart/sweetness.

Valrhona Chocolate Cake is a chocolate mousse with nougat and 2 layers of chocolate sponge cake soaked in rum syrup that's surrounded by a ring of white chocolate. It's topped with slices of caramelized banana and tiny chocolate-covered bananas. It's decorated with a triangle of chocolate, dramatic spirals of spun sugar, tiny banana tuile shaped like miniature sputniks, and small pools of homemade caramel spiced with cinnamon and nutmeg. The mousse is incredibly light and creamy with a slight crunchiness. The caramelized bananas are wonderfully sweet and the caramel sauce is rich and buttery.

The **Double Chocolate Pate** is alternating plugs of dark and milk chocolate pate, separated by dark chocolate disks trimmed with pistachios. They resemble a stack of beautiful gaucho hats. It's served on an over-sized plate with whole huckleberries and huckleberry sauce. The mousses are light-as-air. The chocolate disks are rich with a good bite and the huckleberry sauce adds a tartness that contrasts nicely with the sweet mousses.
Getting there: On University at 4th.

Kaspar's
19 W Harrison Street, Seattle, WA. (206) 298-0123
♥♥♥♥ Low-slung ceilings, a lattice-covered solarium, large

windows, beige shades, tables covered with green and white table-cloths and fresh flowers, hardwood floors and green potted plants all contribute to **Kaspar's** light, almost tropical ambiance. About half the dinner menu changes nightly. Menu standards include dishes like beef tenderloin with café de Paris butter, Muscovy duck breast, rabbit jambalaya, and lamb shank. Nightly specials can include entrees like lamb chops, sautéed scallops with 2 sauces, wild Alaskan salmon with citrus sauce, and halibut in crispy potato crust. Kaspar's desserts change regularly, but he assures chocolate lovers that they can always find a chocolate item like his **Chocolate Truffle Cheesecake**. This slim wedge starts with a shortbread crust that's topped with 2 inches of chocolate cheesecake, garnished with big pieces of white and dark chocolate, a squiggle of raspberry sauce, and a dusting of powered sugar. The result is a lovely blending of cheese and chocolate flavors. The shortbread crust adds a sweet cookie quality to this classic cheesecake and the raspberry puree provides a nice sweet-tart accent.

Kaspar's **Flourless Chocolate Cake with Pecan Filling** is a wedge of 3 layers of dense chocolate cake filled with gooey chocolate and chopped pecans. It's topped with shaved chocolate, dusted with cocoa and powered sugar, and garnished with a strawberry fan. This decadent cake is incredibly rich, moist, and gooey. The pecans add a satisfying crunch. This is great gooey chocolate cake!

The **White Chocolate Espresso Mousse in an Almond Basket** comes with dark chocolate drizzles and slices of fresh pears. The mousse is like pillows of cream with a subtle espresso flavor. The almond basket is thin, lacy, and buttery with a crisp sweetness. This is a wonderful dessert!
Getting there: Near Key Arena on Harrison.

Marco's Supperclub
2510 1st Avenue, Seattle, WA. (206) 441-7801
♥♥♥♥ **Marco's Supperclub's** concrete floors, paint-distressed wooden tables with bottles of rosemary-flavored olive oil, rose and peach-colored walls, and long bar with open shelves of wine bottles all contribute to the casual, funky atmosphere. They serve both lunch and dinner, with dinner entrees like pan-seared duck breast, portobello mushroom steak, Jamaican jerk chicken, tuna with Thai-ginger-carrot sauce, and lamb shank rubbed with garam masala. Desserts, which change regularly, always include a luscious chocolate offering like Chef Donna Moodie's **Pot de Creme**, served in a large coffee cup with whipped cream and chocolate sprinkled on top. It's thick with the consistency of a truffle center rather than a pudding and has a heavenly, rich chocolate flavor. It's one of the best we've tasted. The Pot de Creme is served with a scattering of their delightful cookies—chocolate pepper, chocolate striped peanut butter, and chocolate-dipped macaroon.

Marco's **Chocolate Torte**, is an impressive 5 inches tall with 2 layers of medium-texture cake frosted and filled with grappa-flavored ganache that's thick and rich with a deep chocolate flavor. It's served with lavender vanilla ice cream that's both slightly spicy and lightly flowery. It adds a nice lightness to the intensely chocolate dessert.

Sorry Fido. Chocolate can kill dogs. Theobromine in chocolate stimulates the heart and nervous system, which can be too much for dogs, especially small ones. Baking chocolate, which contains 10 times the theobromine as milk chocolate, is the most deadly.

At Marco's, they also make the desserts for their other restaurant, **Lush Life** (2331 2nd Avenue, (206) 441-9842), where you can enjoy an excellent **Tiramisu**. It's a 4-inch square of layered espresso-soaked lady fingers, flavored with Meyers dark rum, and mascarpone with plenty of shaved chocolate on top. This Italian classic is a difficult dessert to make and Chef Donna does a masterful job of it. The ladyfingers have just the right espresso-rum richness and mascarpone has a light sweetness. The shaved chocolate adds a lovely chocolate interpretation. *Getting there: On 1st at Wall Street.*

Tulio (Hotel Vintage Park)
1100 5th Avenue, Seattle, WA. (206) 624-5500
♥♥♥♥ Seattle continues its tradition of good hotel restaurants with Hotel Vintage Park's **Tulio**, a bustling, boisterous Italian trattoria. Tulio has plenty of dark wood, upholstered booths and small cloth-covered tables with cane-backed chairs, large amber ceiling lights, and an open kitchen with a wood-fired brick oven and a half dozen chefs. The food is contemporary Northern Italian, offering dishes at lunch and dinner like smoked salmon ravioli, linguine with mussels, wood-roasted salmon, pepper-crusted pork loin, and risotto with sea scallops, leeks, orange zest, and saffron butter. Chocolate lovers can look forward to pastry chef Patric Gabre-Kidan's creations like **Semifreddo alla Nicciole**, and airy, half-frozen triangle of milk chocolate, chopped hazelnuts, and dried cherries that's served with vanilla creme anglaise. This semifreddo is smooth with a light milk chocolate flavor. The cherries add an interesting tart contrast and chewiness and the vanilla sauce is delicate. It's a most refreshing chocolate dessert.

The **Torte di Ciccolata di Capri** is Tulio's version of a flourless bittersweet chocolate cake. It's flavored with a touch of espresso and served with walnut sauce. Now this is intense chocolate, chocolate lovers! The cake is thick and rich, with a slightly crumbly, fudgy texture that melts instantly on the tongue. The espresso gives this cake a lovely depth. The walnut sauce, an excellent combination with the cake, has a rich, nutty flavor.

The **Tiramisu de Firenze** is a Florence-style tiramisu with layers of rum- and espresso-soaked sponge cake and mascarpone cream that's topped with shaved chocolate and served with espresso sauce. The sponge cake is ultra-soft with a rum flavor that comes through with authority. The mascarpone adds a light touch and the espresso sauce offers a deep espresso flavor without overpowering. This is a wonderful interpretation of a classic Italian dessert.
Getting there: *Fifth at Spring.*

Canlis
2576 Aurora N, Seattle, WA. (206) 283-3313.
♥♥♥ **Canlis** has been tempting Seattle diners with stunning views of Lake Union and the Cascades and impeccably fresh Northwest cuisine for nearly 50 years. The decor is contemporary with a Japanese flair—natural rock columns, copper kitchen hood and entry, cloth-covered tables with tiny steel lamps and rock flower vases, Japanese-style wall sconces and planters with simple, yet elegant arrangements. Even the waitstaff, most of whom are Japanese, dress in black kimono-style pant suits. Open for dinner, entrees include a large selection of fish such as Alaskan halibut, crab cakes, sole, ahi, scallops, prawns, and wild Pacific Salmon with apples and apple cider butter. They also offer steaks, lamb, pasta, and chicken.

For dessert, dive into their **Lava Cake**, a 4-inch round dome of dark chocolate cake that's served warm with a large rosette of whipped cream, a dark chocolate flower design, and a strawberry fan. This rich cake is soft with a slightly crunchy outside; gooey chocolate goodness on the inside. It's comfort food for chocolate lovers.

They also offer **Chocolate Truffle Cake**, a 4-inch square of 3 layers of Belgian chocolate truffle that's topped with shaved chocolate and powered sugar, garnished with whipped cream, a strawberry fan, and fresh raspberries. It's thick and fudgy, a bit stiff for this reviewer's taste. The shaved chocolate gives a nice textural contrast.
Getting there: *On Aurora (99) at Halladay.*

Dahlia Lounge
1904 4ᵗʰ Avenue, Seattle, WA. (206) 682-4142
♥♥♥ You can't miss **Dahlia's** neon chef with the wagging fish out front. Inside, the fun continues with deep pink walls with faux green columns, floral upholstered booths, big paper fish lamps, a neon café sign, and 2 floor-to-ceiling mirrors that reflect all of the

arty ambiance back on itself. The menu, which changes every 2 months, features lunch and dinner dishes like Moroccan stew, black bean tamales, crab cakes, salmon, guinea hen, and rib eye. For dessert, they offer **Oaxacan Chocolate Pot de Creme**. It's served in an espresso cup topped with whipped cream and dusted with Mexican chocolate. It's rich and creamy just like pot de creme should be. The Mexican chocolate on top adds a slight crunch that's most pleasant.

Getting there: Between Stewart and Virginia.

Fullers (Sheraton Hotel)
1400 6th Avenue, Seattle, WA. (206) 447-5544
♥♥♥ The ambiance at **Fullers** is understated elegance—subtle peach-colored walls, intimate upholstered booths, cloth-covered tables, a fountain with abstract metal sculptures burbling softly. The menu, which changes every 2 months or so, includes entrees like grilled wild Alaskan salmon, roasted breast of pheasant, rack of lamb, and Maine sea scallops. Their signature chocolate dessert is the **Chocolate Mocha Bombe**, a 4-inch, round, flourless chocolate cake filled with chocolate mocha custard served warm with chocolate espresso sauce and java ice cream and almond brittle tuiles. This excellent dessert is rich and gooey—a chocolate lover's delight. The java ice cream with its flecks of espresso beans and the crunchy, buttery almond brittle offer a lovely cold and crunchy contrast to the warm cake. The Chocolate Mocha Bombe is also served cold in the hotel's more casual Pike Street Café, but loses its gooey warmth.

Getting there: Between Pike and Union.

Il Terrazo Carmine
411 1st Avenue S, Seattle, WA. (206) 467-7797
♥♥♥ **Il Terrazo Carmine** has long enjoyed rave reviews from Seattleites who enjoy good food. The rustic red tiles, cloth-covered tables, plants, floral drapes and large windows overlooking an inner courtyard with a waterfall all contribute to the restaurant's light, airy elegance. They serve lunch and dinner with a menu that changes twice a year. For dinner, they offer a large selection of pasta dishes like spaghetti with prawns, mussels, and clams, and fettuccine with smoked salmon, mushrooms, peas, and cream. Non-pasta selections include veal with garlic and scallions, tenderloin with wine and pancetta sauce, venison with junipers, and pork loin with mustard and gorgonzola.

Executive chef Tim Clacy says their desserts change daily, but you'll always find something chocolate and delicious like their **Chocolate Decadence Cake**, a flourless chocolate cake served with raspberry sauce and garnished with whipped cream, fresh raspberries, a mint sprig, and a dusting of powered sugar. It's chocolate heaven—

rich without being overpowering. The cake melts instantly in the mouth, while the chocolate flavor lingers. The tart raspberry sauce adds the right compliment.

Getting there: At the south end of Pioneer Square.

Palace Kitchen

2030 5th Avenue, Seattle, WA. (206) 448-2001

♥♥♥ The neon sign out front announces you're in for something different at **Palace Kitchen**. It's funky and cavernous with high, cranberry-colored ceilings, yellow walls, and a U-shaped bar with wild chandeliers of colorful grapes, apples and other glass ornaments. The over-sized duct work and well-used pots hanging over the open kitchen contribute to an industrial feeling. They serve dinner with selections like lamb mixed grill, maple-cured pork loin, ravioli with pork and chard, and Alaskan halibut, plus daily specials like North Carolina ribs. Their dessert menu, which changes regularly, always features a chocolate item like **Velvet Elvis**, a semi-frozen chocolate peanut pyramid served with banana milkshake sauce and peanut brittle. The bottom of the small pyramid is a 1/2-inch layer of peanut mousse that's light and creamy with a great peanut butter flavor. It's topped with a thick, stiff mousse with a milky chocolate flavor. The sauce tastes exactly like a chocolate banana milkshake.

Getting there: Fifth Aveune at Lenora.

Rover's

2808 Madison E, Seattle, WA. (206) 325-7442

♥♥♥ In a converted house, chef Thierry Rautureau and his **Rover's** restaurant has been wowing Seattlites with gourmet pre-fixe meals for the past 10 years. The *Gourmet Magazine's* Reader's Poll recently voted this restaurant Seattle's best. In several small rooms with pale yellow walls decorated with contemporary paintings of French scenes, diners are served at cloth-covered tables with flickering glass table lamps and single fresh roses. The pre-fixe menu changes regularly and may include dishes like smoked salmon with white Spanish anchovies and Yellow Finn potatoes, Alaskan spot prawns, Alaskan halibut, guinea fowl, pinot noir sorbet, and a dessert sampler. They also offer a vegetarian menu, and a grand menu, which offers even more dishes.

The dessert sampler (or what they call the "symphony of desserts") always includes at least 2 chocolate items, like the **Fallen Chocolate Soufflé**. It's a 31/2 inch individual dark chocolate cake that's served with house-preserved bing cherries and chocolate sauce with tiny creme anglaise hearts swirled in it. Served slightly warm, this soufflé has crispy edges and a fudgy, soft center. The chocolate sauce is ultra rich—some of the best we've tasted—and the cherries add a fresh, deep fruit flavor.

Getting there: On Madison at 28th.

Serafina

2043 Eastlake Avenue E, Seattle, WA. (206) 323-0807

♥♥♥ **Serafina's** is a casual neighborhood Italian place with faux-painted walls in warm rust tones and mural, a blue-green ceiling with skylights that let in plenty of sun, live plants, cloth-covered tables, and open wooden cases of wine stacked along the walls. They serve lunch and dinner with uncommon pasta dishes like rabbit, vegetables, and kalamata olives in cabernet over tagliatelle, bowtie pasta with wild mushrooms, truffle oil, winter greens, and Pecorino cheese, and salmon linguine with leeks and sun-dried tomatoes. Other entrees include lamb chops with porcini mushroom sauce, eggplant with ricotta, and filet mignon with gorgonzola. Their nod to chocolate is their **Mousse de Ciccolata** (chocolate mousse). It comes served in a tall sundae glass topped with commercial whipped cream and shaved chocolate. They call this a chunky mousse and they're right. It's hearty, not airy, and stiffer than most with a creamy texture and satisfyingly deep flavor.

Getting there: On Eastlake at E Boston Street.

The Hunt Club (Sorrento Hotel)

900 Madison, Seattle, WA. (206) 343-6156

♥♥♥ With lots of exposed brick, dark wood, small dining rooms, candle-style sconces and chandeliers, crimson and gold carpeting, crimson upholstered chairs, and cloth-covered tables, **The Hunt Club** has an elegant, clubby feel. Their menu, which changes seasonally, includes entrees like Atlantic salmon, roasted pheasant breast, Chilean sea bass, tiger prawns, rosemary chicken, and N.Y steaks. For dessert, there's the **Soft-centered Chocolate Torte**, a pyramid of dark chocolate cake, drizzled with chocolate sauce, served on a bed of raspberry coulis, with a tiny scoop of creme fraiche sorbet on a chocolate chip cookie. It's garnished with curls of tuile and mint leaves. Served slightly warm, it's an intensely chocolatey, soft cake that melts in the mouth. The raspberry coulis, a bit tart by itself, tastes great with the chocolate cake. The sorbet is light and cool with the warm cake.

If you can't decide, opt for the **Chocolate Sampler**, a selection of chocolate items like a **Chocolate Creme Brulee, Chocolate Chunk Cookies**, and **White and Dark Chocolate Truffles**. The Brulee, which is served in a small espresso cup, comes with a crispy, lacy top crust and the custard is ultra-creamy with a light chocolate flavor. The Chocolate Chunk Cookies have just the right crispy/softness with big hunks of chocolate. The Fudge Cookie is thick and fudgy with plenty of chips. The White Chocolate Truffles are white ganache centers rolled in crunchy, toasted coconut. They're a nice variation on a classic. The Dark Chocolate Truffle, which has a dark chocolate center rolled in crushed dark chocolate, is soft and melts easily in the mouth.

Getting there: Off Madison on First Hill at Terry.

The Painted Table (Alexis Hotel)
92 Madison Street, Seattle, WA. (206) 624-3646
♥♥♥ **The Painted Table** at the Alexis Hotel is famous for the over-sized plates hand-painted by local artists that grace the cloth-covered tables. The 2-level restaurant has a casually elegant feel with its marbled walls with original paintings and large windows. They serve lunch and dinner with the lunch menu featuring dishes like wild mushroom risotto, barbecue pork sandwich, and Thai beef salad. At dinner, the colorful menu offers entrees like duck with huckleberries, sea bass with herbs, morel crusted salmon, and saffron linguine with shellfish.

For dessert, try the Painted Table's signature chocolate dessert, **Valrhona Chocolate Framboise-flavored Truffle Torte**. The 4-inch square starts with a thin layer of vanilla bean shortbread, then alternating layers of Valrhona chocolate soufflé and vanilla buttercream, topped with fresh raspberries, and a lid of Valrhona chocolate. It's served on a bed of orange anglaise and raspberry coulis. This dessert is wonderfully rich without being heavy. The shortbread crust adds a crunchy lightness and the chocolate soufflé has a dark, sweet chocolate flavor. The buttercream, which is less sweet, compliments the chocolate. This is a successful dessert that invites one more bite.
Getting there: *Madison at 1ˢᵗ.*

Andaluca (Mayflower Park Hotel)
407 Olive Avenue, Seattle, WA. (206) 382-6999
♥♥ With its high-backed, upholstered booths, black ceiling, and hand-painted walls in muted shades of blue, green, orange, and red, **Andaluca** has a warm, clubby feel. They serve breakfast, lunch, and dinner, including dishes like shellfish stew, spice crusted sturgeon, pumpkin ravioli, and lamb in vine leaves. Their signature chocolate dessert is **Warm Liquid Chocolate Cake**, a round soufflé cake with a milk chocolate mousse-filled pastry cone (almond tuile) in the center. It's dusted with powered sugar and served warm on a bed of caramel sauce with chocolate and almond shavings. The outside of the soufflé is soft and cake-like; the inside pure liquid chocolate that melts in the mouth. The soufflé is satisfying and doesn't need the crunchy almond pastry cone, which doesn't add to the presentation and is a bit too sweet. The caramel sauce adds a buttery richness.
Getting there: *Corner of Olive and 4ᵗʰ.*

Place Pigalle
81 Pike Street, Seattle, WA. (206) 624-1756
♥♥ **Place Pigalle** is a casual bistro with its black and white checked floor, wood tables and chairs, ceiling fans, and large, original paintings. At dinnertime, it dresses up with linen tablecloths and candles. Perched on a hillside overlooking the sound, window tables have excellent views. The seasonal lunch and dinner menus, which

change 3 times a year, feature dishes like scallop salad with ginger ponzu, steamed mussels, braised halibut with oyster mushrooms, bok choy, and daikon in fish broth, rabbit with roasted eggplant, red pepper, spinach and feta, and pork loin with mole sauce. For dessert, chocolate lovers will enjoy their **Chocolate Pot de Creme**, which comes in a large ramekin topped with a dollop of whipped cream and a mint sprig. It's rich and ultra-creamy with a deep chocolate flavor. This is so rich you could share it with a friend—or not. *Getting there: In Pike Place Market on the south end, bayside.*

Il Bistro
93-A Pike Street, Seattle, WA. (206) 682-3049

♥♥ Located a half-story underground, **Il Bistro** has a dark, cozy feel with cloth-covered tables, wooden chairs, and hardwood floors. First course selections include pasta dishes like gnocchi, Rigatoni Bolognese (ground veal in rosemary tomato sauce), and linguine with shellfish. Second courses include Scaloppine de Vitello (veal), Caretto D'Agnello (rack of lamb with rosemary and garlic), cioppino, and salmon with garlic. Chef Michael Parker's signature chocolate dessert is a **Chocolate Marquise** that comes sliced pate style on a bed of raspberry coulis, garnished with a sliced strawberry, a dollop of whipped cream, and mint, dusted with cocoa and powered sugar. This Marquise, which is made with Venezuelan El Rey chocolate, enriched zabaglione and whipped cream, is very rich and chocolaty. It's like biting into a rich truffle. Definitely share this one. *Getting there: In Pike Place Market, under Read All About It.*

Chez Shea
94 Pike Street, Suite 34, Seattle, WA. (206) 467-9990

♥♥ **Chez Shea**, located on the top floor of the Corner Market Building of Pike Place Market, is a small, bistro-like place with linen-covered iron tables and chairs and crescent-shaped windows overlooking the bay. Their pre-fixe menu, which changes 3 times a year, offers a choice of entrees like salmon, beef tenderloin, Alaskan halibut, lamb shank, and pasta terrine. Desserts (not included in the meal) may include owner Sandy Shea's favorite, **Chocolate Steamed Pudding with Brandied Cherries**. The size of a large muffin, this cake-like pudding is served warm with whipped cream and garnished with shaved chocolate, chopped strawberries, and chocolate sauce squiggles. The result is a warm chocolate cake with pieces of chewy cherries. *Getting there: The corner of Pike at the Market.*

Ruth's Chris Steakhouse
800 Fifth Avenue, Seafirst Plaza Building, Seattle, WA. (206) 624-8524

♥♥ We're suspicious of big chain restaurants and almost didn't review **Ruth's Chris**. They serve huge hunks of prime beef seared at 1800 degrees. If you've got any room after your steak, they also serve a **Chocolate Sin Cake**, a big wedge of dense, fudge-like flourless torte that's served with raspberry puree and fresh raspberries. Extremely rich, this major chocolate hit should be shared with a fellow chocolate lover.

Getting there: Downtown on 5th.

Virazon

1329 1st Avenue, Seattle, WA. (206) 233-0123

♥♥ Elegant best describes **Virazon**—tile floors, blonde chairs, classical music, cloth-covered tables with flickering candles, lace half-curtains on large windows that look out onto busy 1st Avenue. Their menus change daily and may include dishes like Maine lobstercakes and perigord truffles, sauteed sea scallops, African pheasant curry stew, New Zealand venison and Willapa Bay sturgeon and Lopez Island mussel stew. Their desserts change daily too, but, at lunch, you can often find their **Pot de Creme**, garnished with a strawberry fan and spun sugar swirls. It's ultra-creamy with a wonderfully intense chocolate flavor.

At dinner, they offer the **Chocolate Trio**, a selection of tiny, highly architectural desserts that are beautifully presented. The selection might include little scoops of gelato-like **Mocha and Chocolate Sorbet** with praline crunchiness. Or a **Chocolate Napoleon**, a wonderfully rich and creamy, miniature flourless torte served with raspberry glaze and a bittersweet tuile. Or you may be delighted by a **Chocolate Hazelnut Truffle** that comes as little chocolate triangles of hazelnut-chocolate crust and hazelnut truffle artfully stacked and served with black current coulis and chocolate sticks. It's very rich with an intense chocolate flavor. The hazelnut crust adds a lovely textural contrast and a nutty flavor.

> **Cocoa is chocolate liquor with extra cocoa butter, sugar, milk and vanilla added.**

Getting there: At Union, near the Seattle Art Museum.

Reiner's

1106 8th Avenue, Seattle, WA. (206) 624-2222

♥ **Reiner's** sports classic ambiance—carved plaster ceiling, crystal chandelier, heavy pillars, large bouquet of flowers, upholstered chairs, cloth-covered tables with tiny votives and fresh flowers, and large art-print banners that dominate the pale yellow walls. Their menu, which changes seasonally, is classic too with dishes like baked salmon with almond crust, chicken breast with crab meat, rack of lamb, and veal chop with chanterelle mushroom sauce. Reiner's signature chocolate dessert is their **Bittersweet Choco-**

late Mousse in Florentine Basket. It's served on a bed of raspberry sauce and garnished with a rosette of whipped cream, a strawberry fan, and a mint sprig. The mousse has an intensely deep chocolate flavor and the Florentine basket is sweet and crisp, though a bit thick.

Getting there: On 8th at Spring.

Bakeries

Macrina Bakery and Café

2408 1st Avenue, Seattle, WA. (206) 448-4032

♥♥♥♥ Locals in the know crowd into **Macrina's** tiny space for coffees, soups, panini sandwiches and breads (Casera, Organic Sour White, Italian, Potato, Wheat Herb Walnut, Apricot Nut, Greek Olive, Whole Wheat Cider, Cinnamon, Challah, Fresh Herb, Vollkorn, and Sardinian Flat Bread). They also come for Macrina's **Flourless Brownie**, 4 inches of chocolate delight dusted with powered sugar. It's more like a torte than a brownie, with a spongy texture and an intense dark chocolate flavor. Their **Chocolate Pecan Turtle Brownie**, also 4 inches, has a dense, more fudge-like brownie bottom, a thin layer of pecans, topped with $1/2$ inch of buttery, caramel topping. Incredibly rich, the caramel-chocolate combination explodes on the tongue. Caramel lovers rejoice!

Another favorite is **Mom's Chocolate Cake**, 4 layers, $1/2$-inch high, of dark chocolate cake filled and frosted with a dark chocolate buttercream. If you like a good, basic chocolate cake, this is it. The cake is medium-textured and moist and the thick, fudgy buttercream has an intensely chocolate flavor.

Getting there: On 1st at Battery.

Le Panier Bakery

1902 Pike Place Market, Seattle, WA. (206) 441-3669

♥♥♥ **Le Panier**, bills itself as a "very French bakery " and it's just that. They're known for their crusty breads and their flaky, buttery croissants. Chocolate lovers will enjoy their **Pain au Chocolate**, delicate croissants filled with plenty of Barry French Chocolate. For an even richer treat, their **Chocolatine** is a croissant filled with chocolate and hazelnut cream and topped with toasted, slivered Oregon hazelnuts. Outside is the same flaky croissant; inside there's a rich blend of chocolate and hazelnut flavors. Croissant heaven!

Le Panier also makes a **Chocolate Eclair** that's a bit different. The eclair pastry is delicate and chewy and the inside is filled with mousseline (half pastry cream, half chocolate mousse). The result is a wonderfully light, creamy interpretation of an old favorite.

They also make 2 classic French chocolate desserts. Their **Opera Cake** has a biscuit (dry chocolate cake) bottom that's soaked in rum syrup, followed by a layer of chocolate mousse, another layer of biscuit, and another layer of mousse that's dusted with cocoa and garnished with paillete (chocolate pieces) on the sides. The biscuit is soft and delicate with a rich rum flavor. The mousse has an intense bittersweet chocolate taste.

Le Concorde starts with the same rum-soaked biscuit followed by a thick layer of chocolate mousse, topped with ganache and decorated with large, semi-sweet chocolate shavings. The result is a major chocolate hit, chocolate lovers. The mousse is fluffy, floating on the tongue. The biscuit adds just the right cake texture and the ganache and chocolate shavings add to the chocolatey richness.
Getting there: Across from Pike Place Market.

Louisa's Bakery and Café
2379 Eastlake Avenue E, Seattle, WA. (206) 325-0081
♥♥♥ **Louisa's Bakery and Café** is one of those neighborhood gems only the locals seem to know about. It's a casual place with big windows, mismatched tables and chairs, pale yellow and green walls, linoleum tile floor, and original local art on the walls. Patrons belly up to the counter to order breakfast, lunch, dinner, or Louisa's fresh, from-scratch baked goods. Their menu includes plenty of comfort foods like macaroni and cheese, hot turkey sandwich with mashed potatoes and gravy, chicken enchiladas, lasagne, chicken pot pie, and stew—all in hefty portions at bargain basement prices.

The real draw for chocolate lovers is their baked goods like their **Mountain Bar Cookie**, a 5-inch, thick chocolate cookie packed with chocolate chips and walnuts. It's just what a chocolate cookie should be—slightly crunchy outside, soft and chewy inside, with a good, strong chocolate flavor in every bite.

Their **Frosted Brownie** is a 4-inch square, $1\frac{1}{2}$-inch high, dark chocolate, cake-like brownie that's packed with big pieces of walnuts and frosted with dark chocolate ganache. This big, soft brownie has plenty of chocolate flavor and the ganache frosting is sinfully rich. For a more dense brownie, the **Cream Cheese Brownie** has cream cheese swirled into the top layer of batter, giving this a moist, even texture and a good combination of cheese and chocolate flavors. Their **Mexican Tortilla** isn't a tortilla at all, but 4x2 inches of thick, fudgy chocolate brownie. The Mexican chocolate gives it a slightly crunchy texture.

Louisa's makes several varieties of large croissants, including **Chocolate Croissants**. They're buttery and flaky, but stingy on the chocolate. They also make huge cinnamon rolls, Danish (with fresh fruit), scones, and bear claws.

Getting there: *Off I-5, take the Lakeview exit. Louisa's is on Eastlake at E Louisa Street.*

Chocolate Shops

Fran's Chocolates, Ltd.
2805 E Madison, Seattle, WA. (206) 322-6511
2594 NE University Village, Seattle, WA. (206) 528-9969
Also in Bellevue
♥♥♥♥ (chocolates/tortes) Fran Bigelow of **Fran's Chocolates** wants the center and the outside of her **chocolates** to balance one another as a complete unit. To achieve this goal, she makes her chocolates in small batches and combines European chocolate coating (couverture) with American hand-dipping techniques. The result are chocolates that are both elegant and incredibly delicious. Her chocolates are distinctive for their velvety smooth centers, paper-thin chocolate coatings, and flavors that are both complex and subtle. Each box is beautifully wrapped and have descriptions of each chocolate for easy identification.

Blanc et Noir is a white chocolate cream center dipped in dark chocolate that's ultra-buttery with a good contrast between the dark outside and the creamy white center. **Chocolat et Caramel** is a chocolate cream center with a hint of caramel flavor that's dipped in dark chocolate and topped with crushed violets. It's a seamless incorporation of chocolate and caramel. **Gianduja** is a classic blend of milk chocolate and finely ground hazelnuts dipped in milk or dark chocolate that melts in the mouth leaving a heavenly hazelnut flavor lingering on the tongue. The **Mocha Brandy** is like having a smooth brandied coffee.

Chocolate Ginger patty is a thin, sweet layer of ginger enrobed in dark chocolate that will thrill ginger lovers with its fresh, not overly hot flavor.

Fran's **Dark Chocolate Truffles** have centers that melt almost instantly in the mouth, leaving shards of thin, dark chocolate, and inviting another bite. The centers come flavored in **Dark Chocolate, Amaretto, Chambord** (deep, black raspberry flavor), **Irish Whiskey**, and **Kahlua**.

Chocolate-covered Caramels come plain or with pecans or macadamia nuts. They're extremely buttery, rich, and soft–a wonderful marriage of caramel and chocolate.

Fran's signature **Gold Bars** (also **Gold Bites**) are 1.75 ounces of buttery caramel and toasted almonds or macadamia nuts coated in dark Belgian chocolate. They're worth their weight in gold! **Fixations** are half-sized bars (1/2 ounce each) of Belgian chocolate blended with peanut butter, coffee, orange, or mint and enrobed in chocolate. They're all wonderfully flavored.

They make **Praline Bon Bons** that come in an elegant coronet. They are filled with smooth hazelnut cream and have a thicker coating of chocolate than you'll find in most of Fran's chocolates. An elegant dessert offering, Fran's **Figs** are plump, whole Calimyrna figs filled to capacity with creamy chocolate ganache and half-dipped in chocolate. The figs are fresh-tasting and the fig seeds add a lovely crunchy contrast to the creamy, smooth ganache.

Fran's also offers rich **tortes** by the slice or whole, all glazed with a mixture of rich dark chocolate and served with fresh whipped cream. Her **Prince Torte** is a classic torte that's moist, dark, and rich. The small amount of cake flour added to this torte gives it a cake-like texture. The **Espresso Torte** has a denser, more creamy mousse-like texture, like biting into the inside of a luscious truffle. The espresso flavor doesn't overwhelm, but adds a lovely depth to the chocolate. This is torte perfection!

Getting there: On Madison at 28th. The new University Village store is located on University Village next to Briazz.

Chocolatier Profile—
Fran Bigelow, founder and owner
Fran's Chocolates
Seattle, Washington

Fran Bigelow walks through rows of workers rolling ganache, hand-dipping chocolates, wrapping shiny gold foil around bars of caramel and chocolate. She picks a candy off a cart, cuts it in half, and frowns.

"This is too thick," she mutters, closely examining the chocolate coating and holding it out for me to see. The sides are paper-thin. The chocolate on the bottom is a tiny bit thicker.

She cuts open another and frowns again. "This will have to be fixed," she says strongly.

No doubt it will be fixed. It's Fran Bigelow's attention to every detail of her candymaking operation that makes her one of the best chocolatiers in the Northwest.

Always interested in cooking, in the 1970's, Fran went to the California Culinary Academy and learned to make desserts and chocolates. She opened a small dessert shop in Seattle, but what kept customers coming back were her cocoa-dusted truffles. So she ex-

panded her chocolates and, 16 years later, Fran's Chocolates is a $3 million-dollar-a-year business.

Fran's chocolates are distinguished by their lush yet subtle flavors. "I'm interested in the flavor that's going to satisfy that craving for chocolate, not the sweet taste," she says. "If your taste is more sophisticated, you'll want less sugar and more flavor."

Fran uses Callebaut and Belcolade Chocolate from Belgium and El Ray from Venezuela, carefully matching the chocolate with other ingredients to achieve the taste and texture she wants. For instance, the more bittersweet El Ray chocolate stands up well to stronger flavors. Creamy smooth centers match better with the mellower Callebaut.

Fran's coatings marry the centers perfectly for a complete unit. "The first bite has to be that crunch, that snap on the outside," she explains. "The thickness of the chocolate on the outside has to match what's going on in the inside. The center should just dissolve in your mouth, leaving a wonderful sensation."

Even though Fran's Chocolates has grown from its humble beginnings, they still make their chocolates in small batches, hand-piping, hand-dipping, even wrapping by hand. "Our workers are artisans," she says.

"I never get bored in this business because I'm always trying to bring products to another level or explore new flavors. I'm always learning and I'm having fun!"

Bernard C.
1420 5th Avenue, Seattle, WA. (206) 340-0396
♥♥♥ (See review under Bernard Callebaut, Chocolate Shops, Victoria, B.C.)
***Getting there**: On 5th in the US Bank Building.*

Dilettante Chocolates
416 E Broadway Avenue, Seattle, WA. (206) 329-6463
Other Seattle location:
1603 1st Avenue, Seattle, WA. (206) 728-9144
♥♥♥ (chocolates)/♥♥♥ (pastries) Dana Davenport, founder of **Dilettante Chocolates,** is a man in love with intense, masculine flavors. The recipes for his small, dark chocolates come from the notebooks of his grandfather, a master chocolatier who was taught by Julius Rudolph Franzen, pastry chef and candymaker to Czar Nicholas II of Russia. Using Guittard, Merckens, and European chocolate, Dana creates chocolates that have rich, complex fla-

vors. His secret is cooking the butter, sugar, and cream in his ganache to high temperatures, creating centers that have strong caramelized, almost smoky, undertones much like a deep, red wine. Using only the darkest chocolate (even his milk chocolate is a dark variety) with strong acid tones, his chocolates have unique Old World flavors that develop on the tongue as they melt.

His signature chocolate is the **Ephemere Truffle**, a dark chocolate center with a dark chocolate coating that's got a deep caramel-chocolate flavor. The same Ephemere flavor is available in his **Ephemere Truffle Sauce** for use on ice cream or in hot drinks.

In the **Champagne Truffle**, another signature candy, the flavor of champagne comes through strongly and is moderated by the sweet flavor of strawberry crystals that decorate the top. The **Hazelnut Truffle**, made with their own hazelnut paste, is more nutty than sweet. His **Chocolate Espresso** has an intense espresso flavor without being bitter.

Dilettante also makes a large variety of **chocolate-covered hazelnuts, espresso beans, ginger, almonds**, etc. All made with Dilettante's distinctive bittersweet or semi-sweet chocolate.

They make **Czar Bars**, a layer of coconut nougat, caramel with almonds, and chocolate truffle enrobed in a thin layer of dark chocolate. They also come with caramel and honey nougat. Both have the deep, caramel undertones of the Ephemere truffle. Their semi-sweet **Solid Chocolate Bar**, while less intense than the bittersweet chocolate, is still strong on chocolate flavor.

Dilettante also makes a line of **hot chocolate** and **cocoa drinks**, both with and without milk. They all have the caramelized notes of Ephemere.

A local creamery formulates an 18% butterfat vanilla ice cream especially for Dilettante and they make "adult shakes," thick **milk shakes** flavored with Ephemere Truffle Sauce and port, dry sherry or peppermint or peach liqueur. Their hot chocolates and cider can also be spiced up with a shot.

Dilettante carries a line of **pastries** and **desserts**, including **tortes** and **cakes** (available whole or by the slice), **bread pudding, creme brulee, mousse**, and **brownies**. Their signature pastry is the **Rigo Jansci**, a Hungarian torte with a thick layer of chocolate mousse between chocolate genoise, with raspberry preserves and a truffle glaze. It's rich and chocolaty with the Ephemere flavor. Their **brownies**, packed with chopped walnuts and topped with Ephemere glaze, have a wonderfully complex flavor you don't often find in brownies.

Getting there: In the busy Broadway neighborhood.

MERCER ISLAND

Oh Chocolate!
2703 76ᵗʰ Avenue SE, Mercer Island, WA. (206) 232-4974
♥♥♥ (See review under Bellevue.)
Getting there: On 76ᵗʰ street near SE 27ᵗʰ.

BELLEVUE

Just a 10 minute hop to the other side of Lake Washington, Bellevue is a suburban world away from the urban hustle of Seattle.

Restaurants

Tosoni's Café
14320 NE 20ᵗʰ Street, Bellevue, WA. (425) 644-1668
♥♥♥♥ With a name like **Tosoni's**, you'd expect an Italian place. Guess again. Chef/owner Walter Walcher has created an eclectic ambiance with Scandinavian-style booths and chairs, cloth-covered tables, tall cabinets filled with wine, and a scattering of European prints. His dinner menu offers classics like venison steak, Muscovy ducking, pheasant, veal saltimbocca, and rack of lamb, plus several dishes posted on the daily fresh board. Walter offers at least 5 desserts every night, usually a couple of them chocolate. His **Chocolate Decadence** comes as a tiny slice with a scattering of chopped pecans. It's thick, creamy and smooth with a rich, intense chocolate flavor. This dessert is so wonderfully decadent you won't want more than the tiny serving.

In contrast, the **Chocolate Mousse Torte** is a light-as-air dessert that comes in a generous wedge. It starts with a thin layer of sponge cake, then 2 inches of milk chocolate mousse, topped with an inch of whipped cream, and a thin layer of ganache. It's served with a pool of homemade caramel sauce with swirls of raspberry sauce and garnished with fresh raspberries and mint leaves. The mousse is wonderfully fluffy with a creamy milk chocolate flavor and the ganache is richly decadent. The caramel sauce has a delicate caramel flavor and the translucent raspberry sauce is light and fresh-tasting.
Getting there: Just east of 140ᵗʰ.

Azalea's Fountain Court
22 103ʳᵈ Avenue NE, Bellevue, WA. (425) 451-0426
♥♥♥ In a converted house, **Azalea's Fountain Court** offers a lovely respite from busy suburban Bellevue. The blue-green carpeting, gray and white walls, cloth-covered tables, and plenty of light give the feeling of sophistication. There are several dining areas and the back one offers a working fireplace overlooking a

small courtyard. They serve lunch and dinner, with the menu changing seasonally. Lunch offerings include salads (Caesar, wilted spinach, walnut chicken), crab and cheddar melt, and shrimp yakisoba. For dinner, they offer light dishes like smoked salmon quesadilla and grilled vegetable platter or entrees like veal chops with orange green peppercorn demi, tangerine-ginger crusted Chilean sea bass, and alder salmon in a sundried apricot barbecue sauce. Chef Andrew Lam makes 4-5 desserts, plus several fresh fruit sorbets each week. He always includes a chocolate item like **Milk Chocolate Mousse** flavored with rum and Cointreau that comes served with fresh berries. It's airy and ultra-light. There's not much chocolate flavor here, but the rum and Cointreau, which aren't too heavy handed, give a refreshing taste.

Getting there: In old town Bellevue, one-half block off Main Street.

Andre's Eurasian Bistro
14125 NE 20th, Bellevue, WA. (425) 747-6551

♥♥ A small lunch and dinner place off busy 20th, **Andre's** decor combines urban cool and Asian—black naugahyde and purple fabric booths, wooden tables and chairs, a small food bar with tall-backed stools, black and white photos of Asian country scenes, a Chinese statue, and dolls and umbrellas from Bali. Their signature chocolate dessert is the **Chocolate Tower**, 2 squares of dark chocolate cake separated by fresh whipped cream that are topped with a wedge of 2 layers of chocolate cake filled with milk chocolate mousse, frosted with ganache. It's attractively presented on a pool of creme anglaise in which flower designs are swirled in chocolate and raspberry sauces. The top cake wedge is moist and almost fudgy. The mousse, which could be a bit smoother, has a light milk chocolate flavor and the ganache is rich. The bottom cake layers are a bit coarser with a good chocolate cake flavor. The creme anglaise is light, almost custard like. If you're a chocolate cake fan, this one's a creative variation.

> **Normal body temperature is 98.6 F., the same temperature for melting cocoa butter.**

Getting there: In the Highland Park Center (a strip mall), just east of 140th (behind Cameras West and Pro Golf Discount).

Daniel's Broiler
10500 NE 8th Street, Bellevue, WA. (425) 462-4662

♥ On the 21st floor of the Seafirst Building, **Daniel's Broiler** commands stunning views of water and Seattle to the west. Touted as the city's best steakhouse, with marble-topped tables, high-backed booths, and hardwood floors, its ambiance is fitting. They serve lunch and dinner, with entrees heavy on prime USDA beef—sirloin, filet, rib eye, porterhouse, and New York, as well as chops. They also offer a few non-steak items like chicken, fish, and pasta. For dessert, their ode to chocolate is their **Warm Chocolate Cake**, a 3$^1/_2$ inch individual cake that's served warm in a pool of chocolate sauce. It's served with a small scoop of Olympic Mountain vanilla ice cream, 2 thin chocolate tuile cookies and a dusting of powered sugar. The cake's texture is ultra-soft with a good chocolate flavor, though the center could be more gooey for this reviewer. The chocolate sauce is rich and the tuile cookie crisp.

Getting there: In downtown Bellevue, on 8th in the Seafirst Building.

Chocolate Shop

Fran's Chocolates, Ltd.
10305 NE 10th Street, Bellevue, WA. (425) 453-1698
♥♥♥♥ (chocolates)/♥♥♥♥ (tortes) (See full review under Fran's, Seattle.) This is **Fran's** showcase store with its 28-foot case displaying her elegant chocolates on gold serving trays. You can also buy her rich tortes by the slice here and, along with a cup of French press coffee, linger awhile at one of the tiny café tables.
Getting there: On 10th near 103rd.

Oh Chocolate!
Bellevue Place, 10500 NE 8th Street, #108, Bellevue, WA.
(425) 451-1060
♥♥ Started about 15 years ago by Gertrude Krautheim, **Oh Chocolate!** has become a favorite of eastsiders. They use Guittard chocolate, real liqueurs, and they hand-dip their candy. Oh Chocolate! chocolates are pretty and come in some inventive flavors. They carry 17 flavors of truffles, all a delicate size, with just the right thin coatings. The **Amaretto Truffle** has a dark chocolate coating and dark chocolate center that's silky with a subtle Amaretto flavor. The **Raspberry Truffle**, also with dark outside and center, has a wonderful raspberry flavor. The **Champagne Truffle**, dark inside and out, has a light, almost bubbly champagne flavor. **Eastside Latte**, a signature Oh Chocolate! truffle, comes enrobed in white chocolate with a rather stiff dark chocolate center. The white chocolate isn't overly sweet and the coffee-flavored center speaks with authority.

They also make a line of **French Creams**, which they say have a higher percentage of butter and cream than most creams. They have distinct flavors, but their centers tend to be a bit stiff for this reviewer's taste. The **Maui Cream**, one of our favorites, is made with brown sugar, cream, and butter and has a lovely browned butter flavor. The **Raspberry Cream** is a pale pink center with a sweet/tart raspberry flavor that's enrobed in dark chocolate. The **Vanilla Cream,** with its white center and dark coating, is a bit sweet. **Cappuccino Cream**, a dark chocolate with cappuccino-colored cream center, has an intense coffee flavor.

Their caramels are chewy and rich. The **Chocolate Caramel,** with its dark chocolate coating and chocolate caramel, carries a strong chocolate flavor. The **Butterscotch Caramel**, this reviewer's favorite, is a wonderfully buttery caramel with a thin, dark chocolate coating. Their **Peanut Butter Cup** comes with a milk chocolate coating that's mixed with finely ground peanuts enrobing a peanut butter center that has good peanut taste, but is a bit dry.

Recipe:
Hot Fudge
Sauce

Getting there: On NE 8th between Bellevue Way and 106th in the Seafirst Building near the elevators.

KIRKLAND

Chocolate Shop

Bernard C.
128 Central Way, Kirkland, WA. (425) 822-8889
♥♥♥ (See review under Benard Callebaut, Chocolate Shops, Victoia.)

Duck Soup Inn
Friday Harbor, Washington
HOT FUDGE SAUCE

Makes 2¹/₂ cups

1 cup whipping cream
1 cup granulated sugar
9 ounces semi-sweet chocolate, chopped

Combine the cream and sugar in the top of a double boiler over medium heat. Heat, stirring, until the sugar is completely dissolved.

Smooth, silky and rich, this hot fudge sauce will make chocolate lovers weep for joy.

Remove double boiler from heat and stir in chopped chocolate. Allow to stand for 10 minutes and then stir until the chocolate is melted and the sauce is completely smooth. Serve hot over ice cream.

From *The Chocolate Lover's Guide Cookbook*, Pacific Northwest Edition.

WASHINGTON

Puget Sound

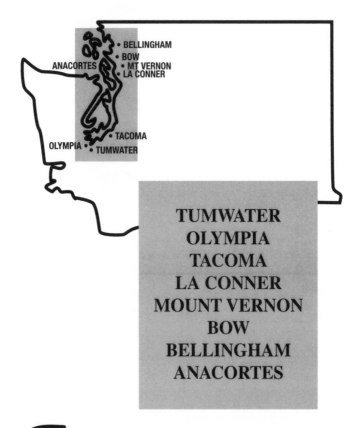

BELLINGHAM
BOW
MT VERNON
LA CONNER
ANACORTES
OLYMPIA
TACOMA
TUMWATER

**TUMWATER
OLYMPIA
TACOMA
LA CONNER
MOUNT VERNON
BOW
BELLINGHAM
ANACORTES**

The Pudget Sound area is defined and dominated by its proximity to water. Vibrant communities cluster along the shores of the Puget Sound, taking their livelihood from its waters.

Great Things to Do

• **View the Snow Geese**, **La Conner, WA**. During the fall and winter months, the elegant white snow geese fly down from Canada to winter in the fields around the quaint town of La Conner. You'll also see trumpeter swans, blue herons, and endless varieties of ducks. Just minutes from town, the **Padilla Bay Reserve** offers even more wild life viewing. The 10,800-acre site features an indoor interpretative center, self-touring exhibits, and viewing areas of tidal flats. For more information, call (360) 428-1558.

• **Take in the Tulips**. **Skagit Valley Tulip Festival, La Conner, Mt. Vernon, Burlington, WA**. (360) 428-5959. During the first few weeks in April, the fields in the Skagit Valley explode with blossoms. More than 1,500 acres of rainbow-colored tulips are available for viewing. The annual celebration also boasts a run, arts and crafts, and flower shows.

• **Take a Chuckanut Drive**. Instead of staying on I-5, take the scenic Chuckanut Drive route between Mt. Vernon and Bellingham, WA. It goes through verdant farmland, skirts the shoreline, and then wends its way through Pacific Northwest rain forest before dropping into South Bellingham.

• **Visit a Garden Art Gallery**. **Chuckanut Bay Gallery,** 700 Chuckanut Drive, **Bellingham, WA**. (360) 734-4885. On Chuckanut Drive, just as you get into South Bellingham, you'll find the Chuckanut Bay Gallery, a fascinating shop filled with enough garden art, fine art, and elegant crafts to keep you visually interested for at least an hour.

Terrific Places to Stay

Puget View Guest House, 7924 61st Avenue NE, **Olympia, WA**. (360) 413-9474. In this secluded cottage, you won't find dataports, fax machines, or voice messaging. You will find a lazy hammock and breath-taking views of Puget Sound and the Olympic Mountains. Puget View Guest House is a place for relaxing. The tiny cottage, nestled next to the host's 1930's log house, has a seating area with a couch, an oak table and chairs, mini-refrigerator, microwave, queen-sized bed, and a deck with a BBQ. Instead of a fitness room, guests hike down a zig-zag path to the beach, walk in nearby Tolmie State Park, or paddle in the Sound. In the morning, your host brings a continental breakfast of fresh-baked goods, fruit, juice, and coffee or tea.

La Conner Channel Lodge, 205 North First Street, **La Conner, WA**. (360) 466-1500. Perched on the Swinomish Channel, the La Conner Channel Lodge is the area's only waterfront hotel. You'll go to sleep with the sound of waves gently slapping the sides of boats docked just a few feet away. (Guests who arrive by boat can moor there.) From the street, the Lodge is understated, but the lobby is charming with its hardwood floors, grand piano, river rock fireplace, coffee, tea, and cookies, and cozy, well-stocked library with comfortable couches that entice guests to linger. All 40 rooms feature gas fireplaces, down comforters, televisions, phones, terry robes, in-room coffee, hair dryers, individual climate controls, and private decks with spectacular views of the busy channel and the picturesque Rainbow Bridge. The 12 fireplace suites have mini-refrigerators and Jacuzzi tubs. Guests enjoy a complimentary breakfast of fresh pastries, homemade granola, yogurt, fresh fruit, juice, and coffee.

The White Swan Guest House, 15872 Moore Road, **Mt Vernon, WA**. (360) 445-6805. Savvy travelers know that The White Swan Guest House is one of the best places to stay in the pastoral Mt. Vernon-La Conner area. Charming host Peter Goldfarb has created an oasis of rest with his well-kept farmhouse on Fir Island, 6 miles from La Conner. Surrounded by flowers both inside and out, the inn offers 3 guest rooms, 2 with shared baths, with lovely brass beds. The Turret Room is especially quaint with its sitting room in the little tower. For those who want more privacy, the cottage, just a few steps from the main house, features a full kitchen and living area with tall windows that overlook the surrounding fields (often filled with swans). The upstairs bedroom is simply and comfortably decorated with fresh flowers and a fluffy comforter to chase away the chill. Guests enjoy a generous continental breakfast and coffee, tea, and Peter's famous chocolate chip cookies are available any time.

Best Western Cottonwood Tree Inn, 2300 Market Street, **Mt. Vernon, WA**. (800) 662-6886. This Best Western has what most travelers look for—comfort and convenience. It's located close to I-5 yet far enough to be away from traffic noise. The rooms are spacious and come with such traveler comforts as hair dryers, irons, extra pillows, coffee makers, and individual heat and air controls. This motor inn features an outdoor pool and 2 restaurants are right across the parking lot. All this at prices that won't break your budget.

Schnauzer Crossing, 4421 Lake Way Drive, **Bellingham, WA.** (360) 733-0055. Schnauser Crossing is one of Bellingham's oldest and most sought-after B&Bs. One of the reasons is that innkeepers Donna and Monty McAllister really love making guests feel at home. Their contemporary home overlooking Lake Whatcom has soaring windows that take in the view of the lake and their Japanese-style garden. Two rooms occupy the main house. The best is a large, elegant suite with a fireplace, Jacuzzi, and TV/VCR. If you really want luxury and privacy, opt for the cottage, with its lake view, kitchenette, fireplace, Jacuzzi, and TV/VCR. All guests enjoy Donna's extras—fluffy towels, bathrobes, fuzzy schnauzer slippers, down comforters, and an outside hot tub. Full breakfast, which may include baked parmesan eggs, fruit compote, and freshly baked apple cobbler, is included.

Big Trees Bed and Breakfast, 4840 Fremont Street, **Bellingham, WA**. (360) 647-2850/(800) 647-2850. Big Trees innkeeper, Jan Simmons, is doing what she's meant to do—living in a big, lively Craftsman bungalow and making her guests feel like family. Under old growth cedars that give the place its name, the 1907 bungalow is a beauty with original woodwork, a stone fireplace, and big wrap-around porch. The guest rooms, which are gaily decorated in bold floral prints, have fresh flowers, comfortable overstuffed chairs, down pillows, and queen or king featherbeds. The downstairs refrigerator is stocked with complimentary drinks and full, delicious breakfasts are served in the diningroom.

TUMWATER

Louisa
205 Cleveland Avenue SE, Tumwater, WA. (360) 352-3732
♥♥♥♥ Tucked into a non-descript building off busy Cleveland Avenue, **Louisa** is a popular little place with blonde wood tables and chairs for 2 or 4, booths with privacy curtains, well-worn Oriental rugs covering a concrete floor, wall sconces that give off soft light, large flower arrangements, and soft jazz. The effect is light, airy, and comfortable. Just off the dining area is an enclosed courtyard for good-weather al fresco dining. They serve lunch and dinner, with several dishes changing daily. Dinner entrees may include dishes like grilled yellow tail, goat cheese phyllo pouch with roma tomato and basil sauce, filet mignon, seafood cannelloni, and grilled chicken breast. They offer several desserts, including **Sweet Pastry Barquette filled with Chocolate Mousse**. About a $1/2$ cup of chocolate mousse is piped into a thin, boat-shaped sweet pastry shell that floats on a bed of creme anglaise, blueberry coulis, and tiny caramel sauce "hearts," garnished with a tiny white chocolate fan. This excellent chocolate mousse offers a rich, deep chocolate flavor and a texture that is creamy rather than airy. The pastry shell is wafer-light, giving the mousse a contrasting crunch. The blueberry coulis has an intense blueberry flavor that's not overly sweet and the creme anglaise is rich and ultra-creamy. It's a most satisfying combination.
Getting there: *On Cleveland between Custer Way and E Bates.*

OLYMPIA

La Petite Maison
1010 Division, Olympia, WA. (360) 943-8812

♥♥♥ In a converted house in suburban Olympia, **La Petite Maison** is a pleasant restaurant with green and burgundy grape print wallpaper, old school-style oak chairs, cloth-covered tables with fresh flowers and silver candle holders, and botanical and French countryside prints on the walls. Focusing on fresh Northwest ingredients, they serve rustic French cuisine at lunch and dinner. Dinner entrees include dishes like rack of lamb, roasted chicken, beef tenderloin with dungeness crab and béarnaise sauce and rainbow trout stuffed with crab and shrimp with mornay sauce. They offer chocolate desserts like Executive Chef Randal Hoff's **Regina Torte**, a generous wedge of flourless torte that's made with bittersweet chocolate, hazelnuts, and flavored with orange and lemon zest. It's served with coffee and creme anglaise and a scoop of Olympic Mountain Madagascar Vanilla ice cream. The cake is served warm and is slightly coarse yet soft with the hazelnuts providing a nutty chewiness. It has a lovely blend of bittersweet chocolate and citrus flavors. The coffee and creme anglaise and ice cream provide a soft, creamy contrast to the cake. It's a delightful combination of textures and flavors. *Getting there: On Division NW ½ block south of Harrison.*

> ### *Chocolate Happening!*
> "A Taste of Chocolate," a fundraiser for The Olympia Symphony, happens every year in mid-May. Chocolate lovers enjoy music, champagne, and plenty of chocolate. Call the Olympia Symphony Office for more information at (360) 753-0074.

Gardner's Seafood and Pasta
111 W Thurston Avenue, Olympia, WA. (360) 786-8466

♥♥ With its open-beam ceiling, hardwood floors, photos depicting Northwest scenes, blonde wooden tables and chairs with fresh flowers in funky art deco vases, **Gardner's** atmosphere is dark, cool, and casual. It's a place where locals come for heaping bowls of fresh steamed clams and cioppino or oyster or crab casserole. They also serve pasta selections like seafood fettuccine Alfredo, cannelloni, and lasagne. Their dessert menu offers several chocolate items like **White Chocolate Mousse**, which comes in a dark chocolate cup with raspberry puree, garnished with rosettes of whipped cream, fresh strawberry, mint, and a chocolate triangle. The mousse is sweet and creamy, almost sticky. The chocolate cup, which is made with good quality dark chocolate, has a deep, dark chocolate flavor and the raspberry sauce has just the right tart/sweetness. The **Chocolate Pecan Mousse Torte** has 2 layers of dark chocolate cake sandwiching an inch of dark chocolate mousse that's frosted with ganache and topped with caramel and chopped pecan sauce. This rich dessert has a moist, fine-textured cake and a dense, slightly sticky mousse. The ganache is thick and the caramel sauce has a wonderful, buttery-caramel flavor.

The chefs often whip up chocolate dessert specials like **German Chocolate Cheesecake** that starts with a thin graham crust, then $2^1/2$ inches of chocolate cheesecake that's topped with coconut, caramel, pecan, and ganache. A nice variation on an old classic, this cheesecake is creamy and tangy. The caramel topping has a lovely buttery flavor and the coconut and pecans add a nutty-chewy effect.

Their **Chocolate Raisin Tart**, this reviewer's favorite, is a big wedge of shortbread crust that's topped with an inch of fudge-like chocolate punctuated with chopped walnuts and raisins and a half-inch of dark chocolate mousse with finely chopped nuts. The raisins and fudgy chocolate are a wonderful combination. With each chocolaty bite, there's a little explosion of raisin flavor. Lovely!
Getting there: In downtown Olympia on Thurston at Capitol.

Budd Bay Café
525 N Columbia Street, Olympia, WA. (360) 357-6963
♥♥ **Budd Bay Café** is a large, light, airy waterfront restaurant overlooking Budd Inlet and the marina. With wood tables and chairs, large nautical murals, a long, blonde bar with comfortable backed stools, and floor-to-ceiling windows, the ambiance is casual, waterfront hip. They serve lunch and dinner, with dinner offerings like grilled peanut black tiger prawns, seafood linguine, grilled Alaskan halibut, and roasted garlic crusted salmon. Non-fish choices include prime rib, sirloin, sesame chicken stir fry and build-your-own pasta (select the pasta and sauce). Their signature chocolate dessert is **French Silk Pie**, which comes with a thin crust of crushed hazelnuts, then $2^1/2$ inches of chocolate mousse that's topped with a thin layer of ganache. It's served with raspberry puree. Surprisingly good, the mousse center is dense yet creamy. The ganache is thick and rich and the hazelnuts add a nice nutty crunch and good hazelnut flavor. However, the raspberry puree is overly thick and adds little.
Getting there: On the waterfront on Columbia between A and B Streets.

The Spar Café and Tobacco Merchant

114 E 4th Avenue, Olympia, WA. (360) 357-6444
Enter **The Spar Café** and you step back to 1935. The café has 20-

foot ceilings with original light fixtures and fans, oak paneling, oak and fabric booths, an extra-long L-shaped counter with wooden swivel seats, neon signs, and walls full of big photos depicting turn-of-the-century logging activities ("spar" means denuded tree trunk). Across from the counter, they sell tobacco, cigars, and cigarettes from old-fashioned, humidified cabinets, with wooden Indians and all. The Spar serves breakfast, lunch, and dinner, with raves from locals for their breakfasts, which they serve until 11:00 a.m. on weekdays and 1:00 p.m. on weekends. For chocolate lovers, they offer The Spar's **chocolate milkshake** made with Darigold hard ice cream. It comes in a big, frosty metal mixing glass with a dollop of whipped cream and a squirt of chocolate sauce. The result is rich and creamy.

Getting there: In downtown Olympia on 4th near Washington.

Bakeries

Desserts by Tasha Nicole
2822 Capitol Boulevard SE, Olympia, WA. (360) 357-6444
♥♥♥♥ If you're a chocolate lover in Olympia, **Desserts by Tasha Nichole** is your Valhalla. A dessert company specializing in cheesecakes (they make 17 kinds). They also make a large variety of **tortes, tarts, cookies, bars**, and **cakes**, by the slice or whole, using French and Swiss chocolate. One of the best ways to get a cross-section of their chocolate delights is to order one of their dessert tray boxes, miniatures of some of their favorites. Their **Chocolate Amaretto Cheesecake Petit Four** is a square of creamy chocolate cheesecake that's a wonderful blending of tangy cheese and chocolate with a hint of Amaretto. Their **Amaretto Cheesecake Dipped in Dark French Chocolate** has more of their delicious cheesy cheesecake with an intense, though not overpowering, taste of Amaretto. The dark chocolate covering gives a good chocolate counterpoint to the tangy cheesecake. **Neapolitan Cheesecake**, a seasonal offering, has a layer of chocolate cheesecake, plain cheesecake, and berry cheesecake, all enrobed in dark chocolate. It's rich and the berry flavor gives it a refreshing lilt. An interesting variation on their cheesecake theme is their **Cheesecake-on-a-Stick**, which is a generous wedge of their creamy, tangy cheesecake dipped in dark chocolate (they specially order their own formulation of dipping chocolate), and then it's frozen. You can eat them frozen or let them warm up to refrigerator temperature, which this reviewer prefers. Their Whidbey Island **Loganberry Cheesecake-on-a-Stick** is wonderfully creamy-cheesy with a delightful tangy accent of loganberry. Other Cheesecake-on-a-Stick flavors include **Amaretto, Blackberry Swirl, Chocolate Hazelnut, Latte, Mocha, New York, Peanut Butter, Raspberry Swirl,** and **White Chocolate**.

Their heart-shaped **Shortbread Cookie Dipped in Dark Chocolate** is slightly crumbly, not overly sweet, with a chocolate accent.

Chocolate Caramel Delight has a shortbread crust and a layer of caramel that's topped with chocolate and chopped pecans. The shortbread is soft; the caramel chewy and buttery; and the chocolate layer densely chocolaty with a good chocolate snap. The **German Chocolate Bar** comes with a brown sugar shortbread crust, a layer of fudgy chocolate, and toasted coconut pecan topping. It's rich and chewy. Yum!

Some of this reviewer's favorites are the tortes like their **Red Knight Wedge**, a chocolate truffle torte that's dipped in dark chocolate. It instantly melts in the mouth with a strong chocolate punch. Wonderful!

Getting there: On Capitol Boulevard at O'Farrell Avenue SE.

Wagner's European Bakery and Café
1013 Capitol Way S, Olympia, WA. (360) 357-7268

♥♥ Rudy Wagner, a European-trained pastry chef, has spent the past 40-plus years baking up European-style tortes and pastries. Peek into their pleasant bakery and café with its big display cases stocked with over-sized **brownies, cookies, bars, cheesecakes,** and **tortes**, all available by the slice, and you'll know why Wagner's is the most popular bakery in Olympia. Their **Chocolate Cheesecake** comes with a dark cookie crust with $2^1/_2$ inches of chocolate cheesecake that's topped with a rosette of whipped cream. It's ultra-creamy, smooth, and tangy/cheesy with a subtle chocolate flavor.

White's Not Real. White chocolate isn't considered chocolate. It has cocoa butter, but no chocolate liquor.

Their **Peanut Butter Torte** is 4 half-layers of dark chocolate cake separated by a peanut butter cream encased with a fudgy, dark chocolate frosting and topped with peanut butter cream and chopped peanuts. The cake has a soft delicate texture and the peanut butter cream is light-as-air with an intense peanut taste. The chocolate frosting is a bit strong-flavored for this dessert.

The **Caramel Torte** is 3 layers of medium chocolate cake that sandwich a $1/_2$ inch layer of caramel and a $1/_2$ inch layer of milk chocolate mousse. It's frosted with dark chocolate frosting and topped with a layer of caramel. This torte is an interesting blend of caramel and chocolate flavors. The cake is moist, but the caramel is a bit sweeter than necessary. Wagner's **M&M Brownie** is a big 4-inch square of dense, chewy brownie with chopped walnuts that's frosted with dark chocolate frosting and caramel and topped with tiny, colorful, M&M candies. This sweet treat is definitely a kid's dessert.

Peanut Butter Brownie is a cake-like chocolate walnut brownie that's frosted with fudge-like chocolate frosting, then topped with big chunks of peanut butter and chocolate and drizzled with chocolate. It's a bit crumbly, with a big peanut butter flavor.

Chocolate Raspberry Truffle is a big 4-inch mound of delight—a shortbread cookie topped with a thin layer of sweet raspberry, a scoop of chocolate truffle center, all enrobed in dark chocolate. The cookie is crumbly-buttery and provides a nice chewiness. The raspberry layer adds a fruity sweetness to the light chocolate center. This is a great dessert to take along on a picnic.

Rudy's **Nougat Log** is a 5-inch Florentine almond cookie that's been rolled and filled with nougat and the ends dipped in dark chocolate. The cookie is crisp and buttery-sweet, if a bit thick, and the nougat is ultra-light and delicate. The chocolate adds an extra delight for chocolate lovers.

Their **Chocolate Eclair** is 7 inches of chewy eclair pastry totally filled with silky Bavarian cream and topped with chocolate icing. It's a sweet way to start the day.
Getting there: *On Capitol near Union Avenue (just north of the Capitol building).*

TACOMA

Stanley and Seaforts Steak, Chop, and Fish House
115 E 34th Street, Tacoma, WA. (253) 473-7300
♥♥ **Stanley and Seafort's** big windows have commanding views of downtown Tacoma and the water. The ambiance is clubby and fun with brass railings, upholstered booths, wooden tables, a large bar with marble tables for light meals, and a big, open kitchen. They serve lunch and dinner, and their Applewood grill focuses on Nebraska steaks, prime rib, chops, and shellfish. They offer 2 chocolate desserts. **Chocolate Indulgence,** made for them by a local baker, is 2 layers of dense chocolate cake filled and frosted with dark chocolate. It's served slightly heated with Madagascar vanilla ice cream and a drizzle of chocolate. The result is gooey and rich, too much even for this chocolate lover.

A more satisfying choice is their **Double Chocolate Bread Pudding**, an individual 5-inch round of chewy, chunky bread pudding served with a scoop of vanilla ice cream. The pudding is slightly crunchy on the outside, soft on the inside. Although it's not long on chocolate flavor, it's a good, comfortable bread pudding that's complimented by the clean-tasting ice cream.

Getting there: *City center exit, take Pacific Avenue (Highway 7) to 34th.*

Candy/Pastry Shop

Affairs Chocolates and Desserts

2811 Bridgeport Way W, Tacoma, WA. (253) 565-8604

♥ **Affairs** is a little dessert and chocolate shop located in a residential area on the west side of Tacoma. Self-taught baker/chocolatier Gay Landry whips up what may be the biggest **truffles** in the Pacific Northwest. These 2-ounce, racquet-ball-sized babies are made with Guittard dark, milk, and white chocolate and traditional ganache with no preservatives. They come in a rainbow of flavors—**Double Chocolate, Amaretto, Kahlua, Grand Marnier, Mt. Tahoma Ice** (dark chocolate and Creme de Menthe), **Praline, Raspberry, Cappuccino, Toasted Almond, Milk Chocolate, Butter Rum, Mocha, Mint Rainier** (Peppermint Schnapps), **Irish Cream, Apricot Rum, White Russian, White Satin**, and **Hazelnut Praline**. The truffle shell has a good snap to it and the centers are well-flavored, but could be smoother.

Affairs makes a variety of **cheesecakes, tortes**, and **cakes**, available whole or by the slice. Their **Chocolate Decadence** is a small wedge of fudge-like flourless torte that's topped with a thin layer of raspberry preserves and a thin layer of ganache. This is a creamy, melt-in-the-mouth dessert.

They offer more than 30 different cheesecakes, including **Bailey's White Chocolate Cheesecake**. It starts with a thin graham cracker crust that's topped with 1 1/2 inches of creamy cheesecake and a 1/3 inch of tangy topping. This cheesecake has a light touch of Bailey's liqueur.

The most popular dessert at Affairs, and this reviewer's favorite, is **Boule de Neige**, a dome-shaped slice of ultra-creamy, truffle-like dark chocolate topped with sweetened whipped cream. It's a sensual, melt-in-the-mouth delight.

Getting there: On Tacoma's west side, on Bridgeport W at 28th.

Chocolate Shop

Brown and Haley

110 E 26th, Tacoma, WA. (253) 620-3067 (Factory "seconds")

Most chocolate lovers know **Almond Roca Buttercrunch**, the crunchy toffee that's enrobed in chocolate and chopped almonds. What they don't know is that **Brown and Haley** is a Tacoma company. While artisan chocolatiers may make toffee that's more buttery and less sweet, Brown and Haley's Almond Roca sets the commercial standard for chocolate-covered toffee.

Brown and Haley has teamed up with Totts, the champagne people, to make **Champagne Truffles**. They're small domes of milk chocolate with creamy dark chocolate centers with a tangy bite of champagne. More in the American than European tradition, some may find these a bit sweet.

> **Unsweetened (also called bitter or baking) chocolate is just pure chocolate liquor. If you've ever tasted it, you know it has no added sugar.**

Their **Belgian Creams** are pretty molded chocolates in milk and dark chocolate. They come in **Amaretto, Black Cherry, Maple, Champagne, Coconut, Mocha, Raspberry, Peanut Butter, Vanilla, Caramel Butter Rum**, and **Pistachio/Orange**. The centers are ultra-creamy with good, distinct flavors, that tend to be quite sweet.

Brown and Haley products are widely available from a variety of retailers throughout the Pacific Northwest. "Seconds" of their products—mis-wrapped and not quite perfect candies—are sold at bargain prices at their factory in Tacoma. It's worth a visit to the industrial side of town.
Getting there: *On the east side of Tacoma in an industrial section of town on E 26th and G.*

LA CONNER

Surrounded by tulip fields and nestled beside the Swinomish Channel, La Conner has plenty of scenery and interesting shops to satisfy the most discriminating visitor. It's also home to some great chocolate.

Restaurants

Palmer's Restaurant and Pub
205 E Washington Street, La Conner, WA. (360) 466-4261
♥♥♥ Upstairs from the pub, **Palmer's Restaurant** is a Northwest fine dining house with a continental feel—exposed beam ceiling, river rock behind an iron fireplace, French prints on the walls, lace curtains, and leaded glass windows. Entrees include lamb with garlic, smoked salmon with wild mushrooms and penne, and grilled pheasant. Palmer's chocolate desserts, all made with Callebaut chocolate, include **Chocolate Mousse**, which is served with whipped cream, and is smooth with a solid chocolate flavor.

Their **Pot de Creme** topped with whipped cream is so thick you have to really push your spoon into it. It's worth the effort for the intense chocolate flavor.
Getting there: *On Washington at 2nd.*

La Conner Seafood and Prime Rib House
614 S 1st Street, La Conner, WA. (360) 466-4014

♥♥ **La Conner Seafood and Prime Rib House** is the town's venerable seafood house. It overlooks the Channel and Rainbow Bridge and you can watch the fishing boats come in from the bar, the outdoor deck, or windowside tables. They serve lunch and dinner, including sandwiches, salads, steaks, and plenty of seafood selections. The chef also makes all his desserts from scratch, including **Deep Dark Chocolate Mousse** made with Grand Marnier, brandy and creme de cacao, and garnished with whipped cream and a rolled cookie wafer. It has a satisfying, rich, dark, chocolate flavor.

Possessed by Chocolate is a fudge-like dark chocolate pie with an almond butter crust on top, garnished with whipped cream, raspberries, and a wafer cookie. This dessert has a smooth, darkly chocolate flavor and the chunky, tart raspberries add a good contrast to the chocolate.

The **Double Chocolate Cheesecake** starts with a graham cracker crust followed by a chocolate cheesecake marbled with Callebaut chocolate topped with bittersweet chocolate, garnished with whipped cream. The graham cracker crust has a wonderfully buttery homemade taste and the cheesecake has a cheesy richness.
Getting there: On the main thoroughfare in downtown La Conner.

Calico Cupboard Café and Bakery
720 S 1st, La Conner, WA. (360) 466-4451
Also in Mt. Vernon and Anacortes, WA.

♥♥ A little café decorated in country style with antique oak tables and chairs and old time ceiling fans, **Calico Cupboard Café and Bakery** is a comfortably casual place for breakfast or lunch. They serve the usual breakfast fare. Lunches include soups, sandwiches, and hot sandwiches like grilled eggplant and roasted red pepper, Thai veggie wrap, and roast turkey—all on their own breads. Their bakery offers a variety of breads, muffins, breakfast rolls, cookies, cobbler, and pies by the slice or whole. Chocolate lovers should try the **Chocolate Silk Pie**, a generous wedge of whipped mousse-like chocolate filling in a flaky crust topped with real whipped cream and garnished with cocoa and chocolate chips. It's smooth, light, and chocolaty.

Their **Fudgy Wudgy Brownie** is a rich 3-inch square of chocolate walnut brownie, topped with a cream cheese layer, garnished with drizzles of melted dark chocolate. It's moist and chock full of nutty/chocolaty goodness.

Calico's **Rocky Road Bar** has a dark brownie layer and sweetened cream cheese layer thickly frosted with milk chocolate frosting with tiny marshmallows. It's moist, but the frosting makes it too sweet for this reviewer.

Getting there: At the south end of 1ˢᵗ.

Bakeries

Georgia's Bakery

109 N 1ˢᵗ Street, La Conner, WA. (360) 466-2149

♥♥ **Georgia's Bakery** is just off the main tourist track, but those in the know still find her. Mornings find locals lining up for freshly baked cinnamon, orange, and blueberry rolls, scones, croissants, a variety of breads such as French, wheat, sunflower, and cinnamon raisin, and cookies like macaroons, rugelah, and chocolate chip. Chocolate lovers will appreciate **Georgia's Brownies**, fat wedges of dark cake-like brownies made with good quality cocoa, unsalted butter, and walnuts.

Also try the **Chocolate-Dipped Orange Biscotti with Almonds**. They have a lovely orange-almond flavor that combines nicely with the Guittard chocolate and, unlike many of these Italian cookies, they won't break your teeth.

Getting there: On N 1ˢᵗ at the corner.

Chocolate Shops

Cascade Candy Company

605 S 1ˢᵗ Street, La Conner, WA. (360) 466-2971

♥♥♥ Nineteen years ago Bob Prince and his wife Peggy started the **Cascade Candy Company**, the most well-known candy company in the Skagit Valley. Keys to their success included using the best ingredients such Guittard chocolate and local ingredients when possible, and keeping the candy very fresh by making it in small quantities. In November 1997, the company was purchased by first-time candy makers, brother and sister team Chuck and Ralynne Kiser. While the candies aren't as pretty, Chuck and Ralynne are moving along the learning curve and they're using the same excellent recipes and techniques as the previous owners.

One of their signature candies is the **Cascade Truffle**. Unlike many oversized truffles, Cascade's are medium-sized and, because they use real essence oils for flavorings, the flavors are intense. They come in milk and dark chocolate in **Irish Cream, Swiss Chocolate with Rum, Lemon, Raspberry, Classic Milk Chocolate, Mocha, Cream Cheese, Mint**, and **Snow Queen** (white chocolate, heavy cream, and pure vanilla centers dipped in white chocolate).

Their **Chocolate-dipped Caramel** is soft, chewy, and buttery. Cascade **Barnacles** (their version of turtles), which come in pecan, macadamia, cashew-macadamia, and almond in milk or dark chocolate, consist of 2 patties of chocolate sandwiching a layer of soft caramel and plenty of nuts.

They seed their **Chocolate Walnut Fudge** with Whidbey's Port Wine rather than with vanilla. The wine acts to inhibit the sweetness slightly and gives the fudge a delightfully rich rather than overly sweet flavor.

Cascade Candy will dip almost anything. Their **Chocolate Potato Chips** dipped half in dark chocolate, half in white chocolate are crunchy and the salty potato chips add an interesting flavor to the chocolate. Bet you can't eat just one! They also dip red licorice, which for this reviewer, is less successful.

In the fall, Cascade doesn't just dip caramel apples, they make their famous **Royal Dessert Apples**, huge (6-7 inches across) Jonagold apples first dipped in soft caramel, then dark chocolate, then drizzled with milk chocolate, and white chocolate, and covered with chopped pecans. The result is nearly 2 pounds of tart, crisp apple, chewy, buttery caramel, and thick chocolate flavors. ***Getting there:*** *About halfway down 1ˢᵗ Street.*

MOUNT VERNON

Wildflowers Restaurant
2001 E College Way, Mt. Vernon, WA. (360) 424-9724
❤❤❤❤ **Wildflowers** is in an old house almost completely hidden by trees and dense foliage off busy College Way and its anonymous strip malls. With subdued lighting, tiny white Christmas lights, fire crackling in the fireplace, and soft classical music, Wildflowers is a wonderfully relaxing place to enjoy such entrees as pan-fried Samish Bay Oysters, New Zealand Lamb with garlic, herbs, and pistachios with zinfandel-orange-mint sauce, or chicken stuffed with sausage, almonds, and dried apricots with port-orange-ginger sauce.

Their chocolate desserts, which are all beautifully and dramatically presented, combine ingredients not often found with chocolate in delicious and complex ways. The **Chocolate Mousse** is Belgian dark chocolate flavored with Whidbey's Loganberry Liqueur. It's served in a fluted glass with whipped cream and "antlers" of dark chocolate. This richly chocolate mousse has a depth not often found in this type of dessert. The Loganberry Liqueur doesn't add a berry flavor, but a wonderful richness that demands another taste.

"Jolt" is a flourless chocolate cake flavored with espresso, Grand Marnier, and fresh orange that's served with a ribbon of whipped cream, shaved chocolate, mint sprigs, and a chocolate fan that looks like a butterfly. It has a lovely fresh orange flavor that blends well with the deep chocolate flavor.

Wildflowers' variation on the Italian classic dessert, **Tiramisu**, includes lemon-orange pound cake, de-caf espresso, sweetened cream cheese instead of Marscapone, and no alcohol. The pound cake recipe is from Grandma Rose of Portland's Roses's Bakery. It's served in an individual soufflé dish with dollops of whipped cream around the edges, garnished with shaved chocolate, mint sprigs, and a chocolate butterfly. The result is creamy with a lovely blending of flavors. Share this one with a friend—it's big.
Getting there: In North Mt. Vernon, just past the Hawthorne Lawn Cemetery on E College Way.

Calico Cupboard Café and Bakery
121 B Freeway Drive, Mt. Vernon, WA. (360) 336-3107
♥♥ (See review under La Conner, WA.)
Getting there: On Freeway Drive near 1st.

City Bakery
514 S 1st, Mt. Vernon, WA. (360) 336-3001
♥♥ Skip the in-store bakeries and head to **City Bakery**, an institution in downtown Mt. Vernon for over 100 years. In this full-service, from-scratch bakery, owner Pat Grenfell and her crew make a large selection of Danish, muffins, cookies, and breads such as egg, white, and their famous Swedish rye. They also sell cakes by the slice or whole, including their **Orange Buttercream Chocolate Cake**, 2 layers of very fine-textured medium chocolate cake filled with dobash (chocolate custard) and lightly frosted with a creamy orange buttercream. Or enjoy their **German Chocolate Cake**, a single layer of the same chocolate cake topped with a thick layer of pecan-coconut and frosted on the sides with chocolate buttercream. The coconut topping is moist and full of coconut flavor. Their **Chocolate Cake with Dobash Topping** tops a single layer of their chocolate cake with a thin layer of chocolate buttercream followed by a thicker layer of chocolate dobash. The sides are frosted with chocolate buttercream. The cake has a good chocolaty flavor, but this amount of dobash is a bit sweet.

Their **Frosted Cream Cheese Brownie** is a 2x3-inch dark chocolate brownie with a thin layer of cream cheese, frosted with dark chocolate. The brownie is dense and chewy and the cream cheese has just the right cheesy flavor.

City Bakery makes **Chocolate-dipped Florentines** by rolling crisp almond cookies and filling them with buttercream and dipping each end in dark chocolate. The result is a cookie that's not long on chocolate flavor, but one that's chewy and full of sweet almond taste.

Their **Macaroon Mountains** are giant (4-inch) macaroons piled high like a mountain with the top dipped in dark chocolate. The macaroons are crispy on the outside, chewy and sweet on the inside. The chocolate is an added treat.

City Bakery also makes their own **truffles** which are surprisingly good—creamy centers, not too much chocolate coating, and rich flavors. They come in **Kahlua, Maple** (this reviewer's favorite), and **Mocha**. Their **Chocolate-covered Caramels** are made with their homemade caramel, which is chewy, medium soft, and not too sweet. They also make nut and raisin clusters.
Traveler's note: They don't make their chocolates during the summer months.
Getting there: *In downtown Mt. Vernon on 1ˢᵗ.*

BOW

Rhododendron Café
5521 Chuckanut Drive, Bow, WA. (360) 766-6667
♥♥♥♥ Amidst the flat, lush farm fields, owner Carol Shank and her husband have carved out a unique dining establishment with the **Rhododendron Café**. Open for lunch and dinner Friday, Saturday, and Sundays, they serve flavorful dishes such as chicken parmesan, Cajun pasta with prawns, oysters, and mushrooms, and pan seared mahi mahi with chanterelles. Even kids have their own menu—pizza, PBJ sandwiches, mac and cheese, and cheese quesadilla. They also have an impressive wine list. Don't miss out on their homemade **Belgian Bittersweet Chocolate Ice Cream**. This is some of the best ice cream this reviewer has ever eaten. If you like rich, fudgy ice cream with an intense chocolate flavor, you'll love this.

*Traveler's Tip: Be sure to stop in the **Rhody Too Gallery and Gifts** next door to the Rhododendron Café. They carry some terrific local pottery, jewelry, and other high quality crafts.*
Getting there: *On Chuckanut Drive at W Bow Hill Drive.*

The Oyster Bar
2578 Chuckanut Drive, Bow, WA. (360) 766-6185
♥♥♥ Perched amidst the trees overlooking Samish Bay, **The Oyster Bar's** wood paneled dining room feels like you're in a treehouse and every table has a great water view. They specialize in fresh seafood and you can't get any fresher than the shellfish

they buy from the Taylor Shellfish Farm just down the hill. They also make all their own desserts, which change seasonally. One of their chocolate staples is **Chocolate Decadence,** a nearly flourless cake made with espresso and served with dollops of lightly whipped cream and raspberry, white chocolate, and dark chocolate sauces. It's exquisitely moist with a rich, melty chocolate flavor.

Getting there: Just a few miles outside of South Bellingham on Chuckanut Drive.

Oyster Creek Inn
2190 Chuckanut Drive, Bow, WA. (360) 766-6816

♥♥♥ A contemporary restaurant along a shady creek, **Oyster Creek Inn** sports a nautical theme with its navigational maps, nautical table lamps, and wooden boat models. Its windows provide wrap-around views of Oyster Creek, where you can watch salmon spawning in season. Oyster Creek serves lunch and dinner, offering dishes such as lamb chops with raspberry sauce, Samish Bay oysters, and veal medallions with crab and béarnaise. For dessert, try their **Chocolate Decadence**, a wedge of thick, fudgy, nearly flourless cake made with Guittard chocolate. It's a cross between fudge and a rich brownie. The chunky raspberry sauce adds just the right sweet/tartness.

Getting there: Just a few miles outside of South Bellingham on Chuckanut Drive.

*Traveler's Tip: If you like fresh shellfish, stop in at the **Taylor Shellfish Farm** (their driveway is right next to the Oyster Creek Inn) and pick up some fresh oysters, crab, or clams. They also smoke their own oysters. They're closed on Mondays and holidays.*

BELLINGHAM

Restaurants

Il Fiasco
1309 Commercial, Bellingham, WA. (360) 676-9136

♥♥♥♥ Bellingham's favorite Italian restaurant, **Il Fiasco** sports high ceilings, Roman columns, and faux marble painted walls adorned with large paintings of Italian market scenes. Their menu includes dishes such as 3 cheese ravioli, grilled rack of lamb in garlic and marsala sauce, and orzo baked with crab, artichokes, and peppers in a garlic cream sauce. Chocolate lovers will go wild for Il Fiasco's rich **Chocolate Mousse Torte**, $2^1/_2$ inches of dark chocolate flourless torte topped with shaved bittersweet chocolate and a sprinkling of powered sugar, served with creme caramel anglaise. Bite into this intensely chocolate dessert and the chocolate flavor immediately goes all the way to the back of the tongue. The caramel creme has a rich, satisfying caramel flavor and a depth

often lacking in dessert sauces. Chocolate fans, this is one wonderful chocolate dessert!
Getting there: Downtown on Commercial.

Pacific Café

100 N Commercial, Bellingham, WA. (360) 647-0800

♥♥♥♥ **Pacific Café** is a comfortable downtown café decorated simply and elegantly with Asian art prints and rice paper screens. Open for lunch and dinner, entrees include dishes like chicken curry, crab cakes, duck Florentine, and calamari. The lunch menu features the same entrees (at reduced prices) as well as pastas and interesting salads like Alaskan prawns with wild greens, feta and green onions.

Do save room for pastry chef Wayne Kent's creations, which include **Danish Cream Tosca**, which starts with butter pastry with a thin layer of raspberry, followed by an almond butter praline center that's topped with toasted almonds in butter. Kent cuts the Tosca into a triangle and dips both ends in dark Belgian chocolate. The result isn't big on chocolate flavor, but it's a buttery almond delight.

It takes 2 pounds of cocoa beans to make 1 pound of cocoa powder.

Serious chocolate lovers will want to try the **Chocolate Decadence**, a slim wedge of fudge-like cake served with mousseline sauce (an egg-sugar base to which lightly whipped cream is added) and a chunky raspberry sauce. It's garnished with whipped cream, a fresh strawberry, mint, and a chocolate pastry curl. This wonderful dessert has a strong, deep chocolate flavor and a melt-in-the-mouth texture. The mousseline is frothy with a light vanilla flavor that adds a light compliment to the intense chocolate flavor.

Getting there: Downtown at the corner of W Champion and Commercial Streets.

Pastazza

Barkley Village, 2945 Newmarket Street, Suite 101, Bellingham, WA. (360) 714-1168

♥♥♥ **Pastazza** owners Fred and Lynn Berman used to own Innisfree, the highly-rated fine dining restaurant near Mt. Baker. This fun, casual, build-your-own-pasta place is their new venture in the rapidly growing North Bellingham area. The menu includes fresh pastas such as linguine, fettuccine, fusili, spaghetti, and penne with sauces like tomato, Alfredo, putanesca (hot red pepper), pesto, gorgonzola, and Mediterranean (eggplant, zucchini, mushroom) and tomato fennel. Then add what you'd like—chicken, sausage, scallops, clams, salmon, mushrooms, prawns, etc.

Fortunately for chocolate lover's, Lynn Berman brought her dessert recipes from Innisfree and her dessert case is bulging with delectable chocolate delights like her signature **Chocolate Pate**, a dark bittersweet truffle cut loaf style and served with mascarpone creme anglaise and raspberry sauce. It has an ultra-smooth texture and a wonderfully rich bittersweet flavor. If chocolate is a sin, this is it.

Pastazza's **Mocha Cheesecake** has a hazelnut crust with mocha flavored chocolate cheesecake drizzled with dark chocolate. The hazelnut crust is buttery with a rich hazelnut flavor and the cheesecake has the perfect, creamy texture with a deep mocha-chocolate flavor. This is something special for cheesecake lovers.

The **Chocolate Hazelnut Torte** is a dark, bittersweet cake with chopped hazelnuts that's served drizzled with chocolate glaze. It's a lot like a rich, dense brownie. The **Chocolate Pecan Pie** has a thin, flaky pie crust that's filled with a praline-chocolate mixture topped with pecan halves. It's a rich treat for pecan lovers.
***Getting there**: In North Bellingham, in Barkley Village off Woburn.*

Wild Garlic
114 Prospect Avenue, Bellingham, WA. (360) 671-1955
♥♥ **Wild Garlic** is a small restaurant with upholstered booths surrounded by exposed brick, deep green walls decorated with black and white photos, and piped-in jazz. They serve lunch and dinner, including dishes like crab crepes, roasted scampi, smoked salmon linguine. For dessert, they offer a dark **Chocolate Raspberry Truffle**, a wedge of thick bittersweet chocolate truffle cake, garnished with raspberry coulis and creme anglaise. It has a good bittersweet flavor and the raspberry sauce is quite tart.

The **White Chocolate Creme Brulee** comes in a custard cup served warm. The top has a lacy baked top and inside the custard is creamy, almost liquid. Allow this dessert to cool down so that it firms up. If it's too hot, the custard is runny.

This reviewer's favorite is the **Chocolate Peanut Butter Pie**, which isn't always on the menu. It starts with a chocolate cookie crust that's filled with 2 inches of peanut butter cream with finely chopped peanuts and topped with chocolate ganache. It's served with creme anglaise and chopped peanuts. The peanut butter cream is silky and the ganache smooth and appropriately chocolately. The creme anglaise, however, is lost with the peanut butter flavor and doesn't really add to this dessert.
***Getting there**: In downtown on Prospect near W Champion.*

Swan Café (At the Food Co-op)
1220 N Forest, Bellingham, WA. (360) 734-0542

♥ With all the fancy chocolate desserts available, sometimes it's tough to find a good, basic chocolate cake. You'll find one at the **Swan Café**. Their **Perfect Chocolate Cake** doesn't quite live up to its name, but it's 4 layers of devil's food cake, filled with whipped cream and frosted with chocolate buttercream. Be sure to ask when the cake was baked. It's best fresh and they sell it for at least 4 days after baking.

Getting there: On Forest, one of the main thoroughfares into the downtown.

Colophon Café

1208 11ᵗʰ Street, Bellingham, WA. (360) 647-0092

In the old Masonic Building sharing quarters with the venerable Village Books, **Colophon Café** may be the only café that runs right through the middle of a bookstore. Upstairs (street level) the Café has old time black and yellow naugahyde booths, a counter with stools, and a big case where they display baked goods. Downstairs are tables. Since 1985, the Colophon has been making a variety of sandwiches, salads, and 5 homemade soups every day. Their soups are so popular, they publish a monthly soup calendar. They also make all their own baked goods from scratch, including pies, cookies, cheesecakes, scones, brownies, and quiches. A signature dessert is their **Chocolate Chunk Cake**, a big slice of a single $2^1/_2$ inch layer of dark chocolate cake, thickly frosted with fudge frosting on the top, sides, and *bottom*! The frosting is fudgy and creamy, but the cake could be a bit more moist.

The **Chocolate Cheesecake** is a large slice that starts with chocolate cookie crust, 3 inches of chocolate cheesecake, topped with a thick chocolate ganache. The cheesecake is creamy and the ganache has a good chocolate flavor.

Getting there: In the old Fairhaven district on 11ᵗʰ, a half block down from Harris.

Bakeries

Suzanne's Specialty Baking

1305 Meador Avenue, suite B#1, Bellingham, WA.
(360) 676-0747

♥♥♥♥ If you've eaten dessert at Il Fiasco, you know that Suzanne Leech is a terrific baker (for a rave review of her **Chocolate Torte**, see Il Fiasco under Restaurants). A confirmed chocoholic, Suzanne knows how to make chocolate lovers beg for more. She makes **Chocolate Ravioli**, a dark chocolate "ravioli" filled with a rich, creamy, truffle-like filling. It's served on a bed of raspberry coulis, sprinkled with grated white chocolate. And you didn't think you liked ravioli!

Suzanne also makes a **Mattonella**, a chocolate walnut fudge brownie covered in dark and white chocolate ganache. It's dense and rich, with the ganache adding that extra chocolate flavor that takes this brownie from ordinary to extraordinary.

Her **Dark Chocolate Fudge Cookies** are made with walnuts and white chocolate chips. They're chewy and loaded with walnut flavor.

The bad news is that Suzanne doesn't have a retail shop. You can special order her goods or find them by the slice at **Il Fiasco, Stuart's Coffeehouse, Tony's Coffeehouse**, and **Bean Blossom Coffee Company**.
Getting there: On Meador Avenue in the Haskell Business Center.

Lafeen's Doughnuts
1466 Electric Avenue, Bellingham, WA. (360) 647-1703
In the mood for **chocolate doughnuts**? Head for **Lafeen's Doughnuts** out by Lake Whatcom. They make a huge selection of chocolate doughnuts, including **Frosted Devil's Food Cake Doughnuts, Frosted Cake Doughnuts With Peanuts, Chocolate Frosted French Cruellers, Chocolate Bars**, and cream-filled **Bismarks**. Their **Glazed Pinwheels** are 5 inches across and come frosted in both **chocolate** and **maple**. Their doughnuts are made fresh daily, they don't skimp on the chocolate icing, and the icing isn't overly sweet.
Getting there: On Electric in the Lake Whatcom area.

Chocolate Shops

Chocolate Necessities
4600 Guide Meridian, #109, Bellingham, WA. (360) 676-0589
♥♥♥ Bellingham chocolate lovers have been keeping **Chocolate Necessities** a secret for more than 10 years. No longer! European-trained chocolatier and owner Kevin Buck is passionate about producing high-quality **chocolates**. He and his staff use the highest grade Callebaut Belgian chocolate, don't add extra sugar, use pastry liquors that have intense flavor, and dip only small quantities to ensure absolute freshness. Chocolate Necessities specializes in gourmet **truffles**, small, elegant, creamy ganache centers dipped in milk or dark chocolate and flavored with **Amaretto, Bailey's Irish Cream, Chambord, Cointreau, Creme de Menthe, Double Chocolate, Frangelico, Grand Marnier, Kahlua, Rum, Triple Chocolate**, and **Nut Crunch**.

They also make a few molded and filled chocolates such as **Chambord-filled seashells** and **tiny monkeys** and **rabbits with Montego rum cream**.
Getting there: They're located in the second building in an industrial park on Guide Meridian, just after Meridian turns into Guide Meridian.

Paper Dreams
1206 11th Street, Bellingham, WA. (360) 676-8676

♥♥ It's actually a gift and card store, but **Paper Dreams** also makes some pretty good **fudge**. (The post mistress in Bow orders large boxes of it.) It's a firm fudge, not overly sweet, and the flavors are distinctive and intense. Chocolate lovers will appreciate their many chocolate flavors, including **Chocolate, Vanilla Chocolate Swirl, Chocolate Mint Swirl, Rocky Road, Peanut Butter Chocolate, Chocolate Rum Raisin, Chocolate Walnut,** and **Snickers**. They also have some unusual flavors like espresso (this reviewer's favorite), pumpkin, pumpkin caramel, and chewy praline.

Getting there: In old Fairhaven, just a few doors down from Village Books.

Ice Creameries

Mallard Homemade Ice Cream (Pastazza Presto)
2945 Newmarket Place, Suite 101, Barkley Village, Bellingham, WA. (360) 734-3884

♥♥♥♥ Pastazza, the pasta restaurant in Barkley Village, is known for desserts and Mike Post Van der Berg, owner of **Mallard Homemade Ice Cream**, makes all of their **ice cream**. You can buy Mallard ice cream to take home by the pint at the Pastazza retail store, Pastazzo Presto. Mallard is premium ice cream with 20% butterfat (most ice creams have 12-16%), which gives it a rich, creamy taste. The ice cream is made using salt and ice, like you would at home, with only 20% air (most ice creams are 35-50% air). The **Raspberry Chocolate** has a rich chocolate flavor with a hint of raspberry. It's creamy without clinging to the palette.

Getting there: In North Bellingham in Barkley Village off Woburn.

ANACORTES

The jump off point for the San Juans and British Columbia, Anacortes has a few places worth stopping for chocolate lovers.

Le Petite Restaurant
3401 Commercial Avenue, Anacortes, WA. (360) 293-4644

♥♥♥♥ A small dinner house known for fresh, seasonal ingredients prepared with a European flair, **Le Petite** serves dishes like Beef Tenderloin with peppercorn cream sauce, lamb marinated in Indonesian spices, and crab stuffed sole with mornay sauce. Their desserts are prepared with equal care, including their **Chocolate Roll**, a chocolate sponge cake, filled with lightly whipped cream, rolled and sliced jelly roll style. The cake is light and creamy, melting in the mouth, leaving a rich bittersweet chocolate taste.
Traveler's note: The entree menu as well as the desserts change

each week. If you have a favorite chocolate dessert, call ahead and ask that it be prepared for your arrival and the chef will try to accommodate your request.
Getting there: *On Commercial Avenue, the main thoroughfare, at 34th Avenue.*

Calico Cupboard Café and Bakery
901 Commercial Avenue, Anacortes, WA. (360) 293-7315
♥♥ (See review under La Conner, WA.)
Getting there: *On Commercial, the main thoroughfare, at 9th.*

Candy Shop

The Dessert Show
2302 Commercial Avenue, Anacortes, WA. (360) 293-8042
♥ You can hardly miss the bright pink building that houses **The Dessert Show**. It's half video store, half confectionery. The candy maker previously worked for Boehm's Candies and now cranks out his own **chocolates**. They're not pretty, but they're fairly tasty. He makes a small selection of **creams, truffles**, and **fudge**. The **Peanut Butter Cream** has an extra soft center with a scattering of peanut pieces and a delicate coating of chocolate. His **Lemon Cream** has a strong lemon flavor. They're known for their **Hennessey Cognac Truffles**, which are creamy with a good, strong cognac flavor. The **Fudge** is a soft, light milk chocolate that's on the sweet side.
Getting there: *On the main thoroughfare in Anacortes (Commercial) at 22nd.*

Bakery

Jim and Kerry's Original Cheesecake Company
2320 Commercial Avenue, Suite B, Anacortes, WA.
(360) 299-3326
♥♥♥ Less than 4 years ago, Jim and Kerry were fighting freeways in Los Angeles. Now, at **Jim and Kerry's Original Cheesecake Company**, they're wrestling vats of cream cheese making terrific **cheesecake.** They make 40 flavors of cheesecake (not all are available at the same time), available by the slice or whole. These are big cheesecakes, a full 3 inches tall, and weighing in at a couple of pounds each. Their **Chocolate Cheesecake** has a thick, sweet crust, followed by cheesy, creamy chocolate cheesecake, topped with chocolate ganache. Their **Chocolate Hazelnut Cheesecake** is the same good-tasting chocolate cheesecake with chopped hazelnuts. Their **White Macadamia Nut Cheesecake** is a traditional white cheesecake with chopped macadamia nuts in the filling and topped with white chocolate drizzles and whole macadamias. It's very creamy and has a nice cheesiness to it.

Jim and Kerry tried dipping their cheesecake in chocolate, but they weren't happy with the thin, tasteless dipping products available. Now they make their own with good quality Guittard chocolate—it's thick, rich, and sweetly dark. They cover slices of frozen cheesecake on a stick with it and call them **Wedgies**. It's heaven on a stick for cheesecake lovers. Let your Wedgie warm up just slightly so you can appreciate the cheesiness of the cheesecake along with the rich chocolate coating.

Jim and Kerry also make a **chocolate cake** they call **Blackout**. It's an impressive 6 inches tall with 2 thick layers of dark chocolate cake, thickly filled and frosted with a dense ganache. It's garnished with dollops of ganache, a solid half-circle of semi-sweet chocolate, and the sides are densely covered with tiny chocolate chips. The cake is moist and fine-textured and the ganache is thick and rich. This is a HUGE piece of cake—share it.

Getting there: *Turn on 24th at Commercial. Jim and Kerry's is located behind Bunnies by the Bay.*

Wildflower Restaurant
Mount Vernon, Washington
CHOCOLATE MOUSSE

8 servings

8 ounces semi-sweet chocolate, chopped (preferably Callebaut)
4 tablespoons butter
$1/2$ cup espresso or very strong coffee
$1/3$ cup Whidbey's Liqueur
$1/4$ cup Whidbey's Port
$3/4$ cup whipping cream
5 egg whites

The liqueurs add a wonderful depth and complexity to this rich chocolate mousse.

Combine the chocolate, butter and espresso in the top of a double boiler over simmering water. Heat, stirring occasionally, over medium heat until chocolate is melted and mixture is smooth. Remove double boiler from heat. Stir in Liqueur and Port. Cool to 90 degrees.

In a medium bowl, whip the cream until soft peaks form. Set aside. In another medium bowl, beat the egg whites until soft peaks form.

Beat the chocolate mixture into the whipped cream. Fold the egg whites into the chocolate mixture 1/3 at a time, folding carefully until well combined.

Spoon into 8 dessert glasses and chill.
See *Raw Egg Warning*, page 17.

San Juan Islands

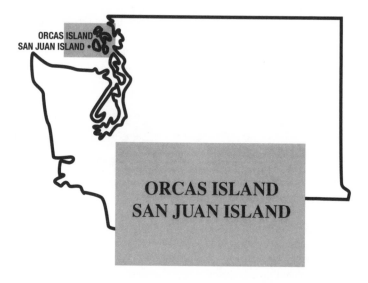

ORCAS ISLAND
SAN JUAN ISLAND •

ORCAS ISLAND
SAN JUAN ISLAND

The San Juan Islands are a cluster of tree-clad rocks in the Georgia Strait just below the Canadian border. They are exceptionally beautiful with soaring eagles, lush seaside meadows, gnarled trees, and colorful wildflowers. Just off shore, seals and Orca whales patrol the waters.

Great Things to Do

• **Watch Whales and Other Wildlife. Western Prince Cruises, Friday Harbor, WA.** (360) 378-5315. The waters around the San Juan Islands are home to a cornucopia of wild life, including Orca "killer" whales. A great way to see and learn more about marine mammals, geology and natural history is to take a naturalist-lead tour.

• **Dig Clams. Spencer Spit, Lopez Island, WA.** Bring your clam shovels and buckets for some great clam digging along Spencer Spit's long rock and sand bar. Check with local authorities for restrictions/permits.

• **Bike Ride.** Bike riding is a favorite past time on the Islands and Lopez Island, with its relatively flat terrain, is one of the favorites. Bring your own or rent a bike at one of the local stands.

• **Check Out the Whale Museum, Friday Harbor** (San Juan Island), **WA.** (360) 378-4710. Nature lovers will appreciate the Whale Museum's fascinating exhibits and programs about underwater creatures that inhabit the waters around the San Juans.

• **Hike a Mountain. Mount Constitution,** Moran State Park, **Orcas Island, WA.** Orcas Island, the biggest, boasts the highest spot in the islands. At 2,407 feet, with plenty of hiking trails, the mountain offers spectacular views of the islands, Canada and the Cascade and Olympic mountain ranges.

• **Retreat to Rosario. Rosario Resort,** One Rosario Way, **Eastsound** (Orcas Island), **WA.** (360) 376-2222. The former home of ship builder Robert Moran, this 1909 home, the centerpiece of Rosario Resort, is a great place for a tour. Listed on the National Register of Historic Places, the Craftsman mansion features walls that are 12 inches thick, 6 tons of copper roofing, and some quirky nautical touches (the mansion was built by Moran's ship carpenters). Some of the rooms are restored with period furniture while others feature nautical displays. A magnificent 1913 Aeolin player organ with more than 1,900 pipes dominates the downstairs and free nightly concerts are offered.

Terrific Places to Stay

Chestnut Hill Inn, P.O. Box 399, **Orcas, Orcas Island, WA.** (360) 376-5157. Situated on a gentle hill overlooking pastures, firs, and a pond for rowing and fishing, Chestnut Hill is about as pastoral and relaxing as it gets. Innkeepers Marilyn and Dan Loewke know how to make guests feel pampered. Their special touches include 4-poster feather beds with Egyptian linens, fluffy robes and slippers, and fireplaces in every room. The 3 rooms upstairs have private baths and lovely views and share a common refrigerator stocked with champagne. The garden room downstairs has a garden patio. For a romantic getaway, the Chestnut Suite is a private retreat with a mini-refrigerator, Jacuzzi tub, special snacks, and a garden veranda. Guests are treated to multi-course breakfasts. November through March, guests can enjoy Marilyn's gourmet dinners by reservation.

Friday's, 35 First Street, **Friday Harbor, San Juan Island**, WA. (360) 376-5157. Situated right in the middle of town next to a pizza and sandwich bistro, Friday's is a fun, casual kind of place that doesn't take itself too seriously. They bill themselves as a "hotel B&B," which means you get the privacy of a hotel with complimentary evening cookies and continental breakfast. Six rooms, some with private balconies, share a bath; 2 others have a private bath with a shower. Three of the rooms come with double Jacuzzi tubs. Two of these, the Chart Room and the Eagle Cove, are billed as "family suites," and come with kitchenettes, private patio or balcony, phone, and cable TV.

ORCAS ISLAND

Ship Bay Oyster House
Horseshoe Highway, Eastsound, WA. (360) 376-5886
♥♥♥♥ In a 130-year-old farmhouse overlooking Ship Bay, **Ship Bay Oyster House** is a favorite with locals and tourists alike for dishes like oysters fried in dijon glaze, crispy panfried osyters, salmon with saffron cream, and halibut marinated in tequila. For non-fish eaters, they also serve steaks and chicken dishes. Chocolate lovers should save room for Pat Anderson's **Chocolate Hazelnut Torte** because this is no run-of-the-mill torte. It's a dark chocolate flourless cake with bits of chopped hazelnuts that's topped with ganache and chocolate shavings. It's ultra-creamy and rich with a delightfully dark chocolate flavor that will make chocolate lovers weep for joy.

Ship's Bay Mud Pie has a chocolate graham cracker crust, Lopez Island Creamery Coffee Ice Cream filled with chopped chocolate Skor bars and it is topped with cocoa and hot fudge. Though it doesn't have a strong chocolate flavor, the ice cream is light and refreshing with a rich coffee flavor.

Traveler's note: Ship Bay Oyster House closes from mid-November until spring.
Getting there: *Off Horseshoe Highway a few miles outside of Eastsound.*

Café Olga
Star Rt. Box 53, Olga, WA. (360) 376-5098
♥♥♥ **Café Olga** is in the barn-like building that houses Orcas Artworks. Open for breakfast and lunch, they serve dishes like eggs ranchero, soups, salads like smoked salmon, sandwiches like

cashew chicken, and hot entrees like chicken enchilada. They bake all their own desserts, including their **French Silk Pie**, which has a flaky crust, a layer of dark chocolate cream, followed by a layer of milk chocolate cream, topped with whipped cream and chocolate shavings. The pie is light and extra creamy with a great blending of chocolate flavors. This is a great chocolate silk pie!

Traveler's Tip: Take some time to browse around Orcas Artworks before or after your meal at Café Olga. They have a good selection of high-quality arts and crafts such as hand-crafted pottery, jewelry, paintings, and woven goods.
Getting there*: At the junction of Horseshoe Highway and Point Lawrence Road (at the Olga Junction on the way to Doe Bay).*

Comet Café
Eastsound Square, Eastsound, WA. (360) 376-4220
♥ A pleasant little breakfast and lunch café in the heart of busy Eastsound, **Comet Café** features small tables and benches where folks enjoy sandwiches, soups, espresso drinks, and a large selection of oven items baked on-site such as croissants, muffins, scones, sticky buns, and pumpkin bread. Their **Devil's Food Chocolate Cake with 7- Minute Frosting** is a standard. It's 2 layers of dark, rich chocolate cake filled and frosted with a fluffy, sweet white cooked frosting that may remind you of your grandmother's cooking.

> *"Don't wreck a sublime chocolate experience by feeling guilty. Chocolate isn't like premarital sex. It will not make you pregnant. And it always feels good."*
> **– Lora Brody, author of *Growing Up on the Chocolate Diet***

Their **Chocolate Zucchini Bread** is moist with flecks of zucchini, but the flavor of nutmeg overwhelms the chocolate flavor. Comet's **Fudgy Brownie** is a 2x2½-inch square of dense, chewy brownie that's moist inside and crisp on top. It's an all-around good brownie.
Getting there*: In Eastsound, on North Beach Boulevard in the Eastsound Square.*

Bakeries

Roses Bread and Specialties
Eastsound Square, Eastsound, WA. (360) 376-5805
♥♥♥ Good wines, a variety of cheeses, and crusty, fresh-baked, hearth breads are the hallmarks at **Roses Bread and Specialties**.

They make a variety of hearth loaves, baguettes, challah, cracked rye, and whole wheat walnut breads. On Tuesdays and Saturdays, they also make **Chocolate Bread with Cherries**, a crusty hearth bread with cocoa-darkened dough that's flecked with chunks of dark Belgian Callebaut chocolate and cherry pieces. Served warm, the bread is chewy and slightly sour with warm, sweet dabs of chocolate and cherry.

They also make cheesecakes, including a **White Chocolate Cheesecake** that has a nut crust topped with 3 inches of creamy-dreamy, rich cheesecake that demands another bite.

Roses' cookies include **Chocolate Dipped Orange Cookies**, slightly sweet cookies, packed with chopped hazelnuts and dipped in dark chocolate. Their **Chocolate Chip Cookies** are classics—large (5 inches), packed with chips and homemade goodness.
Getting there: In Eastsound on North Beach Road, way in the back of Eastsound Square.

SAN JUAN ISLAND

Restaurants

Duck Soup Inn
3090 Roche Harbor Road, Friday Harbor, WA. (360) 378-4878
♥♥♥♥ Tucked in the woods overlooking ponds, **Duck Soup Inn** has an impeccable reputation with people who know great food. They serve dishes such as cilantro crusted smoked chicken breast with goat cheese and cranberry habanero chutney, filet mignon with pecan oregano pesto and beurre rouge, and wild gulf prawns with cherry tomatoes, saffron, orange zest and fresh basil. Chef/owner Gretchen Allison's desserts are equally delightful. Although they change regularly, chocolate lover's can count on treats like **Peppermint Brownies with Vanilla Mint Ice Cream**, a rich chocolate brownie, layered with a mint cream, served with Gretchen's homemade vanilla mint ice cream, garnished with dark chocolate drizzles, mint sprigs, and a dusting of powered sugar. The brownie is rich and chocolatey, chewy and moist in the middle, crunchy on top. The mint ice cream is light, smooth, and refreshing. Chocolate lovers who enjoy mint will love this dessert.

Duck Soup also offers a **Hot Fudge Sundae**, made with Gretchen's vanilla ice cream topped with hot fudge sauce made from dark Callebaut Belgian chocolate and cream. It's rich and creamy!

Traveler's note: Duck Soup is open daily during the summer, but only on weekends in the spring and fall. They close for the winter November 15.

Getting there: On Roche Harbor Road, a few miles outside of Friday Harbor.

Springtree Café

310 Spring Street, Friday Harbor, WA. (360) 378-4848

♥♥♥♥ **Springtree** is famous for the gnarly Camper Down Elm tree that dominates its front courtyard where you can sit and eat, weather permitting. Inside there are peach-colored walls, intimate tables, and soft jazz in the background. The menu is heavy with fresh fish—wild sturgeon, Chilean bass, Alaskan halibut. Chef/owner Jim Boyle whips up dishes like grilled salmon with lemon, olive oil, and basil. He also makes a variety of desserts, including his **Warm and Gooey Chocolate Cake**, flourless cake with chocolate truffles inside that's baked in a mold and then inverted on a bed of espresso sauce and a bit of marionberry sauce for color. It's topped with whipped cream, garnished with handmade, cocoa-dusted truffles, candied lemon, and praline, and served warm. This is a cake that lives up to its name. Push your spoon in and it falls into a pool of warm truffle. The edges of the cake have a lovely crispness and the inside is rich, gooey, and decadent. The espresso sauce is light, yet rich in espresso flavor. This innovative dessert will make chocolate lovers lick their lips, the spoon—maybe even the plate!

Getting there: In downtown Friday Harbor on Spring Street.

Friday Harbor House

130 West Street, Friday Harbor, WA. (360) 378-8455

♥♥ High on a bluff, **Friday Harbor House** and its restaurant have perhaps the best view of the harbor, the marina, and the busy ferry terminal in Friday Harbor. Guests enjoy dinner entrees like chicken stuffed with prosciutto and artichoke puree and coconut green curry seafood pot as well as more traditional dishes like pan-roasted halibut. Their chocolate desserts include a **Bittersweet Chocolate Truffle Cake**, with a chocolate cookie crust, followed by 2 inches of truffle on a bed of raspberry coulis, garnished by lightly whipped cream. This cake is ultra-smooth with a rich bittersweet flavor that lingers on the tongue.

The **Bittersweet Chocolate Ice Cream** is served in a lacy pastry bowl, garnished with milk chocolate filigree. The ice cream, which they make at the restaurant, is medium rich with a clean chocolaty flavor and the pastry bowl is delicate and crispy with a light sweetness.

Getting there: Up the hill from the ferry on West Street.

The Place Next to the San Juan Ferry

1 Spring Street, Friday Harbor, WA. (360) 378-8707

♥♥ Perched right over the water with a bird's eye view of the San Juan Ferry that gives this place its name, **The Place Next to the**

San Juan Ferry is a casual dinnerhouse that serves dishes like tiger shrimp sauté, filet mignon with Whidbey Port sauce, and fresh fish. One of their signature desserts is **Mocha en Forchetta** (mocha on a fork), a custard flavored with espresso and Belgian chocolate that's served in a coffee cup and topped with a mound of whipped cream and garnished with shaved white and dark chocolate and a chocolate-covered espresso bean. This totally creamy dessert is a nice blending of chocolate and espresso flavors. It's a small serving, so make your friend order her own.

A special dessert is their **Chocolate Grand Marnier Truffle Souffle**, which is baked to order (wait 20 minutes). It's a chocolate soufflé with a truffle baked into the middle, served with whipped cream. When it arrives, the aroma of freshly baked chocolate is wonderful. The soufflé has a light chocolate flavor, crispy edges, and a melty truffle center that's almost liquid chocolate. The Grand Marnier sneaks up on the bittersweet chocolate flavor, making for a nice combination.

Getting there: At the foot of Spring Street near the ferry.

Chocolate Shops

San Juan Coffee Roasting Company

18 Cannery Landing, Friday Harbor, WA.
(360) 378-4443/(800) 624-4119

♥♥ The **San Juan Coffee Roasting Company** is famous for their coffee, but they also carry a large selection of **chocolates**. Although they don't make their own, they carry a full line of **truffles** from Bellingham chocolatier Kevin Buck of **Chocolate Necessities** (see Bellingham for review) and a number of different chocolates from Bakers of Seattle including **nut clusters, fruit strings** (jelly sticks)**, seafoam chunks, peanut butter fudge bars**, and **chocolate creams**.

Getting there: In the shopping area right next to the ferry landing.

Chez Daniel
Victoria, British Columbia
CLASSIC TRUFFLES

Makes approximately 3 dozen truffles.

12 ounces semi-sweet chocolate
1 cup heavy cream
$1/4$ cup unsalted butter
1 ounce liqueur (amaretto, kahlua, etc.), optional
unsweetened cocoa

Melt chocolate in a double boiler.

In a heavy saucepan, heat cream and butter over medium heat until bubbles form on the sides of the pan, do not boil.

Mix the cream/butter mixture with the melted chocolate. Stir with a mixer on low speed for 10 minutes to cool. If desired, add 1 ounce of liqueur.

Easy to make and keep in the refrigerator ready for company, these truffles are incredibly silky with a deep chocolate flavor.

Put into covered container and refrigerate overnight.

Spoon out mixture by teaspoon or use a small scoop. Roll in high-quality unsweetened cocoa just before serving.

From *The Chocolate Lover's Guide Cookbook*,
Pacific Northwest Edition.

WASHINGTON

Olympic Peninsula

**POULSBO
PORT ORCHARD
PORT TOWNSEND
PORT ANGELES**

The Olympic Peninsula is home to towns like bustling Port Townsend with its Victorian ambiance. It also encompasses the remote Olympic National Park with a temperate rainforest where the average rainfall is 140 inches per year!

Great Things to Do

• **Visit the Park. Olympic National Park, WA**. With 1,300 square miles of wilderness in the heart of the Olympic Mountains, Olympic National Park may be one of the most beautiful and underused parks in the nation. Its crowing jewel is Mount Olympus, 7,965 feet of glaciers and steep, green valleys. More than 600 miles of trails and a bounty of wildlife, including black bears, mountain sheep, bald eagles, and Roosevelt elk, make this park ideal for hiking, camping, backpacking, or horseback riding.

• **Take the Waters. Sol Duc Hot Springs, Olympic National Park, WA**. (360) 327-3583. Twelve miles south of Lake Crescent in the Olympic National Park, weary travelers will find sublime relief in the 3 hot mineral pools. Follow your soak by a cold swim.

• **Go Naval. Naval Underseas Museum, Bremerton, WA**. (360) 396-4148. A fascinating exhibition of naval history, including the first submarine used in the Civil War, is on display at this one-of-a-kind museum. The **Bremerton Naval Museum**, (360) 479-7447, offers ship building history for the nautically-minded.

• **Get in Touch with Marine Life. Marine Science Center, Port Townsend, WA**. (360) 385-5582. In the summer, travelers can see and touch displays of sea creatures.

• **Tour Historic Homes. Port Townsend, WA**. At one time, residents of Port Townsend were certain their little town was destined to become a major city. Wealthy ship builders, logging tycoons, and others build magnificent Victorian homes on the bluffs. Then fate dealt a cruel blow and the railroad went to Seattle instead of Port Townsend and the town was destined to remain small and quaint. Anytime, you can wander the neighborhoods and marvel at the architectural wonders. In June and September, you can take a tour of historic homes and see inside too.

• **Check Out an Old Fort. Fort Worden State Park, Port Townsend, WA**. Fort Worden used to be part of the defense system protecting the Olympic Peninsula from foreign invaders. It was also the setting for the movie *An Officer and A Gentleman*. Today, the 400-plus acre site is a park with vintage officer's quarters, campgrounds, gardens, a theater, restaurant, and concert hall. The grounds are great for hiking, picnicking, kite flying, and bike riding.

Terrific Places to Stay

The James House, 1238 Washington Street, **Port Townsend, WA**. (360) 385-1238. The James House is perched on a bluff overlooking Port Townsend Bay, the Cascades and the Olympic mountains, and the busy ferry terminal. It's only a short walk to downtown and has exactly what Victorian affectionados look for—beautifully carved and turned woodwork, period tile fireplaces, and lovely antiques—all without being overdone. You won't find Victorian fussiness at The James House, just simple elegance. The best rooms are those that take advantage of the house's million dollar view. The Master/Bridal Suite features a fireplace, sitting room, private balcony, and sweeping views of the water. The Chintz room next door also has a great view and small balcony. Many of the rooms have private baths. All come with niceties like individual climate controls, extra pillows and blankets, and a full breakfast.

POULSBO

Molly Ward Gardens
27462 Big Valley Road NE, Poulsbo, WA. (360) 779-4471
♥♥ **Molly Ward Gardens** is out-of-the-way, but worth the trip. Sam and Lynn Ward have operated this renovated road house for 9 years. Count on filet mignon, fresh wild fish, New Zealand lamb and pork as mainstays of the ever-changing menu. Changes in fare depend on the bounty of the garden and the chef's whim. Sam assures us there is almost always a chocolate dessert like their **Flourless Chocolate Cake** to top off a meal. It's a dense, heavy chocolate with a chocolate wafer crust served with a swirl of blackberry puree. This dessert is for serious chocolate lovers and one not to be missed.
Getting there: On Big Valley Road just past Manor Farm Inn.

Judith's Tearooms and Rose Café
18820 Front Street, Poulsbo, WA. (360) 697-3449
♥ **Judith's Tearooms and Rose Café** has been delighting Poulsbo customers for years. Hospitality and tea luncheons are specialties. Judith greets every customer warmly. When you finish your meal, take time to dip into her dessert menu. The **Old Fashioned Chocolate Cake** is 2 generous layers of dark chocolate cake that's moist and light without being airy. The layers have a thick layer of smooth milk chocolate buttercream frosting, which isn't overly sweet. The cake is served on a bed of freshly whipped cream.
Getting there: On the main thoroughfare in Poulsbo.

PORT ORCHARD

Morningside Bakery
707 Bay Street, Port Orchard, WA. (360) 876-1149
♥♥ **Morningside Bakery** offers the usual breads and pastries— and **fudge**. This creamy, melt-in-your-mouth-fudge will keep your mouth watering as you head down the road. Smooth and creamy, the fudge is a delightful find in this waterside town.
Getting there: On the main street through downtown Port Orchard.

PORT TOWNSEND

A Victorian seaport known for its beautiful old downtown, grand Victorian homes, and spectacular setting, Port Townsend is a favorite with Northwesterners on holiday. Chocolate lovers will find it a delight.

Fountain Café
920 Washington Street, Port Townsend, WA. (360) 385-1364
♥♥♥♥ A little café a block off the main thoroughfare, **Fountain Café** is a culinary find locals know about and more travelers should too. Open only for dinner, they offer sumptuous dishes like roasted walnut and gorgonzola penne. Chef Kate Harrison's **Bittersweet Chocolate Hazelnut Torte** comes in a pool of raspberry puree and is garnished with whipped cream and toasted hazelnut halves. It's moist, rich, and velvet creamy without being overly sweet. The raspberry puree adds a good counterpoint to this rich dessert. It's a chocolate lover's fix for sure.
Getting there: Downtown on Washington near Taylor.

Lonny's
2330 Washington Street, Port Townsend, WA. (360) 385-0700
♥♥♥ Considered by many to be the best fine dining restaurant in Port Townsend, **Lonny's** is located on the edge of town in a light industrial area near a boat repair facility. The faux adobe walls decorated with simple botanical prints and the graceful arches leading from a bar/fireplace room give Lonny's a Mediterranean feel that's soothing. The menu reflects the Mediterranean influence with dishes like rigatoni melanzaone (tubular pasta with eggplant, marinara sauce, fresh mozzarella, sweet basil, and asiago cheese), capellini gamberoni (angel hair pasta with prawns, sweet onions, kalamata olives, roasted tomato, fresh oregano, and white wine), Spanish paella, and Greek scampi sauté. Even the coffee, Torrefazione Italia, has an Italian bite to it. They also have a large selection of nightly specials like fresh halibut with hazelnut crust.

Chef/owner Lonny Ritter serves several desserts made with chocolate. His **Chocolate Pecan Torte**, is a generous wedge of flourless torte topped with a very dark chocolate espresso icing. Beautifully surrounded by orange creme anglaise in which tiny Belgian chocolate hearts float, it's garnished by a fresh flower, a mint sprig, and 2 pecan halves. The torte is rich, yet light, and full of crunchy hazelnuts. The espresso icing is silky smooth with the espresso flavor adding a richness and depth and the creme anglaise brings a creaminess that helps tie all the flavors together.
Getting there: A block off Sims Road (which turns into Water Street), on the water side near Boat Haven.

The Silverwater Café

237 Taylor Street, Port Townsend, WA. (360) 385-6448

♥♥♥ Situated in a venerable old Victorian building with tall windows full of plants, high ceilings with fans, and simple wooden tables and chairs, **Silverwater Café** is a pleasant place for lunch or dinner. At lunch, they serve a variety of hot and cold sandwiches such as green chili and cheddar chicken breast, shrimp burgers, pasta, soups, and salads. The dinner menu features a large selection of seafood imaginatively prepared like prawns with cilantro-ginger-lime butter and Hood Canal oysters in blue cheese sauce, and a number of vegetarian dishes like rotini gorgonzola. Owner and baker David Hero does well by chocolate lovers with a selection of chocolate desserts that includes **Chocolate Truffle Orange Torte**, which starts with an Oreo cookie crust that's topped with 1 inch of very dense Cointreau-flavored chocolate truffle. Rich and full of chocolate-orange flavor, it's like biting into the center of a rich truffle.

David's **Chocolate Cake** is 2 layers of cake topped and filled with dark chocolate ganache and frosted on the outside with a chocolate buttercream. The cake is fine-textured with a good chocolate flavor. The ganache has an ultra-dark bittersweet flavor that's a nice contrast to the cake, and the buttercream is smooth and tangy.

The **Raspberry White Chocolate Cheesecake** has a thin, cake-like crust that's topped with 1½ inches of white chocolate cheesecake that's creamy with a bright, fresh raspberry flavor.

The **Chocolate Hazelnut Mousse** is light, almost airy, with a strong hazelnut flavor. Don't look for much chocolate flavor here, but you'll enjoy it if you're a hazelnut fan.

The **Chocolate Espresso Cheesecake**, this reviewer's favorite, has a thin crust that's topped with a smooth, rich chocolate espresso-flavor cheesecake. The espresso flavor doesn't overwhelm, but adds to the depth of this dessert and enhances the chocolate flavor. Even people who don't like coffee will love this one.

Getting there: Downtown at the corner of Washington and Taylor Streets

The Belmont

925 Water Street, Port Townsend, WA. (360) 385-3007

♥♥ **The Belmont** is located in an 1880's brick building that was formerly a bordello. Decorated in deep burgundy and forest green with exposed brick walls, old hardwood floors, and a deck and windows that overlook Port Townsend Bay, it's got plenty of ambiance. They serve lunch and dinner with dishes like duck with Whidbey Island liqueur, chicken with pistachio nuts and raspberry bacon vinaigrette, and classical dishes like tournedos maison, and filet with crab béarnaise and mushroom demi-glaze. They make some of their own desserts, but their excellent **Chocolate Chambord Cheesecake** comes from **Uptown Custom Catering**. It has a chocolate crust, 1½ inches of chocolate cheese cake, followed by a 1-inch layer of tangy cheese. It's topped with a thick, tart raspberry sauce. This dessert has a wonderfully cheesy flavor that lingers on the tongue. The top cheese layer is velvet smooth. The chocolate cheesecake layer offers a good blend of chocolate and cheese flavors and the raspberry sauce offers a nice accent to the chocolate and cheese.

Getting there: Downtown on Water Street between Taylor and Tyler.

Ice Creamery/Chocolate Shop

Elevated Ice Cream
627 Water Street, Port Townsend, WA. (360) 385-1156
♥♥♥♥ (ice cream)/ ♥♥ (chocolate candy) An institution in Port Townsend for 20 years, **Elevated Ice Cream** got its beginnings when Julie McCullouch started selling scoops of a local dairy's ice cream from an old elevator cage salvaged from St. John's Hospital. Hence the name. She and husband David now make some of the best premium **ice cream** in the Northwest. Their ice cream has only 12% butterfat, which makes it come cleanly off the tongue without any fatty residue. The lower butterfat also allows the flavors to really stand out. Their large volume of sales ensures that the ice cream is very fresh and they use quality ingredients like Guittard chocolate. For chocolate lovers, they always carry plain **Chocolate** and **Swiss Orange Chocolate Chip**, an orange-flavored chocolate ice cream with chocolate chips, that has an intense orange flavor that blends well with the chocolate. Other chocolate flavors rotate. Their **Mexican Chocolate**, this reviewer's favorite, has a wonderful cinnamony bite. At different times, they carry **Chocolate Banana, Chocolate Truffle Mint, Chocolate Hazelnut, Chocolate Chip, Chocolate Almond, Chocolate Malt, Chocolate Maltese Crunch** (chocolate malt-flavored ice cream with Grapenuts)**, Fudge Swirl,** and **Dark Chocolate**, among others.

They also sell **ice cream pies** and **cakes**, by the slice or whole in flavors like **Swiss Orange Chocolate Chip, Mint Chip, Oreo Cookie**, and **Espresso Vanilla**. For a special treat, try a **Tartuffo Ball**, a big scoop of chocolate hazelnut ice cream dusted in cocoa powder and ground hazelnuts. It's a chocolate-hazelnut delight! *Traveler's tip: Let the Tartuffo Ball warm up a bit to fully enjoy the subtleties of the flavors.*

Elevated Ice Cream also offers a small selection of desserts like marionberry pie, pecan pie, and, for chocolate lovers, **Espresso Chip Brownies** and **Black Bottom Cupcakes**, baked exclusively for them by a local wholesale baker. The **Espresso Chip Brownie** is dense, moist, and is topped with chopped walnuts and mini-chips. It's rich and delicious.

They've also been making their own **truffles** for several years in flavors like **Rum, Kahlua, Grand Marnier, Chocolate**, and **Amaretto**. They're small, about the size of a quarter, with thick centers and a thin coating of dark chocolate. They also dip their own **ginger**, a special mild variety from Australia, and the result is a sweet-hot treat ginger lovers will enjoy. Recently, Elevated Ice Cream expanded into a full chocolate shop next door where they sell not only their truffles and ginger, but also a wide selection of chocolates from Bakers of Seattle as well as a variety of other types of candy.
Getting there: *Downtown on Water Street.*

Bakery

Bread and Roses Bakery
230 Quincy Street, Port Townsend, WA. (360) 385-1044
♥♥♥ **Bread and Roses Bakery's** downtown location and big, sun-filled windows make it a place where locals like to linger over coffee with their favorite bakery item. They also serve a few soups, sandwiches, and salads, but the real draw is what comes from the oven. This from-scratch bakery uses quality ingredients like organic flour and turns out a good selection of croissants, scones, muffins, cinnamon rolls, fruit Danish, and breads. For chocolate lovers, they make a **Chocolate Mousse Pie** that has a chocolate cookie crust filled with 3 inches of light, almost airy chocolate mousse filling, topped with shreds of white chocolate. This dessert calls for uncooked eggs, but they use Egg Beaters, so even vegans can enjoy this one. It's ultra-creamy and satisfying.

They also make a wonderful **Death by Chocolate Cookie**, a huge, 6-inch round of crunchy chocolate, half-dipped in dark chocolate (or white chocolate), then drizzled with white chocolate. It's long on chocolate flavor with the excellent dark chocolate adding to the enjoyment.

Their **Double Chocolate Brownie** is 2x4 inches of chewy brownie with walnuts and chocolate chips throughout. It's moist on the inside, slightly crunchy on top—just how a good brownie should be.
Getting there: *Downtown on Quincy between Washington and Water Streets.*

PORT ANGELES

Bonny's Bakery
215 South Lincoln Street, Port Angeles, WA. (360) 457-3585

♥ You're running for the B.C. ferry and your tummy's empty. Take a left at the light, go up a couple of blocks to the old fire house on South Lincoln Street. At **Bonny's Bakery**, you'll find a selection of baked items like eclairs, lemon cake, carrot cake, cinnamon rolls, muffins, and breads (white, cinnamon raisin, sour dough, 10-grain). You'll also find their **Chocolate Heart**, a big cake-like brownie in the shape of a heart that's covered with rich chocolate ganache. It'll hold you until you get to those Victoria chocolate shops.

Getting there: Off the main road into Port Angeles, instead of turning right into the ferry terminal, at the next light (Lincoln), turn right. Go 2 blocks. Bonny's is on the right in the Old Fire House building.

Local Grounds
Redmond, Oregon
HELLO DOLLY BARS

Makes 24 bars

$^1/_2$ cup butter, melted
1 cup graham cracker crumbs
1 cup flaked coconut
1 cup semi-sweet chocolate chips
1 cup chopped pecans
1 cup sweetened condensed milk

Preheat over to 350 degrees.

Pour the melted butter into a 9x9-inch baking pan. Evenly spread the graham cracker crumbs over the butter. Sprinkle the coconut over the graham cracker crumbs. Add the chocolate chips and top with a layer of pecans. Spread the sweetened condensed milk over the chocolate chip layer. Bake for 30 minutes. Cool. Cut into 1x3-inch pieces.

These taste like tiny, buttery pecan pies— with chocolate! This easy recipe is a great one to make with kids. To cut the fat, substitute non-fat sweetened condensed milk. For a Northwest taste, substitute hazelnuts.

From *The Chocolate Lover's Guide Cookbook*, Pacific Northwest Edition.

Southwest Washington Coast and Southwest Washington

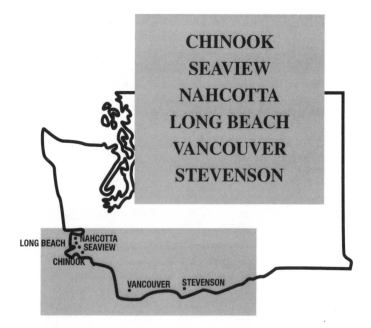

CHINOOK
SEAVIEW
NAHCOTTA
LONG BEACH
VANCOUVER
STEVENSON

*M*uch of the Pacific Northwest coast has the dubious reputation of being a culinary no-man's land. You can go for many miles without finding great food. The south Washington coast is home to the **Long Beach Peninsula**, a skinny finger of land that traces the Washington coastline. It has the distinction of having the longest beach in the Northwest and some of its best restaurants.

Great Things to Do

• **Dig Razor Clams**. **Long Beach Peninsula, WA**. Get up at the crack of dawn, wade out to the tidewaters in warm clothing and rubber boots, and dig furiously in the wet sand whenever you see bubbles. If you're persistent enough and don't mind getting cold and wet, you'll be rewarded with a true Northwest gourmet treat— buttery razor clams. Check with the local authorities for a license and bring your rubber boots.

• **Fly A Kite**. **Long Beach, WA**. Long Beach is perfect for beach kite flying. If you forget to bring your own, check out the selection at Long Beach Kites (360) 642-2202 or Stormin' Norman's (800-288-4512. In August, the **International Kite Festival** (360) 642-2400) fills the sky with hundreds of incredible kites. All year long, you can visit the **Long Beach World Kite Museum and Hall of Fame**, 3rd NW and Pacific Highway, Long Beach, WA. (360) 642-4020.

• **Ride A Moped, Long Beach, WA**. The Long Beach peninsula boasts the world's longest beach—28 miles of uninterrupted sand and waves. It's also one of the best places to hunt for Japanese glass floats that ride the Pacific currents and come to rest on the shore. A good way to explore the beach and find those floats is via moped. They're easy to operate and are legal on the beach. Look for the moped rental center just off main street in Long Beach.

• **Sample the Stinking Rose**. **Garlic Festival, Nahcotta, WA**. (800) 451-2542. The chefs and owner of The Ark Restaurant are garlic affectionados. So much so that they've created the Garlic Festival, a June celebration of the stinking rose in all its forms, including chocolate garlic!

• **Walk Among the Giants**. **Willapa National Wildlife Refuge**, **Seaview, WA**. Tiny Long Island, reachable only by boat, features a 275-acre old growth cedar grove. Stroll through these massive giants (some trunks are 11 feet in diameter) that soar 200 feet and you'll understand why we need to save the little old growth forest that remains in the Pacific Northwest.

Terrific Places to Stay

Shelburn Inn, 4415 Pacific Highway, **Seaview, WA**. (360) 642-2442. Step into the historic Shelburn Inn and you step back in time. The historic 1886 inn is decorated with rich green rugs, lovely period antiques, and unusual artistic touches like an East Indian bull vase complete with head and legs that serves as a coffee table. Half of the 15 rooms are in the original building, the others in the newer half, but they blend seamlessly together. The newer rooms tend to be larger, but all the rooms have niceties like individual heat controls, hair dryers, brass fixtures, and private decks. Although there are no phones or televisions in the rooms, guests are greeted with plates of freshly-baked cookies and coffee and tea are always available near the fireplace in the lobby area. In the morning, host/chef David Campiche treats guests to a sumptuous gourmet breakfast with entree selections like croissant stuffed with egg, ricotta, and winter chanterelles, spiced potato cakes with braised egg, and Willapa oyster scramble. All breakfasts are served with David's delicious country potatoes and freshly baked goods.

Skamania Lodge, 1131 Skamania Lodge Drive, **Stevenson, WA**. (509) 427-7700. Perched high on a cliff on the Washington side of the Columbia River Gorge, Skamania Lodge has the feel of a contemporary hunting lodge. The lobby and common area feature stone floors with throw rugs in Native American patterns, open-beamed ceilings that soar 3 stories, a huge fireplace around which are Arts and Crafts rockers, couches, loveseats, and wicker chairs and floor-to-ceiling windows that capture the view of the Columbia River below. Throughout the lodge are beautiful artworks—wood carvings, replicas of stone petroglyphs, and hand-woven rugs. The 195 contemporary guest rooms, all decorated in warm natural wood, some with fireplaces, wet bars, and balconies, are large and feature views of the river or forest. The fitness center features exercise equipment, with indoor pool, massage service, and a natural rock outdoor spa.

CHINOOK

The Sanctuary
794 Highway 101, Chinook, WA. (360) 777-8380
♥♥♥ If you've ever wanted to eat in church, **The Sanctuary** is the place to go. Geno and Joanne Leech bought the old, decommissioned 1906 Methodist Episcopal Church and changed very little. The ceilings soar to the church's steep roof. Angel wall sconces, an antique leaded glass door, and pews that serve as benches around crimson-clothed tables all add to the sanctuary feeling. Chef Joanne offers dishes like fresh local fish, pan fried oysters, chicken roulade, and rack of lamb. She also makes an excellent **Chocolate Rum Cake** that's a cross between a cake and a mousse pie. It's a wedge of cake topped with ganache, garnished with whipped cream and served on a bed of blackberry sauce. The result is dense, yet light with a rich rum flavor that isn't overpowering.

Pecan pie lovers will enjoy the **Chocolate Bourbon Pecan Pie**, a chocolatey variation on an old favorite. The top has a satisfying crunch while the middle is full of creamy, chocolaty goodness. The crust is delicate and flaky. This one is a winner!
Getting there: On the main highway at Hazel.

SEAVIEW

Cheri Walker's 42nd Street Café

4201 Pacific Highway, Seaview, WA. (360) 642-2323

♥♥ Located in a former Coast Guard barracks, the **42nd Street Café** is a casual, comfortable place with multi-colored vinyl table-cloths, embroidered curtains, and tables for 2 or 4 that serves breakfast, lunch, and dinner. Chef/owner Cheri Walker, formerly chef at the award-winning Shoalwater Restaurant, has created a place that fills the niche between the high-end (and high-priced) restaurants and the local burger and fried fish places. She serves traditional American dishes like fried chicken, sautéed chicken livers, and country fried steaks, lightened up with touches like wild mushrooms, as well as more contemporary offerings like ahi tuna, and sweet pepper ravioli with walnuts.

Chocolate lovers will find at least 1 chocolate dessert on Cheri's ever-changing dessert menu. Her **Chocolate Creme Brulee** is served in an over-sized, individual baking dish with a rosette of whipped cream and a dusting of cocoa. The bigger dish makes for plenty of delicate, lacy caramelized topping covering a creamy custard that's dotted with melted chocolate chips. Lovely!

> *"...the taste of chocolate is a sensual pleasure in itself, existing in the same world as sex.... Furtiveness makes it better."*
>
> –"Dr. Ruth" Westheimer

Raspberry Chocolate Chestnut Gateau is a 3-inch round flourless cake that's topped with whipped cream and served on a bed of raspberry syrup, garnished with chocolate shreds. The texture is a cross between a rich brownie and a mousse. It's rich and chocolaty and the raspberry syrup is sweet and light.

Chocolate Chili Brownie with Vanilla Ice Cream and Hot Fudge Espresso Sauce comes as 2, thin (1/2-inch) 4-inch squares of chili-seasoned brownie, served with a generous scoop of vanilla ice cream, topped with a rich, smooth hot espresso fudge sauce and whipped cream. Though they were a bit spicy for this reviewer's taste, if you like the combination of chocolate and chili, you'll like this. The vanilla ice cream helps cool the heat.

Getting there: On Pacific Highway at 42nd Place.

Shoalwater Restaurant (The Shelburn Inn)

4415 Pacific Highway, Seaview, WA. (360) 642-4142

♥ There's plenty of ambiance in the historic 1896 building that houses the **Shoalwater**. Richly-patterned teal and pink carpeting, red cloth-covered tables, fresh flowers, and plenty of oak woodwork all contribute to a feeling of elegance. For lunch, they serve dishes like mussel and clam chowder, sandwiches like pork, apple, and red onion roast turkey, Cougar Gold and bacon burger (for WSU fans), as well as light meals like crab and shrimp cakes, and Willapa Bay oysters. For dinner, they offer dishes like salmon, Willapa oysters, tiger prawns, and filet as well as a 4-course pre-fixe dinner that includes soup, appetizer, and choice of entree. If you've got any room left after all that food, pastry chef/owner Ann Kischner makes a **Chocolate Pecan Pie** that comes as a generous wedge served with a dollop of whipped cream and a tiny pastry heart. It's gooey with plenty of large pecan pieces.

Her **Gateau Mussoline**, a favorite on the menu, is a big slice of dense, deeply chocolate cake that's served with raspbery sauce and garnished with whipped cream and a chocolate fan. This dessert is crumbly and very rich.

White Chocolate Mousse, which comes in a large, stemmed glass, has a serious lemon flavor. It's light and tangy with a bright lemon flavor that you won't appreciate unless you're a real lemon fan. *Getting there: On the main highway in Seaview.*

NAHCOTTA

The Ark
273rd and Sandridge, Nahcotta, WA. (360) 665-4133
♥♥♥ **The Ark** always feels like a celebration. Tiny, sparkly lights, glitter-dusted garlic braids, colorful garlands, sprays, and ribbons festoon the walls above the linen-covered tables and wooden booths overlooking Willapa Bay. Chef Jamilla Lucas is known for her innovative use of Northwest ingredients, including garlic, and her rich, complex sauces. For dinner, they offer dishes like grilled salmon or Scotch salmon (deglazed with Scotch and orange juice), chicken and scallops tarragon, Willapa Bay oysters, pork or beef tenderloin, and chicken breast stuffed with goat cheese spinach, garlic, and pine nuts, as well as many fresh fish specials.

Pastry Chef Nanci Main, a dedicated chocophile, always offers a large selection of chocolate desserts like **Chocolate Decadence**, a rich, fudge-like torte made with dark, bittersweet chocolate and served with raspberry puree. The chocolate melts instantly in the mouth, leaving an intense chocolate flavor that lingers.

The **Snicker Mousse** alternates layers of peanut caramel and chocolate caramel mousse, whipped cream, and peanuts that are topped with a thin layer of ganache. If you liked Snickers Bars as a kid, you'll like this grown-up interpretation. The peanut butter mousse with its tiny bits of chopped peanuts has a delicate peanut butter flavor. The chocolate mousse is creamy with a rich, chocolate flavor. The layers of whipped cream add a lightness to the dessert and the ganache topping adds a chocolate richness. The result is creamy and crunchy. You'll vow never to eat another Snickers Bar again. *Getting there: On the old Nahcotta dock next to the oyster fleet.*

LONG BEACH

Chocolate Shop/Ice Creamery

Milton York
109 S Pacific, Long Beach, WA. (360) 642-2352   *closed 8/11*
♥♥♥ Started in 1882, **Milton York Candy Company** is the oldest candy company operating continuously in the same location in the country. Twenty years ago when current owners Maxine and Al Levy took over the tiny chocolate shop next door, the old candy recipes were written on the walls. They had them carefully copied onto cards and have followed the time-tested secrets ever since using high-quality Guittard chocolate. One of their signature candies is **Chocolate Velvet**, generous 4x2-inch logs of velvety chocolate cream covered in milk or dark chocolate. They're silky and delicious! Velvets also come in **Rum** and **Peanut Butter**.

Another favorite is the **Peanut Butter No Jell**, a 4-inch square of soft dark chocolate, topped with a thin layer of peanut butter cream. It's soft and creamy with a strong peanut butter flavor. The **Milton York Special** is a milk chocolate sandwich with a center of dark chocolate packed with chopped walnuts. The chocolate has a firm snap when you bite into it and the taste is rich and chocolaty.

Milton York also makes use of local ingredients like cranberries. Their **Cranberry Centers** and **Cranberry Jell Sticks**, made with local cranberries and covered in chocolate, are smooth, the perfect jelly-firm texture, and a good cranberry flavor that is tart/sweet. They also make a **Cranberry Fudge**, a tangy candy that has a beautiful cranberry color and bits of cranberries. It isn't chocolate, but it's quite good.

Their **Butter Creams** such as **Vanilla, Chocolate, Lemon, Orange, Maple Nut, Coffee, Victoria, Strawberry**, and **Raspberry Cream**, are extra creamy with intense flavorings. The **Seafoam** is buttery, crisp, and light honeycomb that's covered in milk or dark chocolate.

If you're lucky enough to be in Long Beach around Christmas, ask for a **Sugar Plum**, rich penoche (maple fudge made with brown sugar and whipping cream) with chopped citrus fruits, dates, and nuts covered in milk chocolate. It's a rich, old-fashioned flavor that's not overly sweet. Or enjoy a holiday **Centennial**, a flat, disk-shaped cream flavored with brandy or Peach Schnapps and covered in chocolate. It's a wonderful treat!

Milton York also sells premium **ice cream** with 18% butterfat and very little air. For chocolate lovers, they offer **Chocolate** and **Rocky Road**. They also make a rich hot fudge sauce. *Traveler's note: The ice cream is best in the summer when it's very fresh.*
Getting there: *In downtown Long Beach on the Pacific Highway near the 4-way stop.*

VANCOUVER

Hudson's Bar and Grill (The Heathman Lodge)
7801 NE Greenwood Drive, Vancouver, WA. (360) 816-6100
♥ Wedged between a freeway and a suburban shopping mall, The Heathman Lodge and its restaurant, **Hudson's Bar and Grill**, is a stunning, peeled log lodge built in the old tradition. The lodge and restaurant are impressive with 20-foot ceilings, oversized wrought iron ceiling fixtures, sconces, and lamps, burgundy upholstery and carpeting in Native American designs, heavy wood tables and arm chairs, exposed timbers, and a rock fireplace hung with a massive dug out canoe. The effect is rustic and comfortable. Hudson's serves breakfast, lunch, and dinner, with dinner entrees like lamb shank, penne pasta with sausage, mustard and herb crusted pork chop, salmon with oyster-corn bread stuffing, and stuffed quail. Their signature chocolate dessert is **Chocolate Torte with Raspberry Sauce**, a generous wedge of flourless torte garnished with a rosette of whipped cream, shaved chocolate, and powered sugar, served with raspberry sauce. While they don't get any awards for originality, this torte has a smooth, soft texture and a rich taste. The sauce, though a bit thick, is tart/sweet.
Getting there: *Off SR 500 near the Vancouver Mall. Take Turston to Parkway.*

> *"We eat, sleep, and even dream chocolate."*
>
> – Iva Elmer, owner
> JiCava's Chocolates
> and Pastries, Portland, OR.

Candy Shop

Van Duyn Chocolates
Vancouver Mall, 8700 NE Vancouver Mall, #125, Vancouver, WA. (360) 254-0413
♥♥♥ (See review under Candy Shops, Portland.)

STEVENSON

Breathtaking scenery defines the Columbia River Gorge, the canyon dredged out by the mighty Columbia River. The good news for chocolate travelers is there's some great chocolate to be found on the Washington side of the Gorge.

Skamania Lodge
1131 Skamania Lodge Way, Stevenson, WA.
(509) 427-7700/(888)-SKAMANIA
♥♥♥ Heavy timbers, open-beam ceilings, wood tables, chairs, and booths, hardwood floors, and huge windows give this contemporary lodge's dining room a casual, warm feel. The lunch menu includes salads (Caesar, cobb, seafood) and sandwiches like burgers, smoked turkey and prime rib. At lunchtime, pastry chef Kristin Wood offers guests beautifully-presented desserts like **Malted White Chocolate Mousse**, scoops of light, subtly malt-flavored mousse that are served in a chocolate cup with a chocolate "straw," a maple tuile (pastry) "saucer" with a tuile "spoon." It looks just like an ice cream soda and is both beautiful and delicious.

Another lunch time offering is the **Mocha Almond Fudge Torte**, 2 layers of chocolate almond torte, coffee buttercream, and devil's food cake, topped with chocolate glaze. This rich, complex torte comes in 2 small triangles and is served in an **Almond Praline Cup with Caramel Ice Cream** with a tuile fan. The ice cream (Alpenrose Vanilla Bean swirled with homemade caramel) is set off beautifully by the crispy, sweet praline cup.

At dinner, chef Wood whips up a dessert buffet that usually includes several chocolate items such as **Chocolate Decadence**, a nearly flourless torte with chocolate ganache topping. It's rich with a brownie-like texture and a deep chocolate flavor. The **Chocolate Hazelnut Tart** comes with a pastry crust filled with a $1/2$ inch layer of butter, chopped nuts, and chocolate. It's drizzled with chocolate and dusted with cocoa. This blending of flavors is buttery and rich.

Kristen's **Chocolate Pot de Creme**, served in a small ramekin, is silky and thick with great chocolate flavor. The dessert buffet usually includes a selection of **petit fours** like **Frangelico Truffles**, little balls of chocolate joy; **tiny eclairs** filled with cream and topped with chocolate glaze; or **Rum Diamonds**, rum-flavored mousse centers covered with dark chocolate.
Getting there: *Forty-five minutes east of Portland. From Portland, take Bridge of the Gods off Highway 84 and follow the signs. From Vancouver, take Highway 14 east. The Lodge is 2 miles west of Stevenson.*

WASHINGTON

Eastern Washington

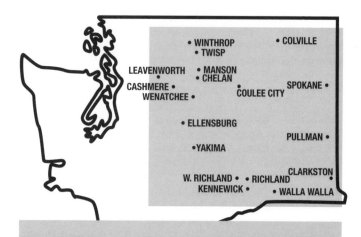

YAKIMA	LEAVENWORTH	CLARKSTON
ELLENSBURG	WINTHROP	WALLA WALLA
WENATCHEE	TWISP	KENNEWICK
CASHMERE	COLVILLE	RICHLAND
MANSON	SPOKANE	WEST RICHLAND
CHELAN	PULLMAN	COULEE CITY

*E*astern Washington is vast, wide open country. We traveled almost 2,000 miles criss-crossing the eastern half of the state in search of great chocolate. We found not only good chocolate, but country that was ever-changing—apple and pear orchards in the fertile Yakima Valley, the soaring Northern Cascade mountains, miles of sagebrush, and the startlingly beautiful wheatfields that undulate across the Palouse Hills.

Great Things to Do

• **Hunt for Blue Agates. Ellensburg, WA**. The Kittitas Valley hills offer rock hounds rare blue agates found no where else. If poking around the hills doesn't produce any gems, try the local rock shop on Main Street.

• **Ride a Painted Pony. Riverfront Park, Spokane, WA**. In the middle of Spokane's downtown, Riverfront Park meanders along the Spokane River, providing locals and travelers with wonderful places to walk, bike, and picnic. A special treat for young and old alike is the original Looff carousel on the south side of the park along Spokane Falls Boulevard. Carved in 1909 by famous carousel master carver Charles Looff, the carousel features 54 horses, a giraffe, a tiger, and 2 Chinese dragon chairs. Each animal has its own specially-carved harness inlaid with a rainbow of German cut glass. The carousel has been beautifully restored and you can take a ride on a painted pony and maybe even catch the brass ring. *Traveler's Note: After the summer season, the carousel is open only on weekends.*

• **Take a Gondola Ride Over the Falls. Riverfront Park, Spokane, WA**. Also in Spokane's largest city park, you can hop aboard a brightly painted gondola sky car for an exciting ride across the spectacular Spokane River Falls. Built for Expo '74, the gondola soars over the churning, cascading falls, giving riders spectacular views and racing hearts.

• **Check Out the Dam. Grand Coulee Dam, Grand Coulee, WA**. (509) 633-3838. Built in 1941, the Grand Coulee is one of those man-made wonders–46 stories high with a spillway that'll make you dizzy looking down. There are self-guided tours every day and a laser light show at night. Call for show times, which change seasonally.

• **Rent a Houseboat. Lake Roosevelt, Wilber, WA**. (800) 648-5253. If you've ever had the yen to captain your own boat, you can rent a houseboat at the Keller Ferry Marina on Lake Roosevelt, the reservoir formed by the Grand Coulee Dam. Everything except towels and bed linens is provided.

• **Take a Boat Tour. Lake Chelan Boat Company, Chelan, WA**. (509) 682-2224. If playing captain isn't your idea of fun, you can let someone else do the driving on Lake Chelan. The lake tour takes you through fjords up to Stehekin, a village full of interesting craft shops. There's a tour that lasts several hours or a shorter 2-hour one.

• **Sip the Vine. Yakima Valley Wine Growers Association, Grandview, WA**. (800) 258-7270. Travelers can visit and sample at more than 2 dozen wineries in the fertile Yakima Valley. Call the Wine Growers Association for a map and listing of all the wineries and their hours.

• **Visit the Fort. Fort Walla Walla Museum, Walla Walla, WA**. (509) 525-7703. In the summer, a great place to go in Walla Walla is the Fort Walla Walla Museum. The 14 historic buildings are packed with pioneer relics that will give you a taste of yesteryear. You can camp or picnic at the park next door.

• **Check Out the Falls**. **Palouse Falls, Pullman, WA**. When the Palouse River meets a 198-foot basalt drop-off, the results are spectacular. You can hike above the falls for a bird's eye view or along the water below the falls. Downstream is the Marmes Rock Shelter, a 10,000-year-old housing project of early area inhabitants. To get to the archaeological site, you can canoe in or take a 2½ mile trail from the Lyons Ferry Marina. The trail is unmaintained. Check at the Marina for more information.

Terrific Places to Stay

Birchfield Manor Country Inn, 2018 Birchfield Road, **Yakima, WA**. (509) 452-1960/ (800) 375-3420. Just 2 miles outside the city limits, but a world away, Birchfield Manor Country Inn's 1910 farmhouse overlooks pastoral fields that will make you think you're a hundred miles from civilization. Birchfield's 4 original manor rooms are upstairs from what is now the Inn's excellent restaurant (see review). All are handsomely decorated with country antiques, have private baths, and share a common room with a television, coffee maker, and refrigerator (some rooms come with their own refrigerators). The newer cottage, just steps away from the original house, offers rooms with even more privacy. Some come with fireplace, private deck, and sauna. Guests are treated to Birchfield's full breakfast. *Traveler's note: Children under 8 years not allowed.*

Wolf Ridge Resort, 412-C Wolf Creek Road, **Winthrop, WA**. (509) 996-2828. Surrounded by the towering North Cascades, Wolf Ridge Resort is situated on 60 acres along the Methow River 5 miles outside of Winthrop, the cross-country ski capitol of the Northwest. Innkeeper and custom furniture maker Lou Childers and his wife have carved out 4 custom log buildings, each filled with Lou's log furniture. The lower units have full kitchens, livingrooms, and patios; the upper units feature microwaves, small refrigerators, and coffeemakers. The units can be combined for larger parties. There's also a 2 bedroom cabin tucked in the trees that has a bedroom, large loft, full kitchen, and livingroom with a pellet stove. With a heated pool, hot tub, recreation room with pool table and games, swing sets, volleyball court, hiking and biking trails, Wolf Ridge is a great place for families. Skiers will be delighted that the resort is located on one of the main cross-country ski trails.

Waverly Place Bed and Breakfast, W 709 Waverly Place, **Spokane, WA**. (509) 328-1856. Waverly is a beautiful 1902 Storybook Victorian perched on the edge of Corbin Park, a historic area of Spokane 5 minutes from downtown. The house is filled with original woodwork, beaded pillars, and built-in window seats. But what makes Waverly Place special are innkeepers Tammy and Marge Arndt, who love old houses and enjoy making their guests feel right at home. Waverly has 4 guest rooms, 2 with private baths. All the rooms are decorated in a simple, yet elegant country style. The Waverly Suite, their newest addition, features a small bedroom downstairs and, upstairs, a large sitting area with a table, couch, and overstuffed chair, and a huge bathroom with a freestanding clawfoot tub and a shower. Guests share a small refrigerator and are greeted in the morning with coffee upstairs and, in the dining room, a full, gourmet breakfast.

Cavanaugh's Inn at the Park, W 303 N River Drive, **Spokane, WA**. (509) 326-8000. Cavanaugh's has 4 hotels in Spokane and the Inn at the Park is by far the finest. It's located at the edge of downtown on the Spokane River and Riverfront Park. Guests can go over a foot bridge right outside the back door and stroll or jog along riverfront paths. Rooms are comfortably decorated with extras like secretary desks, overstuffed chairs, individual heat controls, and clock radios. Some of the rooms in the executive suite have balconies that overlook the river. Rooms in the tower have great city and park views. Guests may use the outdoor or indoor pools, whirlpool, and fitness center. The Inn also features 2 restaurants, the Atrium Café and Deli for light fare and Windows of the Seasons (see review) for fine dining.

Best Western Heritage Inn, 928 NW Olsen, **Pullman, WA**. (509) 332-0928. It's great when a chain hotel has a sense of fun and the Heritage Inn Best Western in Pullman isn't afraid to have a little fun. They offer standard comfortable rooms with all the usual amenities, but, for a real treat, opt for one of their 5 theme suites. The Victorian Suite is decorated in green, white, and burgundy florals with Victorian antiques. The WSU Suite has everything Cougar. The Jazz Suite is musically themed down to the piano key wallpaper trim. The Wheatland's farm implements reflect the Palouse's farm heritage. For a really unusual treat, try the Canyon Suite with its canyon walls festooned with garlands of greenery, an evergreen tree, squirrels, a waterfall in the Jacuzzi, and a floatation bed that looks like a giant rubber raft. Suites come with a double Jacuzzi tub, microwave, and small refrigerator. All rooms have access to the 24-hour indoor pool, spa, and sauna, the continental breakfast, coffee and tea, popcorn, and freshly-baked cookies.

DoubleTree Inn, 2525 N 20th Street, **Pasco, WA**. (509) 547-0701. The cavernous lobby with its carved wooden murals lets you know you're in for fine stay at this DoubleTree. The 279 rooms feature amenities like fluffy, oversized towels, toiletries, and coffeemakers. The suites are large and elegant with living and bedroom areas, recessed lighting, a comfortable couch, overstuffed chairs, secretary desk, dining table, mini-refrigerator, and a television in the livingroom and in the bedroom. Even dog guests are made to feel welcome here. They offer a large outdoor swimming pool and hot tub and guests can dine in one of the Inn's restaurants.

YAKIMA

Yakima is a valley town where you wouldn't necessarily expect sophisticated chocolate, but think again, chocolate lovers.

Birchfield Manor Country Inn
2018 Birchfield Road, Yakima, WA. (509) 452-1960

♥♥♥♥ Located only 2 miles from town, **Birchfield Manor Country Inn** is a lovely 1910 farmhouse in a pastoral setting. Three nights a week, their restaurant serves full dinners—appetizer, salad, a basket of freshly baked bread, vegetables, and hand-dipped chocolates and a choice of entrees, such as salmon wrapped in puff pastry, filet mignon, gingered chicken breast, rack of lamb, or a vegetarian entree like portobello mushroom steak. Pastry chef Greg Masset's chocolate desserts, made with the finest Callebaut chocolate, are divine. His **Double Belgian Chocolate Grand Marnier Cream Torte** is a thin layer of chocolate chiffon topped with 2 inches of French cream, followed by a thin layer of pound cake, covered with Belgian bittersweet icing and served in a pool of sweetened raspberry puree. This dessert has a rich bittersweet chocolate taste, yet is lusciously light. The **Belgian Chocolate Walnut Brownies,** served slightly warm, are chewy and rich with a deep, dark chocolate taste and large chunks of walnuts.

Diners enjoy a basket of Greg's exquisite **hand-dipped chocolates**, which are also available for sale by the box. They may include such delights as **Walnut Fudge, Sliced Toasted Almond Square, Hazelnut Milk Chocolate Desire, Walnut Marzipan**, or a **Crispy Crepe**, all wonderfully fresh and full of chocolate flavor.
Getting there: Two miles from downtown Yakima on Birchfield Road.

Gasperetti's
1013 N 1st, Yakima, WA. (509) 248-0628

♥♥♥♥ **Gasperetti's** doesn't look like much from the outside, but inside it's an intimate retreat filled with beautifully-textured walls, local art work, and linen-covered tables lit by tiny lamps. Gasperetti's has been one of Yakima's finest restaurants for 50 years, so it's no surprise that their chocolate desserts are terrific. Their **Chocolate Decadence** is a rich flourless chocolate cake served in a pool of chocolate creme anglaise. The torte's slightly crunchy top adds a nice contrast to the chewy brownie-like cake.

Their **Chocolate Mousse with Creme Anglaise** is a light chocolate mousse that's velvet smooth and very light. The nutty, slightly sweet creme anglaise provides a wonderful foil for the chocolate flavor.

For this reviewer, their **Belgian White Chocolate Cheesecake,** served with raspberry puree, is a special treat. It's a light, airy New York style cheesecake made satiny by the addition of Belgian white chocolate. This melt-in-your-mouth dessert has just the right cheesy flavor to delight the most discriminating cheesecake lover.
Getting there: On First, north of the downtown area.

Greystone Restaurant
5 North Front Street, Yakima, WA. (509) 248-9801
❤❤❤ **Greystone**, located in the historic Lund Building, gets its name from the wonderful hand-hewn stone wall that dominates the restaurant. The 20-foot high ceilings, antique back bars, brass rails, and cozy linen-covered tables all add to the ambiance. Open for dinner, Greystone offers an upscale menu that includes rack of lamb, prime rib, salmon, oysters, and chicken roulade. They also have a lighter fare menu that's a bit easier on the pocketbook. One of their signature desserts is their **Brownie with Chocolate Sauce**. It's a pie-shaped wedge of rich brownie with walnuts served warm in a giant margarita glass topped with 2 scoops of honey vanilla ice cream and Greystone's own semisweet chocolate sauce. The brownie is chewy with just the right crunch on top. The fudge sauce is thick and rich and the ice cream gives a wonderful cold contrast to the warm brownie and hot fudge sauce. This decadent dessert is like a molten ice cream sundae.
Getting there: In downtown Yakima on North Front.

> *"Chocolate goes well with sex: before, during, after—it doesn't matter."*
> **– Helen Gurley Brown**

Deli De Pasta
7 North Front Street, Yakima, WA. (509) 453-0571
❤❤❤ **Deli De Pasta** isn't a deli at all, but a bright, airy little pasta restaurant that serves fettuccine, steak and pasta, Italian sausage, lasagne, manicotti, and ravioli with a variety of homemade sauces, including pesto, basil cream, clam, lemon, Alfredo, marinara, and tomato meat. Their classic Italian dessert **Tiramisu**, which won first place in the Washington Hills Winery Dessert Contest, achieves new heights here. Lady finger cookies dipped in espresso and kahlua are sandwiched between thick layers of a creamy, mild mascarpone cheese. Then it's sprinkled with a generous layer of sweet dark chocolate flakes. Unlike many tiramisu, Deli De Pasta's is neither

boozy nor soggy. The kahlua taste is subtle and the lady fingers and mascarpone marry into a delicate texture that's just right. The sweet chocolate flakes add a chocolaty compliment to the cheese.

Their **Chocolate Pot De Creme** is a dark chocolate soufflé cup filled with a very dense chocolate custard and garnished with bittersweet fudge sauce, chocolate shavings, a dusting of powered sugar, and a rosette of whipped cream. While it's not up to the caliber of their tiramisu, the bittersweet chocolate is richly flavorful. This is industrial strength chocolate.

Their **Chocolate Chip Cookie,** baked in a tartlet pan, is a half-inch thick and soft, moist, and cake-like. A cross between a brownie and cake, it's loaded with chocolate chips.
Getting there: In downtown Yakima on North Front.

Candy Store

Boehm's Candy Store
910 Summitview Avenue, Yakima, WA. (509) 453-1143
♥♥ Boehm's isn't a hand-made, artisian chocolatier like many of those reviewed in this book. The candies are machine-made in the factory in Issaquah, WA. for a number of retail outlets in the Northwest. This retail store for **Boehm's Chocolates** offers a large variety of Boehm's chocolates, including their buttery creams like **Cherry, Peppermint, Lemon, Orange, Peanut Butter, Mocha, Chocolate**, and **Vanilla**, all in dark, milk, or white chocolate. They carry Boehm's trademark **Mt. Rainer**, a mountain-shaped wedge of chocolate-covered caramel fudge with glazed cherries dusted with coconut shavings. Their truffles are small and elegant. Unlike the more common golf-ball sized **truffles**, Boehm's are about the size of a quarter and come in **Kahlua, Mocha, Grand Marnier, Amaretto, Rum, Grasshopper, Raspberry**, and **Irish Cream**. The flavors are intense and the fine quality chocolate has just the right snap when you bite into it.
Traveler's note: Boehm's has a large chain of retail stores throughout the Pacific Northwest. For other Boehm's retail locations, consult the white pages in the phone book.
Getting there: On Summitview near 9th.

ELLENSBURG

Valley Café
105 W 3rd Avenue, Ellensburg, WA. (509) 925-3050
♥♥♥ A small café designed and decorated in the original Art Deco style of the late 1930's, the Valley Café has been an institution in Ellensburg for nearly 70 years. The dinner offerings include steak, fish, and vegetarian dishes, many with Asian influences. Their

Chocolate Decadence with White Chocolate features a brownie-like bottom, a thick, truffle-like middle, and a velvety smooth white chocolate topping. The creamy white chocolate, which isn't sweet, is perfect for this intense chocolate dessert, softening it and making it truly outstanding.
Getting there: In downtown Ellensburg on 3rd.

Ice Creamery

Winegar Family Dairy
1821 N Main, Ellensburg, WA. (509) 933-1821
❤❤ **Winegar Family Dairy** is THE place in Ellensburg for ice cream. Gary Winegar and his family don't supply the milk for their ice cream anymore, but they still make small batches of creamy ice cream, some of the freshest this reviewer has tasted. Their scoops are a generous 5 ounces with a good chocolate flavor. Chocolate offerings include **Rocky Rodeo (rocky road), Chocolate Gary Dough (chocolate chip cookie dough), Reecer Creek Brownie (chocolate ice cream with pieces of brownie), Riegel Royale (chocolate peanut butter), Holstein Thunder (chocolate), Wildcat Chocomint (chocolate chip mint), Grandma Sarah's Cookies (cookies and cream)**, and **Fudgy Wudgy Ripple (fudge swirl)**.

Winegar ice cream is also sold inside the **18th Street Deli** (1801 N Walnut).
Getting there: On N. Main at 7th.

WENATCHEE

Visconti's
1737 N Wenatchee Avenue, Wenatchee, WA. (509) 662-5013
❤❤❤ You're sure to find something you love on Visconti's extensive dinner menu. They feature Italian favorites like veal and chicken sattimbocca, veal parmesan, cacciatore, and fettuccine with a variety of sauces. We enjoyed their clam linguine, a huge bowl of tiny in-the-shell clams in a light, flavorful cream sauce over fresh linguine, and applewood-roasted salmon, a large piece of salmon infused with a sweet, smoky flavor. Their **White Chocolate Truffle Cheesecake With Raspberry Sauce**, garnished with whipped cream, is worth saving room for (or taking to go). It features a thin graham cracker crust and a light, creamy cheese filling that's a delight.
Getting there: About half-way down Wenatchee Avenue, the main road into town.

Cottage Inn
134 Easy Street, Wenatchee, WA. (509) 663-4435

♥♥♥ The **Cottage Inn** is a family restaurant that's been serving Wenatchee since the 1940's. Their menu features copies of the restaurant's menu from the 1940s and 1960s, as well as old business cards. Voted the best restaurant in 1997 by *Business Journal* readers, they serve a variety of steaks, prime rib and seafood entrees. They also offer **Chocolate Cream Pie**, which should really be called a chocolate mousse pie. It's baked on-site by their baker, Bonnie, and features a walnut/graham crust filled with 4 inches of cream filling that has the lightness of chocolate mousse. It's topped with whipped cream and chocolate shavings. It's a delightful treat!

"When you put good chocolate in your mouth, it has an immediate burst of intense flavor. It hits right in front of your tongue."

**– Iva Elmer, owner
JiCava's Chocolates
and Pastries,
Portland, OR.**

Their **Brownie** is a thin, 4-inch square, frosted with fudge frosting, garnished with walnuts, and served with vanilla ice cream and chocolate sauce. The texture is more like cake than brownie. We'd stick with Bonnie's fabulous chocolate pie.

The other chocolate desserts served by the Cottage Inn come from a food distributor. We always advise opting for homemade when possible.

Getting there: Corner of Penny Road and Easy Street.

John Horan's Steak and Seafood Restaurant
2 Horan Road, Wenatchee, WA. (509) 663-0018
♥♥♥ Located in the middle of an apple orchard in the historic John Horan house, **John Horan's Steak and Seafood** is one of Wenatchee's more upscale dining establishments. The menu, which changes about 4 times a year, features a good selection of steaks, pasta, lamb, duck, chicken, and prawns. They also feature as many as a dozen imaginative and attractive desserts, several of them chocolate, all baked by their full-time pastry chef, Patty Kozlwoski. Their **Aurora Torte**, our favorite, features a thin, flaky pastry crust, followed by thin layers of caramel, chocolate, heavy whipping cream, and chopped, toasted almonds. It's drizzled with chocolate sauce and garnished with whipped cream. The effect is creamy and crunchy with a strong flavor of toasted almonds.

Their **Triple Layer Chocolate Mousse** is 3 mousse layers—white chocolate, milk chocolate, and mocha cream—in a Oreo cookie crust, garnished with chocolate syrup drizzles and a piece of chocolate. This pretty dessert has lovely textures. The mocha flavor dominates the white and milk chocolate flavors, so it's for coffee lovers only.

Their **Grasshopper Cheesecake** has a thick chocolate cookie crust with minty cheesecake topped with a layer of melted dark chocolate. The cheesecake is a bit dry, almost spongy, with a strong mint flavor. Their **Almond Joy Tart** features a crushed almond nut crust and thick coconut cream filling that's topped with dark chocolate ganache swirled with white chocolate. The coconut filling is creamy and the ganache is thick and fudge-like.

Irish Cream Triangle Cake, one of their newest and, in our opinion, least successful entries, alternates layers of white and chocolate sponge cake filled and frosted with Irish cream milk chocolate buttercream garnished with whipped cream. Served as a standing triangle, we found the dessert too dry.
Getting there: *On the way out of Wenatchee, watch for the John Horan signs.*

Prospector Pies
731 N Wenatchee Avenue, Wenatchee, WA. (509) 662-1118
♥♥ **Prospector Pies** is a western theme family restaurant that features booths, wood paneling and horseshoes on the walls, and old time favorites like chicken pot pie, burgers, BBQ ribs, and chicken. They also offer 26 different **pies**, all baked daily on the premises. Their pies all have a flaky crust that holds up to the cream fillings and the pieces are huge. Their **Almond Joy Pie** has a flaky pie crust that's filled with a thick layer of coconut cream filling, a layer of chocolate cream filling, topped with a mound of whipped cream and garnished with dark chocolate cream. It's creamy and loaded with coconut.

Their **Tollhouse Pie**, one reviewer's hand's-down favorite, is a pie crust filled with a layer of chocolate chips and a thicker layer of pecan pie filling. It's served warm and tastes like a just-baked cookie. This rich pie is best served with a scoop of vanilla ice cream.

German Chocolate Cream Pie features pie crust filled with a chocolate/coconut cream filling laced with walnuts and topped with whipped cream and garnished with chocolate cream and chopped walnuts. It's chewy and full of coconut flavor.

Prospector's **Peanut Butter Pie** has a pastry crust, a thick chocolate cream layer, a peanut butter cream layer, followed by whipped cream and chocolate cream for garnish. It's a creamy and tasty blend of peanut butter and chocolate.

Their **Mocha Cheesecake**, one of their few non-pie desserts, has a graham cracker crust, a $1^1/_2$ layer of cheese cake, followed by a

half-inch layer of mocha-flavored chocolate cream, garnished with whipped cream. It's a tangy, cheesy cake that's satisfying.
Getting there: On the main thoroughfare in Wenatchee.

McGlinn's Public House

111 Orondo Street, Wenatchee, WA. (509) 663-9073

♥♥ **McGlinn's** has a fun, tavern-like atmosphere with high ceilings, brick walls, a long, antique bar, old-time baseball photos, and other historical memorabilia. It also features some deliciously unusual sandwiches like the Philly Dip, roast beef, jack cheese, grilled onions, and mushrooms served on crusty al pannette bread with au jus, and their BBTA, fresh basil leaves, bacon, avocado, and tomato on sour dough. Their brick oven churns out inventive pizzas like fresh oyster, BBQ chicken, and scallops and Chilean shrimp. Their signature chocolate dessert is the **Sawmill Toffee Torte**, a thick wedge of buttery graham cracker crust topped with a thick, fudge-like layer of bittersweet chocolate with walnuts and garnished with a dollop of whipped cream. It's like biting into a very creamy piece of dark chocolate fudge on a graham cracker crust.
Getting there: On Orondo between Mission and Wenatchee Avenue.

The Windmill

1501 N Wenatchee, Wenatchee, WA. (509) 663-3478

♥ **The Windmill** has been serving steaks to Wenatchee residents for 65 years. It's a place that's steeped in tradition and new owners Mary Ann Johnson and her husband don't plan on changing a thing, including their **Chocolate Cream Pie**, which is made fresh daily. It's a dark chocolate cream filling in a flaky crust topped with real cream whipped cream, with drizzles of melted chocolate over the top. It's creamy with a rich chocolate flavor.

Their **Chocolate Texas Sheet Cake** is a very thin, soft chocolate cake that's baked on a cookie sheet. It's topped with old-fashioned boiled chocolate frosting and garnished with chopped walnuts. They serve 2 large, 3x3-inch squares with a scoop of vanilla ice cream. Because this cake is made with buttermilk, the cake has a tangy rather than sweet taste. The boiled frosting provides a sweet accent.
Getting there: On the main thoroughfare in Wenatchee.

CASHMERE

Best known as the home of Aplets and Cotlets candies, Cashmere is a village that still retains its small town charm.

Bakeries

Anjou Bakery and Catering

3898 Old Monitor Road, Cashmere, WA. (509) 782-4360

♥♥♥♥ Located in a pear orchard outside of town in an old barn-like building, **Anjou Bakery and Catering** is a from-scratch bakery that's worth searching out. Their specialty is crusty, hearth baked breads such as white, rosemary and olive oil, wheat, and kalamata olive. On Saturday, the special treat is **Pain Chocolate**, chocolate bread. It's a round, 7-inch loaf of dark chocolate dough sprinkled with chocolate chips. The bread, which itself isn't sweet, has a pleasing, fine-grained, chewy texture. It's the chocolate chips that give the bread little surprises of sweet chocolate. This is a wonderful dessert bread that you'll have difficulty waiting until you get home to sample. We love it served slightly warm with cream cheese.

Baker/owner Heather Knight also bakes a **Shortbread Brownie** that's a thin layer of shortbread and a thin layer of brownie. It's a satisfying soft/crunchy variation on the old brownie theme.

Anjou's **Chocolate Smudge** is a double bittersweet/semi-sweet chocolate cookie packed with chopped walnuts. This is a chocolate lover's cookie that's crunchy with a satisfying chocolate flavor.

Getting there: Off Highway 2, take the Old Monitor Road exit, watch for the signs, turn into the first driveway.

Sure to Rise Bakery

115 Cottage Avenue, Cashmere, WA. (509) 782-2424

Sure to Rise is a busy bakery, located in the heart of downtown Cashmere, that makes a variety of breads, rolls, cookies, cinnamon rolls, and tons of doughnuts. Their **Chocolate Frosted Cake Doughnut** is tasty with just the right softness on the inside, crispy outside. Their **German Chocolate Danish** is a chocolate Danish pastry filled with German chocolate coconut filling and frosted with chocolate icing. It's a substantial pastry that's crisp with a chewy softness. For a German chocolate lover, it's the way to start the day.

Tiger Paws are chocolate spritz cookies half-dipped in semi-sweet chocolate. Their **Chocolate-dipped Macaroon,** a local favorite, is a macaroon cookie half-dipped in chocolate. Their **Frosted Chocolate Brownie** is a large, 4-inch brownie with walnuts frosted with chocolate frosting. We found the frosting a bit sweet and layered so thickly that it overwhelmed the brownie.

Getting there: In downtown Cashmere on the main street.

MANSON

The Quail Restaurant at Wapato Point
200 N Quetilaquasoon, Manson, WA. (509) 687-9541

♥♥ Owner Donna Coggins and her daughter, Gail, run **The Quail**, a comfortable, casual family dinnerhouse that's a favorite with locals. They serve pasta, prime rib, steaks, chicken, and salmon dishes at affordable prices. Those in the know save room for the **pies** Donna makes daily. Her **Chocolate Cream Pie** has a flaky crust that's crisp even on the bottom. The cream filling is dark chocolate (she also makes milk chocolate) with a firm texture that's a cross between pot de creme and mousse. Donna says her secret is using cocoa and butter rather than melted chocolate in her filling. The pie is topped with a thin layer of real whipped cream.
Getting there: Just off the main road into Manson.

Village Bake Shop
33 Green Avenue, Manson, WA. (509) 687-3774

♥ The **Village Bake Shop** is a from-scratch bakery that makes bread, muffins, strudels, rolls, and a **Chocolate Mousse Pie** by the slice that's a pie crust filled with a light, milk chocolate mousse filling and topped with a thick layer of whipped cream, garnished with chocolate sauce and slivered almonds. It has a creamy texture that's light without being too airy.

Their **Chocolate Chip Cookies** are thin, chewy, and buttery. One of the closest to homemade these reviewers have found, it's a cookie that goes down easily.

They also make what they call the **"Ultimate Brownie"** that's made with cocoa, chocolate chips, marshmallows, and walnuts. While we don't think it's the ultimate brownie, it is tasty. The marshmallow gives it a soft chewiness and it's chock full of nuts.
Getting there: On Green, just off the main street in Manson.

CHELAN

Goochi's Restaurant
104 E Woodin Avenue, Chelan, WA. (509) 682-2436

♥♥♥ **Goochi's** is a casual, knotty pine paneled place with an eating area and a long bar that has wonderful antique back bar. They serve burgers, pasta, fish, chicken and steaks, and one of the most delightfully unique chocolate desserts these reviewers have experienced, **Oreo Cookie Chocolate Cheesecake**. It's a generous wedge of Oreo cookie crust filled with chocolate cheesecake and huge chunks of Oreo cookies, garnished with a pile of whipped cream and large chocolate curls. It's cut while frozen so you get actual slices of cookie and then it is served chilled. It's refreshing with a creamy, cheesy filling and crunchy, chocolaty crust.

Getting there: On the main street right after you cross the bridge into Chelan.

Peter B's Bar and Grill

116 E Woodin Avenue, Riverfront Shops Building, Chelan, WA. (509) 682-1031

♥♥ This small, casual bar and restaurant sits just off the main street, tucked into the Riverfront Shops Building. The restaurant's large windows overlook the park and the lake. They serve burgers, salads, steaks, and pasta. For the chocolate lover, they make a **Double Chocolate Mousse Cake**, a single layer, dark chocolate, dense truffle-type cake that's topped with sweet chocolate. It's thick and rich. A real chocolate power hit!

Peanut Butter Chocolate Pie is their most popular dessert. It's a graham cracker crust filled with 2 inches of creamy sweet peanut butter filling, topped with a thin layer of dark, sweet chocolate, and garnished with a generous amount of whipped cream and chocolate sauce. It's a delightful blend of flavors and textures—crunchy crust, creamy peanut butter center, and chewy chocolate top.

Getting there: On the main street right after you cross the bridge into Chelan.

Chocolate Shop

Kitchen Kabinet Gourmet Coffee and Gifts

210 E Woodin Avenue, Chelan, WA. (509) 682-4727

♥♥♥ On the main street of Chelan is Ann Fran Seidensticker's Kitchen Kabinet, a kitchen and coffee shop that offers some of the best **fudge** tasted by this reviewer. This is a firm fudge with an intensely chocolate flavor that melts in the mouth. The **Chocolate Peanut Butter** has good peanut butter flavor without being sticky or overwhelming the fudge—a nice blend of 2 favorite flavors. **Carmel Chocolate** fudge is one of the more unique varieties available. The caramel, a firm and rather chewy layer, is sandwiched by chocolate fudge.Their **Chocolate Fudge** is dark and not overly sweet. Like her other varieties, the chocolate fudge is firm without being stiff and soft without being mushy. Ann Fran makes 14 flavors and varies their availability throughout the year. Other flavors to savor include **Mint Chocolate, Amaretto Chocolate, Chewy Praline, Chocolate Walnut, Vanilla Walnut, Espresso, Vanilla Espresso Bean**, and **Penuche**. Her shop is open 7 days a week, year round, and she'll ship to chocolate lovers.

Getting there: On the main street in Chelan.

LEAVENWORTH

Situated in the Cascades, some will find this Bavarian village charming while others may find it's almost too cute.

Café Mozart
829 Front Street, Leavenworth, WA. (509) 548-0600
Located above busy Front Street, **Café Mozart,** serves Bavarian favorites like stuffed cabbage roll, potato pancakes, and sausage. Their most popular dessert is their **Mozart Torte**, a thin layer of cherry filling and sponge cake, followed by thin, alternating layers of sponge cake and marzipan wine cream enrobed in a layer of marzipan and covered with a dark chocolate shell. It's garnished with drizzles of chocolate syrup and a dusting of powered sugar and whipped cream. The sponge cake is light and the chocolate shell provides a crunchy contrast to the soft cake, but the marzipan flavor is a bit intense and sweet for this reviewer.
Getting there: One block off the main road through town, across from the park.

Chocolate Shop

VonWeber's Fudge
224 8th, Leavenworth, WA. (509) 548-4534
♥♥ Owner Shirley VonWeber has been making her **fudge** with dark German chocolate here for 16 years and she's gotten good at it. It's an unusually dark fudge with an intense chocolate flavor and a firm, chewy bite. Her chocolate flavors include **Chocolate, Chocolate Walnut, Chocolate Nut Raisin, Chocolate Coconut, Black Forest, Rocky Road, Chocolate Coconut Nut, Mint Chocolate, Peanut Butter Chocolate, Cookies and Cream, Rum Swirl, Vanilla Chocolate Swirl, Amaretto Swirl**, and **Chocolate Rum Walnut**.
Getting there: On 8th Street, 1/2 block off Front Street.

Das Sweet Shoppe
733 Front Street, Leavenworth, WA. (509) 548-5755
♥ **Das Sweet Shoppe** sells a good selection of chocolate candies from Cascade Candy Company in La Conner, WA. Their chocolate is good quality and has the right bite to it. Their **Chocolate-covered Caramel** is very creamy, almost a gooey caramel. Their **Cream Cheese Truffle** has a dark chocolate center that's a bit stiff, but has an interesting chocolate-cheese flavor. (For a more complete review of Cascade Candy Company, see La Conner, WA.)
Getting there: One block off the main road through town.

Bakery

Home Fires Bakery
13013 Bayne Road, Leavenworth, WA. (509) 548-7362

♥♥♥♥ People drive out of their way for **Home Fires Bakery,** the best bakery in Leavenworth. They're famous for their breads, which include Bavarian farmer's, country French, cranberry whole wheat, and a dozen or so other varieties, but don't miss out on their **Chocolate Hazelnut Brownies**, 3-inch squares of chewy, soft brownie filled with chopped hazelnuts and chocolate chips with a just-right crunchy top. It's a perfect brownie!

Their **Pecan Caramel Bar** is a cookie bottom topped a pecan pie type filling and dipped in bittersweet dark chocolate. It's rich and chewy—a pecan lover's delight. The **Chocolate Fudge Nutter Cookie** is 5 inches of crunchy chocolate cookie filled with oats and peanut butter chips. This is a terrific, rich cookie. Don't leave for home without it!

Food of the Gods. The word "chocolate" is derived from a combination of the Mayan word "xocoatl" and the Aztec word for cocoa, "cacahuatl" or "food of the gods."

Their **Chocolate Cheesecake** has a dark chocolate graham cracker crust topped with a single layer of cheesy filling. It's a light chocolate flavor that's both creamy and delicious.

Home Fires also makes **Chocolate Mint Truffle Cup**, a mousse made of cream cheese and whipping cream in a chocolate wafer crust garnished with swirls of dark chocolate. It's got a light, clean mint taste that's truly refreshing. This is a wonderful dessert to end a meal with.

Getting there: *At the end of town, turn left on Icicle Road and, at the 2 mile point, turn right on Bayne Road.*

WINTHROP

Duck Brand Restaurant and Hotel
248 Riverside Avenue, Winthrop, WA. (509) 996-2192
♥ **Duck Brand Restaurant and Hotel** is a favorite among locals in Winthrop for Mexican food and steaks. They're also noted for their baked goods, including their **German Chocolate Cake**. It's 3 layers of dark chocolate cake, filled and frosted with moist coconutty filling that's loaded with pecans and garnished with chocolate buttercream. Not overly sweet or cloying like many German chocolate cakes can be, Duck Brand's cake is some of the best chocolate cake you'll find in Winthrop. *Traveler's Note: Duck Brand does change their chocolate desserts occasionally, so if you've got your heart set on this German treat, call ahead.*

Their **Chocolate Biscotti** is a long wedge of chocolate flavored with amaretto and filled with chocolate chips and chopped walnuts. It's a treat if you like almond flavor.
Getting there: On the main street through town on Highway 20.

Chocolate Shop/Ice Creamery

Sheri's Sweet Shoppe
207 Riverside Avenue, Winthrop, WA. (509) 996-3834
♥♥♥♥ (chocolate/ice cream) Serious chocolate lovers should to head to Winthrop between mid-April and December to sample some of **Sheri's Sweet Shoppe's** chocolate delights (the shop closes during the height of winter weather). Doug and Sheri Mohre have engineered a chocolate lover's "world of chocolate fun" in Winthrop with over-sized **chocolates, homemade ice cream**, miniature golf, and even special activities like pumpkin carving. You can watch the ice cream being made, the fudge being rolled, the truffles being handcrafted. Their chocolates are huge and made with top quality Guittard—creamy milk chocolate and intensely rich dark chocolate. Their **Sea Foam** is twice the normal size and the golden honeycomb is light and buttery, melting in the mouth quickly. Their **Nut Clusters—Macadamia, Walnut, Peanut, Cashew**, with or without soft **Caramel**—are 4 inches across with at least 2 dozen nuts and a veritable puddle of chocolate. Their **Peanut Butter Cups** are thick bowls of chocolate with a soft, creamy peanut butter filling. Sheri's golf-ball-sized **truffles** have rather stiff centers, but they're richly flavored. Their thick slabs of chocolate **fudge** are very soft, a little sweeter than this reviewer likes.

Sheri's sells what they call "**Fresh Gooey Brownies**," and they're just that. It's a 4x4-inch square that's loaded with chocolate chips. If you prefer a crunchier brownie, ask for an outside piece.

Their ice cream is made on-site from their own recipe. They make 40 different flavors, including **Chocolate, Chocolate Chip Cookie Dough**, and **Semi-Sweet Chocolate**. At 16% butterfat, it's creamy with flavors that explode in the mouth.
Getting there: On the main street through town on Highway 20.

TWISP

Cinnamon Twisp Bakery
116 N Glover Street, Twisp, WA. (509) 997-5030
♥♥ Don't let the whole wheat appearance fool you, **Cinnamon Twisp Bakery** makes some good **chocolate baked goods**. Their **Fudge Brownies**, which are made with whole wheat flour, are moist, cake-like brownies with small pieces of walnuts. Their **Oat Fudgy** has thick, rich fudge between layers of crunchy oat cookie

bar. Made with whole wheat flour, honey, and oats, this delicious cookie is actually good for you! Their **Double Espresso Cookies** are 4 inches of thick chocolate cookie packed with chocolate chips and flavored with espresso. It's a great cookie with a cup of java. The bakery also makes a variety of breads and muffins.

Getting there: One block off of Highway 20 between 1ˢᵗ and 2ⁿᵈ.

COLVILLE

Barman's Historic Country Store
230 S Main Street, Colville, WA. (509) 684-9710
This old-fashioned soda fountain features Darigold Ice Cream in an array of products made the "old-fashioned way." **Chocolate sodas, hot fudge sundaes and chocolate milkshakes** made from hard ice cream make for a delightful break when you're on the road. While you wait for your order, browse owner Jeanie Acorn's renovated 3-story building on Main Street in Colville. You can find everything from antiques to packaged chocolates and assorted candies.

Getting there: Right on Highway 395 (Main Street through downtown).

SPOKANE

Spokane is a city laced by water and accented with lovely parks. It also has some excellent chocolate.

Restaurants

Café Roma
2727 S Mount Vernon, Spokane, WA. (509) 534-5540
♥♥♥♥ **Café Roma** gets high marks for ambiance. It's decorated in deep greens and burgundy with lots of plants, tiny white lights, and a solarium room that brings in the outdoors. Open for lunch and dinner, they offer pastas with a different twist such as Orchietto Sicilian, roasted Italian sausage and peppers, gorgonzola cheese and tomato sauce, and Penne Roma, spinach, grilled artichoke hearts, goat cheese, fresh basil, olive oil and garlic.

Their great selection of desserts comes from **Take the Cake**, folks who know how to make great chocolate. The **Chocolate Marquise** is a flourless mousse torte topped with chocolate ganache in a chocolate cookie crust, garnished with flecks of 22-carat edible gold. This extremely rich, dark chocolate dessert is surprisingly light.

The pretty **Huckleberry Chocolate Mousse** has a dark chocolate cookie crust, an inch of extra-dark chocolate mousse, followed by a lavender layer of huckleberry mousse with flecks of huckleberry pieces. The dark mousse has a rich, almost smokey flavor and the huckleberry mousse has a bright, berry flavor.

Tiramisu is 3 layers of lady fingers soaked in espresso-flavored brandy filled with layers of mascarpone cheese, dusted with cocoa and garnished with dark chocolate curls. The lady fingers are light, not soggy, and the cheese filling is fresh and ultra-light.

Take the Cake's **Nut Caramel Tart** is a combination of walnuts, cashews, macadamia nuts, and caramel in a chocolate cookie crust. The caramel is chewy and buttery. This dessert has a rich nutty flavor people who love nuts will rave about.

Grasshopper Pie starts with a chocolate cookie crust, followed by a layer of dark chocolate mousse, topped with a layer of mint mousse, and garnished with dark chocolate drizzles. The dark chocolate mousse is creamy and chocolaty; the mint mousse soft and lightly minty. It's a surprisingly refreshing dessert.

The **Triple Layer Mousse Cake** has white, milk, and dark chocolate mousse layers in a dark cookie crust. Extra creamy, this light dessert is a wonderful blending of chocolate flavors.
Getting there: *In the South Hill area, just off 29th on the NW corner of Lincoln Heights Shopping Center.*

Lindaman's Gourmet to Go
S 1235 Grand, Spokane, WA. (509) 838-3000
♥♥♥♥ A Spokane favorite for more than 14 years, **Lindaman's Gourmet to Go** is an eat-in or take-out kitchen. For customers who want to eat there, they have a large, casual dining area with lots of windows, wooden tables and chairs, exposed brick walls, hardwood floors, and a long coffee bar that serves excellent espresso. They make more than 400 different food items, which rotate, like prepared salads such as Asian chicken and tortellini and sun dried tomato pesto and entrees like sausage stuffed chicken with lemon caper sauce and pasta with shrimp and feta cheese. They have a huge selection of desserts made from scratch on-site daily, including several chocolate ones like their **Pot de Creme**, which has a chocolate cookie crust that's filled with 3 inches of melt-in-your-mouth creamy chocolate cream. It's a heavenly chocolate treat!

Their **Chocolate Peanut Butter Pie** starts with a chocolate cookie crust that's filled with 4 inches of peanut butter cream and topped with a thin layer of chocolate ganache. The crust is crunchy, the middle is melty-creamy with a good peanut butter taste, and the ganache adds just the right rich chocolate flavor. Peanut butter lovers should line up for this one.

Lindaman's **Mocha Toffee Torte**, this reviewer's favorite, has a pecan toffee crust, a rich chocolate cream layer and a coffee mousse layer that's garnished with chocolate shavings. The chocolate layer is fudgy, the coffee mousse is dreamy creamy with a light coffee flavor, and the pecan toffee crust adds a lovely toffee crunch. Even those who don't love coffee will like this one.

The restaurant has recently added **Chocolate Brownie Pie** to its menu and they're still deciding whether or not to keep it. It's essentially a fudgy walnut brownie in a pastry crust. It's okay, but this reviewer votes no.

"Chocolate is affordable luxury. Chocolate is sensual. It's a treat. You feel good giving it and sharing it. Chocolate is a gift that tells someone they're special."
— Janele Smith, chocolatier, Fenton and Lee, Eugene, OR

Lindaman's makes a traditional, unfrosted **German Chocolate Cake** that's 2 layers of milk chocolate cake filled and topped with a rich coconut-pecan mixture. The cake is fine-grained with a good milk chocolate flavor. The filling is full of buttery coconut flavor.

Traveler's note: The chocolate desserts reviewed here are ones Lindaman's almost always has on hand. However, if you have a favorite and are coming into Spokane, call ahead and request it. Manager John Faley says 3 days notice will guarantee just about any dish you want.
Getting there: *South of downtown, on S Grand at 13ᵗʰ Avenue.*

Milford's Fish House
719 N Monroe, Spokane, WA. (509) 326-7251
♥♥♥♥ If it's fresh fish you want in Spokane, **Milford's** is where to go. Situated in a wonderful 1925 brick building with terra cotta tile, a terrazzo floor, pressed tin ceiling, and lots of woodwork and exposed brick, Milford's has plenty of old time ambiance. It also has a menu of impeccably fresh fish that changes daily. In season, you can get fresh salmon, Alaskan halibut, Hawaiian blue marlin, Chilean sea bass and swordfish, to name a few. They also offer 8-10 desserts, at least half of which are chocolate. They don't make their own, but they buy from the best in town—**Take the Cake, Desserts by Sara**, and **Just American Desserts**. From Just American Desserts, they may offer the seasonal **Raspberry Eggnog**

Chocolate Fudge Cake, 4 layers of dark chocolate cake separated with 2 layers of raspberry filling and 1 of eggnog cream, frosted with chocolate fudge. They also often carry JAD's **Chocolate Mousse Cake**, 2 layers of chocolate cake with a deep, rich chocolate mousse filling, garnished with a dollop of milk chocolate mousse and a tiny chocolate fan.

From Take the Cake, they often carry a **Raspberry Mousse Cake**, a chocolate cookie crust with a layer of dark chocolate mousse with a deep chocolate flavor, topped with a creamy, light white chocolate raspberry mousse. Or try **Chocolate Macadamia Pecan Tart**, this reviewer's favorite, a delightful variation on the pecan pie that's loaded with macadamia nuts, pecans, and chocolate chips and chunks, all in a buttery crust.

(For reviews about these bakers, see Bakeries in this section.)
Getting there: On Milford, north of Riverside Park.

Patsy Clark's

W 2208 2nd Avenue, Spokane, WA. (509) 838-8300
♥♥♥♥ Located in the historic Brown's Addition in the wonderfully ornate and eccentric Patsy Clark Mansion, **Patsy Clark's** is one of Spokane's most elegant dining establishments. The restaurant occupies the lower level of the mansion, including the beautifully restored library, solarium, dining room, and parlor, as well as banquet and meeting rooms on the second level. For lunch, they offer a variety of soups and salads, sandwiches, pasta and special entrees. At dinner, they pull out all the stops with dishes such as Sonoran Duck (citrus marinated duck breast with orange ginger sauce), Thaiger Prawns (prawns in a green curry coconut sauce), and Ravioli Forestierre (portabello filled pasta and hickory smoked chicken).

Do save room for dessert. Although they don't make their own, Patsy Clark's gets kudos for buying wonderful desserts from some of the best pastry chefs in the city, including **Just American Desserts, Divine Elegance**, and **Desserts by Sara**. Sara's **Chocolate Creme de Menthe Cake** is 3 layers of chocolate coconut layered with chocolate mousse, topped with ganache, and garnished with mint drizzles. It's refreshingly minty, rich and moist. The same company also makes a **Cappuccino Cheesecake** that starts with a chocolate cookie crust, followed by a thick layer of cappuccino-flavored cheesecake that's topped with ganache and garnished with a hand-dipped chocolate espresso bean. This creamy dessert is a lovely marriage of cheese and cappuccino flavors. Sara also makes a **Chocolate Decadence** served at Patsy Clark's that's a flourless chocolate torte topped with a thin layer of ganache that's garnished with toasted slivered almonds. It's a dense, chocolaty dessert that's like eating rich, heavy fudge.

Divine Elegance offers their **Chocolate Kahlua Truffle Pie**, a Dilattante chocolate cheesecake with a flourless chocolate layer, and a crushed almond crust. It's finished with a pretty ribbon of chocolate and a cappuccino espresso bean. The result is a melt-in-your-mouth blending of chocolate and kahlua that demands just 1 more bite.

Their **Chocolate Pecan Tart** is made with a pastry crust with a layer of chocolate topped by a layer of pecans. It's served warm with a scoop of vanilla ice cream and the chef's own caramel sauce. It's a rich, wonderful blending of chocolate and caramel. Don't offer to share this one!

Patsy Clark's also serves Divine Elegance's **Chocolate Raspberry Truffle Cake** that has a chopped almond crust, a layer of thick, fudge-like chocolate, followed by a creamy layer flavored with Grand Marnier and Chambord, with a thin layer of raspberry glaze, garnished with a dollop of chocolate ganache and a chocolate covered espresso bean. It's a creamy and crunchy treat for raspberry lovers. Their **Chocolate Grand Marnier Cheesecake** features a chocolate cookie crust with a creamy layer of cheesecake flavored with Grand Marnier, topped with ganache and chocolate ribbons. It's a delight!

Traveler's Note: Some of the chocolate desserts at Patsy Clark's rotate, so call ahead if you have a favorite. Also, be sure to take the self-guided tour of the mansion for a real treat (and to walk off those calories).

Getting there: *Patsy Clark's is 5 minutes from downtown Spokane on 2nd Avenue at Hemlock.*

Clinkerdagger's

621 W Mallon Avenue, Spokane, WA. (509) 328-5965

♥♥♥ Overlooking the Spokane River with dramatic windows that jut toward the rushing waters below, **Clinkerdagger's** is a lunch and dinner favorite for locals. The old flour mill's original brick walls and heavy timbers add to the ambiance. Both their dinner and lunch menus are dauntingly large. For lunch, they serve a variety of soups, salads, hot sandwiches, pasta dishes and fish selections like halibut with rosemary. Dinner includes prawns, aged rock salt prime rib, and a large selection of beef steaks, chops, and roasts. For the chocolate lover, their signature chocolate dessert is **Chocolate Indulgence**, 2 layers of rich chocolate fudge cake thickly filled and frosted with chocolate fudge and garnished with chocolate sauce. Served warm with a scoop of vanilla ice cream, this rich cake is moist and ultra-chocolaty. The fudge filling/frosting is creamy without being cloyingly sweet. It's definitely a chocolate lover's delight.

Getting there: *Located just north of Riverfront Park in the Flour Mill Building on Mallon Avenue.*

Europa

125 S Wall, Spokane, WA. (509) 455-4051

♥♥♥ **Europa** is a casual, comfortable pub and café. The smoke-free pub has an intimate feel with its mahogany and marble bar, Victorian couches and settees, wicker chairs, and small tables. The restaurant invites with brick walls and painted frescos and original artwork adorning the walls. They serve primarily Italian cuisine like roasted garlic linguine, 4 cheese and spinach lasagna, seafood cioppino and a variety of interesting pizzas. This reviewer enjoyed a lunch special of Italian chicken with marinara sauce and parmesan cheese on 2 big slices of crunchy focaccia bread.

Eurpopa also makes all their own desserts, including their **Chocolate Mousse**, which is served with a cookie crust, an inch of fudge-like rum ganache, followed by an inch of a lighter milk chocolate mousse. It's very rich and chocolatey.

Their **Triple Layer Chocolate Mousse** has a graham cracker crust followed by dark chocolate, milk chocolate, and white chocolate mousse. The result is a wonderful combination of flavors and creamy textures with the white mousse adding just the right tang to the chocolate layers.

> **Aztecs believed drinking the chocolate drink, chocolatl, would bring them universal wisdom and knowledge.**

Europa's version of **Tollhouse Pie** is a flaky pie crust followed by a layer of chocolate chips and the walnut-cookie layer. It's served warm with a scoop of vanilla ice cream. One of the best Tollhouse Pies this reviewer has tasted, this dessert has a great chocolate flavor. It's heaven for chocolate chip cookie lovers.

The **Peanut Butter Chocolate Pie** has a chocolate cookie crust, a chocolate custard layer followed by a peanut butter custard layer, topped with a thin chocolate ganache and garnished with a sprinkling of peanuts. It's very creamy with a good blending of chocolate and peanut butter flavors.

Traveler's note: Some of the desserts rotate, so call ahead if you have a favorite.

Getting there: *In downtown, on Wall Street between 1ˢᵗ and 2ⁿᵈ.*

Paprika

S 1228 Grand, Spokane, WA. (509) 455-7545

♥♥♥ **Paprika** is an charmingly intimate café with paprika-colored walls, brightly-colored tablecloths, pounded brass plates, wicker chairs, and original paintings. Open for dinner only, chef/owner Carla Graves whips up gourmet delights like roasted rack of lamb with zinfandel and pear wine sauce, salmon filet with Italian salsa verde and salsa rojo, and polenta lasagne with spicy pizziola sauce. For dessert, save room for her **Chocolate Caramel Nut Tart**, a cookie crust topped with a mixture of caramel, pecans, and chocolate. The presentation is lovely with chocolate sauce squiggles, a big wedge of dark and white chocolate, and cocoa powder. It's served warm with a scoop of Paprika's homemade creme fraiche ice cream. The cookie crust is crisp and melt-in-the-mouth buttery. The big chunks of caramel and chocolate are bathed in a rich, creamy caramel that has just the right sweetness.

They also serve a **Chocolate Bread Pudding** that's a chocolate custard bread pudding with a big dollop of chocolate ganache in the center. It's served warm surrounded by a tart, chunky raspberry sauce, a wedge of chocolate on top, and dusted with cocoa. The result is chewy, gooey, and chocolatey.
Getting there: South of downtown, on Grand near 13th.

Windows of the Seasons (Cavanaugh's Inn at the Park)
W 303 N River Drive, Spokane, WA. (509) 328-9526
♥♥♥ **Windows of the Seasons** is one of the better fine dining restaurants in Spokane serving excellent dishes like grilled salmon with caper butter and filet mignon stuffed with blue cheese. They also have 2 full-time bakers on staff who make desserts that are both innovative and beautiful. Their **Death by Chocolate** has a fudge-like French silk layer nestled in a chocolate cookie crust that's topped with ganache. It's dense and very rich.

Their **Chocolate Medallion,** this reviewer's favorite, starts with a thin medallion of chocolate cake, topped with dark chocolate mousse, raspberries, and macaroon, all encased in a thin shell of dark chocolate. It's garnished with dark chocolate curls and finished with raspberry puree. It's a wonderfully unique blending of flavors with a mousse that has a dark, dense chocolate flavor that chocolate lover's will enjoy.

Egyptian Rush is a beautiful dessert made with triangles of white and dark chocolate stacked pyramid style over dark chocolate hazelnut mousse and Frangelico whipped cream. It's garnished with shaved white chocolate and toasted coconut. While the mousse is smooth and the chocolate triangles tasty, it's a difficult dessert to eat without being messy. The key is to remove the chocolate triangles with your fingers and dive in.
Getting there: On the north side of Riverside Park, just off Division.

Fugazzi
One N Post, Spokane, WA. (509) 624-1133
♥♥ Located right downtown in a light, airy space with modern,

artsy decor, **Fugazzi** has grabbed Spokane's diners' attention with lunch and dinner selections like grilled salmon on a bed of warm potato salad and fresh spinach with lemon vinaigrette and wild mushroom ravioli. Unfortunately for chocolate lovers, when this reviewer visited, chef Meg Rychel-Edwards was going out of town and did not have any of her usual chocolate creations. They were serving a **Chocolate Raspberry Ganache** from the local wholesale baker, **Sweet Cravings** (see review under Bakeries in this section). It's 3 layers of dark chocolate cake filled with raspberry/chocolate cream topped with ganache. It is beautifully presented on an over-sized, hand-painted plate with creme anglaise and raspberry coulis, fresh raspberries, and a sprinkling of cocoa. The cake is fine-textured and the chocolate ganache is smooth with a dark chocolate flavor. While the cake is good, we're looking forward to chef Edwards' own creations in the next edition.

Getting there: Downtown on the corner of Post and Sprague.

Hill's Someplace Else Restaurant and Pub
518 W Sprague, Spokane, WA. (509) 747-3946

♥♥ It was the name that first intrigued us. **Hill's** is a small restaurant with a pub atmosphere—dark, clubby, friendly. They serve some of the best hot sandwiches around like hot pastrami and Swiss on rye that's meaty and spicy. Hill's gets points from chocolate lovers for carrying a good selection of **Just American Desserts** chocolate items such as **Chocolate Mousse Cake, Chocolate Sin, Chocolate Raspberry Pie,** and **Chocolate Truffle Pie** (see review under Bakeries in this section).

Getting there: On the west side of downtown, on Sprague.

Luna
5620 S Perry Street, Spokane, WA. (509) 448-2383

♥♥ **Luna** is a friendly, suburban neighborhood place where regulars are greeted by name and often with hugs. The long, low building with lots of windows and booths with candles on the tables invites casual dining. Their menu changes 4 times a year and includes offerings such as Bangkok pizza (red peppers, zucchini, cilantro, toasted coconut, spicy curry sauce), salmon with lemon dijon sauce, and goat cheese-stuffed ravioli. Just as their dinner menu changes with the seasons, so does their dessert menu. Their dessert case is typically filled with a dozen or so desserts and at least 3 are chocolate. They're open late, especially for dessert and coffee.

Their **Tiramisu** is a different take on this traditional Italian dessert. Made in a large, rectangular pan, it has layers of crushed Amaretto di Saronno cookies, lady fingers, cocoa, mascarpone cheese, marsala wine, and espresso. The result is a very creamy dessert with a slight almond flavor.

Luna's **Chocolate Decadence Cake** is a very dense flourless cake that's served with raspberry or melba sauce and garnished with Belgian chocolate curls and whipped cream. It's a lot like biting into a piece of creamy fudge. Share this one, chocolate lovers.

Their **White Chocolate Caramel Nut Tart** is a pastry shell filled with almonds, pecans, and walnuts in a caramel/white chocolate combination, garnished with raspberry swirls and cocoa and served slightly warm. Although the crust is terrific, the caramel/white chocolate is almost impossible to cut with a fork and too sweet for this reviewer's taste.

The **Macadamia Nut Chocolate Chip Tart**, also served warm, is much more successful. Luna's version of Tollhouse Pie, the crust is flaky and melts in the mouth and the nut/chocolate center is a wonderful combination of nutty chocolaty flavors. It's a winner!
Getting there: Luna is in the South Hill area, at the corner of 57th Avenue and Perry Street.

Cyrus O'Leary's
516 W Main, Spokane, WA. (509) 624-9000
♥ **Cyrus O'Leary's** is a fun place that's, well, wild. It's got antique metal signs, manhole covers, big parrots, birdcages, saxophones, and a gorilla with a huge banana hanging from the ceiling. A large antique bar dominates in green naugahyde on either side and a solarium room on the north. The restaurant is a popular place, especially for lunch or with the munchies and drinks crowd. They serve a large selection of appetizers, hot sandwiches, burgers, pasta, and seafood. They also offer 16 different pies, made daily by Cyrus O'Leary Pies down the street. The slices are generous, the cream fillings thick, and they're topped with real (not canned) whipped cream. For chocolate lovers, they have **Chocolate Cream, Chocolate Peanut Butter, French Silk**, and **Kahlua**, this reviewer's favorite.
Getting there: Near Riverfront Park, at the corner of Main and Stevens.

Bakeries

Desserts by Sara
10502 E Montgomery, Spokane, WA. (509) 922-6039
♥♥♥♥ Don't let the light industrial setting fool you. People know where to find **Desserts by Sara** because she's worth finding. She's primarily a wholesale bakery, selling her cakes and other baked delights to local restaurants like **Patsy Clark's, Milford's Fish House**, and the **DoubleTree**, and by special order, if you call ahead. You can get some of her other chocolate delights on-site with a cup of coffee. In **Derby Bars,** a sugar cookie crust sandwiches a rich, melt-in-the-mouth filling of butter, walnuts, chocolate chips and

whiskey that's drizzled with chocolate. It has a chewy goodness and the liquor adds a richness without a boozy taste.

Sara's **German Nut Squares** have a sugar cookie crust topped with a thick concoction of almonds, walnuts, butter and honey. It's half-dipped in semi-sweet dark chocolate. The effect is buttery, nutty, and simply wonderful.

Super Rich Brownie is a dense brownie packed with walnuts and chocolate chips lightly frosted with a chocolate butter cream cheese frosting. The chocolate flavor is intense, almost smokey, while the cream cheese frosting is light and buttery.

Traveler's Tip: Don't be disappointed. Sara's usually closes by 3:00 p.m.
Getting there: *In the northeast light industrial section of Spokane, on Montgomery off Argonne.*

Sweet Cravings and Classy Cakes
1126 Northwest Boulevard, Spokane, WA. (509) 328-8734
♥♥♥♥ **Sweet Cravings and Classy Cakes** is one of the best specialty bakeries in Spokane. Their **Caramel Crunch Chocolate Cheesecake**, this reviewer's favorite Sweet Cravings dessert, is a big wedge of chocolate cheesecake on a chocolate cookie crust topped with caramel icing and chocolate chips and chopped pecans. A terrific variation on the old cheesecake theme, it's crunchy, creamy, and cheesy with just the right tangy flavor cheesecake lovers crave.

Their **Anika Torte** is 4 layers of dark chocolate cake filled with a buttery coconut filling and frosted with a chocolate buttercream that's garnished with chopped walnuts. **Chocolate Fantasy** has a dark chocolate cookie crust, a thick layer of creamy, tangy cheesecake, and a topping of rich chocolate ganache.

Unfortunately, you can't go to their Northwest Boulevard location and buy a slice of their fabulous cakes, tortes, or cheesecakes. (You *can* call ahead and order a whole dessert.) The good news is you can buy a slice of these and other delights from Sweet Cravings at **Fuggazi's, Clinkerdagger's, The Mustard Seed, Charlie's**, and **Luigi's** restaurants, as well as at **Huckleberry's** market.
Getting there: *On Northwest Boulevard, north of Riverside Park.*

Take the Cake Pastry Shop
139 S Sherman, Spokane, WA. (509) 455-8658
♥♥♥♥ **Take the Cake's** pastry chef/owner Karen Hansen earned her baker's wings at the wonderful Metropol Bakery in Eugene and customers have been flying heavenward with her creations ever since. Her desserts, which are available by the slice or whole

or at a few selected restaurants, are in the European tradition, less sweet and involving more complicated—and delicious—recipes. Her **Chocolate Expresso Cream Roulade** is a flourless chocolate soufflé that's wrapped around a center of whipped cream flavored with espresso. The soufflé, which is sliced jelly roll style, is like dry velvet—slightly crumbly and instantly melting in the mouth, leaving just the rich taste of dark chocolate. The whipped cream is just the right consistency with a hint of espresso to give it depth.

Karen's **Chocolate Chiffon Cake** is 3 layers of light chocolate chiffon cake separated by creamy milk chocolate mousse, frosted with mocha whipped cream. The chocolate cake is soft and fine-textured with a mellow chocolate flavor. The whipped cream's mocha flavor adds a lovely contrast to the cake.

The **Chocolate Hazelnut Terrine** is a melt-in-the-mouth combination of milk chocolate and hazelnut butter with a thin layer of hazelnuts on the bottom enclosed in a rich, bittersweet chocolate glaze. The dessert is sliced much like a chocolate pate, but tastes like a cross between a rich mousse and the inside of a truffle. It's creamy and delicious.

Take the Cake's **Tiramisu** consists of 2 layers of sponge cake soaked with coffee and Meyers Dark Rum, sandwiched between generous layers of mascarpone cheese and ground chocolate. The sponge cake is light, almost airy and the mascarpone tastes sweet and slightly tangy. It's an interesting variation on a traditional dessert.

The **Chocolate Nut Tart** is Karen's version of the pecan pie. Macadamia nuts, pecans, chocolate chips and chocolate chunks are packed into a buttery short crust. It's a pecan lover's delight with the wonderful surprise of chocolate. (For more about Take the Cake's delicious desserts, see Café Roma under Restaurants in this section.)
Getting there: On Sherman at 2nd.

Just American Desserts
10625 E Sprague, Spokane, WA. (509) 927-2253
Other Spokane locations:
2812 E 30th Avenue, Spokane, WA. (509)534-7195 (Southside)
6406 N Monroe, Spokane, WA. (509) 328-5889 (Northside)
♥♥♥ **Just American Desserts**, run by Eva Roberts, (who was formerly a pastry chef at the popular Spokane restaurant Patsy Clark's), and her sister and mom, is a specialty dessert boutique. They make everything from scratch and use ingredients like Guittard and Belgian Callebaut chocolate, butter, and fresh sour cream. They have a huge selection of cakes and other desserts by the piece or whole. **Chocolate Chip Cake**, their #1 seller, is a 3-inch square that's 2 layers of medium chocolate cake filled and frosted with a

tangy cream cheese frosting that's spiked with mini chocolate chips. The cake is light and the frosting has a wonderful cheesiness to it.

Atomic is alternating thin layers of vanilla and chocolate sponge cake filled with raspberry, then a sweet creamy layer, and a hazelnut layer, topped with dark chocolate. The sponge cake is light without being too airy and the raspberry/hazelnut combination is interesting.

Chocolate Truffle Pie comes with a light and flaky pastry crust piled high with a thick French silk filling that's creamy with a rich, intense chocolate flavor. It's garnished with one of their hand-dipped truffles.

Chocolate Fudge Brownie is an intense fudge-like brownie that's lightly frosted with chocolate frosting. **Chocolate Sin** is a large wedge of flourless dark chocolate torte dusted with powered sugar. It's incredibly rich, with chocolate flavor that explodes in the mouth and demands another bite. It's sinfully delicious.

The **Tri-Chocolate Torte** starts with a crunchy brownie-like layer, followed by a dense, dark, chocolate truffle layer, topped with a rich, white chocolate mousse. It's garnished with triangles of white and dark chocolate. The bottom is nutty and chewy; the middle is like biting into a rich truffle; and the white mousse topping is light yet rich.

Chocolate Velvet Mousse Cake is 2 layers of dark chocolate cake filled with an inch of dark chocolate mousse that's covered with a dark chocolate ganache. The mousse is creamy with an intense chocolate flavor that's lightly tinged with rum.

Their **Chocolate Raspberry Cake** is 3 layers of milk chocolate cake filled with raspberry filling. The cake is good-textured, but the raspberry filling is a bit sweet for this reviewer's taste.

Turtle Cheesecake starts with a chocolate cookie crust, followed by a layer of chocolate chips, pecans, and caramel, topped with a 2-inch layer of cheesecake topped with ganache. This rich dessert has lots of pecan flavor.

Their **Chocolate Chip Pie** is a pastry crust filled with chocolate chips, pecans, butter, and bourbon. It's loaded with chips and is best served slightly heated.

They also make softball-sized **Truffles**, thickly coated with creamy, melt-in-the-mouth centers. They come in a variety of flavors, including **Grand Marnier, Bailey's, Kahlua Pecan**, and **Huckleberry**.

Getting there: The mother store, where the desserts are made, is on E Sprague, tucked back into the U-City North Plaza.

The Rocket Bakery
3315 N Argonne Road, Spokane, WA. (509) 927-2340
Other Spokane locations:
903 W Garland Avenue, Spokane, WA. (509) 325-8009
1301 14th, Spokane, WA. (509) 456-3534
S 18 Monroe, Spokane, WA. (509) 455-5282
♥ The eastside **Rocket Bakery** with its green awnings, long coffee bar with stools, and outside tables is a welcoming retreat from busy Argonne Road. The bakery, whose motto is "come in and blast off," offers coffee drinks and an array of scones, muffins, thick slices of banana, cranberry/orange, and date nut breads, and big cookies. For the chocolate lover, they have a **Devil's Food Cake** that is 2 layers of medium-grained cake frosted with a fudge frosting, garnished with chopped pecans. The cake is moist, but the frosting is a bit sweet.

Use only the best. If you use the best, you'll get the best out of it."

– Hans Weiss, owner/ pastry chef, Hans, Bend, OR.

A better choice is their **Chocolate Cascade Cake**, 2 layers of dark chocolate cake flavored with espresso and thinly frosted and filled with an intensely coffee-flavored icing with flecks of finely ground espresso beans. This moist cake has a terrific coffee flavor that java lovers will enjoy.

Mixed Nut Torte is a pastry shell with a soft, buttery, nut-filled mixture that's topped with melted dark chocolate. There's not much chocolate flavor, but plenty of nuts.

Chocolate No-bake Cookie is the coconut-chocolate-oatmeal recipe you remember from childhood. Rocket's 4-inch version will take you right back to those good old days.
Getting there: The eastside Rocket is on Argonne Road between Liberty Avenue and Dalton.

Ice Creameries

The Corner Fountain and Books
N 3301 Argonne, Spokane, WA. (509) 921-9253
♥♥♥ Located in historic Millwood, **The Corner Fountain and Books** sign says, "Might be open at 10:00 a.m.—11:00 a.m. for sure." That's not the only thing different about this wonderful old soda fountain. Artist Betsy Mott, whose paintings of movie stars adorn the café's walls, and her partners Gregory Mott and Bobbie

Beese, serve 50 different flavors of **milkshakes** behind the old marble soda fountain. Their **Chocolate Espresso Milkshake**, made with chocolate and vanilla ice cream, chocolate syrup, and a shot (or more) of espresso, is smooth, thick, and rich. The espresso adds an unusual richness that's terrific. They also serve **malts, sundaes,** and **ice cream sodas**, all made with local, premium ice cream from Doyles or Mary Lou's. If you're in the mood for lunch, they serve a variety of deli sandwiches, salads, and soups. And don't forget to browse their selection of new and used books.

Getting there: On the corner of Argonne and Dalton in Millwood.

Chocolate Shops

Hallet's Chocolate and Treats
1419 E Holyoke, Spokane, WA. (509) 484-6454 (factory and retail shop)
Other Spokane location:
2525 E 29th, Spokane, WA. (509) 535-7077

♥♥ Even though **Hallet's** chocolate factory is located in a light industrial section of Spokane, fans have no problem finding them. Using Guittard chocolate and a variety of interesting flavors, including local huckleberries, they produce a wide array of **chocolate candies**, including **creams, truffles**, and **caramels**. Their Jelly Sticks, which come in **Orange, Raspberry**, and **Huckleberry**, have vibrant flavors that leap onto the tongue. Their **Huckleberry Cream** shouts, "Huckleberry!"

Hallet's **Truffles** are delicately small, with a thick coating of chocolate, and creamy centers. Their **Chocolate-covered Caramels** are creamy, if a bit sweet.

Getting there: In the northern section of town, off Francis on Holyoke between Helena and Perry Streets

Other Chocolate Outlets

Huckleberry's Fresh Market
926 S Monroe, Spokane, WA. (509) 624-1349
Huckleberry's is part gourmet grocery, part health food store. It's an upscale market that sells organic produce, bulk foods, food supplements, and herbal remedies, as well as specialty cheeses, sausages, meats, and other high-end items. It also has a good selection of New Age books and a bistro selling soups, salads, sandwiches, and espresso. For the chocolate lover, Huckleberry's has gathered items from some of the best local bakeries and chocolatiers, including **Sweet Cravings, Fery's Catering, Sweet Swiss**, and **Seattle's 60th Street**. Sweet Cravings' **Anika Torte** is 4 layers of dark chocolate cake filled with a buttery coconut filling and frosted with a chocolate buttercream that's garnished with chopped walnuts. Also from Sweet Cravings, the **Chocolate Fantasy** has a dark chocolate cookie crust, a thick layer of creamy, tangy cheesecake, and a topping of chocolate ganache.

60th Street's **Chocolate Decadence** is an intensely rich, flourless torte that has the texture of a thick truffle. Their **Chocolate Pecan Tart** features a flaky pastry crust filled with a buttery pecan mixture with chocolate chunks, garnished with a dollop of thick ganache. This is a taste that'll make you wish you were born in the South.

The **Chocolate Mousse Cake** from Fery's Catering is 2 layers of milk chocolate cake filled and frosted with a milk chocolate mousse. It's light and creamy with a lilt of rum flavor.

They also carry truffles from Sweet Swiss and other chocolates from Roger's Chocolates in Canada.
Getting there: *On S Monroe at 10th.*

PULLMAN

Hilltop Restaurant
Davis Way, Pullman, WA. (509) 334-2555
♥♥ **Hilltop Restaurant** has been an institution in Pullman for nearly 50 years. With a great view of town, Hilltop has evolved from a family steak house to a fine dining establishment serving not only flavorful steaks, but also prime rib, pasta, chicken, and salmon. Do save room for their chocolate desserts. Their **Chocolate Mousse** is 3 generous scoops of light chocolate mousse garnished with chocolate sprinkles and a rolled wafer cookie. It has a light cocoa flavor and an airy, whipped texture that invites another bite.

Their **Black Forest Cake** is 3 layers of medium chocolate cake filled with white buttercream and cherry chunk filling, frosted with buttercream. This cake has a good homemade from-scratch taste. Unlike many Black Forests, it's subtle rather than cloyingly sweet. The buttercream is airy and light.

The **Rum Cake With Chocolate** is a rich, buttery, bundt-style pound cake flavored with rum. The rum isn't overly done and semi-sweet chocolate topping is thick, fudge-like, and rich.

Hilltop's **Chocolate Truffle Cake** is a generous wedge that begins with a crunchy, crisp chocolate layer, followed by an inch of dense truffle cake that's a cross between the inside of a truffle and a brownie, topped with bittersweet chocolate ganache that's garnished with white chocolate swirls. The truffle melts in the mouth while the crust adds an interesting chewiness. The ganache is just the right bittersweet flavor to compliment the sweeter truffle layer.
Getting there: *Up the hill from 270 off of 195.*

Combray
215 E Main Street, Pullman, WA. (509) 334-9024

♥ **Combray** features an open kitchen and a large dining room decorated in minimalist fashion. Their menu, which changes weekly, features 3-course, pre-fixe meals with a choice of entrees such as petrale sole with crab, saffron risotto, or beef tenderloin. Their dessert menu changes too, but often includes their **Pot de Creme**, a milk chocolate pudding with the texture of flan, beautifully presented with vanilla and chocolate sauce and a caramel cage. It's light on chocolate flavor, but the texture is very creamy. Another favorite is **Chocolate Raspberry Decadence**, a raspberry layer sandwiched between 2 layers of dense chocolate cake, topped with dark chocolate ganache. It's thick and rich with chocolate flavor.
Getting there: Just off Grand on Main Street.

Swilly's
200 Kamiaken Street, Pullman, WA. (509) 334-3395

♥ **Swilly's** is a pleasant little bistro in downtown Pullman that serves pasta, calzone, soups, salads, hot and cold sandwiches, and steaks. They also make a **Chocolate Truffle Cake**, a single layer of dense chocolate cake frosted with a thick, stiff layer of dark chocolate ganache, garnished with white and milk chocolate savings. The cake has a dense texture and the ganache has a rich, dark chocolate flavor.

Nanimo Bar, one of the best this reviewer has tasted, isn't overly sweet and features a bottom brownie layer loaded with chopped coconut and walnuts, a middle cream cheese layer, followed by a thick, dark chocolate layer. The marriage of flavors is most satisfying.

Their **Frosted Brownie** is a thin layer of chewy, medium chocolate flavor brownie (no nuts) topped with a thick coating of rather sticky fudge frosting. We'd opt for the Nanimo Bar.
Getting there: 1 block east of Grand.

Ice Creamery
Ferdinand's Creamery
2 blocks east of Stadium Way on the WSU campus, Pullman, WA. (509) 335-6392

♥♥♥♥ There's a reason people in Idaho and Southern Washington drive for miles to buy WSU's **Ferdinand's Ice Cream**. This is great ice cream—smooth, creamy, fresh tasting without clinging to the palette. Operated by the University's Agricultural Department, the creamery makes ice cream in small batches using its own milk, ensuring it's some of the freshest ice cream you'll ever taste. Their chocolate flavors include **Chocolate, Chocolate Almond, Cookies and Cream**, and **Chocolate Peanut Butter**, made with big chunks of peanut butter. A single scoop is the size of a softball.

Also check out some of their famous Cougar Gold Cheese.

Traveler's Note: Don't miss out—the Creamery is only open Monday through Friday 9:30 a.m.-4:30 p.m.
Getting there: *Follow the signs to the WSU Stadium on campus and then follow the signs to Ferdinand's.*

CLARKSTON

4-10 Drive-In
1296 Bridge Street, Clarkston, WA. (509) 758-4908
It's been a long way down the highway from Spokane and a long time without some chocolate. The **4-10 Drive-In**, "keeping the spirit alive since '55," offers thick **chocolate malts** or **milkshakes** made from soft ice cream. It's a real yesteryear drive-in with car hop service and those old trays that fit on the car window.
Getting there: *Corner of 13th and Bridge Street.*

WALLA WALLA

Ice-Burg Drive-In
616 W Birch, Walla Walla, WA. (509) 529-1793
♥♥♥ The **Ice-Burg Drive-In** advertises "the best shakes in the NW," and they may be right. Made with soft ice cream, their **Hot Fudge Shake** is thick, creamy and satisfying. In addition to hot fudge and **Chocolate**, they have enough flavors to satisfy anyone—**Coffee, Vanilla, Lemon, Banana, Orange, Rootbeer, Peanut Butter, Marshmallow, Peppermint, Strawberry, Blackberry, Pineapple,** and **Raspberry**.
Getting there: *Off 9th at Birch Street.*

Coffee Perk
4 S First, Walla Walla, WA. (509) 526-0636
Coffee Perk is an intimate coffee house complete with comfortable booths, couches, a river rock fireplace, and covered outdoor seating. They specialize in coffee and espresso drinks and desserts. They don't make their own desserts, but their **White Chocolate Cheesecake** is interesting. It's a chocolate crust with 2 inches of white chocolate cheesecake filling, topped with dark chocolate. It's velvet soft and cheesy. Their **French Raspberry Cake** is 3 layers of extra dark chocolate cake with chocolate-raspberry filling, frosted with a dark fudge. The cake is moist, but the raspberry

is a bit sweet and the frosting sticky. They also serve a **Cappuccino Brownie**, a cake-like brownie frosted with a light, whipped cappuccino frosting. It's less successful than their cheesecake, but an interesting twist on old favorite.

Getting there: Downtown on South 1st Street.

Bakery

Chocolate Expectations

213 S 9th, Walla Walla, WA. (509) 529-6354

♥♥ **Chocolate Expectations** is a wholesale cookie and brownie bakery that uses quality ingredients like Guittard chocolate, butter, real vanilla, and no preservatives. They make 2 types of cookies. **Super Hunk** is a 4-inch tollhouse cookie with big, semi-sweet chocolate chunks and big pieces of walnut. It's chewy, not overly sweet, with big hits of chocolate. Their **Hunca Blanca**, a white chocolate macadamia cookie, is the same jumbo size with a lovely chewy crunchiness and plenty of macadamia flavor.

They make 5 different **brownies**. Their **Fudge Chunk** and **Super Fudge** are both fudge-like and moist with big pieces of walnut. **Death by Chocolate**, their #1 seller, is a white chocolate brownie filled with big pieces of semi-sweet, dark chocolate. It's a little gooey with a good white chocolate taste. Their **Cappuccino Brownie** is very moist and tinged with the flavor of espresso. **Euphoria** is a dark chocolate brownie with big slabs of white chocolate and walnuts. It's chewy, moist, and the white chocolate adds a nice contrast to the dark chocolate. *You can find Chocolate Expectations cookies and brownies at many local convenience stores in the area. Or you can call the bakery and find out where the nearest retail outlet is to you.*

Getting there: On S 9th at Birch Street.

Money Trees! Cocoa beans were so valued by early Indian people that they were used as units of calculation and as payment for goods and services. It is said that 10 cocoa beans would pay for a rabbit; 100 beans a slave. Money really did grow on trees!

John's Wheatland Bakery

1828 East Issacs, Walla Walla, WA. (509) 522-BAKE

♥ **John's Wheatland Bakery** specializes in breads such as sourdough, cinnamon swirl, rye, and raisin. They also make **cakes**— **German Chocolate, Chocolate Mousse, Truffle Torte,** and **Chocolate Angel Food**. Their **Chocolate Mousse Cake** is 2 layers of fine-grained, medium chocolate cake filled and frosted with a light chocolate mousse, garnished with semi-sweet chocolate shavings. The cake is very soft with a hint of cinnamon and the mousse is creamy and light with a soft chocolate flavor.

Their **Chocolate Croissant** is a big 7-incher stuffed with dark, intensely chocolate filling. Their **Chocolate Chip Cookie** is crunchy with a buttery flavor and is filled with walnuts and chocolate. Their **Brownie** is a soft, cake-like half-inch layer lightly frosted with a dark ganache. It has good flavor, but let these refrigerated brownies warm up before enjoying.

Traveler's note: If you have a Wheatland favorite, call ahead and ask them to put it aside. They tend to run out of favorites later in the day.
Getting there: *Take the Issac Street exit off Highway 12.*

Chocolate Shop

Bright's
5 S First Street, Walla Walla, WA. (509) 525-5533/(800) 350-5533
♥♥ **Bright's** has been in business since 1934. New owners Tiffany and Paul Jenes use the original tried and true recipes and Guittard Chocolate to make hand-dipped **chocolates, truffles**, and homemade **fudge**. This store is also known for mints, popcorn, cheesecorn, and fresh caramel corn, Jelly Bellys, unique gift items, and specialty-shaped chocolates (i.e., seasonal lollipops, cowboys, bowling pins and bowling balls, and state shapes).

Their **Caramel Nut** and plain **Nut Clusters**, which are 2 inches across, have a good balance of ingredients and come in creamy milk or dark chocolate. Their **Truffles** are soft centered with an almost whipped texture and a thin chocolate coating with just the right snap to it. The truffles are intensely flavored. Count on these chocolates to be fresh and full-bodied.
Getting there: *Downtown on South 1ˢᵗ Street.*

KENNEWICK

Chez Chaz Bistro and Catering
5011 W Clearwater Avenue, Kennewick, WA. (509) 735-2138
♥♥♥ Off busy Clearwater Avenue, **Chez Chaz Bistro and Catering** is a popular lunch and dinner bistro that offers a large selection of sandwiches such as Little Italy—ham, salami, provolone on French—homemade soups, pasta and chicken dishes. Weekends the chef pulls out all the stops and offers a pre-fixe menu with entrees such as Cajun prime rib, chicken with prawns and hollandaise sauce, salmon with almonds and cracked peppercorns,

and linguine with chicken and hazelnuts. Their desserts, all made on-site from scratch, are worth saving room for. Their signature dessert is their **Chocolate Cabernet Cake**, a soft-textured, dark chocolate cake flavored with cabernet, frosted with chocolate buttercream and drizzled with dark chocolate and sliced almonds. The cabernet adds an almost tangy depth to this cake without being boozy. The chocolate buttercream/drizzled chocolate combination is ultra-creamy with a deep, intense chocolate flavor that's delightfully good. Two reviewers fought over the last bite of this dessert!

Their **Chocolate Hazelnut Torte** is 2 layers of dark chocolate cake sprinkled with chopped hazelnuts, filled and frosted with dark chocolate buttercream, garnished with chopped hazelnuts. The cake is very moist and rich and the toasted hazelnuts offer a wonderful nutty flavor.

Getting there: On Clearwater Avenue at Edison.

Henry's
3013 W Clearwater Avenue, Kennewick, WA. (509) 735-1996
♥♥ (See review under Henry's, Richland, WA.)
Getting There: On W Clearwater near Hwy 395.

The Country Register Café and Tea Room
8310 Gage Boulevard, Kennewick, WA. (509) 783-7553
In a barn-like building behind the Columbia Center Mall, **The Country Register Café and Tea Room** is a pleasant lunch place that's decorated with ivy trim, ceiling fans, and floral tablecloths. In addition to afternoon tea with all the trimmings, they serve light lunch fare such as salads, sandwiches, and tortilla wraps. For chocolate lovers they offer a **Kahlua Brownie**, a large triangle of soft, airy, cake-like brownie infused with chocolate chips, served with vanilla bean ice cream and garnished with a dollop of whipped cream, chocolate syrup, and a cherry.

Getting there: Behind the Columbia Center Mall off Gage.

Candy Shop

Sweet Cravings
201 N Edison, Suite 244, Kennewick, WA. (509) 735-8658
♥♥♥ For the past 9 years, Trudy Anderson and her daughter, Monica Devine, have been delighting folks in Kennewick with **Sweet Cravings' hand-dipped chocolates**. Made with high-quality Merkens chocolate, their **Truffles**, which come in the usual flavors and some less common ones like **Cabernet, Piña Colada, Malted Milk, Peppermint Schnapps**, and **Dark Chocolate With Cinnamon**, are large, creamy, and full of flavor. Their signature **Death by Truffle**, which won 1st place in a local chocolate extravaganza, is a square truffle layered with kahlua, amaretto, and dark chocolate. It's rich and a different take on the usual truffles.

Their **Chocolate-covered Caramel** is dense and chewy with a bright caramel flavor. Their **Orange Sticks** are full of fresh orange flavor. They also make a variety of **Nut Clusters**, which tend to be a bit small and more chocolate than nuts.

Getting there: South on Edison exit off Highway 240.

RICHLAND

Henry's

1435 George Washington Way, Richland, WA. (509) 946-8706
Other Washington location:
3013 West Clearwater Avenue, Kennewick, WA. (509) 735-1996
♥♥ Right off busy George Washington Way and decorated in brass and soothing forest green, **Henry's** is a nice retreat. They serve a large selection of steaks, including blackened cajun, burgers, and chicken dishes. Henry's famous **"Mile High" Mudpie** is a huge slice of chocolate chip mocha ice cream in a thin cookie crust that's covered with chocolate sauce and smothered with whipped cream and garnished with chopped almonds. Unlike many mudpies, this one isn't heavy. Instead, it's refreshing, light on the coffee flavor, and big enough to split with a friend.
Getting there: North on George Washington in Richland.

Candy Shop

Baum's Candies

2147 Van Giesen, Richland, WA. (509) 943-5830
♥♥♥ Kathy Baumgarter was the first to introduce the Tri-Cities area to great **hand-dipped chocolates** 16 years ago and she's still going strong. **Baum's** features small, elegant chocolates made from Guittard chocolate in the European tradition—flavors that are subtle rather than obvious, candies that are beautiful to look at as well as to eat. Her **Truffles** are the size of a quarter, but so rich you don't need more. The centers are a little stiffer than some we've had, but they have with a creamy, melt-in-the mouth texture. A new line for Baum's is **Belgian Truffles**—hazelnut-based and rum-based fillings that are richly flavored. Her **Chocolate-covered Toffee** is rich and buttery, inviting another bite. The **Peanut Butter Cup** is a soft peanut butter filling enrobed by just the right amount of milk or dark chocolate. They're creamy and delicious.
Getting there: West on Van Giesen from George Washington or, from Highway 240, East on Van Giesen.

WEST RICHLAND

Green Gage Plum Restaurant
3892 West Van Giesen, West Richland, WA. (509) 967-2424

♥♥♥♥ It doesn't look like much from the outside, but chef/owner Sue Needham has created a veritable oasis of culinary delights in her tiny **Green Gage Plum Restaurant** (Green Gage, by the way, is a type of small plum). She offers usual lunch fare like burgers, soups, and hot and cold sandwiches. Chef Sue really shines at dinner when she serves entrees like Halibut St. Charles, halibut satueed with fresh mushrooms and artichokes in a rich sherried dijon cream, and chicken scallopine, chicken breast sauteed in white wine with fresh mushrooms, garlic, and parmesan. They make their own sauces, breads, soups, and even salad dressings. Chocolate lover's shouldn't pass up Green Gage Plum's **Pot de Creme**, a ramekin of deep, dark chocolate topped with a generous amount of real whipped cream and dusted with cocoa. This is a cross between a smooth mousse and the inside of a truffle—creamy, rich, sensuous. It's one of the best pot de cremes we've enjoyed.

Getting there: West on Van Giesen from Highway 240 or from George Washington Boulevard. (crossing the Yakima River).

COULEE CITY

Steamboat Rock Restaurant
420 W Main, Coulee City, WA. (509) 632-5452

You're really out in the middle of no where and it's been a long time since your last chocolate fix. You pull off Highway 17 and into the **Steamboat Rock Restaurant**, a little diner with a handful of tables and a counter. Ask for one of their big **Chocolate Chocolate Chip Muffins**. Okay, they don't make them, but they're served warm and are full of melted chips. It's a fix that'll hold you.

Getting there: On the main street in Coulee City.

Campagne
Seattle, Washington
CINNAMON ICE CREAM

Makes 8 servings

2 cups whole milk
1 cup granulated sugar
1 tablespoon ground cinnamon
Zest of 1 orange
6 egg yolks
2 cups whipping cream

In a heavy-bottomed sauce pan, heat milk, sugar, cinnamon and orange zest until scalded, whisking occasionally to incorporate ingredients. Mixture is scalded when tiny bubbles form around the edges of the pan. Do not boil.

Whisk together egg yolks. Ladle a small amount of the scalded milk into the yolks and whisk thoroughly. Whisk the egg mixture back into the sauce pan. Using a rubber spatula, stir the mixture over low heat, using a figure 8 motion with the spatula. When the creme anglaise is done, it will coat the spatula with a fine film. Do not boil!

Remove immediately from heat and strain into a plastic bowl or container. Whisk in cream. Place the mixture into a bowl of ice and stir occasionally until completely cool. Pour into container of ice cream freezer and freeze according to manufacturer's directions. Serve with the Hot Fudge Sauce on page 183.

This ice cream from one of Seattle's best restaurants has a lovely orange-cinnamon flavor.

From *The Chocolate Lover's Guide Cookbook*, Pacific Northwest Edition.

CANADA

British Columbia

VANCOUVER

VICTORIA

*C*anadians have long been famous for their love of good chocolate. In addition to breath-taking scenery, British Columbia boasts some of the best chocolate in the Pacific Northwest. For chocolate lovers, we've limited our review of chocolate sources to B.C.'s 2 great cities, Vancouver and Victoria.

VANCOUVER

If location is everything, Vancouver has it all. The city is surrounded by water and soaring, snow-capped mountains. Vancouver has a decidedly international flair and many of the city's best chefs and chocolatiers come from Europe. Get ready, chocolate fans, the city of chocolate awaits.

Great Things to Do

• **Stroll in Stanley Park. Stanley Park, Vancouver, B.C.** Just northwest of downtown, Stanley Park is 1,000 acres of rolling hills and trees surrounded by a seawall that surrounds the park. It's a great place to walk, run, bike, or rollerblade. For a bird's eye view, you can ride in an enclosed gondola up Grouse Mountain. Or drive to Cypress Bowl for a breathtaking view of the city. In the summer, the Vancouver Symphony Orchestra holds a concert at the top of the mountain.

• **Window Shop. Robson Street, Vancouver, B.C.** The most fashionable shopping district in Vancouver is Robson Street. Since many of the prices are comparable to Rodeo Drive, you may need to content yourself with window shopping.

• **Get the Low Down On Native Culture. Museum of Anthropology**, University of British Columbia, 6393 NW Marine Drive, **Vancouver, B.C.** (604) 822-3825. Much of Vancouver's art and tradition can be traced back to the native peoples who lived in the area thousands of years before Europeans arrived. A great way to learn about native culture, including their beautiful totem poles, is to spend an afternoon in the Museum of Anthropology. They have an extensive collection of native artifacts.

• **Take in the Symphony. Vancouver Symphony Orchestra**, 884 Granville, **Vancouver, B.C.** (604) 876-3434. Starting in October, the Vancouver Symphony begins its season.

• **Check Out Gastown**. In Vancouver's oldest neighborhood, the old and new combine seamlessly. You'll find old architecture, antique shops, and cobblestone streets as well as trendy art galleries and restaurants. At the corner of Water and Cambie Streets, the old Gastown Steam Clock chimes every 15 minutes.

• **See Sun Yat-Sen. Dr. Sun Yat Sen Park**, 578 Carrall Street, **Vancouver, B.C.** (604) 662-3207. If you enjoy lovely gardens, you'll appreciate the classical Chinese garden named after the Asian scholar Dr. Sun Yat Sen. The many beautiful pavilions and walkways will help melt away accumulated stress.

Terrific Places to Stay

Wedgewood Hotel, 845 Hornby, **Vancouver, B.C.** (604) 689-7777/ (800) 663-0666. Sophisticated elegance and flawless service is what the Wedgewood Hotel is about. Located in the heart of the downtown district across from the gardens of Robson Square, this 94-

room hotel has all the qualities of a first-rate city hotel with the intimate feel of a country inn. The guest rooms and suites are large and well-appointed with English antiques, sculpted wall paper, and private balconies that allow guests to take in the city lights. Niceties include nightly turn down service, cookies and mineral water at bedside, phones, color televisions, coffee pots, hair dryers, fluffy robes, valet parking, and 24-hour room service. Guests would do well to skip the bare-bones fitness room and head instead for the popular, clubby lounge or the Bacchus Ristorante (see review). This is a place you'll want to return to again and again.

Metropolitan Hotel, 645 Howe Street, **Vancouver, B.C.** (604) 687-1122. Located downtown, the Metropolitan Hotel is a luxury hotel with a contemporary elegant feel. The 197 rooms are large and beautifully decorated with oak cabinetry, wool carpets, and large marble bathrooms with separate walk-in showers and soaker tubs. Extras include silky Italian linens, European down duvets, turn down service, an in-room coffee pot, hair dryers, terry robes, and morning newspaper. Guests can enjoy a full-service health club and spa with an indoor pool in an enclosed atrium, a whirlpool, men's and women's saunas, a fully-equipped workout area, and squash and racquetball courts. Massage and personal trainers are available for an extra fee. Diva at the Met, an award-winning restaurant, is just off the lobby area (see review).

Four Seasons, 791 West Georgia, **Vancouver, B.C.** (604) 689-9333. Four Seasons Hotels are renown for excellence and the Four Seasons Hotel in Vancouver is no exception. Located in the ultramodern Pacific Centre, the Four Seasons offers guests 385 beautifully-appointed guest rooms, including large suites with 2 bathrooms equipped with their own telephones. Amenities include turn down service, morning newspaper, 24-hour room service, complimentary limousine, valet parking, hair dryers, soft robes, exquisite bed linens, and over-sized towels. The large glassed-in health club, one of the best hotel clubs in the city, is well-equipped with the latest aerobic and weight training equipment and an indoor-outdoor pool. Guests can enjoy the rooftop garden, complete with waterfall, and dine at the notable Chartwell Restaurant (see review), or the more casual, sunlit Garden Terrace.

Sutton Place Hotel, 845 Burrard Street, **Vancouver, B.C.** (604) 682-5511/(800) 961-7555. Sutton Place Hotel is a luxury hotel with a warm, residential feeling. The 397 rooms, from guest rooms to elegant suites, are spacious and beautifully decorated with English antiques. All feature air conditioning, radios, remote-control televisions, mini-bars, terry robes, hair dryers, umbrellas, 2 or more phones with messaging and dataports, toiletries, the finest linens, and fresh flowers. Morning newspapers, free limousine service, turn down service, and even personalized stationary raise the level of service even higher. The staff is friendly, attentive and accomplished. Le Spa, a full-service health club, offers a complete workout area, indoor pool and jacuzzi, outdoor sundeck, sauna, and steamroom. Massage, reflexology, and body care are also available. Guests can dine at the Fleuri Restaurant with its Chocoholic Bar (see review). *Traveler's note: Dog guests welcome.*

Restaurants

Allegro Café
1G-888 Nelson, Vancouver, B.C. (604) 683-8485
♥♥♥♥ Tucked a few steps below Nelson Square, **Allegro** is an intimate little café that seats 30. Green, semi-circular booths, tables covered with mustard-colored cloths, wooden chairs, the cement floor, and bar with tall chairs all contribute to the casual, comfortable feeling. Lunch offerings include dishes like frittata, fettuccine with spring salmon and Spanish paella. Dinner entrees include angel hair pasta with black tiger pawns, ravioli with crab, mascarpone, and eggplant, veal osso buco, and salmon and asparagus, as well as a large selection of nightly specials. *Do* save room for chef Barbara Reese's desserts. A confirmed chocolate lover, Barbara makes sure there are 8-9 dessert selections each day, many of them chocolate.

Her **Chocolate Pate** is a thick slice of dark chocolate flavored with dark rum. It's incredibly rich with a silky texture that floats on the tongue. The dark rum gives it an extra flavor kick.

The **White Chocolate Creme Brulee** comes in a small ramekin, garnished with a rosette of whipped cream. The caramelized top is extra thick with a lacy, crunchy sweetness. The custard is ultra-creamy with a delicate white chocolate flavor. This is one of the best creme brulees this reviewer has tasted.

Chef Barbara's husband's family are the people who brought us Reese's Peanut Butter Cups. So it's no wonder that her **Reese's Peanut Butter Pie** is a delight. It comes as a thick wedge with a chocolate cookie crust, $2^1/_2$ inches of peanut butter cream with pieces of peanut, topped with a thin layer of ganache, and garnished with a bit of whipped cream and a dark chocolate triangle. It's served frozen, which gives the dessert a refreshing lilt. The peanut butter cream has a good peanut flavor without being overwhelming; the crust, which isn't really sweet, adds a lovely crunch. Peanut butter fans will go crazy for this one.

Barbara also makes an **Amaretto White Chocolate Cheesecake** that has a graham crust with 2 inches of thick, crumbly, cheesy cake. The amaretto isn't too heavy-handed and gives the dessert a lift.

Bailey's Chocolate Chip Cheesecake starts with a thick graham crust. The Bailey's-flavored cheese is packed with tiny chocolate chips and topped with a thick layer of ganache. While it's interesting, it lacks distinctiveness and isn't as successful as her other wonderful desserts.

Getting there: On Nelson between Howe and Hornby below Nelson Square.

Chartwell Restaurant (Four Seasons Hotel)
791 Georgia Street, Vancouver, B.C. (604) 689-9333
♥♥♥♥ **Chartwell** has long been one of Vancouver's most celebrated restaurants and with good reason. The attention to detail in both the food and service is without parallel. The oak dining room with its hand-painted countryside panels and marble fireplace is classic, elegant, and formal without being stuffy. Wedgewood plates and fresh flowers grace each cloth-covered table and comfortable arm chairs encourage diners to take their time. Chartwell's dinner menu includes entrees like steamed Atlantic salmon with seafood mousse, scallion-studded swordfish, rack of lamb, venison loin, and sweet potato and vegetable lasagna, in addition to nightly specials.

Diners should save room for dessert because, if there's an award for the best pastry chef in Vancouver, it belongs to executive pastry chef Thomas Haas. Anything this man makes is going to be terrific. His **Milk Chocolate and Dark Chocolate Mousse** starts with a thin, lacy crust (made from sweet, flaky wheat flour mixed with hazelnuts), then a layer of dark chocolate mousse, followed by a layer of milk chocolate mousse, which is dusted with bittersweet cocoa. The result is a wonderful blending of milk and dark chocolate flavors with the cocoa adding a bittersweet contrast to the sweet mousses. The crisp crust adds a delicate crunch.

The **Chocolate Banana Soufflé** comes warm in a cup with a tuile (pastry) "spoon," dusted with powered sugar and served with warm chocolate sauce on the side. The top is crisp and chewy, a lovely mixture of liquid chocolate and banana. It's a wonderfully warm and comforting dessert.

Chartwell's **Chocolate Cinnamon Sorbet**, which is served on a triangle of dark chocolate, has a spicy cinnamon flavor that lifts it head and shoulders above most chocolate sorbets. This is one of the best chocolate sorbets this reviewer has tasted.

The **Opera Cake** has thin, alternating layers of sponge cake and coffee and almond cream, topped with ganache. The cake adds texture to this otherwise creamy dessert and the ganache adds a rich chocolate goodness.

The **Chocolate Pudding Cake with Chocolate Sauce** has a delightfully moist, cake-like texture outside, a gooey, soft pudding-like texture inside. The **Chocolate Marquise,** a standard on the dessert menu, is shaped like a small cylinder with truffle cream inside, dark chocolate ganache outside. The truffle cream is incredibly rich, yet light. This is a dessert that melts in the mouth, chocolate lovers.

Getting there: Howe and Georgia in the Four Seasons Hotel.

Diva at the Met (Metropolitan Hotel)
645 Howe Street, Vancouver, B.C. (604) 602-7788
♥♥♥♥ Diva at the Met has been recognized by *Gourmet* magazine as the best restaurant in Vancouver. It's a busy, exciting place with a contemporary feel with its etched glass wall in the lounge, wall of glass bricks in the dining area, Italian linens and tiny glass oil lamps on the tables, and a large, open kitchen (ask for a table in the upper tier of the dining area if you want quiet). Dinner includes selections like their grilled salmon with roasted apples and wild rice pancakes, sun-dried tomato crusted swordfish, porcini crusted veal steak, and venison medallions. Chocolate lovers will do well to order their **Valhrona Creme Brulee,** which comes wrapped in a sun-dried cherry chocolate brioche "sack," topped with a scoop of their **Chocolate Fudge Ice Cream.** It's served on a compote of sour cherries and is garnished with creme anglaise, chocolate sauce, and a chocolate triangle. The result is ultra-creamy, soft, rich, and interesting. The sour cherries add a lovely sweet/sour flavor. The chocolate ice cream has a clean, intensely chocolate flavor that's sure to please.

> **"As long as you eat chocolate, you'll live a long time."**
> – Marguerite Phillips, 87, chocolatier and owner of Phillips Candies of Seaside, who has been making chocolate candy for 72 years—and eating it even longer.

Getting there: On Howe between Dunsuir and Georgia.

Il Giardino di Umberto
1382 Hornby Street, Vancouver, B.C. (604) 669-2422
♥♥♥♥ **Il Giardino di Umberto** feels like old Italy—high, timbered ceilings, paned windows painted forest green and brick red wainscoting, yellow textured walls, tile floors that look like they've seen 100 years of footsteps, Italian prints and posters, large ceramic pots and greenery, cloth-covered tables with wrought-iron

table lamps, and Italian opera playing in the background. They serve lunch and dinner, with dinner selections including a large selection of pasta dishes like spaghetti carbonara, fettuccine with sun-dried tomatoes, goat cheese, and arugula, cannelloni filled with game meats, as well as grilled salmon, reindeer loin with port peppercorn sauce, pheasant breast stuffed with wild mushrooms, and veal with rosemary and lemon. While they have a set dessert menu, executive chef Pino Posteraro likes to offer at least 2 daily dessert specials like **Chocolate Ganache**. It's a light, espresso-flavored mousse that's wrapped with a chocolate band and served on a compote of citrus and melon and garnished with white and dark chocolate straws. It's served with **Valhrona Chocolate Ice Cream**. The mousse is rich, yet incredibly light with a dense chocolate flavor. The texture is a cross between a light mousse and a ganache. The chocolate ice cream has a fabulous rich chocolate flavor.
Getting there: On Hornby at Pacific.

Sausi's Bar and Grill
3005 West Broadway, Vancouver, B.C. (604) 734-3005
♥♥♥♥ Formerly Paradiso, **Sausi's** is hip and contemporary with its mustard-colored walls, black vinyl bench seats and booths, tables covered with navy blue cloths, industrial stainless steel posts, fanciful wrought iron, geometric windows, and a colorful, free-form mural that runs along one wall. The menu has been tweaked to reflect more emphasis on West Coast tastes with dinner selections like Asian risotto, Thai chicken curry, handrolled potato gnocchi with caramelized pears and gorgonzola, rack of lamb, veal tenderloin, and roasted chicken with garlic, rosemary, and lemon. For dessert, their **Chocolate Pudding Cake** is not to be missed. It's sliced pate style and served with sliced strawberries, whipped cream, candied orange peel, raspberry puree, and a dusting of powered sugar. It's thick, rich and deeply chocolaty, like biting into a velvety dark truffle. This one is so chocolaty you might consider sharing it with a friend.
Getting there: On West Broadway near Bayswater.

Teahouse Restaurant at Ferguson Point
7501 Stanley Park Drive, Vancouver, B.C. (604) 669-3281
♥♥♥♥ The **Teahouse Restaurant at Ferguson Point** in Stanley Park offers stunning views of English Bay and Vancouver Island. In addition to plenty of view windows, the dining room features mustard-colored walls, floral patterned carpets and upholstered chairs, cloth-covered tables, and soft, classical music. The popular Conservatory, entirely glassed-in and dominated by a giant rubber tree, and the Drawing Room with its half-glass ceiling and center stage ficus, both offer refreshing retreats on a dreary winter's afternoon. The Teahouse serves brunch, lunch, dinner, and afternoon tea. Lunch and dinner selections include dishes such as crab and spinach ravioli, salmon wrapped in pastry, roast duck, rack of lamb,

and scallops and prawns. Their signature chocolate dessert is the **Torta Milano**, a Belgian truffle torte with almond mascarpone mousse. The wedge comes with a thin graham crust that's filled with creamy dark and milk chocolate and almond-flavored mascarpone that's topped with ganache and garnished with a chocolate fan, creme anglaise, caramel, and chocolate sauces. The chocolate truffle is an excellent marriage of dark and milk chocolate flavors; the mascarpone mousse has a light almond flavor that doesn't overwhelm. It has a velvety texture that lingers on the tongue. The ganache is rich and provides a deep chocolate accent. The result is a dessert that works entirely, chocolate fans.
Getting there: In Stanley Park at Ferguson Point.

Villa del Lupo
869 Hamilton Street, Vancouver, B.C. (604) 688-7436
♥♥♥♥ When you walk into the converted house that's **Villa del Lupo**, it feels like you've entered an exclusive, private club. There's a working fireplace in the front room, red tile floors, cloth-covered tables with fresh flowers, cinnamon-colored walls with modern, original art work, floral fabric-covered chairs, and wrought-iron lamps that give off soft lighting. Their dinner menu includes dishes like fettuccine with walnut pesto, seafood cannelloni, veal medallion, and rabbit braised with Pinot Grigio wine and basil, as well as a selection of daily specials. Their desserts, which change often, may include Chef Julio Gonzalez-Perini's excellent **Chocolate and Mascarpone Semifreddo**. It comes served as a small, molded dome, artistically garnished with white and dark chocolate swirls, a pastry star, mint leaves, and raspberry and chocolate sauce squiggles. Served cool, not frozen, it's silky and creamy with a light chocolate flavor that's most satisfying.
Getting there: On Hamilton at Smithe.

Bacchus Ristorante (Wedgewood Hotel)
845 Hornby, Vancouver, B.C. (604) 689-7777
♥♥♥ Located inside the elegant Wedgewood Hotel, **Bacchus Ristorante** overlooks a lively lounge area with live, soft pop music from a grand piano. The cloth-covered tables with fresh flowers and candles contribute to the clubby, classic feel. They serve breakfast, lunch, and dinner. Dinner selections include cioppini, beef tenderloin, pan-seared salmon with mussels and red wine pan glaze, rack of lamb with goat cheese, and penne with quattro funghi, bocconcini, olives, parsley, and basil, and linguine with clams. Pastry chef Kimberly Heideman tempts guests with her **Ravioli di Banana**, 3 crisp pastry "ravioli," filled with warm chocolate and banana chunks and dusted with powered sugar, surrounding a scoop of handmade vanilla ice cream. It's beautifully presented with a caramelized sugar fan, caramel and chocolate sauces, mandarin oranges and mint leaves. The pastry ravioli is crisp and flaky; the warm filling wonderfully blends banana and chocolate.

Kim's **Chocolate Semifreddo** comes as an impressive 8-inch cone of milk chocolate cream with slivered hazelnuts punctuated with orange and rum-soaked raisins, garnished with squiggly tuile pastry decorations, chopped pistachio nuts, chocolate sauce and creme anglaise. The semifreddo has an airy lightness and smoothness with a soft milk chocolate flavor. The rum raisins add little surprises of rum.

For diners who can't decide, there's always the **Chocolate Fantasia**, a generous selection of several small chocolate delights such as the **Flourless Chocolate Cake**, a slice of thick, fudgy, ultra-chocolaty richness. The **White Chocolate/Milk Chocolate Terrine**, served as a layered triangle, has white chocolate that is tangy and light, and milk chocolate that's softly chocolaty. It's a lovely combination. Kim's **Chocolate Salami** is a dense chocolate terrine with chopped pistachios and chopped lady fingers sliced salami style that's chewy and nutty, with a deep chocolate flavor. The **Double Chocolate Gateau** is alternating layers of thin chocolate cake and white chocolate orange mousse with brandied cherries, topped with ganache. It's a delicate treat with mousse that's light and airy with a chewiness added by the cherries.

Kim makes all the ice cream at Bacchus and her **Chocolate Ice Cream in an Almond Lace Tuile Cup** comes garnished with a chocolate triangle decorated with coffee bean transfers. The ice cream is light and clean-tasting and the tuile cup is very crisp, not overly sweet.

For a special treat, try the **Grand Marnier Chocolate Soufflé**, served warm in a large soufflé dish dusted with powered sugar with rich cream poured into a slit in the middle. Made fresh daily with real chocolate, not cocoa, this soufflé is worth the 20 minute preparation time. It's rich, yet very light with a satisfying cake-like texture. Excellent!
Getting there: On Hornby near Robson.

Seasons in the Park
7501 Stanley Park Drive, Vancouver, B.C. (604) 874-8008
♥♥♥ **Seasons in the Park** is sophisticated yet comfortable. Situated on the highest point in Vancouver, the restaurant offers excellent views of the Vancouver skyline, the North Mountains, and the water. The glassed-in gazebo room with its fireplace, resident pine tree, and wrap-around windows offers the most spectacular viewing. However, the tiered seating ensures there isn't a bad seat in the house, and all the dining areas feature plenty of glass, greenery, and cloth-covered tables. They serve brunch, lunch, and dinner, with entrees like B.C. salmon, smoked Chilean sea bass, lobster ravioli, grilled prawns, lemon pepper linguine, herbed loin of veal, and curried lentils in phyllo. For dessert, their **White Chocolate**

Ganache comes with a chocolate crust that's made with graham crackers and crushed biscotti, white chocolate ganache, and praline. It's artfully presented with a pansy, mint leaves, and chocolate sauce swirls with dollops of organic blackberry and orange coulis. It's slightly cheesy with a delicately soft texture.

Executive chef Pierre Delacorte and pastry chef Michael Fitzgerald couldn't agree whether the restaurant's chocolate truffle should be made with dark or milk chocolate. So they mixed the 2 and came up with a **Double Chocolate Truffle** that blends the best of milk and dark chocolate. This popular dessert starts with a thin layer of genoise cake with light and dark chocolate mousse lightly flavored with rum and topped with ganache. It's garnished with raspberry coulis, mint and chocolate sauces, brandied cherries, and a chocolate fan. The genoise adds a bit of cake texture to this very creamy dessert.

A special dessert (as yet unnamed) that we'll call the **Orange Brownie Cake**, is 3 layers of a brownie-like cake flavored with orange and filled and frosted with ganache. It's chewy, moist, and a lovely combination of chocolate and orange flavors. Look for this one to earn a permanent place on Seasons' menu.
Getting there: 33rd and Cambie in Queen Elizabeth Park.

Cin Cin
1154 Robson Street, Vancouver, B.C. (604) 688-7338
♥♥ Above busy Robson Street, **Cin Cin** is a happening, upscale Italian eatery that features a huge marble bar, tile floors, brass pots hanging over the open kitchen, large, arched windows, cloth-covered tables, and big Italian murals. It's a popular lunch and dinner place with both locals and tourists. Dinner selections include pasta dishes like paella, angel hair pasta with garlic, basil, and tomatoes, prawns and scallops in pesto cream; alder wood grilled and baked items like rare ahi tuna, herb marinated rack of lamb, salmon, sea bass with porcini horseradish cream, and roasted chicken with pesto and sundried tomatoes.

For chocolate lovers, pastry chef Sergio Salamonvitz makes beautiful, architectural desserts every day, many of them chocolate. Sergio's **Cioccolata e Bacca** comes as a semi-circle of decorative white and chocolate cake (joconde) that's filled with a layer of meringue-like finely ground almond meal (dacquoise), white chocolate ganache, a dollop of a gelatin-like raspberry puree (glee), topped with bittersweet chocolate mousse. It's served on a bed of thin pomegranate sauce and garnished with crushed raspberries and a dark chocolate star with tiny musical scales. The result is complex and rich. The cake is rich, almost creamy; the mousse is chocolaty. This is an entirely satisfying dessert.

Sergio's **Tiramisu** is equally beautiful. It's alternating round layers of homemade ladyfingers soaked in espresso and kahlua and thick mascarpone, topped with a white chocolate disk with gold lips transferred onto it and dark chocolate squiggles dramatically flowing out of the top. It's served on a bed of cappuccino and vanilla creme anglaise. The mascarpone is wonderfully velvety and slightly sweet, but the ladyfingers are too heavily soaked in kahlua/espresso for this reviewer.

Getting there: On Robson near Bute.

Fleuri (Sutton Place Hotel)
845 Burrard, Vancouver, B.C. (604) 682-5511

♥♥ Unlike many of the city's hotel fine dining restaurants, **Fleuri's** dining room exudes lightness—cream-colored wainscoting, boxed ceiling and wood trim, wall paper in cream and beige, white cloth-covered tables with glass oil lamps and tiny roses, and wall sconces that soften the whole effect. They serve breakfast, lunch, and dinner with dishes like ravioli with ricotta and arugula, halibut in bouillabaisse, salmon lasagna with Pinot Noir butter sauce, pork tenderloin with tarragon sauce, and rack of lamb with lavender and grapefruit crust.

Fit for a King. Reserved for royalty in Mexico, the chocolate drink, chocolatl, was a thick drink the consistency of honey made from chocolate flavored with vanilla and spices and served cold.

Fleuri is famous with chocolate lovers for their **Chocoholic Bar**, served every Thursday, Friday, and Saturday night. It's a beautiful presentation of more than a dozen different chocolate desserts. The selection changes, but diners are likely to find the **Chocolate Truffle Cake**, with a light genoise cake on the bottom, then ultra-creamy chocolate truffle that's covered with dark chocolate curls that give it a bittersweet flavor. There's often a large selection of delicate **Petit Fours**, tiny bite-sized gems that are exquisitely decorated. Their **Triple Croissant Pudding** is a traditional bread pudding that's served warm and made even richer with buttery croissants and bits of Callebaut chocolate.

Their **Chocolate Pecan Pie** has a chocolate tart crust and thick chocolate that's packed with pecans that give it a nutty flavor. The **White Chocolate Bavaroise**, which is served with a strawberry puree, has a texture that's a cross between pudding and mousse and a soft white chocolate flavor. **Belgiun Chocolate Towers** are little triangles of dense chocolate with bits of chewy, soft coconut.

If that's not enough, you may also find selections like **White Choco-late Charlotte, Chocolate Mousse, Chocolate Cheesecake, Chocolate Profiteroles, Chocolate-dipped Fruits**, and **Choco-late Crepes** that are made on the spot with the choice of fruits, liqueurs, and toppings.
Getting there: On Burrard between Robson and Howe in the Sutton Place Hotel.

Le Crocodile
#100-909 Burrard, Vancouver, B.C. (604) 669-4298
♥♥ At **Le Crocodile**, the mustard-colored walls, burgundy up-holstered/rosewood chairs, hardwood floor, cloth-covered tables, wall sconces and tiny table lights, and bouquets of fresh flowers all add to the casual elegance. They serve classic French cuisine with lunch entrees like tenderloin with pepper sauce and crab ravioli. At dinner, the large menu includes selections like grilled Atlantic salmon with fresh spinach, tiger prawns and sea scallops with an-gel hair pasta, grilled lamb chops, duck breast, prime rib with béarnaise sauce, and pheasant with port wine sauce. In addition to 3-4 nightly dessert specials, their dessert menu includes regulars like **Chocolate Mousse**, served in a large wine glass. It's light-as-air without being frothy. This is an excellent mousse!

Their **Flourless Hazelnut Chocolate Cake** is served as a 4-inch square, sliced pate style, and topped with a thin layer of ganache. The cake is moist with a cakey texture that's punctuated with chopped hazelnuts throughout. The ganache is rich, if a bit stiff.

You can also order a selection of their sorbets, including **Choco-late Sorbet**, which is intensely chocolate.
Getting there: On Smithe at Burrard in the Vancouver Tower Build-ing.

Lumiere
2551 West Broadway, Vancouver, B.C. (604) 739-8185
♥♥ **Lumiere's** ambiance comes from its contemporary, minimalist decor—walls in shades of gray, blonde hardwood floors and chairs, cloth-covered tables with tiny votive lights, green upholstered bench seats around the perimeter, and large black and white photographs. Dinner includes cutting-edge choices like Chilean sea bass in mirin, ginger, soy, and scallion broth, lobster in vanilla saffron sauce, as well as more traditional dishes like duck and B.C. spot prawns and deer loin wrapped in maple bacon.

Their chocolate offering is a **Valrhona Chocolate Trio**, which in-cludes a **Jivara Milk Chocolate Tart with Candied Lemons and Meringue, Gianduja Dark Chocolate Mousse with Roasted Hazelnuts**, and **Ivoire White Chocolate Tulipe with a Cocoa Sorbet**. They're all delicate and served in a minimalist style with

only 3 chocolate "L's" decorating the large serving plate. The tart is a 3-inch round of thin, crumbly tart pastry that's topped with milk chocolate mousse covered in a soft meringue that's been piped on and lightly baked. The tart is crisp. The mousse is light, but its chocolate flavor is overwhelmed by the slightly bitter lemon. The meringue is soft and fluffy. The Gianduja mousse is more successful. It comes surrounded by a thin, dark chocolate wrapping that's soft enough to easily spoon into. The mousse is perfectly light with a deep chocolate flavor and the roasted hazelnuts add a lovely, nutty crunch. The sorbet is a small scoop served on a tiny chocolate pastry "plate" and has an intense chocolate flavor sorbet fans will appreciate. The tulipe pastry is paper-thin, light, and crisp.
Getting there: On Broadway between Larch and Trafalgar.

Sophie's Cosmic Café
2095 West 4th Avenue, Vancouver, B.C. (604) 732-6810

♥♥ **Sophie's Cosmic Café**—it's funky, it's hip, it's happening. The giant coffee cup protruding from an exterior wall and the huge stainless steel knife and fork (with bent tines) on either side of the entrance say you're in for some fun. The walls are festooned with a bit of everything—chalk murals of cows and coffee bean people, kid's lunch boxes, a pool table complete with balls, sticks, and a lobster, peddle cars, a rocking horse, and more, much more. People crowd into the naugahyde booths where giant breakfasts are an all-day happening. Eggs are served anyway you can think of—rancheros, Mexicana, benedict, omlettes, chorizo or Italian sausage and eggs, and smoked salmon and eggs. Or you can order waffles, French toast, or pancakes. If you're more in the mood for lunch, Sophie's offers a large selection of burgers as well as some vegetarian sandwiches and salads. Chocolate lovers should ante up for Sophie's **Chocolate Shake**. Made with hard ice cream and Hershey's syrup, it's big and so thick you can't sip it through the straw. You can order your shake "fortified" with Irish cream, cream de cacao, creme de menthe, or Sambuca liqueur. Yum!
Getting there: On W 4th Avenue at Arbutus.

Biship's
2183 W 4th, Vancouver, B.C. (604) 738-2025

♥♥ Simple and elegant sums up **Biship's** with its white walls, tall candles flickering on white, cloth-covered tables, and huge bouquets of fresh flowers as accents. Dinner entrees include scallops with lemon grass, chive, and lobster sauce, chicken breast on wild mushroom risotto, duck with sun-dried fruit and candied ginger glacé, smoked black cod, rack of lamb, and venison medallions with steamed corn pudding. Their nod to chocolate is **Death by Chocolate**, a chocolate pate served with organic raspberry puree. It's simply presented with the puree poured on top and spattered on a white plate. The pate is thick—so thick it's difficult to cut—like a thick fudge with a velvety texture. The tart raspberry puree

adds an interesting contrast to the chocolate.
Getting there: On 4th between Arbutus and Yew.

William Tell Restaurant (Georgian Court Hotel)
765 Beatty Street, Vancouver, B.C. (604) 688-3504
♥ The Swiss restaurant, **William Tell**, has a classic, formal feel with its green upholstered chairs, cloth-covered tables, sterling plates and flatware, brass chandeliers, and green fabric-covered walls with old European lithographs. They serve breakfast, lunch, and dinner, with dinner entrees such as grilled salmon, roast duck breast in sun-dried cranberry and mango sauce, pheasant in maple glaze, veal chop, and beef tenderloin with a black calamata olive crust. For dessert, they offer their signature **Meringue Glace au Chocolate**, which comes as a circular layer of meringue that's covered with a scoop of vanilla ice cream, topped with another circle of meringue and a thick layer of whipped cream. It's served with warm chocolate sauce and garnished with fresh berries and a chocolate fan. The meringue is crisp, offering a crunchy contrast to the creamy homemade ice cream and the warm chocolate sauce is rich. It's not a lot of chocolate, but it's very creamy, very Swiss.

William Tell offers a trio of sorbets or ice creams, often 2 fruit sorbets with a chocolate ice cream. But chocolate lovers in the know can order a **Trio of Chocolate Ice Creams** such as **Chocolate Tea**, made tangy with the addition of Earl Grey Tea; **Chocolate Cinnamon**, a wonderfully spicy Mexican chocolate flavor (this reviewer's favorite); or **Double Chocolate**, with an intense chocolate flavor. All of their ice creams, which are made in-house, are rich without clinging to the palette.

Their **Double Chocolate Ganache Torte** comes as 3 layers of dense chocolate cake frosted and filled with thick ganache and

> **Keep Your Cool When Cooking with Chocolate.** *"People get chocolate too hot in their home kitchens. The kitchen is too warm. Then they get the chocolate too warm. It'll be thick and so they'll heat it up a little more. You should keep the room around 68 degrees. You want low humidity and low temperatures when working with chocolate."*
>
> — Janele Smith, chocolatier, Fenton and Lee, Eugene, Oregon

garnished with white chocolate shavings, a dark chocolate fan and kiwi and raspberry puree and served with vanilla bean ice cream. The cake is moist, but it lacks a deep chocolate flavor and the texture is a bit too dense for this reviewer's taste. The vanilla bean ice cream, however, is wonderfully light and refreshing.

The **White Chocolate Chestnut Cheesecake** is a generous slice topped with white chocolate ganache. It comes garnished with sugared zucchini strips, white chocolate curls, and mango, raspberry, and chocolate sauces. The chestnut adds a soft, subtle flavor that doesn't overwhelm the white chocolate.
Getting there: On Beatty between Robson and Georgia.

Bakeries

au Chocolat
1702 Davie Street, Vancouver, B.C. (604) 682- 3536
♥♥♥ (pastries) **au Chocolat** offers a selection of cakes by the slice as well as small pastries. **Their Old Fashioned Chocolate Cake** is 4 layers of dark chocolate cake filled and frosted with dark chocolate buttercream that's dusted with bittersweet cocoa. For those who love dark chocolate, this cake has a deep, satisfying dark chocolate flavor. The cake is moist with just the right texture and the buttercream is silky. It's a lovely chocolate cake.

au Chocolate's **Petit Fours** are tiny, elegant, and each is distinctive. They're just right for a party or afternoon tea. Their **Chocolate Mousse Cup** has a small, dark chocolate shell that's filled with folds of dark chocolate mousse topped with dark chocolate curls. Their **Opera Cake** consists of thin layers of jaconde biscuit (light cake) and coffee buttercream that has a creamy, rich coffee taste, and topped with ganache. The **Monte Cristo** is jaconde biscuit topped with milk chocolate mousse nougatine, then entirely covered in chocolate. It's creamy and rich with a terrific hazelnut flavor. The **Grenoble** has a jaconde biscuit layered with ganache, nougatine, and topped with a sprinkling of praline, which gives it a delicious praline flavor with a bit of crunch. The **Cypress** is a white chocolate mousse cup that's filled with light-as-air, tangy white mousse. The **Day and Night** is a rich and creamy white chocolate mousse and ganache enrobed in dark chocolate.

au Chocolat also makes truffles, but this reviewer found them much less successful than their pastries.
Getting there: On Davie Street at Bidwell.

Patisserie Bordeaux
3675 W 10th Avenue, Vancouver, B.C. (604) 731-6551
♥♥♥ (pastries)/♥♥♥ (chocolates) **Patisserie Bordeaux** is a classic French bakery. Its cases are filled with stunningly beautiful cakes, pastries, mousses, cookies, and hand-made chocolates. Their

Chocolate Mousse in a Chocolate Cup is a 4-inch tall dark chocolate cup generously filled with dark chocolate mousse that's flavored with dark rum. The mousse is thick and frothy with deep undertones of rum.

Their **Chocolate Mousse** comes surrounded by sponge cake—a thin layer of chocolate cake on the bottom; white and chocolate cake on the sides. It's filled with thick, dark chocolate mousse and topped with a rich chocolate ganache. The **Carre au Chocolat** has thin layers of chocolate cake filled with raspberry jam and buttercream that's lightly flavored with rum. The sides and top are coated with dark chocolate ganache. The rum and essence of raspberry make a lovely combination. The **Morcoain** is a 4-inch round of 2 layers of almond chocolate cake filled and frosted with an ultra-light chocolate buttercream.

Patisserie Bordeaux carries a large selection of cookies like **Biscuit Pralines**, 5-inch shortbread cookies filled with praline cream and half-dipped in dark chocolate. Their Florentines, half-dipped in chocolate, are crispy and chewy. Their **Rum Balls**, which are the size of a racquetball, feature moist, rum-flavored chocolate cake that's covered in dark chocolate and rolled in dark chocolate sprinkles. The **Almond Square**, a favorite of this reviewer, is shortbread covered with a crisp, buttery almond topping, then half-dipped in dark chocolate. It's super!

The bakery also makes a small selection of **hand-made chocolate candies**. They use good quality chocolate and their fillings, often creamy milk chocolate, hazelnut, or marzipan, are flavorful. *Getting there: On 10th Avenue at Alma.*

Chocolate Shops

Chocolate Art
2037 W 4th Avenue, Vancouver, B.C. (604) 739-0475
♥♥♥♥ If you want **artisan chocolates**, look no further than **Chocolate Art**. Their company motto is "Fine Chocolate is an Art" and chocolatier Greg Hook uses Callebaut and Valhrona chocolate like some artists use clay or paint. They are famous for their intricately molded **Chocolate Medallions**, small masks that use native designs. Originally designed and carved by Native Canadian artist, Robert Davidson, the moon, frog, and killer whale designs are so exquisite you'll want to save them instead of eat them.

Greg makes small batches of elegant chocolates every day, using no preservatives, local organic nuts, and organic fruits (they dry their own). **Rhubarb Rhapsody** has a rhubarb and milk chocolate ganache coated in dark chocolate and lightly dusted with powered sugar. The vibrant rhubarb flavor gives the ganache a wonderful complexity you won't soon forget. The chocolate coating is so light and delicate, it gently cups the soft ganache.

Their **Classic Truffle** is a rich, dark chocolate ganache in bitter Valhrona Cocoa. The result is an intense chocolate flavor with a center that melts delightfully on the tongue. Their **Raspberry Passion** comes in a heart-shape and features finely-chopped pieces of tart raspberry leather in white (or milk) chocolate highlighted with dark chocolate. The white chocolate is creamy and subtle tasting; the firm center offers mini-bursts of raspberry flavor.

Another unusual combination is their **Basil and Lemon Truffle**, with a light, lemony flavor punctuated by fresh-tasting basil. It's refreshing! **Romeo** is a pyramid of dark fruity blackberry ganache and whipped blackberry buttercream in a dark chocolate shell. The ganache is incredibly creamy. The blackberry flavor is subtle, yet rich—a wonderful combination.

Their **Poire** offers creamy ganache with a tiny piece of fresh-tasting pear. Their **Chocolate Ginger** features a subtle, clean-tasting ginger that won't singe the tongue. **Palates** are creamy milk chocolate disks topped with a single whole roasted almond, pistachio, and organic raisin. They're simple, yet elegant.
Getting there: On 4th a block down from Sophie's Cosmic Café.

Chocolaterie Bernard Callebaut
2698 Granville Street, Vancouver, B.C. (604) 736-5890
♥♥♥♥ (See review under Chocolate Shops, Victoria, B.C.)
Getting there: On Granville at 11th Avenue.

Over the Moon Chocolate Company
2868 West Broadway, Vancouver, B.C. (604) 737-0880
♥♥♥♥ Some of the best filled European-style chocolates can be found at **Over the Moon Chocolates**. Using Callebaut Chocolate and no preservatives, chocolatiers Maria Lutz and Rob Greenhowe create molded chocolates that have fresh-tasting, velvety centers with some unusual flavors like **Mandarin Orange Cream, Apricot, Passion Fruit**, and **Black Currant**. The chocolate coatings are delicate, never interfering with the center's flavor, and they're often hand-painted with designs in dark or white chocolate. For instance, a molded dark chocolate might feature a delicate white chocolate rose or a cameo design.

Their **Almond Cream** has a soft, melt-in-the-mouth center that's accented with crunchy praline. **Pistachio Crunch** combines the velvet softness of pistachio cream with tiny bits of chewy pistachio. **Tiramisu** comes with a rum-flavored chocolate center with a white cheesy filling that actually tastes like the real thing.

If you love caramel, don't miss their **Chocolate-covered Caramel**, which is almost liquid with a buttery richness that marries well with the rich chocolate. For a bit more crunch, the **Hazelnut Buttercrunch** features a crunchy, buttery center with a subtle hazelnut flavor that's dipped half in milk chocolate and half in white chocolate. It's delicious! **Kit's Delight**, one of their signature candies, is a disk of Belgian chocolate, nougat, caramel, and roasted almonds, hazelnuts, and pistachios that is rich, crunchy, and satisfying.

They also have fun molding items out of chocolate like toothbrushes and giant clamshells that are filled with seashells.
Getting there: On W Broadway near Mackenzie Street.

Le Chocolat Belge Daniel
124 W 3rd Avenue, Vancouver, B.C. (604) 879-7782 (factory)
Vancouver retail shops:
1105 Robson Street, Vancouver, B.C. (604) 688-9624
North Park Royal, #805 Central Entrance, West Vancouver, B.C. (604) 925-2213
2820 Granville Street, Vancouver, B.C. (604) 733-1994
4447 W 10th Avenue, Vancouver, B.C. (604) 224-3361
♥♥ "Everyone deserves good chocolate," says chocolatier Daniel Poncelet. That's why **Le Chocolate Belge Daniel** makes good quality, **molded Belgian chocolates** and sells them at bargain prices. He uses no preservatives, coloring agents, oils, or artificial substances and molds his chocolate into beautiful shapes like snail shells, hearts, octagons, and tiny baskets. His flavors are intense, with centers that are slightly stiff, and coatings that can be a bit too thick at times. Each box comes with a "map" that decodes his more than 40 different chocolates.

His **Caramel** is thick, rich, and toothsome. **Advocat Ganache** comes with a white center that's heavily flavored with bourbon. **Orange Ganache** features a creamy ganache with a slightly bitter orange flavor. His **Chocolate Ganache** has an intense, rich chocolate flavor and his **Raspberry Ganache** comes with white ganache with bits of raspberry covered in white chocolate.
Getting there: The Robson and Granville stores are located downtown. The 10th Avenue store is across the Granville Bridge from downtown.

Purdy's Chocolates
2777 Kingsway, Vancouver, B.C. (604) 454-2777
(factory and factory store)
Other Vancouver retail locations:
Purdy's has more than 40 stores in the Vancouver area. Check the white pages of the phone book.
♥♥ In a city in love with Belgian molded chocolates, **Purdy's**

makes a large selection of traditional "North American" creams, fruits, nuts and chews. Unlike many hand-made artisan chocolates, Purdy's chocolates are machine-made using time-tested recipes developed more than 90 years ago. In fact, owner Charles Flavelle has designed many of the high-tech machines that enable Purdy's to supply their 44 retail stores. Their chocolates come boxed in eye-pleasing purple and gold boxes and come with a legend that describes each chocolate.

Hedgehogs, hazelnut cream centers enrobed in chocolate that are molded to look like tiny hedgebogs, are one of the company's signature candies. The center is creamy with an excellent hazelnut flavor and the milk chocolate coating is extra creamy. It's no wonder they sell these little critters by the box.

Their **Coconut Caramel** is a new twist on an old theme. The caramel is quite stiff and the coconut adds an interesting flavor and texture. The **Peanut Butter Daisy** is a peanut butter cream enrobed in chocolate that's molded into a daisy shape. It's long on peanut butter flavor.

Raspberry Cream has a loose, almost liquid center, with an intense raspberry flavor. The **Coconut Cluster** is solid milk chocolate with chopped coconut. **Snowball** is a creamy coconut center that's coated in chocolate and rolled in coconut. Their **Chocolate-covered Cashew** has a good roasted cashew flavor.

Bonte is Purdy's line of **Belgian molded chocolates**. The beautiful shapes—roses, logs, moons, stars, hearts, grapes, cameos, bees—come artistically packaged in red, purple, and gold boxes, and have a shorter shelf life than their North American chocolates. Although many of the Bonte line are quite good, this reviewer felt their traditional line was tastier and more consistent in quality and flavor.
Getting there: *On the east side of Vancouver on Kingsway. Other retail locations situated throughout Vancouver.*

Ice Creamery

Mum's Gelati
855 Denman, Vancouver, B.C. (604) 681-1500
Other Vancouver retail location:
2028 Vine Street, Vancouver, B.C. (604) 738-6867
♥♥♥♥ Tucked into a tiny storefront on Denman, **Mum's Gelati** is an ice cream lovers dream. For 25 years, Mum's has been making homemade **Italian ice cream** that uses all natural ingredients, no preservatives, no added air, no eggs, less sugar, and half the fat of regular ice cream. Made fresh every day, their ice cream, which is made with milk rather than cream, is light and refreshing with intense flavors. The flavors change, but they always have Moka

and 1 or 2 other chocolate flavors. **Moka** is chocolate with ground cocoa and espresso beans and big hunks of chocolate. Java lovers will love the big coffee taste. Their **Choconut,** made with chocolate gelati, coconut, and almonds, has a delightful chocolate/coconut flavor nicely accented by the crunch of roasted almonds. **Chocolate Peanut Butter**, this reviewer's favorite, has a surprisingly rich peanut butter flavor.

Mum's also makes a line of sorbetto, or **sorbet**, non-dairy "ice fruit" made with fresh fruits like mangos, raspberry, guava, kiwi, and lemon. The sorbet is light, almost creamy, with just-picked fruit flavors.

Getting there: On Denman a few blocks east of Robson.

VICTORIA

Victoria has shed its stogy image and has become a place travelers from all over the world flock to for its wonderful gardens, interesting shops and galleries, world-class museum, and quaint carriage rides and double-decker buses. It's also a place you can count on for good chocolate.

Great Things to Do

• **Check Out the Museum. Royal British Columbia Museum**, 675 Bellville Street (Bellevue and Government), **Victoria, B.C.** (250) 387-3701. Victoria's museum houses one of the best exhibits of Northwest Native artifacts, including an excellent collection of totem poles. In addition, they have extensive dioramas of natural landscapes and special exhibitions like a recent one on whales.

• **Stroll the Park. Beacon Hill Park, Victoria, B.C.** Surrounded by water, the 184-acre Beacon Hill Park is a popular place for walking, biking, or reading a book under the trees. The park's landscaping is largely natural and the park offers excellent views of the water.

• **Take a Harbor Tour**. You've walked your feet off and you're in need of a break. A wonderful respite is the tiny Harbor Taxis, miniature boats that buzz in and around the harbor. For a small fee, the taxi will take you all around the harbor and back. Or you can get off at any stop and another taxi will be along shortly. Catch the taxi at the stand along Inner Harbor.

• **Walk the Songhee Path along the Harbor, Victoria, B.C**. A great way to get a little exercise and an up close and personal look at the harbor is to take a stroll along the harbor. There's a wonderful walking path that runs in front of the Ocean Pointe Resort to the end of the harbor.

• **Take a Tally Ho Tour**. You seen them everywhere—wagons pulled by huge Belgian draft horses filled with tourists. Cheaper than the individual horse-drawn carriages, the Tally Ho Tours are relaxing and informative. They take you through some of the oldest parts of residential Victoria and through Beacon Hill Park, providing tid bits of gossip and history. The carriages line up near the Parliament Buildings on Government Street.

• **Spend an Afternoon with Greenery. Crystal Garden**, 715 Douglas Street, **Victoria, B.C.** (250) 381-1213. It used to be an indoor swimming pool. Now the wonderful 1900's glass conservatory is filled with lush plants and tropical birds. It's an especially lovely way to spend a rainy day.

• **Tour a Castle. Craigdarroch Castle,** 1050 Joan Crescent, **Victoria, B.C.** (250) 592-1225. Coal baron Robert Dunsmuir built this 19th century castle for his homesick wife. You can tour the opulent mansion every day and get a peek at what it was like to be wealthy at the turn of the century.

Terrific Places to Stay

Ocean Pointe Resort, 45 Songhees Road, **Victoria, B.C.** (250) 360-2999. You can't miss the Ocean Pointe Resort when you sail into Victoria's Inner Harbor. It stands like a grand sentinel on Songhees Point overlooking the water. The 250-room hotel features both standard guest rooms and suites with conveniences like coffee makers, mini-bars, and hair dryers. Some of the rooms have excellent views while others have nominal views. However, the lounge, bistro and fine dining restaurant all have good views. A distinction for Ocean Pointe is their fully-equipped gym with trainers, an indoor pool, hot tub, sauna, and complete spa treatments.

Laurel Point Inn, 680 Montreal Street, **Victoria, B.C.** (250) 386-8721. If you want an elegant yet friendly resort-style hotel where every room has outstanding views of Victoria's Harbor, the Laurel Point Inn is a great choice. The decor is simple and contemporary with natural colors and Asian accents. In the older wing, they offer reasonably-priced standard hotel rooms, each with water views and balconies. In the newer South wing, beautifully-appointed suites have huge marble bathrooms with deep, extra-long soaking tubs, glassed-in free-standing showers, and even mini-televisions. They also feature balconies and glass walls that look onto a serene Japanese reflecting pond and the busy harbor. For those really special occasions, they offer 3 ultra-luxurious penthouse suites with panoramic views of the water, the city, and the surrounding Olympic and Cascade mountain ranges. The lounge offers nightly complimentary snacks and live piano music. The Café Laurel serves breakfast, lunch, and dinner, including an excellent **Chocolate Mousse** and **Chocolate Ganache Torte**.

Restaurants

Camille's
45 Bastion Square, Victoria, B.C. (250) 381-3433

♥♥♥♥ **Camille's** feels like walking into a 100-year-old French farmhouse where your favorite aunt waits with a terrific meal. The front room is light and cheery; the back room, intimate and cozy. Cloth-covered tables are lit by candlelight, making the original art works glow on the old brick walls. Imaginatively prepared with fresh, local ingredients, dinner entrees include dishes like salmon filet in lime/mango vinaigrette, caramel and almond-crusted duck, pork loin glazed in pear, honey, and calvados, and rack of lamb with dijon, mint, and blackberry/port sauce. Camille's achieves what many restaurants do not—dishes that taste as good as they look. Their wine list is impressive too.

Desserts change regularly, but there's always great chocolate. Their **Dark Belgian Chocolate Truffle Torte** is served in stacked triangles surrounded by spun caramel sugar strings, chocolate "cages," and creme anglaise and chocolate sauce. The torte is rich and cake-like with a complex and satisfying flavor.

This reviewer's favorite is Camille's **Dark Chocolate Grand Marnier Coffee Mousse with Chanilly Creme** (vanilla-laced whipped cream). This mousse has rich depth and a complex blending of flavors not often found in chocolate mousse. The delicate chantilly creme adds a light elegance.

Camille's **Butterscotch Chocolates** are little swirls of butterscotch-flavored chocolate cream dusted with cocoa, which are often presented to diners at the end of the meal. They have a rich butterscotch flavor that lingers on the tongue.
Getting there: On Bastion Square at Government and Fort Streets.

Café Brio
944 Fort Street, Victoria, B.C. (250) 383-0009

♥♥♥♥ Tucked behind a Mediterranean style courtyard, **Café Brio** is a loud, upbeat, happening kind of place, especially with locals who know great food. With its tall ceilings, U-shaped bar center stage, simple wooden tables and chairs, hardwood floors, and mustard-and rust-colored walls adorned with original paintings, the ambiance says relax and enjoy yourself. The menu changes 4 or 5 times a year. The lunch menu may feature dishes like prawns and white beans with roasted artichokes, preserved lemon and leeks, and roasted pork loin with caramelized onions, raddichio, and barbecue sauce on country bread. Dinner items can include roasted sea bass and free range chicken with gorgonzola and salmon with chanterelles, corn and potato hash.

British Columbia

Pastry chef Marcie Kurbis regularly changes the dessert menu, but chocolate lovers can always count on wonderful chocolate items. Her **Chocolate Mousse** is something special. It comes in a large stemmed glass topped with kahlua whipped topping and garnished with chocolate shavings, 2 delicate cookies, and a sprig of mint. The mousse is silky and light with rich chocolate and kahlua flavors. The whipped topping is even lighter (if that's possible) with a subtle kahlua flavor. Chocolate lovers, this is terrice mousse.

The **Very Chocolate Torte** is a good-sized flourless wedge that's garnished with tiny orange and grapefruit slices and candied orange peel, a Cape gooseberry, and chocolate zabaglione, and a mint sprig. It's heavenly—moist, fudge-like yet light on the tongue. The zabaglione adds a lovely, light contrast.
Getting there: On Fort Street near Vancouver.

Chez Daniel

2524 Estevan, Victoria, B.C. (250) 592-7424
♥♥♥♥ Step into **Chez Daniel's** and you feel as if you're in an intimate restaurant in the French countryside. It's decorated simply and elegantly—green linen tablecloths, soft classical music, and walls adorned with shiny copper cooking pans, original artwork, and chef Daniel Rigollet's numerous awards. The dinner menu is classically French with dishes like chateaubriand with bordelaise sauce, filet mignon with red wine sauce, rabbit with dijon and cream, roast duck, and filet of sole poached in wine. Wine lovers will enjoy the award-winning wine selection of more than 500 labels. For dessert, enjoy Daniel's **Chocolate Truffles**—7 of the most heavenly ganache morsels you'll ever savor. Deliciously rich with heavy cream, fresh butter, and Callebaut chocolate, and perhaps a liqueur like amaretto, these truffles are "au natural," rough formed as they come off the spoon, and rolled into unsweetened cocoa and served with a scattering of pomegranate seeds or other simple garnish. This is chocolate nirvana!
Getting there: In Oak Bay at Estevan and Beach, about 15 minutes from downtown.

> **An Early Chocolate Lover.** The Mayan Emperor Montezuma was said to have drank as many as 50 golden goblets of the chocolate drink, chocolatl, every day.

Herald Street Caffe

546 Herald Street, Victoria, B.C. (250) 381-1441
♥♥♥♥ Rave reviews have followed chef and owner Daniel Lacy ever since he opened **Herald Street Caffe** in 1982. He broke with Victoria tradition by offering a busy, bistro-like atmosphere with

Pacific Northwest cuisine with Italian and Asian influences. Open for lunch, dinner, and brunch (weekends only), you'll find dishes like chicken breast in crispy cashew crust with lemon rosemary sauce and scallops pan-fried in tomato-chili oil with Thai salsa and scallions. Specials change daily, depending on what's fresh. Their chocolate desserts vary too, but chocolate lovers will always find Herald Street's **Chocolate Almond Pave**, a dense, flourless torte made with ground almonds instead of flour. It comes sliced like pate, garnished with chocolate buttercream and toasted, candied almonds. The result is a cake-like texture that's extremely creamy with a dense chocolate flavor. The ground almonds add a richness and the buttercream is velvety.

Getting there: One block past Chinatown, on Herald between Store and Government Streets.

Decadence Café and Catering
1724 Douglas, Victoria, B.C. (250) 389-0383
♥♥♥ A bit off the beaten tourist track, **Decadence Café and Catering** is a wonderfully pleasant retreat with high ceilings, small wooden tables with iron chairs, and mustard-colored walls that are accented with curly twigs and tiny white lights. For breakfast, they serve a selection of baked goods and, for lunch, salads, sandwiches, and hot entrees like chicken lasagne, eggplant parmigiana, and ginger-garlic prawn stir-fry. Owner and chef Debbie Harding is a graduate of the Cordon Bleu School and the training really shows in her exquisite desserts like **White Chocolate Creme Brulee**. It's a rich, thick, silky custard topped with crunchy, sweet espresso and brown sugar that's served in a large, individual soufflé pan. Her **Chocolate Lover's Torte** is 3 layers of dark chocolate cake spiked with rum, sandwiched with bittersweet chocolate mousse, and frosted with white butttercream. The moist cake is dense and fine-grained. The mousse has a deep chocolate flavor and the buttercream is incredibly light and smooth. It's most satisfying!

For white chocolate fans, Debbie's **White Chocolate Cheesecake** starts with a crunchy chocolate crust topped with 2½ inches of cheesecake made with Callebaut white chocolate that's served with a tart raspberry coulis and garnished with a chocolate fan. It's smooth, rich, and very tangy. Decadence also offers **Chocolate Chunk Pecan Brownies**, a 4x5-inch, dense, chewy brownie chock full of chopped pecans, topped with pecans and drizzled chocolate. It's chewy and rich. Their **Decadence Nanimo** bars have a layer of chocolate-coconut-walnut, followed by a thin layer of sweetened cheese, and a layer of dark chocolate with white chocolate drizzles. Interesting, but on the overly sweet side. A better choice is **Debbie's Truffles**, small gobs of rich, firm truffle center rolled in cocoa, that they'll make for you if you call ahead.

Getting there: Downtown on Douglas between Fisgard and Herald.

La Ville D'Is
26 Bastion Square, Victoria, B.C. (250) 388-9414

♥♥ **La Ville D'Is** is an intimate restaurant that will make you think you're in a tiny French village. Owner Michelle Duteau was born in Brittany and its influence shows in this French seafood restaurant. The menu offers dishes like lobster soufflé, scallops cooked in garlic, green peppers, onion, and tomatoes, and braised sturgeon in Chablis sauce. Michelle offers chocolate lovers his **Mousse Maison**, made from his "secret" recipe with Callebaut chocolate, whipped cream, and no alcohol. The result is creamy with a texture that's a cross between custard and pudding. There's little air here, just intense chocolate flavor.

Getting there: Downtown in Bastion Square.

Pescatore Fish and Oyster Bar
614 Humbolt, Victoria, B.C. (205) 385-4512

♥♥ **Pescatore** is considered one of the better fish houses in Victoria. With its faux marble walls in orange and yellow hues, over-sized ceiling fans, original paintings, wooden tables and upholstered booths with tiny flickering oil lamps, and center bar with a mermaid diving from the ceiling, Pescatore has a fun, bistro atmosphere that invites diners to relax and enjoy themselves. They feature plenty of oysters—raw, pan-fried, baked, or roasted with cheese and salmon. They also offer dishes like Sooke trout stuffed with crab and French brie and salmon seared with orange balsamic vinaigrette, and pasta dishes like smoked chicken fettuccine and seafood cannelloni. Their signature chocolate dessert is **Le Concorde Direct from Paris**, a large wedge of 2 layers of chocolate cake thickly filled with a dark chocolate mousse that's topped with chocolate meringue. It's served garnished with creme anglaise and dark chocolate, a rosette of whipped cream, and dusted with powered sugar and cocoa. The result is INTENSE. The menu says, "For those who crave an intensely chocolate flavor." They're not kidding. The cake is moist with a good dark chocolate flavor. The mousse is fudgy with a deep chocolate taste and the meringue is light with a soft crunchiness. Together, they produce a chocolate experience that's almost too much chocolate, even for this dedicated chocolate lover. If you opt for this one, plan to share it with another chocolate affectionado.

Getting there: Across from the Empress Hotel on Humbolt.

Marina Restaurant
1327 Beach Drive, Victoria, B.C. (250) 598-8555

♥ **Marina** is a circular, tiered restaurant that overlooks the Oak Bay Marina, Haro Strait, the San Juans, and Mount Baker. The dinner menu features pastas like lemon chicken penne and puttanesca (calamari and clams), crab cakes, salmon, prime rib, veal, and a large selection of steaks. The daily fresh sheet offers dishes like tuna filet with peppercorns and scallop fritters. Their signature chocolate dessert is the **Chocolate Fetish**, a sampler of chocolate items, some of which are quite good, while others are less successful. The **Warm Milk Chocolate Soufflé** is served warm and is light and fluffy with a light chocolate flavor. The **Chilled White Chocolate Cointreau Parfait**, which is served with a beautiful dark chocolate butterfly, is a small tower of refreshing white chocolate custard with a strong flavor of orange. The **Bittersweet Truffle Torte with White Chocolate Sauce** is a tiny triangle of cake-like torte that lacks sufficient chocolate taste. The **Hazelnut Nougatine Mousse** is a silver-dollar-sized button of smooth hazelnut mousse punctuated by finely-chopped hazelnuts and garnished with a tiny dollop of chocolate ganache and toasted hazelnuts. The scoop of **Chocolate Ice Cream** is golf ball-sized and sits in a pool of chocolate sauce. It's refreshing and smooth, but could be more chocolaty. The **Spicy Chocolate Creme Brulee** comes in a tiny cup and it's a good thing. The smooth chocolate custard is seasoned with chilies with a heat that sneaks up and sends you back to the cooling ice cream.

Getting there: On Beach Road at Currie Drive, about 10 minutes from downtown.

Empress Room

721 Government Street, Victoria, B.C. (250) 389-2727

♥ The **Empress Room** in the Empress Hotel with its heavy, carved timbers, patterned fabric wall coverings, chandeliers, huge fireplace, fresh orchids on each table, and harp playing in the background, is ornate and formal. They offer a nightly pre-fixe menu with entrees such as roasted quail or ala carte selections like tuna, salmon, duck breast, rack of lamb, and filet of beef, all classically prepared. Desserts come on a 4-tiered, rosewood dolly from which the waiter cuts and plates each dessert tableside. A standard on their menu is the **Empress Sacher Torte**, 2 layers of dark chocolate sponge cake filled with chocolate fondant and raspberry sauce that's topped with chocolate ruffles. It's beautifully presented in a pool of creme anglaise with mango puree in a star shape, surrounded by raspberry hearts. The chocolate cake is fine-textured; the ganache thick. The creme anglaise is perfectly light and creamy and the raspberry puree has a bright, fresh raspberry flavor. This dessert may be served too cold to really enjoy. Have a cup of tea and let it warm up.

> *"What you see before you, my friend, is the result of a lifetime of chocolate. A pound a day often."*
> — **Katherine Hepburn**

Their **Chocolate Truffle Torte** is a wedge of dense torte topped with a white chocolate triangle and chocolate arrow that's garnished with chocolate sorbet and a Cape gooseberry. It's lovely to look at and is thick and fudge-like with a good chocolate flavor. The sorbet, however, is a bit chalky.

The **Empress Chocolate Mousse**, the best of the lot, is a generous portion served in a stemmed dessert glass and garnished with the orange Cape gooseberry, a white chocolate rectangle, and a whipped cream swirl. An excellent mousse, it's light and creamy without clinging to the tongue.

Getting there: In the Empress Hotel right in the center of the Inner Harbor.

Bakeries

Patisserie Daniel
768 Fort, Victoria, B.C. (250) 361-4243
♥♥♥♥ **Patisserie Daniel** is a tiny French bakery that makes some terrific baked goods. They offer a large selection of scones, breads like country, peasant (rye with seeds) and stollen (a holiday fruit bread with marzipan and brandy), cookies like Florentines, biscotti, and almond crescents, scones (almond, cranberry oat), and a large selection of big muffins (raisin bran, cappuccino chocolate chip, poppyseed, apricot oat, blueberry, sour cherry, and date bran, among others).

For chocolate lovers, they make **Chocolate Truffle Tarts**, sweet pastry cups filled with soft, mousse-like centers and topped with soft chocolate curls. It's a buttery blend of rich almond and chocolate. Their **Florentine** cookies, are 5 inches of sweet, crispy almonds dipped in dark chocolate. Daniel's **White Chocolate Raspberry Cookies,** made with 2 (6-inch) rounds of buttery shortbread cookie filled with raspberry and frosted with white chocolate glaze, are a bit sweet for this reviewer's taste.

If you're more in the mood for bread, their **Chocolate Baguette** is a braid of chewy chocolate bread filled with plenty of sweet, dark chocolate. They also make **Mocha Chocolate Truffle Triangles,** 6-inch long icicles of creamy truffle with crunchy flecks of espresso, covered with dark chocolate and dusted with cocoa. They're a real delight for those who like chocolate and coffee.

The Patisserie also makes a number of **chocolate cakes** available whole such as chocolate truffle torte with Kirsch, chocolate sponge with sour cherries, chocolate truffle and whipped cream, and hazelnut and praline truffle layered with sponge cake with rum.

Getting there: Between Blanchard and Douglas.

Dutch Bakery and Café
718 Fort Street, Victoria, B.C. (250) 385-1012
♥♥ (pastries)/♥♥ (chocolates) **The Dutch Bakery** has a window display case that's full of some of the most beautiful pastries

and cakes in Victoria—Sacher tortes, chocolate eclairs, meat pies, sausage rolls, and fruit, custard, nut, and ginger tarts. Inside, it gets even better. The Dutch Bakery has been Victoria's most authentic Dutch bakery since 1956. Kees and Jack Schaddelee, who both started baking in Holland with their father, take pride in doing things the old way. They make their own almond paste with almonds they import from Spain. They make their own fondant and hazelnut paste. They use quality ingredients like Callebaut chocolate and fresh creamery butter. They make 25 different types of butter **cookies** and dozens of almond, halfways, and cream nut cookies, cakes, and tarts. In addition, they make a large variety of **tea fancies**, **small cookies**, **tarts**, and **cream-filled delights** to serve at tea time. They make a huge variety, but only make a few at a time to keep them as fresh as possible. Their cookies are small and elegant, with silky creams, crunchy, light-as-air almond-bases, and dark, chocolaty coatings.

If that isn't enough for chocolate lovers, The Dutch Bakery also hand-dips their own **chocolates**. Their dark chocolate is smooth with a satiny sheen. The milk chocolate is milky and creamy. If you're tired of the same old chocolates, you'll be delighted by the unusual textures and flavors of Dutch Bakery chocolates. You'll find whipped centers with surprising crunch or crunchy textures with lacy, wafer-like airiness. Their **Chocolate-covered Ginger**, which uses Australian ginger, is a real treat—tart, tangy, and refreshing without being too hot.

Getting there: On Fort Street near Douglas.

Chocolate Shops

Chocolaterie Bernard Callebaut
623 Broughton, Victoria, B.C. (250) 380-1515
Other Victoria locations:
#520 777 Royal Oak Drive, Broadmede Village Mall, Victoria, B.C. (250) 744-1596
1140 Government Street (Bedford Regency Hotel), Victoria, B.C. (250) 380-1510
♥♥♥♥ The name **Callebaut** has long been associated with fine **Belgian chocolate**, especially among bakers. Luckily for chocolate travelers, son Bernard has opened several chocolate shops bearing his name which use Callebaut chocolate made exactly to his specifications. His shops are a cornucopia of beautifully molded and filled chocolates using European molds such as leaves, swirls, flowers, clovers, flames, and hearts. Many of them have an incredibly high sheen that's achieved by specially tempering the chocolate. The chocolates are made without preservatives in small batches weekly as each store orders them. So insistent are they on freshness, they ask customers to keep the chocolates at the right temperature and eat them within 8 days of purchase. All the chocolates come beautifully packaged in foil boxes with ribbon imported from

Europe and each box is packed with a special pictorial menu so you can identify each candy.

They make chocolates filled with **buttercream, ganaches, caramel, fresh cream** (creme fraiche), which is made with fresh whipping cream, and **truffles (Espresso, Champagne, Butter, Brussels, Celeste (dark chocolate)**, and **Raspberry)**. Bite into a Bernard Callebaut chocolate and you're transported to chocolate heaven. They're sensual and incredibly silky, melting in the mouth quickly, leaving just a sweet memory. The fresh creams are especially delightful with the cool, fresh taste of whipped cream in each morsel. Bernard Callebaut is a 10th degree black belt of chocolatiers.

Traveler's note: Bernard Callebaut chocolates are now available in the United States (sold under the Bernard C. name). We reviewed Callebaut chocolates in Canada and the U.S. and found the Canadian chocolates fresher. Hence, we awarded the Canadian stores ♥♥♥♥ *and the stores in the U.S.* ♥♥♥.
Getting there: *Their downtown store is on Broughton near Blanchard. They also have a kiosk downtown in the lobby of the Bedford Regency Hotel.*

Fat Phege's Fudge Factory
560 Johnson, Victoria, B.C. (250) 383-3435
♥♥ If it's **fudge** you want in Victoria, **Fat Phege's Fudge** is the place to visit. Owner and candy maker Herman Friesen makes all of the fudge by hand using time-tested recipes. The result is fudge that's creamy and silky smooth. His chocolate fudge comes in **Chocolate, Chocolate Peanut Butter, Chocolate Walnut, Chocolate Grand Marnier, Chocolate Marshmallow, Chocolate Amaretto**, and **Rocky Road**. Non-chocolate flavors include maple walnut, vanilla, and Bailey's Irish Cream.

Though it's not chocolate, Herman's old fashioned Opera Roll, nougat, currants, and chopped cherries, rolled in handmade caramel and pecan halves, is definitely worth a try.
Getting there: *Tucked in an upper corner of Market Square.*

Homefires Bakery
Leavenworth, Washington
CHOCOLATE MINT TRUFFLE PIE

Recipe:
Chocolate
Mint Truffle
Pie

Makes 1 9-inch pie

Crust: 1/4 cup chocolate wafer crumbs
(4 or 5 chocolate wafer cookies)
6 tablespoons vanilla wafer crumbs
(about 7 vanilla wafers)
2 tablespoons melted butter
Filling: 1/2 envelope unflavored gelatin (1 teaspoon)
1/4 cup water
1 1/2 teaspoons peppermint extract
6 tablespoons semi-sweet chocolate chips
1 8-ounce package cream cheese
1 cup granulated sugar
1 cup whipping cream
1 1/2 teaspoons vanilla
Topping: 3 tablespoons semi-sweet chocolate chips

A cool, refreshing combination of mint and chocolate, this surprisingly light dessert is a great way to end a meal. It can also be made in muffin cups for individual desserts or in tiny confectionery cups for bite-sized delights.

Preheat oven to 300 degrees.

For Crust: Stir together the chocolate and vanilla crumbs and the butter. Pat evenly onto the bottom and up the sides of a 9-inch pie pan. Bake for 5 minutes. Set aside to cool.

For Filling: Melt the chocolate in the top of a double boiler. Set aside to cool.

Soften the gelatin in water, let stand for 5 minutes. Heat over low heat until clear and then add the peppermint extract and stir well. Add the gelatin mixture to the melted chocolate and blend. Meanwhile, in a large mixing bowl, beat cream cheese until fluffy. Add the sugar and beat again until fluffy. Add the chocolate mixture to the cream cheese mixture and blend well. Set aside.

In a large bowl, whip the cream until soft peaks form. Add the vanilla and beat until firm peaks form. Fold the whipped vanilla cream into the chocolate mixture and pour into the prepared pie crust. Smooth with a spatula. Chill until set.

For Topping: Melt the chocolate and drizzle in an attractive pattern over the top of the pie. Chill to set. Pie can be frozen and served directly from the freezer.

British
Columbia

From *The Chocolate Lover's Guide Cookbook*,
Pacific Northwest Edition.

Index

The Chocolate Lover's
PERSONAL LIFE LIST

*Bird lovers keep life lists of bird sightings. Why shouldn't choco-
late lovers have a life list of favorite chocolate delights? Keep
track of your favorite chocolate desserts, confections, ice creams,
etc. and where you found them, so you can enjoy them again and
again (or so you can tip off The Chocolate Lover's Guide
reviewer(s)).*

Date	Chocolate Item	Location

Date	Chocolate Item	Location

Personal
Life List

BACK TALK/TALK BACK

Have we missed your favorite chocolate spot? Do you agree/dis-
agree with a particular review? Let us know! *If you're the first to
send us a lead that we end up reviewing and including in our
next edition, we'll send you a chocolate lover's bumper sticker as
a way of saying thanks.* Fill out the form below with as much
information as you have.

Name of establishment:_____

Address: _____

City, State or Province:_____

Phone: _____

Your Report (please include any must-have chocolate items):

_____

_____

_____

_____

_____

_____

_____

_____

_____

Name:_____

Your Address: _____

_____

Your phone number: _____

Date: _____

Thanks for your help, chocolate lovers!
Please address to *The Chocolate Lover's Guide*,
Wordsworth Publishing, P.O.Box 311,
Beavercreek, OR 97004.
You can also e-mail us at hasselbring@msn.com
or fax (503) 632-6754

ORDER FORM

The Chocolate Lovers Guide to the Pacific Northwest makes a great gift for yourself or for chocolate-loving friends, family, and co-workers. **Order 3 or more copies and get 10% off.**

Send me ____ books @ $ 17.95 U.S. each $ _____

Shipping and handing up to 2 books $ ___ **3.00** ___

     For additional books add $1.00 each $ _____

10% discount (3 or more books) $ _____

Total order amount $ _____

Name _____

Address _____

City, State or Province, Zip _____

Country _____

Daytime phone number (_____) _____

I'd like my copy autographed _____

Any special message _____

_____

Mail this order form with a check or money order to:
Wordsworth Publishing
P.O. Box 311
Beavercreek, OR. 97004

Phone or Fax Orders:
Call **(503) 632-4610** (Portland area) or toll-free **1-877-800-7700** (outside Portland area only) or fax **(503) 632-6754**.

Credit Card No. _____

❑ Visa ❑ MC *(check one)*   Expiration date_____

Signature _____

The Chocolate Lover's Guide Cookbook

IS COMING!

Enjoy more than 90 outstanding chocolate recipes from chefs, pastry chefs, bakers, and chocolatiers throughout the Pacific Northwest

- **Celebrity TV Chef Caprial Spence** contributes her **Chocolate Turtle Torte** and **Chocolate Silk**.
- **Genoa**, one of Portland's best restaurants for more than 25 years, shares its classic **Torta di Santa Maria**, an exquisite blend of chocolate, nuts, and raisins.
- **Black Butte Ranch** offers **Sourdough Chocolate Cake**, a luscious warm chocolate cake slathered in homemade chocolate sauce.
- **Canlis**, a top Seattle restaurant for 50 years, gives the recipe for **Chocolate Lava Cake**, a veritable explosion of chocolate flavor.
- **Diva at the Met**, named Vancouver, B.C.'s top restaurant in 1998 by *Gourmet Magazine*, shows you how to make its **Chocolate Crème Brulee**.
- Also:
  How to cook with chocolate.
  ✔ Tools ✔ Tips ✔ Techniques ✔ Temperatures
  Where to find the best ingredients.

Yes, let me know when
The Chocolate Lover's Guide Cookbook, Pacific Northwest Edition comes out.

Name_____

Address_____

City/State/ProvinceZip_____

Country_____

Daytime phone number (_____)_____